The Stylistics Reader
From Roman Jakobson to the present

Andrew Lim
Sheffield 1997

The Stylistics Reader

From Roman Jakobson to the present

Edited by

Jean Jacques Weber
University Centre Luxembourg

A member of the Hodder Headline Group
LONDON • NEW YORK • SYDNEY • AUCKLAND

First published in Great Britain 1996 by
Arnold, a member of the Hodder Headline Group,
338 Euston Road, London NW1 3BH
175 Fifth Avenue, New York, NY 10010

Distributed exclusively in the USA by St. Martin's Press, Inc.
175 Fifth Avenue, New York, NY 10010

British Library Cataloguing in Publication Data
A catalogue record for this book is available from the British Library

Library of Congress Cataloging-in-Publication Data
The stylistics reader: from Roman Jakobson to the present/edited by
Jean Jacques Weber.
      p.   cm.
   Collection of sixteen previously published essays, articles, etc.
   Includes bibliographical references and index.
   ISBN 0-340-64621-7.—ISBN 0-340-64622-5 (pbk.)
   1. Language and languages—Style.   2. Style, Literary. I. Weber,
Jean Jacques.
P301.S879   1996
808—dc20   95-38118
                                                                CIP

ISBN 0 340 64621 7 (hb)
ISBN 0 340 64622 5 (pb)

Typeset in 10/12pt Times and produced by Gray Publishing, Tunbridge Wells
Printed in Great Britain by J. W. Arrowsmith Ltd, Bristol

Contents

Contributors

Derek Attridge, Rutgers University, USA

David Birch, University of Central Queensland, Australia

Deirdre Burton, formerly of Birmingham University, UK

Ronald Carter, University of Nottingham, UK

Stanley E. Fish, Duke University, USA

Roger Fowler, University of East Anglia, UK

Donald C. Freeman, University of Southern California, USA

M. A. K. Halliday, University of Sydney, Australia

Roman Jakobson (deceased), formerly of Harvard and MIT, USA

Sara Mills, Sheffield Hallam University, UK

Mary Louise Pratt, Stanford University, USA

Mick Short, University of Lancaster, UK

Dan Sperber, Ecole Polytechnique, France

Talbot J. Taylor, College of William and Mary, USA

Michael Toolan, University of Washington, USA

Jean Jacques Weber, University Centre Luxembourg

H. G. Widdowson, University of London, UK

Deirdre Wilson, University College London, UK

Acknowledgements

I would like to thank all the contributors for generously making their work available, as well as Naomi Meredith and all the others at Arnold and Gray Publishing for their unfailing support with problems of editing and compiling.

Acknowledgement is due to the copyright holders of the following texts for their kind permission to reprint them in this book: Ch. 1: MIT Press; from *Style in language* (1960) ed. T. Sebeok. Ch. 2: Manchester University Press; from *The linguistics of writing* (1987) ed. N. Fabb, D. Attridge, A. Durant and C. MacCabe. Ch. 3: Professor Seymour Chatman; from *Literary style: A symposium* (1971) ed. S. Chatman. Ch. 4: Julius Groos Verlag; from *Journal of Literary Semantics* 13 (1984) 57–62. Ch. 5: Columbia University Press; from *Approaches to poetics* (1973) ed. S. Chatman. Ch. 6: Routledge; from *The stylistics of fiction* (1990) by M. Toolan. Ch. 7: Oxford University Press; from *The Edinburgh course in applied linguistics, vol. 3, Techniques of applied linguistics* (1973) ed. J. P. B. Allen and S. Pit Corder. Ch. 8: Oxford University Press; from *Literature and Language Teaching* (1986) ed. C. J. Brumfit and R. A. Carter. Ch. 9: Oxford University Press; from *Applied Linguistics* 2 (1981) 180–202. Ch. 10: Duke University Press and The Porter Institute for Poetics and Semiotics, Tel Aviv University; from *Poetics Today* 7 (1986) 59–72. Ch. 11: Rodopi, Amsterdam; from *Linguistics and the study of literature* (1986) ed. T. D'Haen. Ch. 12: Routledge (Unwin Hyman); from *Language, discourse and literature* (1989) ed. R. Carter and P. Simpson. Ch. 13: Routledge (Allen & Unwin); from *Language and literature* (1982) ed. R. Carter. Ch. 14: Routledge; from *Language, text and context* (1992) ed. M. Toolan. Ch. 15: Elsevier Science B.V., Amsterdam; from *Lingua* 87 (1992) 53–76. Ch. 16: Longman; from *Language and Literature* 2 (1993) 1–18.

Material quoted within chapters: 'Futility' by Wilfred Owen, from *The Collected Poems of Wilfred Owen*, copyright © 1963 Chatto & Windus, reprinted by permission of The Estate of Wilfred Owen, Chatto & Windus and New Directions Publishing Corp.; an extract from 'The Man with the Scar' by W. Somerset Maugham, from *Collected Short Stories of W. Somerset Maugham*, published by William Heinemann Ltd, reprinted by permission of Reed Consumer Books Ltd and A.P. Watt Ltd on behalf of The Royal Literary Fund; an extract from *A Christmas Garland* by Max Beerbohm, reprinted by permission of Mrs Eva Reichmann; extracts from *The Inheritors*, copyright © 1955 by William Golding, reprinted by permission of Harcourt, Brace and Company and Faber & Faber Ltd; extracts from *Waiting for Godot* by Samuel Beckett and *Enter a Free Man* by Tom Stoppard, reprinted by permission of Faber & Faber Ltd and Grove/Atlantic Inc.; 'Trouble in the Works' by Harold Pinter, from *Plays: Two*, reprinted by permission of Faber & Faber Ltd and Grove/Atlantic Inc.; extracts from *A Man For All Seasons* by Robert Bolt, reprinted by permission of Heinemann; an extract from *The Bell Jar* by Sylvia Plath, copyright © 1971 Harper & Row Publishers Inc., reprinted by permission of Faber & Faber Ltd and HarperCollins Publishers Inc.; an extract from *The Sound and the Fury* © 1929 by William Faulkner, reprinted by permission of Curtis Brown, Random House Inc. and the Estate of William Faulkner; an extract from *One Way Pendulum* by N. F. Simpson, reprinted by kind permission of the author; 'Steel', 'May 1954', 'Fifteen Years After' by Edwin Thumboo, reprinted by kind permission of the author.

Every effort has been made to contact copyright holders of the works reproduced in this volume. Should anyone have any copyright queries, the publishers will be happy to hear from them.

Towards contextualized stylistics: An overview

Jean Jacques Weber

This book focuses on the main problems that have fascinated scholars working at the interface between language and literature: what is literature? How does literary discourse differ from other discourse types? How do we read and interpret literary texts? What is style? What is the relationship between language, literature and society? Each section introduces a particular approach, thus covering the major tendencies in stylistics in the last 35 years (from Roman Jakobson to the present). The early chapters introducing approaches current in the 1960s and 1970s are each followed by a more recent paper which takes issue with some of the assumptions behind these theories. In this way, readers are encouraged to take up their own position in these fundamental debates.

The second part of the book presents the main currents in contemporary stylistics: pedagogical stylistics and the different types of contextualized stylistics practised nowadays, each movement being represented by two chapters (they include pragmatic, critical, feminist and cognitive approaches).[1] The major principles of contemporary stylistics are highlighted, and readers are introduced to the debates that concern not only stylisticians but also linguists and literary critics.

Here I shall attempt to put these key issues into a historical perspective by presenting a very brief and personal overview of the development of stylistics as a discipline in the last 40 years. I shall take as my starting-point Roman Jakobson's seminal essay 'Closing statement: Linguistics and poetics' (ch. 1), presented at the *Style in Language* conference in 1958, in which he calls for an explicit, objective, scientific and structuralist stylistics, to be modelled on the scientific, structuralist linguistics of the time. What makes such a scientific approach possible is that Jakobson sees style as an inherent property of the literary text, to the exclusion of the reader. He sets up a structural distinction between literary and non-literary texts, with the former marked by a dominance of the poetic function, which he defines as a focus or set upon the message ('message' is a misleading term, by which he means something more akin to what would normally be referred to as 'text').

In an interesting paper entitled 'Closing statement: Linguistics and poetics in retrospect' (ch. 2), Derek Attridge points to a fundamental flaw in Jakobson's reasoning here. He claims that Jakobson is not successful in his attempt to exclude the reader from the concerns of stylistics. Jakobson's definition of the poetic function as a focus or set upon the message in fact presupposes the reader: literary texts are those which are marked by *the reader's* focus upon the message.

So ultimately Jakobson's distinction between literary and non-literary texts turns out to be a sociocultural rather than a structural one.

Jakobson and his followers, however, exclude the reader from consideration and set out to study the intricate patterning of literary texts. They have no difficulty in identifying the relevant stylistic features, since the selection is made on the basis of purely formal criteria. They study all the instances of repetition and parallelism, as well as all the instances where the language of the literary text deviates from assumed linguistic norms. The problem with these formalist stylistic analyses is that they strike one as mechanical, lifeless, sterile exercises, and largely irrelevant to the interpretation of the literary work that they are describing. And if the critics try to ascribe some function or meaning to the formal patterns that they have uncovered, then a huge leap of faith is required to move from description to interpretation.

Functionalist stylistics evolved as an attempt to solve this fundamental problem of Jakobsonian, formalist stylistics, to close or at least narrow the gap between analysis and interpretation. In order to achieve this goal, the functionalist introduces a new criterion of stylistic significance: namely, obviously enough, direct functional relevance to the interpretation of the literary text. In other words, a formal feature is only considered stylistically significant if it is functional, if it has a particular meaning or effect or value. This considerably increases the power of stylistic description, since the latter becomes directly relevant to interpretation, but it does not really solve the problem: like formalist stylisticians, many functionalists still assume a fixed correlation between form and meaning, and ignore the indeterminacy and plurality of the functions and meanings of particular language items. So we still find interpretive leaps from form to function, as when M. A. K. Halliday, in his analysis of William Golding's *The Inheritors* (ch. 3), which is probably the best-known functionalist stylistic analysis, interprets systematic choices in the area of transitivity as creating a particular world-view. This general problem, faced by all functionalist stylisticians, is lucidly discussed by Talbot Taylor and Michael Toolan in chapter 4.

As a result of these continuing problems which beset the very nature of the stylistic enterprise, there were more and more attacks against the discipline, the most influential of which was doubtlessly Stanley Fish's 'What is stylistics and why are they saying such terrible things about it?' (ch. 5). What Fish attacks in the work of both formalists and also functionalists such as Halliday is precisely the interpretive leaps from 'syntactic preferences' to 'habits of meaning'. He insists that every 'act of description is itself an interpretation', in other words, that stylistic analysis is an interpretive act right from the beginning and hence cannot be objective and scientific. Therefore, also, a stylistic analysis cannot be a means of validating other critical interpretations.

Fish rejects Jakobson's view of style as an inherent property of the text and sees style as dynamic effects produced by the reader in the process of reading the text. He locates stylistic effects not in the text but in the activity of reading, and advocates an affective or reader-oriented stylistics in which it becomes paramount to study the reader's assumptions, expectations and interpretive processes.

ENKVIST: STYLO BEHAVIOURISTICS

Fish is fully aware of the danger of relativism in such a stylistics, with every reader using different assumptions and different interpretive processes. In his book *Is There a Text in this Class?* (1981), he therefore introduces the notion of 'interpretive communities' in order to keep in check the danger of relativism: he claims that readers' interpretive processes are determined by the particular interpretive community to which they belong. However this does not really banish the threat of relativism for, as Michael Toolan (ch. 6) shows, the notion of 'interpretive community' is notoriously hard to define; and for this as well as some other reasons (such as its lack of a political dimension), Fish's notion as it stands turns out to be a rather vacuous one.

In the late 1970s, stylistics was still reeling from the onslaughts of Fish and other critics. But it managed to gather strength and developed in two highly promising directions, the first of which is pedagogical stylistics. These stylisticians turn away from theoretical matters, and from bold claims of scientificity: stylistic analysis may not be objective and scientific but, they contend, it can be rigorous, systematic and replicable, and hence achieve inter-subjective validity and pedagogical usefulness. Their much more modest aim is simply to demonstrate that stylistic analysis as a *way* of reading can be of direct use to students, both in mother-tongue language learning and in an English as a foreign language context – something that had already been advocated by Henry Widdowson since the early 1970s (see ch. 7). Now, in the 1980s, and with the support of the British Council, more and more stylisticians worked towards an integration of language and literature study, and developed what they called 'pre-literary' language-based activities (unscrambling, gap-filling, intertextual comparison, rewriting and other creative writing exercises). Such activities will, it is hoped, not only improve the students' reading and writing skills, but also awaken their awareness of, and sensitivity to, different (literary and non-literary) uses of language. For a good example of this kind of work in an EFL context, see chapter 8 by Ronald Carter.

The other important development which took place in stylistics at that time was an orientation towards contextualization, which gathered a new momentum under the influence of similar trends in mainstream linguistics, where the increasing importance of context was acknowledged through the rise of such subdisciplines as pragmatics and discourse analysis. It became increasingly clear that style is not either inherent in the text (as the formalists claimed) or totally in the reader's mind (as Fish and other reader-response theorists claimed) but an effect produced in, by and through the interaction between text and reader. Thus meaning and stylistic effect are not fixed and stable, and cannot be dug out of the text as in an archaeological approach, but they have to be seen as a potential which is actualized in a (real) reader's mind, the product of a dialogic interaction between author, the author's context of production, the text, the reader and the reader's context of reception – where context includes all sorts of sociohistorical, cultural and intertextual factors.

The movement towards greater contextualization in stylistic analysis could be thought of as a succession of concentric circles representing the gradual widening of the text's contextual orbit. The first development was speech-act stylistics, where the analyst is interested not only in what the speaker says but also in what the speaker is *doing* when she says something, in other words, what speech acts she is performing (making a promise, uttering a command or a threat, etc.). Mary Louise Pratt, one of the first practitioners of this type of stylistic analysis (see Pratt 1977), is also one of its first critics: in 'Ideology and speech-act theory' (ch. 10), she points to the limitations of speech-act analysis and debunks the reactionary ideological assumptions upon which it is based.

Very soon, stylisticians such as Mick Short (ch. 9) were also interested in other aspects of language in use, other forms of implicit meaning, which were being studied concurrently in linguistic pragmatics: in particular, presuppositions and inferences (or implications, implicatures). They ask questions such as the following: what does the speaker presuppose when she produces a particular utterance? What inferences can be drawn from what the speaker says, on the basis of such general principles of communication as cooperation or politeness? The interesting thing here is that it is not clear any longer whether presuppositions and inferences are a matter of form or content or both, so this kind of analysis successfully avoids falling into the crippling form/content dichotomy.

In the late 1970s and early 1980s, linguistic pragmatics split into social pragmatics and cognitive pragmatics. Mary Louise Pratt's chapter is already a good example of a more socially oriented pragmatics, the practitioner of which tends to be concerned with the social and political ideologies constructed in texts. 'Ideology' here is used not in its negative sense of false consciousness but in a more neutral sense of the often disjointed common-sensical assumptions and values which are shared by a particular social group and which make up the world-view of that group. It is because of this critical sociopolitical concern that work in this area is usually referred to as critical linguistics and critical stylistics.

Critical-stylistic analyses are largely based on a linguistics which is explicitly constructivist in its underlying assumptions: namely, Halliday's systemic-functional grammar, which sees language as a resource for making meaning, a meaning potential in and through which social reality is constructed and reproduced, a social semiotic that constitutes the 'reality' of the culture (for details, see ch. 11 by Roger Fowler). Halliday talks about language *construing* experience: by construal he means the semiotic construction of reality; and he says *experience* rather than reality, because he does not want to deny the existence of external physical reality. The point he makes is that we cannot experience it in an unmediated way, every representation through language being a constructive process and only an approximation to reality.

Critical stylisticians thus reject the mimetic view of language as a value-free, transparent medium reflecting reality. They deny the possibility of a neutral representation of reality, and consequently see their own role as being demystificatory: to unmask ideologies, to denaturalize common-sense assumptions and, ultimately, to enable and empower readers.

However, if this meant a simple reading of ideological structures off linguistic structures, it would mean falling back into the old form/content dichotomy that crippled the work of many functionalist stylisticians. But critical stylisticians have learnt from past mistakes: they insist that the relationship between language and ideology is complex and indirect, that other (social, historical, cultural, intertextual) factors which determine the meanings of particular language items for the reader have to be taken into account, that ideologies should be associated with cultural schemata rather than with individual language items and, finally, that ideologies, which in earlier studies were often assumed to be simple, unitary and static, in fact tend to be far more complex, dynamic and full of internal contradictions. Thus, quite explicitly, critical stylistics sees itself not as an objective and scientific, but as an interpretive and interested enterprise, with the critic being fully aware of his or her own ideological situatedness, and of the inevitable historicity of all interpretive acts (see ch. 12 by David Birch).

The concern of critical stylisticians with ideology and representation is shared by feminist stylisticians, who are also interested in unmasking (patriarchal) ideologies and denaturalizing (patriarchal) assumptions. In fact, feminist stylisticians often use Hallidayan transitivity analysis to examine critically the representations of women in literature and popular culture (see e.g. ch. 13 by Deirdre Burton). They study the ways in which images of women are constrained by language, and work towards a critical feminist awareness, which might lead to resistance and, ultimately, linguistic and/or social change. For example, in Sara Mills' analysis of a poem by John Fuller (ch. 14), the stylistic features she identifies in the text do not point to a particular interpretation but to the way in which the reader is addressed and positioned by the text. She shows how Fuller's poem constructs a masculine reading position from which the dominant meanings are to be read, and calls on all 'female-affiliated' readers to take up resisting readings. It is of course their constructivist assumptions that commit both critical and feminist stylisticians to the view that new modes of discourse such as critical and feminist discourses can change culture (as well as vice-versa), that because reality is at least to some extent linguistically constructed more positive alternative constructions of reality become possible.

Cognitive pragmaticists, on the other hand, focus on mental processes, on how the assumptions, expectations and beliefs of speaker and hearer enter into their construction of the meaning of the text. This has led to the development of a number of theories of cognitive pragmatics, the most influential of which, at least in stylistics, are Dan Sperber and Deirdre Wilson's relevance theory and George Lakoff's cognitive linguistics.

Sperber and Wilson deny that there is a fixed correlation between form and meaning, by means of a conventional code, so that the meaning of a text could simply be 'decoded'. They insist that the creation of meaning is an inferential process, which can lead to different interpretations, because different readers use different assumptions in their processing of the text. The reader thus plays an active role in constructing the indeterminate implicit content of utterances. In their theory, indeterminacy is not denied (as it often was in formalist stylistics) nor allowed to go wild (as in Fish and much contemporary deconstructive criticism) but it is contained by a principle of relevance, which they see as a universal principle underlying all cognitive processing and which directs the reader to try and maximize the number of contextual implications while at the same time minimizing the processing costs of deriving them.

This seems a promising foundation for stylistic work, and it has in fact been applied to the stylistic analysis of (literary and non-literary) texts both by Sperber and Wilson themselves and by others, though an obvious limitation is that relevance theorists tend to ignore the ideological aspect of all reader construction. The analyses have mostly concentrated on the interpretation of tropes, especially metaphor and irony (see ch. 15). For example, when readers process a metaphorical utterance, they typically draw a large array of what Sperber and Wilson call 'weak implicatures'. What is interesting here is that the writer did not specifically intend the readers to draw these weak implicatures, but merely gave them a licence to explore the implications of the text in this particular direction. How far they go is up to each individual reader, and largely determined by the reader's cultural and intertextual context (the role of which is acknowledged but otherwise ignored in Sperber and Wilson's analyses). The reader takes the responsibility for these weak implicatures, which are 'authorized' by the text rather than 'intended' by the writer. Sperber and Wilson refer to this process, in which the reader plays a highly creative role, as the 'exploitation' of the text by the reader.

The other theory of potential use to stylistics is cognitive linguistics and the associated metaphor theory developed by George Lakoff, Mark Turner and Mark Johnson (Lakoff *et al.* 1989), and applied to Shakespearean texts by Donald Freeman (ch. 16). Like Hallidayan linguistics, cognitive linguistics, too, is based on explicitly constructivist assumptions. Lakoff rejects the correspondence view that formal features reflect, imitate or correspond to a reality which exists out there independently of language. He insists that the coding relation between language and the world is not an objectivist one: the categories of language do not mirror the categories of the world, since the latter is an unlabelled, uncategorized place. So categories are not given but imposed. Moreover, to characterize category structure, we need not only propositional but also metaphoric and metonymic models, which provide motivation for the extension of a particular category. In other words, form-meaning correspondences are not arbitrary but motivated by, among others, conceptual metaphors.

Hence it becomes important to study these conceptual systems and metaphors. Lakoff and his co-workers see metaphor as an ontological and epistemic mapping across conceptual domains, from a source domain to a target domain. For instance, argument (the target domain) can be metaphorically conceptualized as war (the source domain). Note that this conceptualization has many different linguistic realizations (*attacking* or *shooting down* somebody's arguments, *defending* one's own position, using a particular *strategy* in order to *wipe out* one's opponent in a debate, etc.). Therefore cognitive linguists see metaphor not just as a matter of language but of thought and reason.

Interestingly, it is in the area of metaphor studies that the analyses of cognitive and social pragmaticists are most compatible. The latter emphasize the sociopolitical consequences of our conceptual systems. For instance, David Lee (1992, pp. 71–6) points out that our culture's way of looking at arguments in terms of war is not natural but highly ideological; another culture might well understand arguments as a form of dance. Lee admits that the metaphor is not constraining: we, too, can look at arguments in terms of dance (e.g. 'Richard waltzed through Alan's objections quite effortlessly'), but the metaphors current in a particular culture are bound to influence the cognitive outlook of a child during his or her acquisition of the language. This means that conceptual metaphors may not determine our cognitive outlook but certainly predispose us to see aspects of reality in certain ways rather than others.

Social linguists have also studied the ways in which wars, epidemics and other sociopolitical situations are metaphorically represented in the media. They show that the choice of metaphor provides insights into the assumptions, values and attitudes which are part of the common sense of a particular culture, and they examine its ideological and social consequences. An example here would be Norman Fairclough's discussion of a newspaper article describing social riots in terms of the spread of cancer. He demonstrates that this metaphor implies a particular way of dealing with the problem: 'one does not arrive at a negotiated settlement with cancer ... Cancer has to be eliminated, cut out' (1989, p. 120; for literary stylistic studies which combine a cognitive with a critical perspective, see e.g. Simon-Vandenbergen 1993 and Weber 1995).

The picture that emerges is that of a contextualized stylistics which is far more sophisticated than earlier forms of stylistic practice: it tends to be explicitly constructivist in its underlying assumptions, and often it openly acknowledges itself to be interpretive and interested. It is also much more directly in line with modern literary theory, since the latter is similarly characterized by a move away from essentialism and towards constructivism (though see what Freeman, ch. 16, says in his polemical note 16). The challenge for future researchers and practitioners now is to work towards a greater synthesis of cognitive and social approaches, a synthesis which, as we have seen, has already been partially achieved in the study of metaphor.

Note

1 What Easthope and McGowan (1992, p. 2) say about their *A Critical and Cultural Theory Reader* obviously applies to all Readers of this kind, including the present one:

> there is no self-evident selection of texts for [a Reader]. We are conscious that this book constructs a version of history, and one that can be contested and of course should be.

References

EASTHOPE, A. and McGOWAN, K. (eds) 1992: *A critical and cultural theory reader*. Buckingham: Open University Press.

FAIRCLOUGH, N. 1989: *Language and power*. Harlow: Longman.

FISH, S. 1981: *Is there a text in this class?* Cambridge, Mass.: Harvard University Press.

LAKOFF, G. and TURNER, M. 1989: *More than cool reason: A field guide to poetic metaphor*. Chicago: Chicago University Press.

LEE, D. 1992: *Competing discourses: Perspective and ideology in language*. Harlow: Longman.

PRATT, M. L. 1977: *Toward a speech-act theory of literary discourse*. Bloomington: Indiana University Press.

SIMON-VANDENBERGEN, A.-M. 1993: Speech, music and dehumanisation in George Orwell's *Nineteen eighty-four*: A linguistic study of metaphors. *Language and Literature* 2, 157–82.

WEBER, J. J. 1995: How metaphor leads Susan Rawlings into suicide: A cognitive-linguistic analysis of Doris Lessing's 'To room nineteen'. In Verdonk, P. and Weber, J. J. (eds), *Twentieth-century fiction: From text to context*. London: Routledge, 32–44.

Part I

Formalist stylistics

1

Closing statement: Linguistics and poetics

Roman Jakobson

Fortunately, scholarly and political conferences have nothing in common. The success of a political convention depends on the general agreement of the majority or totality of its participants. The use of votes and vetoes, however, is alien to scholarly discussion, where disagreement generally proves to be more productive than agreement. Disagreement discloses antinomies and tensions within the field discussed and calls for novel exploration. Not political conferences but rather exploratory activities in Antarctica present an analogy to scholarly meetings: international experts in various disciplines attempt to map an unknown region and find out where the greatest obstacles for the explorer are, the insurmountable peaks and precipices. Such a mapping seems to have been the chief task of our conference, and in this respect its work has been quite successful. Have we not realized what problems are the most crucial and the most controversial? Have we not also learned how to switch our codes, what terms to expound or even to avoid in order to prevent misunderstandings with people using different departmental jargon? Such questions, I believe, for most of the members of this conference, if not for all of them, are somewhat clearer today than they were three days ago.

I have been asked for summary remarks about poetics in its relation to linguistics. Poetics deals primarily with the question, 'What makes a verbal message a work of art?' Because the main subject of poetics is the *differentia specifica* of verbal art in relation to other arts and in relation to other kinds of verbal behavior, poetics is entitled to the leading place in literary studies.

Poetics deals with problems of verbal structure, just as the analysis of painting is concerned with pictorial structure. Since linguistics is the global science of verbal structure, poetics may be regarded as an integral part of linguistics.

Arguments against such a claim must be thoroughly discussed. It is evident that many devices studied by poetics are not confined to verbal art. We can refer to the possibility of transposing *Wuthering Heights* into a motion picture, medieval legends into frescoes and miniatures, or *L'Après-midi d'un faune* into music, ballet, and graphic art. However ludicrous the idea of the *Iliad* and *Odyssey* in comics may seem, certain structural features of their plot are preserved despite the disappearance of their verbal shape. The question of whether W. B. Yeats was right in affirming that William Blake was 'the one perfectly fit illustrator for the *Inferno* and the *Purgatorio*' is a proof that different arts are comparable. The problems of the baroque or any other historical style transgress the frame of a single art. When handling the surrealistic metaphor, we could hardly pass by Max Ernst's pictures or Luis Buñuel's films, *The Andalusian Dog* and *The Golden Age*. In short, many poetic features belong not only to the science of language but to the whole theory of signs, that is, to general semiotics. This statement, however, is valid not only for verbal art but also for all varieties of language, since language shares many properties with certain other systems of signs or even with all of them (pansemiotic features).

Likewise, a second objection contains nothing that would be specific for literature: the question of relations between the word and the world concerns not only verbal art but actually all kinds of discourse. Linguistics is likely to explore all possible problems of relation between discourse and the 'universe of discourse': what of this universe is verbalized by a given discourse and how it is verbalized. The truth values, however, as far as they are – to say with the logicians – 'extralinguistic entities', obviously exceed the bounds of poetics and of linguistics in general.

Sometimes we hear that poetics, in contradistinction to linguistics, is concerned with evaluation. This separation of the two fields from each other is based on a current but erroneous interpretation of the contrast between the structure of poetry and other types of verbal structure: the latter are said to be opposed by their 'casual', designless nature to the 'noncasual', purposeful character of poetic language. In point of fact, any verbal behavior is goal-directed, but the aims are different and the conformity of the means used to the effect aimed at is a problem that evermore preoccupies inquirers into the diverse kinds of verbal communication. There is a close correspondence, much closer than critics believe, between the question of linguistic phenomena expanding in space and time and the spatial and temporal spread of literary models. Even such discontinuous expansion as the resurrection of neglected or forgotten poets – for instance, the posthumous discovery and subsequent canonization of Emily Dickinson (d. 1886) and Gerard Manley Hopkins (d. 1889), the tardy fame of Lautréamont (d. 1870) among surrealist poets, and the salient influence of the hitherto ignored Cyprian Norwid (d. 1883) on Polish modern poetry – finds a parallel in the history of standard languages that tend to revive outdated models, sometimes long forgotten, as was the case in literary Czech, which toward the beginning of the nineteenth century leaned toward sixteenth-century models.

Unfortunately, the terminological confusion of 'literary studies' with 'criticism' tempts the student of literature to replace the description of the intrinsic values of a literary work with a subjective, censorious verdict. The label 'literary critic' applied to an investigator of literature is as erroneous as 'grammatical (or lexical) critic' would be applied to a linguist. Syntactic and morphologic research cannot be supplanted by a normative grammar, and likewise no manifesto, foisting a critic's own tastes and opinions on creative literature, may act as substitute for an objective scholarly analysis of verbal art. This statement should not be mistaken for the quietist principle of *laissez faire*; any verbal culture involves programmatic, planning, normative endeavors. Yet why is a clear-cut discrimination made between pure and applied linguistics or between phonetics and orthoëpy, but not between literary studies and criticism?

Literary studies, with poetics as their focal point, consist like linguistics of two sets of problems: synchrony and diachrony. The synchronic description envisages not only the literary production of any given stage but also that part of the literary tradition which for the stage in question has remained vital or has been revived. Thus, for instance, Shakespeare, on the one hand, and Donne, Marvell, Keats, and Emily Dickinson, on the other, are experienced by the present English poetic world, whereas the works of James Thomson and Longfellow, for the time being, do not belong to viable artistic values. The selection of classics and their reinterpretation by a novel trend is a substantial problem of synchronic literary studies. Synchronic poetics, like synchronic linguistics, is not to be confused with statics; any stage discriminates between more conservative and more innovative forms. Any contemporary stage is experienced in its temporal dynamics, and, on the other hand, the historical approach both in poetics and in linguistics is concerned not only with changes but also with continuous, enduring, static factors. A thoroughly comprehensive historical poetics or history of language is a superstructure to be built on a series of successive synchronic descriptions.

Insistence on keeping poetics apart from linguistics is warranted only when the field of linguistics appears to be illicitly restricted, for example, when the sentence is viewed by some linguists as the highest analyzable construction, or when the scope of linguistics is confined to grammar alone or uniquely to nonsemantic questions of external form or to the inventory of denotative devices with no reference to free variations. Voegelin has clearly pointed out the two most important and related problems that face structural linguistics, namely, a revision of 'the monolithic hypothesis about language' and a concern with 'the interdependence of diverse structures within one language' (1960, p. 57). No doubt, for any speech community, for any speaker, there exists a unity of language, but this over-all code represents a system of interconnected subcodes; every language encompasses several concurrent patterns, each characterized by different functions.

Obviously we must agree with Sapir that, on the whole, 'ideation reigns supreme in language' (1921, p. 40), but this supremacy does not authorize linguistics to disregard the 'secondary factors'. The emotive elements of speech, which, as Joos (1950) is prone to believe, cannot be described 'with a finite number of absolute categories', are classified by him 'as nonlinguistic elements of the real world'. Hence, 'for us they remain vague, protean, fluctuating phenomena', he concludes, 'which we refuse to tolerate in our science'. Joos is indeed a brilliant expert in reduction experiments, and his emphatic demand for the 'expulsion' of emotive elements 'from linguistic science' is a radical experiment in reduction – *reductio ad absurdum*.

Language must be investigated in all the variety of its functions. Before discussing the poetic function we must define its place among the other functions of language. An outline of these functions demands a concise survey of the constitutive factors in any speech event, in any act of verbal communication. The ADDRESSER sends a MESSAGE to the ADDRESSEE. To be operative the message requires a CONTEXT referred to (the 'referent' in another, somewhat ambiguous, nomenclature), graspable by the addressee, and either verbal or capable of being verbalized; a CODE fully, or at least partially, common to the addresser and addressee (or in other words, to the encoder and decoder of the message); and, finally, a CONTACT, a physical channel and psychological connection between the addresser and the addressee, enabling both of them to enter and stay in communication. All these factors inalienably involved in verbal communication may be schematized as follows:

CONTEXT

ADDRESSER   MESSAGE   ADDRESSEE

CONTACT

CODE

Each of these six factors determines a different function of language. Although we distinguish six basic aspects of language, we could, however, hardly find verbal messages that would fulfill only one function. The diversity lies not in a monopoly of some one of these several functions but in a different hierarchical order of functions. The verbal structure of a message depends primarily on the predominant function. But even though a set (*Einstellung*) toward the referent, an orientation toward the context – briefly the so-called REFERENTIAL, 'denotative', 'cognitive' function – is the leading task of numerous messages, the accessory participation of the other functions in such messages must be taken into account by the observant linguist.

The so-called EMOTIVE or 'expressive' function, focused on the addresser, aims a direct expression of the speaker's attitude toward what he is speaking about. It tends to produce an impression of a certain emotion, whether true or feigned; therefore, the term 'emotive', launched and advocated by Marty (1908), has proved to be preferable to 'emotional'. The purely emotive stratum in language is presented by the interjections. They differ from the means of referential language both by their sound pattern (peculiar sound sequences or even sounds elsewhere unusual) and by their syntactic role (they are not components but equivalents of sentences). '*Tut! Tut!* said McGinty': the complete utterance of Conan Doyle's character consists of two suction clicks. The emotive function, laid bare in the interjections, flavors to some extent all our utterances, on their phonic, grammatical, and lexical level. If we analyze language from the standpoint of the information it carries, we cannot restrict the notion of information to the cognitive aspect of language. A man, using expressive features to indicate his angry or ironic attitude, conveys ostensible information, and evidently this verbal behavior cannot be likened to such nonsemiotic, nutritive activities as 'eating grapefruit' (despite Chatman's bold simile). The difference between [big] and the emphatic prolongation of the vowel [bi:g] is a conventional, coded linguistic feature like the difference between the short and long vowel in such Czech pairs as [vi] 'you' and [vi:] 'knows', but in the latter pair the differential information is phonemic and in the former emotive. As long as we are interested in phonemic invariants, the English /i/ and /i:/ appear to be mere variants of one and the same phoneme, but if we are concerned with emotive units, the relation between the invariants and variants is reversed: length and shortness are invariants implemented by variable phonemes. Saporta's surmise that emotive difference is a nonlinguistic feature, 'attributable to the delivery of the message and not to the message' (1960, p. 88), arbitrarily reduces the informational capacity of messages.

A former actor of Stanislavskij's Moscow Theater told me how at his audition he was asked by the famous director to make forty different messages from the phrase *Segodnja večerom* (This evening), by diversifying its expressive tint. He made a list of some forty emotional situations, then emitted the given phrase in accordance with each of these situations, which his audience had to recognize only from the changes in the sound shape of the same two words. For our research work in the description and analysis of contemporary Standard Russian (under the auspices of the Rockefeller Foundation) this actor was asked to repeat Stanislavskij's test. He wrote down some fifty situations framing the same elliptic sentence and made of it fifty corresponding messages for a tape recording. Most of the messages were correctly and circumstantially decoded by Moscovite listeners. May I add that all such emotive cues easily undergo linguistic analysis.

Orientation toward the addressee, the CONATIVE function, finds its purest grammatical expression in the vocative and imperative, which syntactically, morphologically, and often even phonemically deviate from other nominal and verbal categories. The imperative sentences cardinally differ from declarative sentences: the latter are and the former are not liable to a truth test. When in O'Neill's play *The Fountain*, Nano '(in a fierce tone of command)' says 'Drink!' – the imperative cannot be challenged by the question 'is it true or not?' which may be, however, perfectly well asked after such sentences as 'one drank', 'one will drink', 'one would drink'. In contradistinction to the imperative sentences, the declarative sentences are convertible into interrogative sentences: 'did one drink?', 'will one drink?', 'would one drink?'

The traditional model of language as elucidated particularly by Bühler (1933, pp. 19–20) was confined to these three functions – emotive, conative, and referential – and the three apexes of this model – the first person of the addresser, the second person of the addressee, and the 'third person' properly (someone or something spoken of). Certain additional verbal functions can be easily inferred from this triadic model. Thus the magic, incantatory function is chiefly some kind of conversion of an absent or inanimate 'third person' into an addressee of a conative message. 'May this sty dry up, *tfu, tfu, tfu, tfu*' (Lithuanian spell; Mansikka 1929, p. 69). 'Water, queen river, daybreak! Send grief beyond the blue sea, to the sea bottom, like a gray stone never to rise from the sea bottom, may grief never come to burden the light heart of God's servant, may grief be removed and sink away' (North Russian incantation; Rybnikov 1910, pp. 217–8). 'Sun, stand thou still upon Gibeon; and thou, Moon, in the valley of Aj-a-lon. And the sun stood still, and the moon stayed' (Joshua 10.12). We observe, however, three further constitutive factors of verbal communication and three corresponding functions of language.

There are messages primarily serving to establish, to prolong, or to discontinue communication, to check whether the channel works ('Hello, do you hear me?'), to attract the attention of the interlocutor or to confirm his continued attention ('Are you listening?' or in Shakespearean diction, 'Lend me your ears!' – and on the other end of the wire 'Um-hum!'). This set for CONTACT, or in Malinowski's (1953) terms PHATIC function, may be displayed by a profuse exchange of ritualized formulas, by entire dialogues with the mere purport of prolonging communication. Dorothy Parker caught eloquent examples: ' "Well!" the young man said. "Well!" she said. "Well, here we are," he said. "Here we are," she said, "Aren't we?" "I should say we were," he said, "Eeyop! Here we are." "Well!" she said. "Well!" he said, "well." ' The endeavor to start and sustain communication is typical of talking birds; thus the phatic function of language is the only one they share with human beings. It is also the first verbal function acquired by infants; they are prone to communicate before being able to send or receive informative communication.

A distinction has been made in modern logic between two levels of language: 'object language' speaking of objects and 'metalanguage' speaking of language (Tarski 1936). But metalanguage is not only a necessary scientific tool utilized by logicians and linguists; it plays also an important role in our everyday language. Like Molière's Jourdain who used prose without knowing it, we practice metalanguage without realizing the metalingual character of our operations. Whenever the addresser and/or the addressee need to check up whether they use the same code, speech is focused on the CODE: it performs a METALINGUAL (i.e. glossing) function. 'I don't follow you – what do you mean?' asks the addressee, or in Shakespearean diction, 'What is't thou say'st?' And the addresser in anticipation of such recapturing questions inquires: 'Do you know what I mean?' Imagine such an exasperating dialogue: 'The sophomore was plucked.' 'But what is *plucked*?' '*Plucked* means the same as *flunked*.' 'And *flunked*?' '*To be flunked* is *to fail an exam*.' 'And what is *sophomore*?' persists the interrogator innocent of school vocabulary. '*A sophomore* is (or means) a *second-year student*.' All these equational sentences convey information merely about the lexical code of English; their function is strictly metalingual. Any process of language learning, in particular child acquisition of the mother tongue, makes wide use of such metalingual operations; and aphasia may often be defined as a loss of ability for metalingual operations.

I have brought up all the six factors involved in verbal communication except the message itself. The set (*Einstellung*) toward the MESSAGE as such, focus on the message for its own sake, is the POETIC function of language. This function cannot be productively studied out of touch with the general problems of language, and, on the other hand, the scrutiny of language requires a thorough consideration of its poetic function. Any attempt to reduce the sphere of the poetic function to poetry or to confine poetry to the poetic function would be a delusive oversimplification. The poetic function is not the sole function of verbal art but only its dominant, determining function, whereas in all other verbal activities it acts as a subsidiary, accessory constituent. This function, by promoting the palpability of signs, deepens the fundamental dichotomy of signs and objects. Hence, when dealing with the poetic function, linguistics cannot limit itself to the field of poetry.

'Why do you always say *Joan and Margery*, yet never *Margery and Joan*? Do you prefer Joan to her twin sister?' 'Not at all, it just sounds smoother.' In a sequence of two coordinate names, so far as no problems of rank interfere, the precedence of the shorter name suits the speaker, unaccountably for him, as a well-ordered shape for the message.

A girl used to talk about 'the horrible Harry'. 'Why horrible?' 'Because I hate him.' 'But why not *dreadful, terrible, frightful, disgusting*?' 'I don't know why, but *horrible* fits him better.' Without realizing it, she clung to the poetic device of paronomasia.

The political slogan 'I like Ike' /ay layk ayk/, succinctly structured, consists of three monosyllables and counts three diphthongs /ay/, each of them symmetrically followed by one consonantal phoneme, /..l..k..k/. The make-up of the three words presents a variation: no consonantal phonemes in the first word, two around the diphthong in the second, and one final consonant in the third. A similar dominant nucleus /ay/ was noticed by Hymes (1960, pp. 123–6) in some of the sonnets of Keats. Both cola of the trisyllabic formula 'I like / Ike' rhyme with each other, and the second of the two rhyming words is fully included in the first one (echo rhyme), /layk/ – /ayk/, a paronomastic image of a feeling which totally envelops its object. Both cola alliterate with each other, and the first of the two alliterating words is included in the second: /ay/ – /ayk/, a paronomastic image of the loving subject enveloped by the beloved object. The secondary, poetic function of this campaign slogan reinforces its impressiveness and efficacy.

As I said, the linguistic study of the poetic function must overstep the limits of poetry, and, on the other hand, the linguistic scrutiny of poetry cannot limit itself to the poetic function. The particularities of diverse poetic genres imply a differently ranked participation of the other verbal functions along with the dominant poetic function. Epic poetry, focused on the third person, strongly involves the referential function of language; the lyric, oriented toward the first person, is intimately linked with the emotive function; poetry of the second person is imbued with the conative function and is either supplicatory or exhortative, depending on whether the first person is subordinated to the second one or the second to the first.

Now that our cursory description of the six basic functions of verbal communication is more or less complete, we may complement our scheme of the fundamental factors with a corresponding scheme of the functions:

REFERENTIAL

EMOTIVE   POETIC   CONATIVE

PHATIC

METALINGUAL

What is the empirical linguistic criterion of the poetic function? In particular, what is the indispensable feature inherent in any piece of poetry? To answer this question we must recall the two basic modes of arrangement used in verbal behavior, *selection* and *combination*. If 'child' is the topic of the message, the speaker selects one among the extant, more or less similar nouns like child, kid, youngster, tot, all of them equivalent in a certain respect, and then, to comment on this topic, he may select one of the semantically cognate verbs – sleeps, dozes, nods, naps. Both chosen words combine in the speech chain. The selection is produced on the basis of equivalence, similarity and dissimilarity, synonymy and antonymy, while the combination, the build-up of the sequence, is based on contiguity. *The poetic function projects the principle of equivalence from the axis of selection into the axis of combination.* Equivalence is promoted to the constitutive device of the sequence. In poetry one syllable is equalized with any other syllable of the same sequence; word stress is assumed to equal word stress, as unstress equals unstress; prosodic long is matched with long, and short with short; word boundary equals word boundary, no boundary equals no boundary; syntactic pause equals syntactic pause, no pause equals no pause. Syllables are converted into units of measure, and so are morae or stresses.

It may be objected that metalanguage also makes a sequential use of equivalent units when combining synonymic expressions into an equational sentence: $A = A$ (*'Mare* is *the female of the horse'*). Poetry and metalanguage, however, are in diametrical opposition to each other: in metalanguage the sequence is used to build an equation, whereas in poetry the equation is used to build a sequence.

In poetry, and to a certain extent in latent manifestations of the poetic function, sequences delimited by word boundaries become commensurable whether they are sensed as isochronic or graded. 'Joan and Margery' showed us the poetic principle of syllable gradation, the same principle that in the closes of Serbian folk epics has been raised to a compulsory law (cf. Maretic 1907, secs 81–3). Without its two dactylic words the combination '*in*nocent *by*stander' would hardly have become a hackneyed phrase. The symmetry of three disyllabic verbs with an identical initial consonant and identical final vowel added splendor to the laconic victory message of Caesar: 'Veni, vidi, vici.'

Measure of sequences is a device that, outside of the poetic function, finds no application in language. Only in poetry with its regular reiteration of equivalent units is the time of the speech flow experienced, as it is – to cite another semiotic pattern – with musical time. Gerard Manley Hopkins, an outstanding searcher in the science of poetic language, defined verse as 'speech wholly or partially repeating the same figure of sound' (1959, p. 289). Hopkins' subsequent question, 'but is all verse poetry?' can be definitely answered as soon as the poetic function ceases to be arbitrarily confined to the domain of poetry. Mnemonic lines cited by Hopkins (like 'Thirty days hath September'), modern advertising jingles, and versified medieval laws, mentioned by Lotz (1960, p. 137), or finally Sanskrit scientific treatises in verse which in Indic tradition are strictly distinguished from true poetry (*kāvya*) – all these metrical texts make use of the poetic function without, however, assigning to this function the coercing, determining role it carries in poetry. Thus verse actually exceeds the limits of poetry, but at the same time verse always implies the poetic function. And apparently no human culture ignores verse making, whereas there are many cultural patterns without 'applied' verse; and even in such cultures as possess both pure and applied verses, the latter appear to be a secondary, unquestionably derived phenomenon. The adaptation of poetic means for some heterogeneous purpose does not conceal their primary essence, just as elements of emotive language, when utilized in poetry, still maintain their emotive tinge. A filibusterer may recite *Hiawatha* because it is long, yet poeticalness still remains the primary intent of this text itself. Self-evidently, the existence of versified, musical, and pictorial commercials does not separate the questions of verse or of musical and pictorial form from the study of poetry, music, and fine arts.

To sum up, the analysis of verse is entirely within the competence of poetics, and the latter may be defined as that part of linguistics which treats the poetic function in its relationship to the other functions of language. Poetics in the wider sense of the word deals with the poetic function not only in poetry, where this function is superimposed upon the other functions of language, but also outside poetry, when some other function is superimposed upon the poetic function.

The reiterative 'figure of sound', which Hopkins saw as the constitutive principle of verse, can be further specified. Such a figure always utilizes at least one (or more than one) binary contrast of a relatively high and relatively low prominence effected by the different sections of the phonemic sequence.

Within a syllable the more prominent, nuclear, syllabic part, constituting the peak of the syllable, is opposed to the less prominent, marginal, nonsyllabic phonemes. Any syllable contains a syllabic phoneme, and the interval between two successive syllabics is, in some languages, always and, in others, overwhelmingly carried out by marginal, nonsyllabic phonemes. In so-called syllabic versification the number of syllabics in a metrically delimited chain (time series) is a constant, whereas the presence of a nonsyllabic phoneme or cluster between every two syllabics of a metrical chain is a constant only in languages with an indispensable occurrence of nonsyllabics between syllabics and, furthermore, in those verse systems where hiatus is prohibited. Another manifestation of a tendency toward a uniform syllabic model is the avoidance of closed syllables at the end of the line, observable, for instance, in Serbian epic songs. Italian syllabic verse shows a tendency to treat a sequence of vowels unseparated by consonantal phonemes as one single metrical syllable (cf. Levi 1930, secs 8–9).

In some patterns of versification the syllable is the only constant unit of verse measure, and a grammatical limit is the only constant line of demarcation between measured sequences, whereas in other patterns syllables in turn are dichotomized into more and less prominent, or two levels of grammatical limits are distinguished in their metrical function: word boundaries and syntactic pauses.

Except the varieties of the so-called vers libre that are based on conjugate intonations and pauses only, any meter uses the syllable as a unit of measure at least in certain sections of the verse. Thus in purely accentual verse ('sprung rhythm' in Hopkins' vocabulary), the number of syllables in the upbeat (called 'slack' by Hopkins 1967, p. 45) may vary, but the downbeat (ictus) constantly contains one single syllable.

In any accentual verse the contrast between higher and lower prominence is achieved by syllables under stress versus unstressed syllables. Most accentual patterns operate primarily with the contrast of syllables with and without word stress, but some varieties of accentual verse deal with syntactic, phrasal stresses, those which Wimsatt and Beardsley cite as 'the major stresses of the major words' (1959, p. 592) and which are opposed as prominent to syllables without such major, syntactic stress.

In quantitative ('chronemic') verse, long and short syllables are mutually opposed as more and less prominent. This contrast is usually carried out by syllable nuclei, phonemically long and short. But in metrical patterns like Ancient Greek and Arabic, which equalize length 'by position' with length 'by nature', the minimal syllables consisting of a consonantal phoneme and one mora vowel are opposed to syllables with a surplus (a second mora or a closing consonant) as simpler and less prominent syllables opposed to those that are more complex and prominent.

The question still remains open whether, besides accentual and chronemic verse, there exists a 'tonemic' type of versification in languages where differences of syllabic intonations are used to distinguish word meanings (Jakobson 1923). In classical Chinese poetry (Bishop 1955), syllables with modulations (in Chinese *tsê*, deflected tones) are opposed to the nonmodulated syllables (*p'ing*, level tones), but apparently a chronemic principle underlies this opposition, as was suspected by Polivanov (1924) and keenly interpreted by Wang Li (1958); in the Chinese metrical tradition the level tones prove to be opposed to the deflected tones as long tonal peaks of syllables to short ones, so that verse is based on the opposition of length and shortness.

Joseph Greenberg (1960) brought to my attention another variety of tonemic versification – the verse of Efik riddles based on the level feature. In the sample cited by Simmons (1955, p. 228), the query and the response form two octosyllables with an alike distribution of *h*(igh)- and *l*(ow)-tone syllabics; in each hemistich, moreover, the last three of the four syllables present an identical tonemic pattern: *lhhl/hhhl///lhhl/hhhl//*. Whereas Chinese versification appears as a peculiar variety of quantitative verse, the verse of the Efik riddles is linked with the usual accentual verse by an opposition of two degrees of prominence (strength or height) of the vocal tone. Thus a metrical system of versification can be based only on the opposition of syllabic peaks and slopes (syllabic verse), on the relative level of the peaks (accentual verse), and on the relative length of the syllabic peaks or entire syllables (quantitative verse).

In textbooks of literature we sometimes encounter a superstitious contraposition of syllabism as a mere mechanical count of syllables to the lively pulsation of accentual verse. If we examine, however, the binary meters of strictly syllabic and at the same time accentual versification, we observe two homogeneous successions of wavelike peaks and valleys. Of these two undulatory curves, the syllabic one carries nuclear phonemes in the crest and usually marginal phonemes in the bottom. As a rule the accentual curve superimposed upon the syllabic curve alternates stressed and unstressed syllables in the crests and bottoms respectively.

For comparison with the English meters that we have discussed at length, I bring to your attention the similar Russian binary verse forms which for the last fifty years have undergone an exhaustive investigation (see particularly Taranovsky 1955). The structure of the verse can be very thoroughly described and interpreted in terms of enchained probabilities. Besides the compulsory word boundary between the lines, which is an invariant throughout all Russian meters, in the classic pattern of Russian syllabic accentual verse ('syllabo-tonic' in native nomenclature) we observe the following constants: (1) the number of syllables in the line from its beginning to the last downbeat is stable; (2) this very last downbeat always carries a word stress; (3) a stressed syllable cannot fall on the upbeat if the downbeat is fulfilled by an unstressed syllable of the same word unit (so that a word stress can coincide with an upbeat only as far as it belongs to a monosyllabic word unit).

Along with these characteristics compulsory for any line composed in a given meter, there are features that show a high probability of occurrence without being constantly present. Besides signals certain to occur ('probability one'), signals likely to occur ('probabilities less than one') enter into the notion of meter. Using Cherry's (1957) description of human communication, we could say that the reader of poetry obviously 'may be unable to attach numerical frequencies' to the constituents of the meter, but as far as he conceives the verse shape, he unwittingly gets an inkling of their 'rank order'.

In the Russian binary meters, all odd syllables counting back from the last downbeat – briefly, all the upbeats – are usually fulfilled by unstressed syllables, except some very low percentage of stressed monosyllables. All even syllables, again counting back from the last downbeat, show a sizable preference for syllables under word stress, but the probabilities of their occurrence are unequally distributed among the successive downbeats of the line. The higher the relative frequency of word stresses in a given downbeat, the lower the ratio shown by the preceding downbeat. Since the last downbeat is constantly stressed, the next to last has the lowest percentages of word stresses; in the preceding downbeat their amount is again higher, without attaining the maximum, displayed by the final downbeat; one downbeat further toward the beginning of the line, the amount of the stresses sinks once more, without reaching the minimum of the next-to-last downbeat; and so on. Thus the distribution of word stresses among the downbeats within the line, the split into strong and weak downbeats, creates a *regressive undulatory curve* superimposed upon the wavy alternation of downbeats and upbeats. Incidentally, there is also the captivating question of the relationship between the strong downbeats and phrasal stresses.

The Russian binary meters reveal a stratified arrangement of three undulatory curves: (I) alternation of syllabic nuclei and margins; (II) division of syllabic nuclei into alternating downbeats and upbeats; and (III) alternation of strong

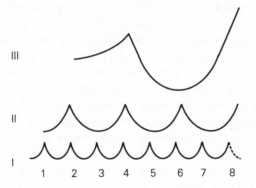

Figure 1.1

and weak downbeats. For example, the Russian masculine iambic tetrameter of the nineteenth and present centuries may be represented as in Figure 1.1, and a similar triadic pattern appears in the corresponding English forms.

Three out of five downbeats are deprived of word stress in Shelley's iambic line 'Laugh with an inextinguishable laughter'. Seven out of sixteen downbeats are stressless in the following quatrain from Pasternak's late iambic tetrameter 'Zemlja' (Earth):

> I úlica za panibráta
> S okónnicej podslepovátoj,
> I béloj nóči i zakátu
> Ne razminút'sja u rekí.

Since the overwhelming majority of downbeats concur with word stresses, the listener or reader of Russian verses is prepared with a high degree of probability to meet a word stress in any even syllable of iambic lines, but at the very beginning of Pasternak's quatrain the fourth and, one foot further, the sixth syllable, both in the first and in the following line, present him with a *frustrated expectation*. The degree of such a 'frustration' is higher when the stress is lacking in a strong downbeat and becomes particularly outstanding when two successive downbeats carry unstressed syllables. The stresslessness of two adjacent downbeats is the less probable and the most striking when it embraces a whole hemistich, as in a later line of the same poem: 'Čtoby za gorodskóju grán'ju' [stəbyzəgərackóju grán'ju]. The expectation depends on the treatment of a given downbeat in the poem and more generally in the whole extant metrical tradition. In the last downbeat but one, unstress may, however, outweigh the stress. Thus in this poem only 17 of 41 lines have a word stress on their sixth syllable. Yet in such a case the inertia of the stressed even syllables alternating with the unstressed odd syllables prompts some expectancy of stress also for the sixth syllable of the iambic tetrameter.

Quite naturally it was Edgar Allan Poe, the poet and theoretician of defeated anticipation, who metrically and psychologically appraised the human sense of gratification from the unexpected which arises from expectedness, each unthinkable without its opposite, 'as evil cannot exist without good' (1855, p. 492). Here we could easily apply Robert Frost's formula from 'The Figure a Poem Makes' (1939): 'The figure is the same as for love.'

The so-called shifts of word stress in polysyllabic words from the downbeat to the upbeat ('reversed feet'), which are unknown to the standard forms of Russian verse, appear quite usually in English poetry after a metrical and/or syntactic pause. A notable example is the rhythmical variation of the same adjective in Milton's 'Infinite wrath and infinite despair'. In the line 'Nearer, my God, to Thee, nearer to Thee', the stressed syllable of one and the same word occurs twice in the upbeat, first at the beginning of the line and a second time at the beginning of a phrase. This license, discussed by Jespersen (1933) and current in many languages, is entirely explainable by the particular import of the relation between an upbeat and the immediately preceding downbeat. Where such an immediate precedence is impeded by an inserted pause, the upbeat becomes a kind of *syllaba anceps*.

Besides the rules that underlie the compulsory features of verse, the rules governing its optional traits also pertain to meter. We are inclined to designate such phenomena as unstress in the downbeats and stress in upbeats as deviations, but it must be remembered that these are allowed oscillations, departures within the limits of the law. In British parliamentary terms, it is not an opposition to its majesty the meter but an opposition of its majesty. As to the actual infringements of metrical laws, the discussion of such violations recalls Osip Brik, perhaps the keenest of the Russian Formalists, who used to say that political conspirators are tried and condemned only for unsuccessful attempts at a forcible upheaval, because in the case of a successful coup it is the conspirators who assume the role of judges and prosecutors. If the violences against the meter take root, they themselves become metrical rules.

Far from being an abstract, theoretical scheme, meter – or in more explicit terms, *verse design* – underlies the structure of any single line – or, in logical terminology, any single *verse instance*. Design and instance are correlative concepts. The verse design determines the invariant features of the verse instances and sets up the limits of variations. A Serbian peasant reciter of epic poetry memorizes, performs, and, to a high extent, improvises thousands, sometimes tens of thousands of lines, and their meter is alive in his mind. Unable to abstract its rules, he nonetheless notices and repudiates even the slightest infringement of these rules. Any line of Serbian epics contains precisely ten syllables and is followed by a syntactic pause. There is furthermore a compulsory word boundary before the fifth syllable and a compulsory absence of word boundary before the fourth and the tenth syllable. The verse has, moreover, significant quantitative and accentual characteristics (cf. Jakobson 1933 and 1952).

This Serbian epic break, along with many similar examples presented by comparative metrics, is a persuasive warning against the erroneous identification of a break with a syntactic pause. The obligatory word boundary must not be combined with a pause and is not even meant to be audible to the ear. The analysis of Serbian epic songs phonographically recorded proves that there are no compulsory audible clues to the break, and yet any attempt to abolish the word boundary before the fifth syllable by a mere insignificant change in word order is immediately condemned by the narrator. The grammatical fact that the fourth and fifth syllables pertain to two different word units is sufficient for the appraisal of the break. Thus verse design goes far beyond the questions of sheer song shape; it is a much wider linguistic phenomenon, and it yields to no isolating phonetic treatment.

I say 'linguistic phenomenon' even though Chatman states that 'the meter exists as a system outside the language' (1960, p. 158). Yes, meter appears also in other arts dealing with time sequence. There are many linguistic problems – for instance, syntax – which likewise overstep the limit of language and are common to different semiotic systems. We may speak even about the grammar of traffic signals. There exists a signal code, where a yellow light when combined with green warns that free passage is close to being stopped and when combined with red announces the approaching cessation of the stoppage; such a yellow signal offers a close analogue to the verbal completive aspect. Poetic meter, however, has so many intrinsically linguistic particularities that it is most convenient to describe it from a purely linguistic point of view.

Let us add that no linguistic property of the verse design should be disregarded. Thus, for example, it would be an unfortunate mistake to deny the constitutive value of intonation in English meters. Not to mention its fundamental role in the meters of such a master of English free verse as Whitman, it is hardly possible to ignore the metrical significance of pausal intonation ('final juncture'), whether 'cadence' or 'anticadence' (Karcevskij 1931) in poems like 'The Rape of the Lock' with its intentional avoidance of enjambments. Yet even a vehement accumulation of enjambments never hides their digressive, variational status; they always set off the normal coincidence of syntactic pause and pausal intonation with the metrical limit. Whatever is the reciter's way of reading, the intonational constraint of the poem remains valid. The intonational contour specific to a poem, to a poet, to a poetic school is one of the most notable topics brought to discussion by the Russian Formalists (Ejxenbaum 1969 and Zirmunskij 1928).

The verse design is embodied in verse instances. Usually the free variation of these instances is denoted by the somewhat equivocal label 'rhythm'. A variation of *verse instances* within a given poem must be strictly distinguished from the variable *delivery instances*. The intention 'to describe the verse line as it is actually performed' is of lesser use for the synchronic and historical analysis of poetry than it is for the study of its recitation in the present and the past. Meanwhile the truth is simple and clear: 'There are many performances of the same poem – differing among themselves in many ways. A performance is an event, but the poem itself, if there *is* any poem, must be some kind of enduring object.' This sage memento of Wimsatt and Beardsley (1959, p. 587) belongs indeed to the essentials of modern metrics.

In Shakespeare's verses the second, stressed syllable of the word 'absurd' usually falls on the downbeat, but once in the third act of *Hamlet* it falls on the upbeat: 'No, let the candied tongue lick absurd pomp'. The reciter may scan the word 'absurd' in this line with an initial stress on the first syllable or observe the final word stress in accordance with the standard accentuation. He may also subordinate the word stress of the adjective in favor of the strong syntactic stress of the following head word, as suggested by Hill (1953): 'Nó, lèt thĕ cândĭed tóngue lîck ăbsùrd pómp', as in Hopkins' conception of English antispasts – 'regrét néver' (1959, p. 276). There is, finally, the possibility of emphatic modifications either through a 'fluctuating accentuation' (*schwebende Betonung*) embracing both syllables or through an exclamatory reinforcement of the first syllable [àb-súrd]. But whatever solution the reciter chooses, the shift of the word stress from the downbeat to the upbeat with no antecedent pause is still arresting, and the moment of frustrated expectation stays viable. Wherever the reciter puts the accent, the discrepancy between the English word stress on the second syllable of 'absurd' and the downbeat attached to the first syllable persists as a constitutive feature of the verse instance. The tension between the ictus and the usual word stress is inherent in this line independently of its different implementations by various actors and readers. As Hopkins observes, in the preface to his poems, 'two rhythms are in some manner running at once' (1967, p. 46). His description of such a contrapuntal run can be reinterpreted. The superinducing of the equivalence principle upon the word sequence or, in other terms, the *mounting* of the metrical form upon the usual speech form necessarily gives the experience of a double, ambiguous shape to anyone who is familiar with the given language and with verse. Both the convergences and the divergences between the two forms, both the warranted and the frustrated expectations, supply this experience.

How the given verse instance is implemented in the given delivery instance depends on the *delivery design* of the reciter; he may cling to a scanning style or tend toward prose-like prosody or freely oscillate between these two poles. We must be on guard against simplistic binarism which reduces two couples into one single opposition either by suppressing the cardinal distinction between verse design and verse instance (as well as between delivery design and delivery instance) or by an erroneous identification of delivery instance and delivery design with the verse instance and verse design.

> 'But tell me, child, your choice; what shall I buy
> You?' – 'Father, what you buy me I like best.'

These two lines from 'The Handsome Heart' by Hopkins contain a heavy enjambment which puts a verse boundary before the concluding monosyllable of a phrase, of a sentence, of an utterance. The recitation of these pentameters may be strictly metrical with a manifest pause between 'buy' and 'you' and a suppressed pause after the pronoun. Or, on the contrary, there may be displayed a prose-oriented manner without any separation of the words 'buy you' and with a marked pausal intonation at the end of the question. None of these ways of recitation can, however, hide the intentional discrepancy between the metrical and syntactic division. The verse shape of a poem remains completely independent of its variable delivery, whereby I do not intend to nullify the alluring question of *Autorenleser* and *Selbstleser* launched by Sievers (1924).

No doubt, verse is primarily a recurrent 'figure of sound'. Primarily, always, but never uniquely. Any attempts to confine such poetic conventions as meter, alliteration, or rhyme to the sound level are speculative reasonings without any empirical justification. The projection of the equational principle into the sequence has a much deeper and wider significance. Valéry's view of poetry as 'hesitation between the sound and the sense' is much more realistic and scientific than any bias of phonetic isolationism (cf. Valéry 1958).

Although rhyme by definition is based on a regular recurrence of equivalent phonemes or phonemic groups, it would be an unsound oversimplification to treat rhyme merely from the standpoint of sound. Rhyme necessarily involves a semantic relationship between rhyming units ('rhyme-fellows' in Hopkins' [1959, p. 286] nomenclature). In scrutinizing a rhyme we are faced with the question of whether or not it is a homoioteleuton, which confronts similar derivational and/or inflexional suffixes (congratulations – decorations), or whether the rhyming words belong to the same or to different grammatical categories. Thus, for example, Hopkins' fourfold rhyme is an agreement of two nouns – 'kind' and 'mind' – both contrasting with the adjective 'blind' and with the verb 'find'. Is there a semantic propinquity, a sort of simile between rhyming lexical units, as in dove – love, light – bright, place – space, name – fame? Do the rhyming members carry the same syntactic function? The difference between the morphological class and the syntactic application may be pointed out in rhyme. Thus in Poe's lines, 'While I nodded, nearly *napping*, suddenly there came a *tapping*. As of someone gently *rapping*', the three rhyming words, morphologically alike, are all three syntactically different. Are totally or partly homonymic rhymes prohibited, tolerated, or favored? Such full homonyms as son – sun, I – eye, eve – eave, and on the other hand, echo rhymes like December – ember, infinite – night, swarm – warm, smiles – miles? What about compound rhymes (such as Hopkins' 'enjoyment – toy meant' or 'began some – ransom'), where a word unit accords with a word group?

A poet or poetic school may be oriented toward or against grammatical rhyme; rhymes must be either grammatical or antigrammatical; an agrammatical rhyme, indifferent to the relation between sound and grammatical structure, would, like any agrammatism, belong to verbal pathology. If a poet tends to avoid grammatical rhymes, for him, as Hopkins said, 'There are two elements in the beauty rhyme has to the mind, the likeness or sameness of sound and the unlikeness or difference of meaning' (1959, p. 286). Whatever the relation between sound and meaning in different rhyme techniques, both spheres are necessarily involved. After Wimsatt's (1954) illuminating observations about the meaningfulness of rhyme and the shrewd modern studies of Slavic rhyme patterns, a student in poetics can hardly maintain that rhymes signify merely in a very vague way.

Rhyme is only a particular, condensed case of a much more general, we may even say the fundamental, problem of poetry, namely *parallelism*. Here again Hopkins, in his student papers of 1865, displayed a prodigious insight into the structure of poetry:

> The artificial part of poetry, perhaps we shall be right to say all artifice, reduces itself to the principle of parallelism. The structure of poetry is that of continuous parallelism, ranging from the technical so-called Parallelisms of Hebrew poetry and the antiphons of Church music up to the intricacy of Greek or Italian or English verse. But parallelism is of two kinds necessarily – where the opposition is clearly marked, and where it is transitional rather or chromatic. Only the first kind, that of marked parallelism, is concerned with the structure of verse – in rhythm, the recurrence of a certain sequence of syllables, in metre, the recurrence of a certain sequence of rhythm, in alliteration, in assonance and in rhyme. Now the force of this recurrence is to beget a recurrence or parallelism answering to it in the words or thought and, speaking roughly and rather for the tendency than the invariable result, the more marked parallelism in structure whether of elaboration or of emphasis begets more marked parallelism in the words and sense ... To the marked or abrupt kind of parallelism belong metaphor, simile, parable, and so on, where the effect is sought in likeness of things, and antithesis, contrast, and so on, where it is sought in unlikeness.
>
> (Hopkins 1959, p. 85)

Briefly, equivalence in sound, projected into the sequence as its constitutive principle, inevitably involves semantic equivalence, and on any linguistic level any constituent of such a sequence prompts one of the two correlative experiences which Hopkins neatly defines as 'comparison for likeness' sake' and 'comparison for unlikeness' sake' (1959, p. 106).

Folklore offers the most clear-cut and stereotyped forms of poetry, particularly suitable for structural scrutiny (as Sebeok [1960] illustrated with Cheremis samples). Those oral traditions that use grammatical parallelism to connect consecutive lines, for example, Finno-Ugric patterns of verse (see Austerlitz 1958 and Steinitz 1934) and to a high degree also Russian folk poetry, can be fruitfully analyzed on all linguistic levels – phonological, morphological, syntactic, and lexical: we learn what elements are conceived as equivalent and how likeness on certain levels is tempered by conspicuous difference on other ones. Such forms enable us to verify Ransom's wise suggestion that 'the meter-and-meaning process is the organic art of poetry, and involves all its important characters' (1941, p. 295). These clear-cut traditional structures may dispel Wimsatt's (1960, p. 205) doubts about the possibility of writing a grammar of the meter's interaction with the sense, as well as a grammar of the arrangement of metaphors. As soon as parallelism is promoted to canon, the interaction between meter and meaning and the arrangement of tropes cease to be 'the free and individual and unpredictable parts of the poetry'.

Let me translate a few typical lines from Russian wedding songs about the appearance of the bridegroom:

> A brave fellow was going to the porch,
> Vasilij was walking to the manor.

The translation is literal; the verbs, however, take the final position in both Russian clauses (*Dobroj mólodec k séničkam privoráčival,/ Vasílij k téremu prixá žival*). The lines wholly correspond to each other syntactically and morphologically. Both predicative verbs have the same prefixes and suffixes and the same vocalic alternant in the stem; they are alike in aspect, tense, number, and gender; and, moreover, they are synonymous. Both subjects, the common noun and the proper name, refer to the same person and form an appositional group. The two modifiers of place are expressed by identical prepositional constructions, and the first one stands in a synecdochic relation to the second.

These verses may occur preceded by another line of similar grammatical (syntactic and morphologic) make-up: 'Not a bright falcon was flying beyond the hills' or 'Not a fierce horse was coming at gallop to the court'. The 'bright falcon' and the 'fierce horse' of these variants are put in metaphorical relation with the 'brave fellow'. This a traditional Slavic negative parallelism – the refutation of the metaphorical state (vehicle) in favor of the factual state (tenor). The negation *ne* may, however, be omitted: *Jasjón sokol zá gory zaljótyval* (A bright falcon was flying beyond the hills) or *Retív kon' kó dvoru priskákival* (A fierce horse was coming at a gallop to the court). In the first of the two examples the *metaphorical* relation is maintained: a brave fellow appeared at the porch like a bright falcon from behind the hills. In the other instance, however, the semantic connection becomes ambiguous. A comparison between the appearing bridegroom and the galloping horse suggests itself, but at the same time the halt of the horse at the court actually anticipates the approach of the hero to the house. Thus, before introducing the rider and the manor of his fiancee, the song evokes the contiguous, *metonymical* images of the horse and of the courtyard: possession instead of possessor, and outdoors instead of inside. The exposition of the groom may be broken up into two consecutive moments even without substituting the horse for the horseman: 'A brave fellow was coming at a gallop to the court,/ Vasilij was walking to the porch.' Thus the 'fierce horse', emerging in the preceding line at a similar metrical and syntactic place as the 'brave fellow', figures simultaneously as a likeness to and as a representative possession of this fellow, properly speaking – *pars pro toto* for the horseman. The horse image is on the border line between metonymy and synecdoche. From these suggestive connotations of the 'fierce horse' there ensues a metaphorical synecdoche: in the wedding songs and other varieties of Russian erotic lore, the masculine *retiv kon'* becomes a latent or even patent phallic symbol.

As early as the 1880s, Potebnja (1883 and 1887), a remarkable inquirer into Slavic poetics, pointed out that in folk poetry symbols are, as it were, materialized (*oveščestvlen*), converted into an accessory of the ambiance. Still a symbol, it is put, however, in a connection with the action. Thus a simile is presented in the shape of a temporal sequence. In Potebnja's examples from Slavic folklore, the willow, under which a girl passes, serves at the same time as her image; the tree and the girl are both present in the same verbal simulacrum of the willow. Quite similarly, the horse of the love songs remains a symbol of virility not only when the maid is asked by the lad to feed his steed but even when being saddled or put into the stable or tied to a tree.

In poetry not only the phonological sequence but in the same way any sequence of semantic units strives to build an equation. Similarity superimposed on contiguity imparts to poetry its thoroughgoing symbolic, multiplex, polysemantic essence, which is beautifully suggested by Goethe's 'Alles Vergängliche ist nur ein Gleichnis' (Anything transient is but a likeness). Said more technically, anything sequent is a simile. In poetry, where similarity is superinduced upon contiguity, any metonymy is slightly metaphoric and any metaphor has a metonymic tint.

Ambiguity is an intrinsic, inalienable character of any self-focused message, briefly, a corollary feature of poetry. Let us repeat with Empson (1947): 'The machinations of ambiguity are among the very roots of poetry.' Not only the message itself but also its addresser and addressee become ambiguous. Besides the author and the reader, there is the 'I' of the lyrical hero or of the fictitious storyteller and the 'you' or 'thou' of the alleged addressee of dramatic monologues, supplications, and epistles. For example the poem 'Wrestling Jacob' is addressed by its title hero to the Saviour and simultaneously acts as a subjective message of the poet Charles Wesley (1707–88) to his readers. Virtually any poetic message is a quasi-quoted discourse with all those peculiar, intricate problems which 'speech within speech' offers to the linguist.

The supremacy of the poetic function over the referential function does not obliterate the reference but makes it ambiguous. The double-sensed message finds correspondence in a split addresser, in a split addressee, as well as in a split reference, as is cogently exposed in the preambles to fairy tales of various peoples, for instance, in the usual exordium of the Majorca storytellers: 'Aixo era y no era' (It was and it was not; see Giese 1952). The repetitiveness effected by imparting the equivalence principle to the sequence makes reiterable not only the constituent sequences of the poetic message but the whole message as well. This capacity for reiteration whether immediate or delayed, this reification of a poetic message and its constituents, this conversion of a message into an enduring thing, indeed all this represents an inherent and effective property of poetry.

In a sequence in which similarity is superimposed on contiguity, two similar phonemic sequences near to each other are prone to assume a paronomastic function. Words similar in sound are drawn together in meaning. It is true that the first line of the final stanza in Poe's 'Raven' makes wide use of repetitive alliterations, as noted by Valéry (1958, p. 319), but 'the overwhelming effect' of this line and of the whole stanza is due primarily to the sway of poetic etymology.

> And the Raven, never flitting, still is sitting, *still* is sitting
> On the pallid bust of Pallas just above my chamber door;
> And his eyes have all the seeming of a demon's that is dreaming,
> And the lamp-light o'er him streaming throws his shadow on the floor:
> And my soul from out that shadow that lies floating on the floor
>   Shall be lifted – nevermore!

The perch of the raven, 'the pallid bust of Pallas', is merged through the 'sonorous' paronomasia /pǽləd/–/pǽləs/ into one organic whole (similar to Shelley's molded line 'Sculptured on alabaster obelisk' /sk.lp/–/l.b.st/–/b.l.sk/). Both confronted words were blended earlier in another epithet of the same bust – *placid*/plǽsɪd/ – a poetic portmanteau, and the bond between the sitter and the seat was in turn fastened by a paronomasia: '*b*ird or *b*east upon the ... *b*ust'. The bird 'is sitting/ On the pallid bust of Pallas just above my chamber door', and the raven on his perch, despite the lover's imperative 'take thy form from off my door', is nailed into place by the words /ʒʌst əbʌv/, both of them blended in /bʌst/.

The never-ending stay of the grim guest is expressed by a chain of ingenious paronomasias, partly inversive, as we would expect from such a deliberate experimenter in anticipatory, regressive *modus operandi*, such a master in 'writing backwards' as Edgar Allan Poe. In the introductory line of this concluding stanza, 'raven', contiguous to the bleak refrain word 'never', appears once more as an embodied mirror image of this 'never': /n.v.r/ – /r.v.n/. Salient paronomasias interconnect both emblems of the everlasting despair, first 'the Raven, never flitting', at the beginning of the very last stanza, and second, in its very last lines the 'shadow that lies floating on the floor' and 'shall be lifted – nevermore': /névər flítíng/ – /flótíŋ/ ... /flɔ́r/ ... /líftəd névər/. The alliterations that struck Valéry build a paronomastic string: /stí ... / – /sít .../–/stí .../ – /sít .../. The invariance of the group is particularly stressed by the variation in its order. The two luminous effects in the chiaroscuro – the 'fiery eyes' of the black fowl and the lamplight throwing 'his shadow on the floor' – are evoked to add to the gloom of the whole picture and are again bound by the 'vivid effect' of paronomasias: /ɔ́lðə símɪŋ/ ... /dímənz/ ... /ɪz drímɪŋ/ – /ɔ́rɪm strímɪŋ/. 'That shadow that lies /láyz/' pairs with the raven's 'eyes' /áyz/ in an impressively misplaced echo rhyme.

In poetry, any conspicuous similarity in sound is evaluated in respect to similarity and/or dissimilarity in meaning. But Pope's alliterative precept to poets – 'the sound must seem an echo of the sense' – has a wider application. In referential language the connection between *signans* and *signatum* is overwhelmingly based on their codified contiguity, which is often confusingly labeled 'arbitrariness of the verbal sign'. The relevance of the sound-meaning nexus is a simple corollary of the superposition of similarity upon contiguity. Sound symbolism is an undeniably objective relation founded on a phenomenal connection between different sensory modes, in particular between the visual and the auditory experience. If the results of research in this area have sometimes been vague or controversial, it is primarily due to an insufficient care for the methods of psychological and linguistic inquiry. Particularly from the linguistic point of view the picture has often been distorted by lack of attention to the phonological aspect of speech sounds or by inevitably vain operations with complex phonemic units instead of with their ultimate components. But when on testing, for example, such phonemic oppositions as grave versus acute we ask whether /i/ or /u/ is darker, some of the subjects may respond that this question makes no sense to them, but hardly one will state that /i/ is the darker of the two.

Poetry is not the only area where sound symbolism makes itself felt, but it is a province where the internal nexus between sound and meaning changes from latent into patent and manifests itself most palpably and intensely, as was noted in Hymes's stimulating paper (1960). The super-average accumulation of a certain class of phonemes or a contrastive assemblage of two opposite classes in the sound texture of a line, of a stanza, of a poem acts like an 'undercurrent of meaning', to use Poe's picturesque expression (1895, p. 46). In two polar words phonemic relationship may be in agreement with their semantic opposition, as in Russian /d'en'/ 'day' and /noč/ 'night', with the acute vowel and consonants in the diurnal name and the corresponding grave vowel in the nocturnal name. A reinforcement of this contrast by surrounding the first word with acute phonemes, in contradistinction to the grave phonemic neighborhood of the second word, makes the sound into a thorough echo of the sense. But in the French *jour* 'day' and *nuit* 'night' the distribution of grave and acute vowels is inverted, so that Mallarmé's *Divagations* (1899) accuse his mother tongue of a deceitful perversity in assigning to day a dark timbre and to night a light one. Whorf states that when in its sound shape 'a word has an acoustic similarity to its own meaning, we can notice it ... But when the opposite occurs, nobody notices it.' Poetic language, however, and particularly French poetry in the collision between sound and meaning detected by Mallarmé, either seeks a phonological alternation of such a discrepancy and drowns the 'converse' distribution of vocalic features by surrounding *nuit* with grave and *jour* with acute phonemes; or it resorts to a semantic shift and its imagery of day and night replaces the imagery of light and dark by other synesthetic correlates of the phonemic opposition grave/acute and, for instance, puts the heavy warm day in contrast to the airy, cool night – because 'human subjects seem to associate the experiences of bright, sharp, hard, high, light (in weight), quick, high-pitched, narrow, and so on in a long series, with each other; and conversely the experiences of dark, warm, yielding, soft, blunt, heavy, slow, low-pitched, wide, etc., in another long series' (Whorf 1956, pp. 276–7).

However effective is the emphasis on repetition in poetry, the sound texture is still far from being confined to numerical contrivances, and a phoneme that appears only once, but in a key word, in a pertinent position, against a contrastive background, may acquire a striking significance. As painters used to say, 'Un kilo de vert n'est pas plus vert qu'un demi kilo.'

Any analysis of poetic sound texture must consistently take into account the phonological structure of the given language and, beside the overall code, the hierarchy of phonological distinctions in the given poetic convention as well. Thus the approximate rhymes used by Slavic peoples in oral and in some stages of written tradition admit unlike consonants in the rhyming members (e.g., Czech *boty, boky, stopy, kosy, sochy*) but, as Nitsch (1954) noticed, no mutual correspondence between voiced and voiceless consonants is allowed, so that the quoted Czech words cannot rhyme with *body, doby, kozy, rohy*. In the songs of some American Indian peoples such as the Pima-Papago and Tepecano, according to Herzog's observations – only partly communicated in print (1946, p. 82)

– the phonemic distinction between voiced and voiceless plosives and between them and nasals is replaced by a free variation, whereas the distinction between labials, dentals, velars, and palatals is rigorously maintained. Thus in the poetry of these languages consonants lose two of the four distinctive features, voiced/voiceless and nasal/oral, and preserve the other two, grave/acute and compact/diffuse. The selection and hierarchic stratification of valid categories is a factor of primary importance for poetics both on the phonological and on the grammatical level.

Old Indic and medieval Latin literary theory keenly distinguished two poles of verbal art, labeled in Sanskrit *Pāñcālī* and *Vaidarbhī* and correspondingly in Latin *ornatus difficilis* and *ornatus facilis* (Arbusow 1948), the latter style evidently being much more difficult to analyze linguistically because in such literary forms verbal devices are unostentatious and language seems a nearly transparent garment. But one must say with Charles Sanders Peirce: 'This clothing never can be completely stripped off, it is only changed for something more diaphanous' (1931, p. 171). 'Verseless composition', as Hopkins calls the prosaic variety of verbal art – where parallelisms are not so strictly marked and strictly regular as 'continuous parallelism' and where there is no dominant figure of sound (1959, pp. 267, 107) – present more entangled problems for poetics, as does any transitional linguistic area. In this case the transition is between strictly poetic and strictly referential language. But Propp's (1958) pioneering monograph on the structure of the fairy tale shows us how a consistently syntactic approach can be of paramount help even in classifying the traditional plots and in tracing the puzzling laws that underlie their composition and selection. The studies of Lévi-Strauss (1955, 1958 and 1960) display a much deeper but essentially similar approach to the same constructional problem.

It is no mere chance that metonymic structures are less explored than the field of metaphor. Allow me to repeat my old observation that the study of poetic tropes has been directed mainly toward metaphor and that so-called realistic literature, intimately tied to the metonymic principle, still defies interpretation, although the same linguistic methodology that poetics uses when analyzing the metaphorical style of romantic poetry is entirely applicable to the metonymical texture of realistic prose (Jakobson 1956).

Textbooks believe in the occurrence of poems devoid of imagery, but actually a scarcity of lexical tropes is counterbalanced by gorgeous grammatical tropes and figures. The poetic resources concealed in the morphological and syntactic structure of language – briefly, the poetry of grammar and its literary product, the grammar of poetry – have been seldom known to critics and mostly disregarded by linguists but skillfully mastered by creative writers.

The main dramatic force of Antony's exordium to the funeral oration for Caesar is achieved by Shakespeare's playing on grammatical categories and constructions. Mark Antony lampoons Brutus' speech by changing the alleged reasons for Caesar's assassination into plain linguistic fictions. Brutus' accusation of Caesar, 'as he was ambitious, I slew him', undergoes successive transformations. First Antony reduces it to a mere quotation which puts the responsibility for the statement on the speaker quoted: 'The noble Brutus / Hath told you.' When repeated, this reference to Brutus is put into opposition to Antony's own assertions by an adversative 'but' and further degraded by a concessive 'yet'. The reference to the alleger's honor ceases to justify the allegation when repeated with a substitution of the merely copulative 'and' instead of the previous causal 'for', and when finally put into question through the malicious insertion of a modal 'sure':

> The noble Brutus
> Hath told you Caesar was ambitious ....
> For Brutus is an honourable man ....
> But Brutus says he was ambitious,
> And Brutus is an honourable man ....
> Yet Brutus says he was ambitious,
> And Brutus is an honourable man ....
> Yet Brutus says he was ambitious,
> And, sure, he is an honourable man.

> (III.ii)

The following polyptoton – 'I speak ... Brutus spoke ... I am to speak' – presents the repeated allegation as mere reported speech instead of reported facts. The effect lies, modal logic would say, in the oblique context of the arguments adduced, which makes them into unprovable belief sentences:

> I speak not to disprove what Brutus spoke,
> But here I am to speak what I do know.

> (III.ii.102–3)

The most effective device of Antony's irony is the *modus obliquus* of Brutus' abstracts changed into a *modus rectus* to disclose that these reified attributes are nothing but linguistic fictions. To Brutus' saying 'he was ambitious', Antony first replies by transferring the adjective from the agent to the action ('Did this in Caesar seem ambitious?'), then by eliciting the abstract noun 'ambition' and converting it into the subject of a concrete passive construction 'Ambition should be made of sterner stuff' and subsequently to the predicate noun of an interrogative sentence, 'Was this ambition?' – Brutus' appeal 'hear me for my cause' is answered by the same noun *in recto*, the hypostatized subject of an interrogative, active construction: 'What cause withholds you?' While Brutus calls 'awake your senses, that you may the better judge', the abstract substantive derived from 'judge' becomes an apostrophized agent in Antony's report: 'O judgment, thou art fled to brutish beasts.' Incidentally, this apostrophe with its murderous paronomasia *Brutus–brutish* is reminiscent of Caesar's parting exclamation 'Et tu, Brute!' Properties and activities are exhibited *in recto*, whereas their carriers appear either *in obliquo* ('withholds you', 'to brutish beasts', 'back to me') or as subjects of negative actions ('men have lost', 'I must pause'):

> You all did love him once, not without cause;
> What cause withholds you then to mourn for him?

O judgment, thou art fled to brutish beasts,
And men have lost their reason!

(III.ii.104 – 7)

The last two lines of Antony's exordium display the ostensible independence of these grammatical metonymies. The stereotyped 'I mourn for so-and-so' and the figurative but still stereotyped 'so-and-so is in the coffin and my heart is with him' or 'goes out to him' give place in Antony's speech to a daringly realized metonymy; the trope becomes a part of poetic reality:

My heart is in the coffin there with Caesar,
And I must pause till it come back to me.

(III.ii.108–9)

My attempt to vindicate the right and duty of linguistics to direct the investigation of verbal art in all its compass and extent can come to a conclusion with the same burden which summarized my report to the 1953 conference here at Indiana University: 'Linguista sum; linguistici nihil a me alienum puto' (in Lévi-Strauss *et al.* 1953). If the poet Ransom is right (and he is right) that 'poetry is a kind of language' (1938, p. 235), the linguist whose field is any kind of language may and must include poetry in his study. The present conference has clearly shown that the time when both linguists and literary historians eluded questions of poetic structure is now safely behind us. Indeed, as Hollander stated, 'there seems to be no reason for trying to separate the literary from the overall linguistic' (1959, p. 295). If there are some critics who still doubt the competence of linguistics to embrace the field of poetics, I believe that the poetic incompetence of some bigoted linguists has been mistaken for an inadequacy of the linguistic science itself. All of us here, however, definitely realize that a linguist deaf to the poetic function of language and a literary scholar indifferent to linguistic problems and unconversant with linguistic methods are equally flagrant anachronisms.[1]

Note

1 This paper was originally presented at a conference on style held at Indiana University in the spring of 1958, then it was revised and published in *Style in Language*, ed. T. A. Sebeok (Cambridge, Mass.: MIT Press, 1960).

References

ARBUSOW, L. 1948: *Colores rhetorici*. Göttingen: Vandenhoeck and Ruprecht.
AUSTERLITZ, R. 1958: Ob-Ugric metrics. *Folklore Fellows Communications* 174.
BISHOP, J. L. 1955: Prosodic elements in T'ang poetry. Indiana University Conference on Oriental-Western Literary Relations. Chapel Hill, 49–63.
BUEHLER, K. 1933: Die Axiomatik der Sprachwissenschaft. *Kant-Studien* 38, 19–90.
CHATMAN, S. 1960: Comparing metrical styles. In Sebeok, T.A. (ed.), *Style in language*. Cambridge, Mass.: MIT Press, 149–72.

CHERRY, E. C. 1957: *On human communication*. New York: Wiley.

EJXENBAUM, B. M. 1969(1922): Melodika russkogo liričeskogo stixa. In *O poèzii*. Leningrad.

EMPSON, W. 1947: *Seven types of ambiguity*. New York: Chatto and Windus.

FROST, R. 1939: *Collected poems*. New York: Halcyon House.

GIESE, W. 1952: Sind Märchen Lügen? *Cahiers S. Puscariu* 1, 137–50.

GREENBERG, J. 1960: Survey of African prosodic systems. In Diamond, S. (ed.), *Culture in history: Essays in honour of Paul Radin*. New York: Columbia University Press, 925–50.

HERZOG, G. 1946: Some linguistic aspects of American Indian poetry. *Word* 2, 82.

HILL, A. A. 1953: Review of Kökeritz *Shakespeare's pronunciation*. *Language* 29, 549–61.

HOLLANDER, J. 1959: The metrical emblem. *Kenyon Review* 21, 279–96.

HOPKINS, G. M. 1959: *Journals and papers*, ed. H. House and G. Storey. London: Oxford University Press.

—1967: *Poems*, ed. W.H. Gardner and N.H. Mackenzie, 4th ed. London: Oxford University Press.

HYMES, D. H. 1960: Phonological aspects of style: Some English sonnets. In Sebeok, T. A. (ed.), *Style in language*. Cambridge, Mass.: MIT Press, 109–31.

JAKOBSON, R. 1923: O češskom stixe preimuščestvenno v sopostavlenii s russkim. Berlin and Moscow.

—1933: Ueber den Versbau der serbokroatischen Volksepen. *Archives néerlandaises de phonétique expérimentale* 7–9, 44–53.

—1952: Studies in comparative Slavic metrics. *Oxford Slavonic Papers* 3, 21–66.

—1956: The metaphoric and metonymic poles. In Jakobson, R. and Halle, M. *Fundamentals of language*. The Hague: Mouton, 76–82.

JESPERSEN, O. 1933: Cause psychologique de quelques phénomènes de métrique germanique. In *Psychologie du langage*. Paris.

JOOS, M. 1950: Description of language design. *Journal of the Acoustical Society of America* 22, 701–8.

KARCEVSKIJ, S. I. 1931: Sur la phonologie de la phrase. *Travaux du Cercle Linguistique de Prague* 4, 188–223.

LEVI, A. 1930: Della versificazione italiana. *Archivum Romanicum* 14, 449–526.

LEVI-STRAUSS, C. 1955: The structural study of myth. In Sebeok, T. A. (ed.), *Myth: A symposium*. Philadelphia: American Folklore Society, 50–66.

—1958: *La geste d'Asdival*. Paris: Ecole Pratique des Hautes Etudes.

—1960: Analyse morphologique des contes russes. *International Journal of Slavic Linguistics and Poetics* 3.

—JAKOBSON, R., VOEGELIN, C. F. and SEBEOK, T. A. 1953: *Results of the conference of anthropologists and linguists*. Baltimore: Waverly Press.

LOTZ, J. 1960: Metric typology. In Sebeok, T. A. (ed.), *Style in language*. Cambridge, Mass.: MIT Press, 135–48.

MALINOWSKI, B. 1953: The problem of meaning in primitive languages. In Ogden, C. K. and Richards, I. A. (eds), *The meaning of meaning*, 9th ed. New York: Routledge and Kegan Paul, 296 – 336.

MALLARME, S. 1899: *Divagations*. Paris: E. Fasquelle.

MANSIKKA, V. 1929: Litauische Zaubersprüche. *Folklore Fellows Communications* 87.

MARETIC, T. 1907: Metrika narodnih naših pjesama. *Rad Yugoslavenske Akademije* 168, 170.

MARTY, A. 1908: *Untersuchungen zur Grundlegung der allgemeinen Grammatik und Sprachphilosophie*, Vol. 1. Halle.
NITSCH, K. 1954: Z historii polskich rymów. *Wybór pism polonistycznych* 1, 33–77.
PEIRCE, C. S. 1931: *Collected papers*, Vol. 1. Cambridge, Mass.: Harvard University Press.
POE, E. A. 1855: Marginalia. In *Works*, Vol. 5. New York.
—1895: The philosophy of composition. In *Works*, Vol. 6, ed. E. C. Stedman and G. E. Woodberry. Chicago.
POLIVANOV, E. D. 1924: O metričeskom xaraktere kitajskogo stixosloženija. *Doklady Rossijskoj Akademii Nauk*, serija 5, 156–8.
POTEBNJA, A. A. 1883 + 1887: *Ob''jasnenija malorusskix i srodnyx narodnyx pesen.* Warsaw, 1 (1883) and 2 (1887).
PROPP, V. 1958: *Morphology of the folktale*. Bloomington: Indiana University Research Center in Anthropology, Folklore and Linguistics.
RANSOM, J. C. 1938: *The world's body*. New York: C. Scribner's Sons.
—1941: *The new criticism*. Norfolk, Conn.: New Directions.
RYBNIKOV, P. N. 1910: *Pesni*, Vol. 3. Moscow.
SAPIR, E. 1921: *Language*. New York: Harcourt, Brace and World.
SAPORTA, S. 1960: The application of linguistics to the study of poetic language. In Sebeok, T. A. (ed.), *Style in language*. Cambridge, Mass.: MIT Press, 82–93.
SEBEOK, T. A. 1960: Decoding a text: Levels and aspects in a Cheremis sonnet. In *Style in language*. Cambridge, Mass.: MIT Press, 221–35.
SIEVERS, E. 1924: *Ziele und Wege der Schallanalyse*. Heidelberg: Winter.
SIMMONS, D. C. 1955: Specimens of Efik folklore. *Folk-lore* 66, 417–24.
STEINITZ, W. 1934: Der Parallelismus in der finnisch-karelischen Volksdichtung. *Folklore Fellows Communications* 115.
TARANOVSKY, K. 1955: *Ruski dvodelni ritmovi*. Belgrade.
TARSKI, A. 1936: Der Wahrheitsbegriff in den formalisierten Sprachen. *Studia Philosophica* 1.
VALERY, P. 1958: *The art of poetry. Collected works*, Vol. 7. New York: Pantheon Books.
VOEGELIN, C. F. 1960: Casual and noncasual utterances within unified structures. In Sebeok, T. A. (ed.), *Style in language*. Cambridge, Mass.: MIT Press, 57–68.
WANG LI 1958: *Han-yü Shih-lü-hsüeh* (Versification in Chinese). Shanghai: Jiaoyu Chubanshe.
WHORF, B. L. 1956: *Language, thought, and reality*, ed. J. B. Carroll. New York: Wiley.
WIMSATT, W. K. 1954: *The verbal icon*. Lexington: University of Kentucky Press.
—and BEARDSLEY, M. C. 1959: The concept of meter: An exercise in abstraction. *Publications of the Modern Language Association of America* 74, 585–98.
—1960: The concept of meter (abstract, followed by Comments). In Sebeok, T. A. (ed.), *Style in language*. Cambridge, Mass.: MIT Press, 193–209.
ZIRMUNSKIJ, V. M. 1928: *Voprosy teorii literatury*. Leningrad.

2

Closing statement: Linguistics and poetics in retrospect

Derek Attridge

In so far as these words call to mind a famous paper by Roman Jakobson, the gesture of opening with a 'closing statement' is an obvious one, perhaps even an inevitable one.[1] The 'Linguistics of Writing' conference was planned to commemorate, to emulate, and to mark our distance from, an earlier conference, held at Indiana University in 1958 and published two years later in a volume edited by Thomas Sebeok under the title *Style in Language* (1960). That collection turned out to be one of the founding documents in English of what we can call 'literary linguistics', and one of the most memorable papers in it was Jakobson's 'Closing statement, from the viewpoint of linguistics', which he entitled 'Linguistics and poetics'. This paper has been reprinted, summarized, quoted from, and alluded to with remarkable frequency since its publication, and anyone who wishes to write or speak about the linguistic characterization of poetic discourse is obliged to take account of it.

But if my own comments – which will pretend to none of the magisterial sweep and penetration of that earlier piece – also constitute some kind of 'closing statement', they will do so by registering, and setting up for debate, a sense of the completion or exhaustion of the long and fruitful enterprise for which Jakobson's 'Closing statement' can stand as an initiating moment. Such a point of exhaustion would also, of course, be a turning-point, and my retrospective look at Jakobson's achievement from our present vantage point is intended not as an act of interment or disavowal but as a preparation of the ground for a new 'linguistics of writing' – which will remain deeply indebted to Jakobson's work. In returning once more to that earlier 'Closing statement' I wish to consider some of the reasons for its immediate impact and lasting influence, and to ask to what extent its arguments and its aims have survived the mutations and revolutions in literary and linguistic thought that have marked the intervening decades.

That the essay in question achieved such a remarkable status points, I would contend, not only to its own intrinsic value but to a widely felt need in the 1950s for an authoritative statement about the special qualities of literary language. For some time literary studies, in Britain and America at least, had tended, in the name of critical sensitivity or empirical history, to dissolve the boundaries between literary and other uses of language; and though there were rumours that the story was rather different in places such as Russia and Czechoslovakia, full communication had been inhibited by barriers of language, culture, and politics.[2] At this historical moment Jakobson spoke with the immense prestige of one who had been centrally involved in those goings-on in Moscow and Prague, and he presented his argument *ex cathedra*, as though these were not matters for debate but truths he was laying before the expectant audience.[3] Jakobson confidently defines 'poetics' as what most of us would now call 'stylistics', and proceeds to claim for it an unparalleled importance in the literary domain:

> Poetics deals primarily with the question, 'What makes a verbal message a work of art?' Because the main subject of poetics is the *differentia specifica* of verbal art in relation to other arts and in relation to other kinds of verbal behavior, poetics is entitled to the leading place in literary studies.

> (p. 10)

And he has no hesitation in situating the flagship of literary studies in what he sees as its wider context: 'Since linguistics is the global science of verbal structure, poetics may be regarded as an integral part of linguistics' (p. 10). While this was a claim guaranteed to amuse or outrage most traditional literary critics and to disturb many theoretical linguists, it was a call to arms for the stripling discipline of stylistics.

Jakobson's thought is energized by an unquestioning faith in the power of positivistic thinking which must have been particularly appealing in the late 1950s. He can declare ringingly: 'No manifesto, foisting a critic's own tastes and opinions on creative literature, may act as substitute for an objective scholarly analysis of verbal art' (p. 11), without evincing the slightest fear that his own analyses might be subject to his particular literary predilections or ideological biases. He thus offers an attractively democratic vision: no longer will literary analysis be the exclusive preserve of those who have mysteriously imbibed the capacity to make sensitive judgements. The insistence on complete explicitness, as in the then fledgling discipline of generative linguistics, will take away the mystique from literary criticism, and reveal the real and unchanging reasons why literary texts function as they do.

In facing the question of the *differentia specifica* of the language of literature, therefore, Jakobson is seeking clear definitions and distinctions which will, at the same time as offering a sharp focus, do justice to the evident lack of absoluteness in the relation between literary and non-literary language. His solution, an extension of the proposals of Bühler and Mukařovský, is the famous map of linguistic functions, six in number, which characterize different kinds of linguistic event according to the different hierarchic relations of these functions. Poetry, in this scheme, is a use of language in which the poetic function dominates any of the others which might be present – the referential, the emotive, the conative, the phatic, and the metalingual. By this means, Jakobson appears to avoid many of the problems inherent in the notion of a norm against which a deviant poetic language is defined; any comparisons would have to be made five ways to encompass all the other possible functions of language. One of the recurrent problems of norm-and-deviation arguments – that whatever feature you come up with as the distinguishing mark of poetry turns out to exist in nonpoetic texts as well – appears to be solved: of course the poetic function occurs outside poetry, but it is only in poetry that it predominates over the others. The language of a poetic utterance, Jakobson asserts, is orientated, not toward the world it refers to, not toward the one who utters or the one who reads or hears, not toward the code or the channel of communication being utilized, but toward 'the message as such'.[4] Poetry is distinguished by its self-referentiality, which takes precedence over all the other operations performed by its language.[5]

How does the language of poetry achieve this state of self-referentiality? 'What', in Jakobson's words, 'is the empirical linguistic criterion of the poetic function?' (p. 17). Jakobson's pronouncement on this question is one of his most-quoted utterances: *'The poetic function projects the principle of equivalence from the axis of selection into the axis of combination'* (p. 17). It isn't surprising that this single sentence made a strong and continuing impact: it is impressively technical in its vocabulary, assured in its rhetoric, and free of any interference from the messy world of judgements, values, and power-relations; and it offers an objective and purely linguistic method of identifying what counts as poetry and what doesn't.[6] It provides just what was wanted – a key to the sealed chamber that had baffled literary thought for centuries.

It also dismisses as irrelevant several issues that have troubled accounts of literary language since Plato and Aristotle. The principle of projection has nothing to tell us about the difference between a good and a bad poem – just as the identification of the emotive function says nothing about the success or otherwise of any given expression of emotion and the referential function is in play whether the speaker is telling the truth or not.[7] It has no necessary relation to the author's intentions – if I wrote a text that was not a poem in terms of the projection principle, it would do no good to write *Poem* at the top of the page. And most significantly, perhaps, it excludes the *reader* from any role in the determination of what is or is not poetic language. Jakobson's stated position is clear: the reader is in the position of the 'addressee', the goal of the communicative channel, whose only requirement is that he or she is in a position to receive the message and has access to the code being used. It is therefore the message itself, which, by virtue of its inherent properties – that is, in its adherence to the principle just enunciated – proclaims itself as poetic.[8] Those properties are empirical features of the text, available to objective analysis; and any reader, or body of readers, who insisted on the title 'poem' for a particular text which lacked these features would simply be wrong (unless the analysis of the text which claimed to show their absence were itself inadequate).[9]

There may, however, be a price to be paid for this assured singleness of purpose, and we need to scrutinize Jakobson's writing for any signs that what he has excluded remains a force to be reckoned with, even within his own argument. I am not proposing this from a position of superiority, as though I were capable of achieving a consistency unattained by Jakobson, but in the recognition that Jakobson's work necessarily looks different in the light of subsequent work, including that of the contributors to this book. My own text is therefore a product, both deliberately and inevitably, of the situation we found ourselves in in 1986.

The question I am posing in particular is whether Jakobson's exclusion of the reader, and the collectivity to which the reader belongs, is, or could ever be, successful; do his formulations manage to contain the determination of the literary *within* the text, and thus to achieve the cross-cultural and trans-historical universality he is seeking? We can begin with the familiar formula which encapsulates the proposed invariant of all poetic language: 'The set (*Einstellung*) toward the MESSAGE as such, focus on the message for its own sake, is the POETIC function of language' (p. 15). We may note, first of all, that in this definition Jakobson uses not a linguistic but a psychological terminology: the three words 'set', '*Einstellung*', and 'focus' all imply a mental attitude on the part of the reader – in spite of the fact that Jakobson's project is to define the 'poetic' in structural terms, not in terms of effect.[10] What one might have expected Jakobson to begin with is a specification of the exact linguistic and structural properties of poetry, that is, with the famous dictum about projection from one axis to the other; he could then have followed with the logically additional information that the effect of this property of poetic texts is to produce a set toward the message in the minds of its readers.

But the ordering of the argument as we have it indicates the force of the position Jakobson is attempting, but failing, to abandon: that the determination of what counts as poetry and what does not is ultimately in the hands of its readers, and any particular feature we might care to advance as the distinguishing characteristic of poetry can be tested only in the sociocultural arena. A 'set toward the message' – assuming that we do not limit the word 'message' too narrowly – is a plausible definition of poetry precisely because it describes a cultural evaluation, a society's categorization of certain texts as deserving a particular kind of attention and offering a particular kind of satisfaction. But a description of a defining structural property can never anticipate or exhaust a culture's behaviour (least of all when what is being attempted is a definition which takes account of cross-cultural variation). There are bound to be many other ways in which a set toward the message can be induced, such as a text's physical appearance or its categorization within a particular institutional framework. There are also ceaseless historical changes at work, shifting the boundaries between the poetic and the non-poetic, which Jakobson, in his grand synchronicity, ignores. What Jakobson is trying to establish is that a text's poetic status is an inherent property, which survives movement in time and space: thus he remarks 'A filibusterer may recite *Hiawatha* because it is long, yet poeticalness still remains the primary intent of this text itself' (p. 18).

This may help us to explain why the promise of a theory of linguistic functions which escapes the problems produced by norm-and-deviation approaches to poetic language is in fact never fulfilled. Jakobson makes it quite clear that the 'referential' function is to be thought of as the norm, the unmarked member of the set: 'Obviously we must agree with Sapir that, on the whole, "ideation reigns supreme in language" ..., but this supremacy does not authorize linguistics to disregard the "secondary factors" ' (p. 12).[11] As Stanley Fish (1980) has shown, any notion of an 'ordinary language' against which a 'literary language' is defined, in terms of special features which it possesses (or lacks), impoverishes both terms in the distinction. What such theories are designed to counter is the view that the difference between the 'literary' and the 'non-literary' is produced historically by a particular culture, and Jakobson, were he genuinely to present his six functions in such a way as to privilege none of them, would be on the way to accepting such a view. (The general theory of markedness, so central to Jakobson's thinking, seems to me at times to run the risk of converting contingent hierarchies into universal ones, especially when what is at issue is not a physiologically determined feature but a socially constructed one.)[12] The relativity of the various functions, their determination by the uses to which they are put in specific contexts by speakers and hearers, writers and readers, cannot, for Jakobson, be allowed to threaten the founding distinction between the poetic and the non-poetic, which must be protected as an essential, inherent, structural difference.

Let us return to the description of the defining feature of poetry: 'The set toward the MESSAGE as such, focus on the message for its own sake, is the POETIC function of language.' At first sight, this seems an odd use of the word *function*, which is usually equated with some effective activity, not a state. It can best be understood as a residue from an earlier stage in Jakobson's intellectual career, since the same word (in Czech) played a central part in the formulations of the Prague Linguistic Circle, of which Jakobson was of course a leading member; but we find a very different emphasis is given it by, for instance, Jan Mukařovský, whose arguments at other points come very close to Jakobson's. Any function, for Mukařovský, is a question of three factors: the object itself – in our case, the poem; the social consciousness – the cultural conventions in force; and the individual – the reader. Peter Steiner notes that 'The most common error in attributing a function to an object according to Mukařovský is to proceed from the object alone' (1978, p. 361). The individual operates in terms of the social collectivity, which determines the function that is dominant in any object.

In the case of the other five functions which Jakobson enumerates, the social and psychological purpose of the particular kind of language is evident – it is serving to maintain a contact, express and convey an emotion, produce an effect upon a listener, check on the code, or, of course, communicate a cognitive content. But in the case of poetry there is a curious silence about its role in the sociolinguistic framework. We can no doubt deduce from Jakobson's comments a quite traditional aesthetic argument about the value and function of literature; we learn in the course of the description of the poetic function that it promotes 'the palpability of signs' (p. 16), that its employment in an election slogan 'reinforces its impressiveness and efficacy' (p. 16) and that it adds 'splendor' to Caesar's message, *'Veni, vidi, vici'* (p. 17); but in his definitions he seems to present poetry not only as self-referential but also as self-justifying. This avoidance of any appeal to the reader, and to the values or expectations he or she brings to the text, is part of a wider elision of the cultural determination of literature itself, in its many changing and differently interpreted forms, though the word 'function' remains like the ghost of these excluded possibilities.

We find a similar hesitation in the statement that is intended as an empirical description of the *differentia specifica* of verbal art, that which induces, automatically it would appear, a set toward the message: 'The poetic function projects the principle of equivalence from the axis of selection into the axis of combination.' Here we again have a rather odd use of the word *function*, as though it were some force acting within the poem, or operating upon it; and this sense is strengthened when Jakobson states that texts like advertising jingles 'make use of the poetic function without, however, assigning to this function the coercing, determining role it carries in poetry' (p. 17–18). Mary Louise Pratt has pointed out that if the projection principle is operative in such texts but not to the extent that would make them poetry, 'some systematic way of measuring this lack in terms of the axes of selection and combination must be appended to the projection principle and must be testable against the available examples of versified laws, advertising jingles, and so on' (1977, p. 36).[13] In the absence of such a principle, we must suspect that in the final analysis the poetic function is determined not by the projection principle but some other principle, not necessarily intrinsic to the poem.[14]

Furthermore, the statement seems to be inverted: it asserts that the poetic function is active in *producing* a particular structural disposition, when one might expect Jakobson to say that it is produced by the disposition.[15] If this is not the case, what determines the domination of a message by the poetic – or any other – function? Again there is the lurking possibility that the classification of a text as a poem may in fact *precede* the special qualities it possesses, which then become a matter of reading strategies or sociocultural categorization and not empirical differences.

What is projected from the axis of selection – the associative or paradigmatic axis – to the axis of combination – the syntagmatic axis – is 'the principle of equivalence'; and Jakobson is at pains to explain, though he has not always been understood, that this does not mean merely 'the principle of similarity'.[16] Dissimilarity and antonymity are mentioned as well as similarity and synonymity, and the example he offers by way of immediate illustration is the equalization of one syllable with another, one word-stress with another, one word-boundary with another, and so on. That is, in poetry, features of language which are usually merely the *carriers* of semantic content and have no importance in themselves and therefore no relations among themselves other than contiguity, gain that importance and enter into such relations. Any form of versification which uses syllables as a measure, for instance, has introduced a principle of equivalence along the sequence; so would a verse form which employs one sentence per line. Jakobson's account of all poetic features is in fact an extrapolation from his account of metrical form. (Indeed, as he himself once suggested, his whole intellectual career can be seen as growing out of his 'undergraduate attempt of 1911 to outline the formal properties of the earliest Russian iambs'.)[17]

He has often been taken to mean that poetry is definable in terms of the additional patterning it introduces into language, the regular recurrence of similar items in the sequence.[18] Such a reading, though it is not strictly what Jakobson's theory states, is understandable, since it provides the kind of objective, empirical criterion that the argument appears to need. Patterns of similar items can be empirically identified, and perhaps some kind of cut-off point established at which the poetic function could be declared dominant over the others. Many of Jakobson's analyses of poems suggest that he did indeed believe that intricate patterning was a distinctive and discoverable feature of poems, and he certainly remained unconvinced by demonstrations that with an interpretative machinery as powerful as his, intricate patterns could be detected in virtually *any* stretch of language;[19] but in setting out the theory he avoids – and one can understand why – reducing poetry to a mechanically specifiable set of texts. The notion of 'equivalence', like the notions of 'set', and 'focus', is oriented toward the reader. The poetic function, in effect, *invites* the reader to treat as equivalent items in the sequence which would have simply been contiguous in non-poetic language; thus the hypothetical verse-form made up of one sentence per line does not in itself make the sentences similar or dissimilar, but encourages the reader to treat them as having a relation of 'similarity or dissimilarity'. Jakobson's liking for Hopkins's word *parallelism* points in the same direction: items in parallel to one another invite an act of comparison, whereas items in a pattern imply no activity other than passive apprehension.[20]

Jakobson's insistence on the *semantic* aspect of his principle confirms the role of the reader, even though it is introduced with a flourish of positivism:

> No doubt, verse is primarily a recurrent 'figure of sound'. Primarily, always, but never uniquely. Any attempts to confine such poetic conventions as meter, alliteration, or rhyme to the sound level are speculative reasonings without any empirical justification. The projection of the equational principle into the sequence has a much deeper and wider significance. Valéry's view of poetry as 'hesitation between the sound and the sense' is much more realistic and scientific than any bias of phonetic isolationism.
>
> (p. 25)

Thus in rhyme, the semantic relation between rhyme words is as important as the phonetic relation – and since the former relation is not itself marked, but can vary over the whole range of possibilities, the only applicable model is one that involves the reader, who takes the rhyme as an instruction to carry out a semantic comparison. Jakobson quotes Hopkins's definition of what the latter calls the two 'correlative experiences' involved in semantic equivalence: 'comparison for likeness' sake' and 'comparison for unlikeness' sake'; for Hopkins, too, the poetic function is posited upon the interpretative activity of the reader. Whether this process of comparison is a *necessary* and *universal* feature of the reading of poetry, as Jakobson wants it to be, becomes therefore an empirical question about traditions of reading in different periods and cultures; and it is Jakobson's generalizing account itself that stands in danger of being accused of 'speculative reasonings without any empirical justification'.

A particularly interesting development of the argument occurs when Jakobson moves from the fusion of phonetic and semantic relations to the operation of semantic units themselves, which he does in order to bring the widely-observed phenomenon of poetic ambiguity within the compass of his explanation. 'In poetry not only the phonological sequence but in the same way any sequence of semantic units strives to build an equation' (p. 28). Again there is an odd displacement from the reader's interpretative activity to the language itself, as though the poem were struggling of its own accord towards its entelechy, but the argument indicates something of the real power of Jakobson's proposal. It seems to me very helpful to think of poetic discourse – at least that which characterizes one identifiable type of poetry – as a discourse in which the reader is encouraged, by the text itself and by the cultural matrix within which it is presented, to derive 'meaning' (let us leave that word as vague as we can) from a number of linguistic features over and above the usual operations of lexis and syntax. The notion of ambiguity, while it appears to signify to Jakobson multiple meanings which any reader will perceive, could also suggest a range of potential meanings, not all of them available to any single reader, and it would then be possible to agree with Jakobson that 'ambiguity is an intrinsic, inalienable character of any self-focused message' (p. 28), since the diversion of attention away from the semantic content to other features of the text is bound to complicate the simple transmission of meaning.[21] One might question whether the notion of 'projection' from one axis to another is necessary (apart from giving Jakobson's own sentence the very qualities of parallelism that it is referring to, making it an example as well as a definition of the poetic function); but the idea that poetic language often involves a number of additional possibilities in the interrelations among linguistic and semantic elements, brought into play by a heightened sense of potential equivalences, is not one that can be easily dismissed.

That is not to say that it will do as the single explanation of poetic distinctiveness; we are only likely to accept it as that if we assume from the beginning that a single explanation is necessary, and we are probably less prone to that assumption today than we would have been in 1958. We might want, for instance, to insist that the other kind of poetic distinctiveness to which the discipline of stylistics has paid great attention – the contravention of linguistic rules – is equally important in focusing attention on the poetic message. But as one aspect of that complex set of procedures, historically-conditioned and always subject to historical change, which produces a special psychic and cultural space – or one had better say a number of such spaces – for certain texts we label 'poetic', the theory of multiple equivalences retains its value.

But how might we follow through the implication, suppressed in Jakobson, that readers are active in determining what is poetry and what is not? We would need some account of the role of ideology, of gender, of institutional practices, perhaps of the unconscious; and we would need to take account of our own position as culturally and ideologically situated readers. Upon these foundations we might attempt to build a theory of pleasure (which would need to be a fully historicized theory to do justice to the changing modes and functions of pleasure) in its relation to the phenomenon of poetry. The question would then arise: how does the operation of Jakobson's projection principle, in however complex a form, relate to the production of pleasure and to the value judgements associated with it? It must be something other than a simple correlation between the extent to which the principle of equivalence is exploited and the degree of pleasure produced by the poem; many a poem has been condemned as unpleasant or bad because of the excess of its parallelisms and repetitions.[22] It seems impossible at this point to avoid invoking some such notion as 'subtlety', 'judgement', or 'taste', and once we admit to this, we have to admit to the cultural production of the entire value-system within which poetry is appraised and authorized, since these terms represent systems that are neither individual nor universal. The more general issue that is touched on here is that the necessary idealizations and abstractions of 'theory' as understood in linguistics, especially since Saussure, appear to anyone who is engaged in 'theory' as understood currently within literary studies as simplifications of complex cultural and philosophical phenomena – since a great deal of recent literary theory has been devoted to showing the unworkability (and sometimes the unacknowledged political force) of such simplifications. This is one of the reasons why the work of the Bakhtin–Vološinov school has held much greater appeal to literary theorists in recent years than the work of Jakobson and the Russian Formalists.[23]

Jakobson clearly would not admit that his judgements were part of a culturally-produced value system. However, it is difficult to analyse poetry without making any explicit or implicit evaluative judgements; and Jakobson's 'empirical' studies of poems are perhaps not as far removed from the maligned activity of critics who 'foist their own tastes and opinions on creative literature' as he liked to think. Let us examine his description of the type of poetic analysis he championed in a paper roughly contemporary with the 'Closing statement':

> Any unbiased, attentive, exhaustive, total description of the selection, distribution and interrelation of diverse morphological classes and syntactic constructions in a given poem surprises the examiner himself by unexpected, striking symmetries and anti-symmetries, balanced structures, efficient accumulation of equivalent forms and salient contrasts, finally by rigid restrictions in the repertory of morphological and syntactic constituents used in the poem, eliminations which, on the other hand, permit us to follow the masterly interplay of the actualized constituents.
>
> (Poetry of grammar and grammar of poetry, in Jakobson 1985, p. 42)

This is the extraordinary Jakobsonian rhetoric at full stretch: the analysis is presented as a demanding but essentially mechanical procedure, needing not taste or discrimination to achieve its purpose but patience, thoroughness, and accurate linguistic knowledge. Although, as Jonathan Culler has shown, the notion of exhaustiveness is a fiction, since the capacity to produce descriptive linguistic categories is infinite, and the analyst's choice of a very few to focus on must be guided by some initial decision about what is important and what is not.[24] The statement is impressive for its consistency with Jakobson's central argument about the poetic function as an objective property – except in one respect: it is shot through with a sense of admiration for the poets who are able to achieve such effects with language. Their work 'surprises' the examiner, its symmetries and antisymmetries are 'unexpected' and 'striking', its accumulations are 'efficient', and its interplay of constituents is 'masterly'. This response is understandable, and increases rather than diminishes one's respect for Jakobson as a reader of poetry, but it sits uneasily in a demonstration that poetry as such, good or bad, can be objectively defined. What would be the conclusion to be drawn from a poem whose symmetries did not surprise or impress? Would it be a bad poem or not a poem at all?

In fact, when we turn to Jakobson's analyses of particular poems we find that they are not simply demonstrations of the poetic function at work, but are clearly designed, like most traditional literary criticism, to persuade the reader of the magnitude of the poet's achievement. It is not just that the principle of equivalence allows poems to function differently from other kinds of language, it is that in the hands of great poets (or a productive oral tradition) the principle of equivalence is a resource which produces networks of association and contrast, interrelations of sound and sense, of remarkable unity, intricacy, and subtlety. (Jakobson's critical method, like any critical method, privileges certain kinds of writing – poetry over prose, the short poem over the long poem, the lyric over the narrative, the formally patterned over the freely varying, etc.; and Krystyna Pomorska, summarizing Jakobson, can call the 'short lyric poem' 'poetry in its epitome' without any recognition that this valuation is produced by the theory rather than the other way round.)[25] The following are some of Jakobson's comments on individual poets and poems:

On Pushkin's lyric poetry (1936):

> A masterful alternation of grammatical categories of person becomes a means of intense dramatization. There can hardly be an example of a more skillful poetic exploitation of morphological possibilities.
>
> (Two poems by Pushkin, in Jakobson 1985, p. 47)

On Yeats, 'The Sorrow of Love' (1977):

> The exacting selection and arrangement of verbal symbols summoned in 'The Sorrow of Love' to build a harmonious system of rich semantic correlations ... indeed warrant the poet's assertion: *And words obey my call.*
>
> (Yeats' 'Sorrow of Love' through the years, in Jakobson 1985, p. 106)

e. e. cummings, 'love is more thicker than forget' (1979):

> Close attention to 'love is more thicker' shows how sound correspondences acquire or enhance a semantic propinquity and how they act as kindred submorphemes upheld by a mysteriously complex and cohesive network of metrical, strophic, and compositional means.
>
> (Jakobson and Waugh 1979, p. 228)

Similarly, Jakobson and Jones find in Shakespeare's Sonnet 129 an 'amazing external and internal structuration palpable to any responsive and unprejudiced reader' and refer to the 'cogent and mandatory unity of its thematic and compositional framework' (1970, pp. 31, 32).

Even if he had excised all evaluative comments from his writing, however, the rhetorical function of Jakobson's minutely-detailed analyses is clear: it is not to show that the object before him is a poem, or, since we know it is a poem, that his definition of the poetic function holds good for one more example; it is to persuade by the amassing of detail that this verbal artefact has remarkable qualities of intricate structuration and cohesion – and that they enforce a particular interpretation, for in spite of the argument for the importance of poetic ambiguity, when it came to interpretation Jakobson had no doubt that poems possess fixed, timeless, and strictly limited meanings. (A secondary purpose of the exercise is to persuade the reader that only a Jakobsonian linguistic analysis can reveal these qualities, while of course claiming that they are there to be seen by any reader whose head isn't full of foolish literary prejudices.) The tools may be different, but the job is a time-honoured one: to persuade others to share one's preferences, and to show off one's skills as a critic.[26] Each analysis is an intervention in a cultural (and ultimately political) struggle, and the use of empirical vocabulary and the rhetoric of objectivity is, like the use by others of an impressionist vocabulary and the rhetoric of subjectivity, a strategy with its own advantages and disadvantages. But as I have tried to show, the rhetoric of objectivity, like all rhetorics, reveals itself as such in its language; to define is to attempt an act of exclusion, keeping out that which would threaten the logical form of the definition. Jakobson's definition of the poetic function attempts in the same gesture to protect both poetry and his own discourse from those forces which would render it impermanent, inconsistent with itself, and open to an infinity of future contexts, but it can succeed in doing neither. Both poems and academic papers, including this one, have their existence in a culture within which they are generated, fought over, prized or dismissed. One of the functions of poetry as a historically mobile cultural practice is to test and undermine existing norms (and one might say the same about conference presentations); Jakobson's attempt to fix, once and for all, the parameters of poetic language fails to take account of this function.

The critical assumptions in Jakobson's poetic analyses are, in fact, as traditional as his purposes: that the value of a poem inheres in its capacity to produce maximal unity from maximal diversity, and to fuse the realms of form and meaning. These assumptions, which he does not raise for questioning, can be traced to Romantic notions of organic form, and in the English tradition relate most closely to the critical practice and pronouncements of another lifelong seeker for universal keys, Samuel Taylor Coleridge,[27] though their pedigree goes back much further in Western culture. Jakobson's theory of poetic language, then, can be seen as belonging to, and participating in, a specific cultural history, which is also a social and political history, of which we too are a part.

Jakobson approaches the problem of poetic language not only with post-Romantic assumptions about literary form but also with a particular commitment to linguistic explanations – a prior commitment, if you like, to 'the message as such'. The diagram of the six fundamental factors in verbal communication, and the translation of this into the six functions of language is a masterly piece of theoretical rhetoric, with its implication that poetry's place is set out for it *in advance* by the necessary structure of the speech event; once the other five factors have had functions assigned to them, there remains only the 'message' to be taken care of, and only poetry is available to fill that slot. That the whole structure is only one of many possible ways of categorizng speech events, that the sense of an exhaustive covering of the ground is only a convincingly-managed illusion, that the existence of an inherent property of poetic language remains to be demonstrated, are suspicions that fade in the bright sunlight of Jakobson's apodictic prose.

This feat of exclusion, echoed so often in linguistic and literary theory since then, is all the more striking when Jakobson's position in 1958 is compared with that of his earlier self and his former colleagues. It was Jakobson himself who, in Prague in 1928, produced with Jurij Tynjanov a manifesto which moves away from the Formalist isolation of the work of art from its context, at a time when Mukařovský was still arguing that literary analysis must stay within the boundaries of the work itself;[28] and the Prague Linguistic Circle, in which Jakobson played a leading part, was to develop a theoretical position 'emphasizing above all', as Peter Steiner puts it, 'the social context of the phenomena under study rather than the question of their invariants' (1978, p. 381, n. 48).[29] But in the United States in the 1950s, after a World War and during a Cold War, Jakobson's work seems to be driven by the pursuit of the invariant, transcending the social and cultural differences which occur across space and time. He liked to look back on his career as an unwavering search for universals and essences; and all his detailed empirical investigations can be seen to be in the service of a totalizing drive.[30] In his unquestioning dedication to a model of explanation based on Occam's razor – the best account is the one which subsumes the widest variety of phenomena under a single rule – he was scarcely an unbiased researcher (who is?), and the influence of this cast of thought on linguistic theory has been immense in this century.

We are left, then, with a sense of Jakobson's achievement as residing more in the questions his work provokes than in the confident maxims it proclaims. One of the questions is obviously whether the methods and the aims of objective analysis as understood by Jakobson are appropriate in the literary domain. Does a linguistics of writing – however broadly or narrowly we wish to define the latter word – require different objectives, different tools? And if the answer is yes, the further question remains: does linguistics proper, which has tended to see itself as concerned primarily with speech, have something to learn from this encounter with the written word and with literature? The work of Jacques Derrida would suggest that Jakobson's confident incorporation of literary studies into linguistics might be reversible, and that the particular problems which arise when we try to define, to categorize, to fix literary or philosophical writing might be characteristic of all uses of language. To close the chapter which Jakobson opened thirty years ago is by no means to reach the end of the story.

Notes

1 This paper was originally presented as the opening lecture of the 'Linguistics of Writing' conference held at Strathclyde University in July 1986, then it was published in *The Linguistics of Writing*, ed. N. Fabb *et al*. (Manchester: Manchester University Press, 1987).

 Roman Jakobson's paper is reprinted in chapter 1 of this volume. Page references to Jakobson's paper as it appears in chapter 1 will be given in the text.

2 Nine years earlier, René Wellek and Austin Warren had published their *Theory of Literature* (1949), with many intriguing references to Russian Formalism, and six years after that Victor Erlich's *Russian Formalism: History – Doctrine* (1955) provided the first full introduction for the English-speaking world.

3 The section of the paper outlining the six linguistic functions, including the description of the poetic function in terms of a 'set toward the message', was originally given as part of Jakobson's Presidential Address to the Annual Meeting of the Linguistic Society of America in 1956; it has been published as 'Meta-language as a linguistic problem', in Jakobson (1980, pp. 81–92).

4 Jakobson does not elaborate on the meaning of 'message' in this context. In particular, he appears to want it both to involve and to exclude semantic content; on the one hand, he makes it clear that he is not limiting the poetic function to a heightened attention to the sounds of language, or more generally to the *signans*, but, on the other hand, to emphasize the existence in poetry of a set towards the meaning, the *signatum*, would leave the referential function – which he also calls the 'denotative' and 'cognitive' function (p. 13) – with a very limited role. Furthermore, such a separation of meaning and reference would contradict the coalescence of these two terms which was an increasingly important feature of Jakobson's thinking (see Waugh 1976, pp. 28–31). His position in the 1920s had been more clearly based on Husserlian phenomenology: poetry is characterized by a set toward 'expression', a term derived from Husserl in an attempt to name inherent as opposed to referential meaning; see Steiner (1984, pp. 201–5). I discuss this tension within Jakobson's theory, which is most acute in the consideration of sound-symbolism, in 'Literature as imitation: Jakobson, Joyce, and the art of onomatopoeia', ch. 5 of Attridge (1988).

5 Although Jakobson avoids the word, this principle is of course derived from the notion of 'foregrounding', developed in Russian Formalism and of central importance in the discussions of the Prague School. In Mukařovský's account, for instance, 'the function of poetic language consists in the maximum of foregrounding of the utterance' – but this can be achieved in a number of ways, one of which must, in any given case, be dominant (Standard language and poetic language, in Garvin 1964, p. 19).

6 Saussure's associative relations, called by later writers 'paradigmatic' or 'systematic', become Jakobson's relations of similarity, operating on the axis of selection, and manifested in metaphor; Saussure's syntagmatic relations become – without any insistence on linearity – Jakobson's relations of contiguity, manifested in metonymy. See 'Two aspects of language and two types of aphasic disturbances', in Jakobson and Halle (1956).

7 Cf. Waugh's comment: 'Nor, as should be obvious, is the poetic function to be equated with "great" poetry; the poetic function may also occur in "doggerel"'

(The poetic function and the nature of language, in Jakobson 1985, p. 146).

8 See Waugh's summary: 'The "function" of a given message is, in Jakobson's terminology, an *intrinsic quality* of the message itself; thus, the focus upon the message is an inherent quality of the poem' (The poetic function and the nature of language, in Jakobson 1985, p. 148).

9 Another question, which, as Mary Louise Pratt and David Lodge have both emphasized, receives only a fudged answer from Jakobson, is: 'How does this definition of the poetic function bear upon prose literature?' (See Pratt 1977, pp. 34–5 and Lodge 1977, pp. 91–2.) The best Jakobson can do when he poses this question to himself is to categorize literary prose as a 'transitional linguistic area', existing somewhere between 'strictly poetic and strictly referential language' (p. 31): presumably in this case the two functions in question are nicely balanced. This marginalization of a major component of the Western literary tradition indicates that something is amiss with the theory that necessitates it, and the notion that, say, Swift's *Gulliver's Travels* is different from Wordsworth's *Prelude* in that the former is halfway to being a referential text is plainly unsatisfactory.

10 This choice of words no doubt betrays the influence of Gestalt psychology and Husserl's phenomenology on the Prague School; see Steiner (1978 and 1984). A full study of Jakobson's debt to Husserl is Holenstein (1976).

11 Waugh, in summarizing Jakobson's argument, has no hesitation in reinforcing this statement:

> The referential function seems to be that function which is the unmarked one in the system of six ... As evidence of the unmarked nature of the referential function, we may cite the fact that in many linguistic and philosophical studies of language, the referential function has been said to be the *only* function of language, or, if (some of) the other functions have been discerned, they have been declared to be 'deviant' or 'unusual' or needing special consideration. And even in our parlance about language, the referential function is spoken of as 'ordinary language'.
>
> (The poetic function and the nature of language, in Jakobson 1985, p. 144)

12 See, for instance, 'The concept of the mark', in Jakobson and Pomorska (1980, pp. 93–8). Jakobson's comments indicate that, on the one hand, there was an early emphasis on the concept of markedness as a tool for examining cultural variety ('correlations encountered in the history of culture, such as life/death, liberty/oppression, sin/virtue, holidays/workdays, etc., can always be reduced to the relation α/not α; the relevant thing is to establish what constitutes the marked set for each period, group, people, and so on' – from a letter to Trubetzkoy in 1930); on the other, there is a tendency to equate the 'unmarked' with the 'natural', which gives rise to a number of problems always associated with the specification of that which is 'natural' in human behaviour as opposed to that which is 'non-natural'. I discuss these problems in Attridge (1988, especially chs 2 and 3).

13 Pratt's whole chapter, entitled 'The "poetic language" fallacy', is a valuable discussion of these issues.

14 Samuel R. Levin, while using a model very similar to Jakobson's, is rather more modest in his claims: 'We are not presuming, however, to give necessary or

sufficient conditions for poetry; we are simply asserting that the exploitation of such equivalences seems to be manifest in most of those utterances or texts that we agree to call poems' (1962, p. 30, n. 1). Levin in fact defines a much more precise and objectively identifiable feature in his notion of 'coupling' — the occurrence of items which are phonetically or semantically equivalent in equivalent positions in a syntactic or poetic structure. This might seem to move away from Jakobson's unacknowledged implication that what determines poetry is a reading strategy, but it is still a reading convention that chooses to make something of such linguistic phenomena, and the whole question of what might *count* as phonetic and semantic equivalence is not at all an objective matter. We are back with the historical question of what a culture makes of its texts (implicit in Levin's 'texts that we agree to call poems'); and Jakobson's discussion, in its vaguer account of the criteria involved, comes nearer to acknowledging this.

15 Earlier, Jakobson had offered the general statement: 'The verbal structure of a message depends primarily on the predominant function' (p. 13). The undecideability of this moment in the argument is dramatized in Waugh's description of poetic discourse as understood by Jakobson: 'The combination is built upon *and/or* produces equivalence and similarity relations between the combined elements' (The poetic function and the nature of language, in Jakobson 1985, p. 152, my emphasis).

16 Thus the Group μ paraphrase Jakobson's dictum as 'the projection of the principle of *similarity* from the paradigmatic axis onto the syntagmatic axis' (1981, p. 18, my emphasis). They also write of a 'law of similarity', which they see as 'an imposition added to the sequence' (1981, p. 11).

17 'My favorite topics', in Jakobson (1985, p. 3).

18 Thus Jonathan Culler writes, after quoting Jakobson's dictum, 'In other words, the poetic use of language involves placing together in sequence items which are phonologically or grammatically related. Patterns formed by the repetition of similar items will be both more common and more noticeable in poetry than in other kinds of language' (1975, p. 56).

19 See Culler (1975, ch. 3). Jakobson's failure to be impressed is amusing:

> A short time ago I was even asked the same question in print, by a lecturer at Oxford University, who had published a book, *Structuralist Poetics*, in which a chapter is devoted to my attempts at applying linguistics to poetics. The author made the experiment of taking a few lines out of one of my essays in order to interpret them from the point of view of poetics. The result was really extremely negative. I told him – I had a discussion with him in Oxford quite recently – that if it were a work of poetry, it would be an awfully bad poem.
> (On poetic intentions and linguistic devices in poetry, in Jakobson 1985, p. 70.)

> That Jakobson should raise the issue of evaluation as a way out of this problem is not as surprising as might at first appear, as we shall see. He discusses the issue in Jakobson and Pomorska (1980), but his defence is little more than an appeal to subjective impressions: 'The idea that it is possible to discover as many symmetrical properties as one wants is firmly contradicted by the concrete experience of analysis' (1980, p. 118).

20 It is interesting to note that in discussing parallelism in music and painting, Jakobson is careful to qualify his position by a reference to the particular conven-

tion in force: 'In the musical art the correspondences of elements that are recognized, *in a given convention*, as mutually equivalent or in opposition to each other, constitute the principal, if not the only, semiotic value'; 'The laws of opposition and equivalence which govern the system of the spatial categories that are at work in a painting offer an eloquent example of similarities *imputed by the code of the school, in the epoch, of the nation*' (A glance at the development of semiotics, in Jakobson 1980, pp. 24, 25; my emphases).

21 When Jakobson moves on to one of his favourite topics, sound-symbolism, a rather different claim emerges; if there were, as Jakobson believes there is, an 'undeniably objective' relation between a word's sound and its meaning which is reinforced in poetry (p. 29), then poetic language would be likely to narrow and constrain rather than complicate and generalize meaning.

22 Levin is very aware of this, acknowledging that 'it would be a mistake to conclude that the more couplings one finds or puts in a poem, the better is that poem'. But the only answer he has is in terms of 'the simultaneous action and interaction of all the other factors that operate in a poem' (1962, p. 48), which sounds very much like a matter of traditional critical judgement and techniques of persuasion.

23 Tzvetan Todorov (1984, pp. 54–6) constructs a Bakhtinian model of the linguistic event to place side-by-side with Jakobson's, and quotes a passage from Medvedev attacking Jakobson's model for its static, simplified presentation of a changing, interacting complex.

24 See Culler (1975, pp. 56–8). Paul Kiparsky (1973, p. 235) has suggested a limitation of the possible range of items in terms of the dictum: *the linguistic sames which are potentially relevant in poetry are just those which are potentially relevant in grammar*. While it is doubtless true that the perception of language is focused on those categorizations which are operative in normal linguistic structures, it is always open to a poet – or a culture – to produce a form of writing which makes use of other categorizations. The Renaissance placed the highest valuation on Latin and Greek verse organized in terms of the quantities of syllables, whereas these languages as they were spoken at this time did not possess quantitative distinctions of this kind (see Attridge 1974). Kiparsky's careful use of 'potential' also leaves open a space for the determining role of cultural norms.

25 'Poetics of prose', in Jakobson (1985, p. 171).

26 There is also an implication in Jakobson's phrasing that the *poet* is to be accorded admiration for the intricate work entailed in creating such an object, though this doesn't square very well with his insistence that his analyses make no assumptions about the consciousness with which any of these properties are imparted – see, for instance, 'Subliminal verbal patterning in poetry' and 'On poetic intentions and linguistic devices', both reprinted in Jakobson (1985). Commentators have often rewritten Jakobson's description of poetic language as though it referred to the act of composition; thus, Terry Eagleton states, 'What happens in poetry ... is that we pay attention to "equivalences" in the process of *combining* words together as well as in selecting them: we string together words which are semantically or rhythmically or phonetically or in some other way equivalent' (1983, p. 99).

27 At times Jakobson's formulations come very close to Coleridge's; compare the former's statement – cited by Waugh as Jakobson's definition of a poem (in

Jakobson 1985, p. 148) – that a structure is 'not a mechanical agglomeration but a structural whole and the basic task is to reveal the inner ... laws of this system' with Coleridge's influential distinction (derived from A. W. Schlegel) between 'mechanical' and 'organic' form. Tzvetan Todorov (1977, p. 340) has argued, in fact, that there is a chain of influence from Coleridge and the German Romantics via Poe, Baudelaire, and Mallarmé, whom Jakobson acknowledges as an important early source of ideas.

28 Tynjanov and Jakobson (1971, pp. 79–81). Other Jakobson texts from this period which show the same willingness to consider literature in its relation to the social and ideological environment are cited by Erlich (1955, pp. 207–8, 257). See also Winner (1978, p. 435).

29 See also Bennett (1979) for a valuable discussion of the openness of Formalist arguments to a concern with the social determination of literature and literary value.

30 'The question of invariance in the midst of variation has been the dominant topic and methodological device underlying my diversified yet homogeneous research work', 'My favorite topics', in Jakobson (1985, p. 3). Of course, to interpret a long and varied career as 'diversified yet homogeneous', given focus by a single quest, is itself an example of this motif in Jakobson's thought.

References

ATTRIDGE, D. 1974: *Well-weighed syllables: Elizabethan verse in classical metres*. Cambridge: Cambridge University Press.

—1988: *Peculiar language: Literature as difference from the Renaissance to James Joyce*. Ithaca: Cornell University Press.

BENNETT, T. 1979: *Formalism and marxism*. London: Methuen.

CULLER, J. 1975: *Structuralist poetics*. London: Routledge and Kegan Paul.

EAGLETON, T. 1983: *Literary theory: An introduction*. Oxford: Blackwell.

ERLICH, V. 1955: *Russian formalism: History – doctrine*. The Hague: Mouton.

FISH, S. 1980: How ordinary is ordinary language? In *Is there a text in this class?* Cambridge, Mass.: Harvard University Press, 97–111.

GARVIN, P. L. (ed.) 1964: *A Prague School reader on esthetics, literary structure and style*. Washington, DC: American University Language Center.

GROUP μ 1981: *A general rhetoric*, trans. P. B. Burrell and E. M. Slotkin. Baltimore: Johns Hopkins University Press.

HOLENSTEIN, E. 1976: *Roman Jakobson's approach to language: Phenomenological structuralism*. Bloomington: Indiana University Press.

JAKOBSON, R. 1960: Concluding statement: Linguistics and poetics. In Sebeok, T. A. (ed.), *Style in language*. Cambridge, Mass.: MIT Press, 350–77.

—1980: *The framework of language*. Michigan Studies in the Humanities 1. Ann Arbor: University of Michigan.

—1985: *Verbal art, verbal sign, verbal time*. Oxford: Blackwell.

—and HALLE, M. 1956: *Fundamentals of language*. The Hague: Mouton.

—and JONES, L. G. 1970: *Shakespeare's verbal art in 'Th' Expense of Spirit'*. The Hague: Mouton.

—and POMORSKA, K. 1980: *Dialogues*. Cambridge, Mass.: MIT Press.

—and WAUGH, L. 1979: *The sound shape of language*. Brighton: Harvester Press.

KIPARSKY, P. 1973: The role of linguistics in a theory of poetry. *Daedalus* 102, 231–44.

LEVIN, S. R. 1962: *Linguistic structures in poetry*. The Hague: Mouton.

LODGE, D. 1977: *The modes of modern writing*. London: Edward Arnold.

PRATT, M.L. 1977: *Toward a speech-act theory of literary discourse*. Bloomington: Indiana University Press.

STEINER, P. 1978: The conceptual basis of Prague structuralism. In Matejka, L. (ed.), *Sound, sign and meaning*. Michigan Slavic Contributions 6. Ann Arbor: University of Michigan, 351–85.

—1984: *Russian formalism: A metapoetics*. Ithaca: Cornell University Press.

TODOROV, T. 1977: *Théories du symbole*. Paris: Seuil.

—1984: *Mikhail Bakhtin: The dialogical principle*, trans. W. Godzich. Manchester: Manchester University Press.

TYNJANOV, J. and JAKOBSON, R. 1971: Problems in the study of literature and language. In Matejka, L. and Pomorska, K. (eds), *Readings in Russian poetics: Formalist and structuralist views*. Cambridge, Mass.: MIT Press, 79–81.

WAUGH, L. R. 1976: *Roman Jakobson's science of language*. Lisse: de Ridder.

—1985: The poetic function and the nature of language. In Jakobson, R. *Verbal art, verbal sign, verbal time*. Oxford: Blackwell.

WELLEK, R. and WARREN, A. 1949: *Theory of literature*. New York: Harcourt Brace.

WINNER, T. G. 1978: Jan Mukařovský: The beginnings of structural and semiotic aesthetics. In Matejka, L. (ed.), *Sound, sign and meaning*. Ann Arbor: University of Michigan, 433–55.

Part II

Functionalist stylistics

3

Linguistic function and literary style: An inquiry into the language of William Golding's The Inheritors

M. A. K. Halliday

My main concern, in this paper, is with criteria of relevance. This, it seems to me, is one of the central problems in the study of 'style in language': I mean the problem of distinguishing between mere linguistic regularity, which in itself is of no interest to literary studies, and regularity which is significant for the poem or prose work in which we find it. I remember an entertaining paper read to the Philological Society in Cambridge some years ago by Professor John Sinclair (1965), in which he drew our attention to some very striking linguistic patterns displayed in the poetry of William McGonagall, and invited us to say why, if this highly structured language was found in what we all agreed was such very trivial poetry, we should be interested in linguistic regularities at all. It is no new discovery to say that pattern in language does not by itself make literature, still less 'good literature': nothing is more regular than the rhythm of *Three Blind Mice*, and if this is true of phonological regularities it is likely to be true also of syntactic ones. But we lack a general criteria for determining whether any particular instance of linguistic prominence is likely to be stylistically relevant or not.

This is not a simple matter, and any discussion of it is bound to touch on more than one topic, or at the least to adopt more than one angle of vision. Moreover the line of approach will often, inevitably, be indirect, and the central concern may at times be lost sight of round some of the corners. It seems to me necessary, first of all, to discuss and to emphasize the place of semantics in the study of style; and this in turn will lead to a consideration of 'functional' theories of language and their relevance for the student of literature. At the same time these general points need to be exemplified; and here I have allowed the illustration to take over the stage: when I re-examined for this purpose a novel I had first studied some four years ago, *The Inheritors* by William Golding, there seemed to be much that was of interest in its own right.[1] I do not think there is any antithesis between the 'textual' and the 'theoretical' in the study of language, so I hope the effect of this may be to strengthen rather than to weaken the general argument. The discussion of *The Inheritors* may be seen either in relation to just that one work or in relation to a general theory; I am not sure that it is possible to separate these two perspectives, either from each other or from various intermediate fields of attention such as an author, a genre, or a literary tradition.

The paper will fall into four parts: first, a discussion of a 'functional theory of language'; second, a reference to various questions raised at the Style in Language conference of 1958 and in other current writings; third, an examination of certain features of the language of *The Inheritors*; and fourth, a brief résumé of the question of stylistic relevance. Of these, the third part will be the longest.

The term *function* is used, in two distinct though related senses, at two very different points in the description of language. First it is used in the sense of 'grammatical' (or 'syntactic') function, to refer to elements of linguistic structures such as actor and goal or subject and object or theme and rheme. These 'functions' are the roles occupied by classes of words, phrases, and the like in the structure of higher units. Secondly, it is used to refer to the 'functions' of language as a whole: for example in the well-known work of Karl Bühler, in which he proposes a three-way division of language function into the representational, the conative and the expressive (Bühler 1934; see also Vachek 1966, ch. 2).

Here I am using 'function' in the second sense, referring, however, not specifically to Bühler's theory, but to the generalized notion of 'functions of language'. By a functional theory of language I mean one which attempts to explain linguistic structure, and linguistic phenomena, by reference to the notion that language plays a certain part in our lives, that it is required to serve certain universal types of demand. I find this approach valuable in general for the insight it gives into the nature and use of language, but particularly so in the context of stylistic studies.

The demands that we make on language, as speakers and writers, listeners and readers, are indefinitely many and varied. They can be derived, ultimately, from a small number of very general headings; but what these headings are will depend on what questions we are asking. For example, if we were to take a broadly psychological viewpoint and consider the functions that language serves in the life of the individual, we might arrive at some such scheme as Bühler's, referred to above. If on the other hand we asked a more sociological type of question, concerning the functions that language serves in the life of the community, we should probably elaborate some framework such as Malinowski's (1935) distinction into a pragmatic and a magical function. Many others could be suggested besides.

These questions are extrinsic to language; and the categorizations of language function that depend on them are of interest because, and to the extent that, the questions themselves are of interest. Such categorizations therefore imply a strictly instrumental view of linguistic theory. Some would perhaps reject this on the grounds that it does not admit the autonomy of linguistics and linguistic investigations. I am not myself impressed by that argument, although I would stress that any one particular instrumental view is by itself inadequate as a general characterization of language. But a purely extrinsic theory of language functions does fail to take into account one thing, namely the fact that the multiplicity of function, if the idea is valid at all, is likely to be reflected somewhere in the internal organization of language itself. If language is, as it were, programmed to serve a variety of needs, then this should show up in some way in an investigation of linguistic structure.

In fact this functional plurality is very clearly built into the structure of language, and forms the basis of its semantic and 'syntactic' (i.e. grammatical and lexical) organization. If we set up a functional framework that is neutral as to external emphasis, but designed to take into account the nature of the internal, semantic, and syntactic patterns of language, we arrive at something that is very suggestive for literary studies, because it represents a general characterization of semantic functions – of the meaning potential of the language system. Let me suggest here the framework that seems to me most helpful. It is a rather simple catalogue of three basic functions, one of which has two sub-headings.

In the first place, language serves for the expression of content: it has a representational, or, as I would prefer to call it, an *ideational* function. (This is sometimes referred to as the expression of 'cognitive meaning', though I find the term *cognitive* misleading; there is, after all, a cognitive element in all linguistic functions.) Two points need to be emphasized concerning this ideational function of language. The first is that it is through this function that the speaker or writer embodies in language his experience of the phenomena of the real world; and this includes his experience of the internal world of his own consciousness: his reactions, cognitions, and perceptions, and also his linguistic acts of speaking and understanding. We shall in no sense be adopting an extreme pseudo-Whorfian position (I say 'pseudo-Whorfian' because Whorf himself never was extreme) if we add that, in serving this function, language lends structure to his experience and helps to determine his way of looking at things. The speaker can see through and around the settings of his semantic system; but he is aware that, in doing so, he is seeing reality in a new light, like Alice in Looking-glass House. There is, however, and this is the second point, one component of ideational meaning which, while not unrelatable to experience, is nevertheless organized in language in a way which marks it off as distinct: this is the expression of certain fundamental logical relations such as are encoded in language in the form of co-ordination, apposition, modification, and the like. The notion of co-ordination, for example, as in *sun, moon, and stars*, can be derived from an aspect of the speaker's experience; but this and other such relations are realized through the medium of a particular type of structural mechanism (that of linear recursion) which takes them, linguistically, out of the domain of experience to form a functionally neutral, 'logical' component in the total spectrum of meanings. Within the ideational function of language, therefore, we can recognize two sub-functions, the *experiential* and the *logical*; and the distinction is a significant one for our present purpose.

In the second place, language serves what we may call an *interpersonal* function. This is quite different from the expression of content. Here, the speaker is using language as the means of his own intrusion into the speech event: the expression of his comments, his attitudes, and evaluations, and also of the relationship that he sets up between himself and the listener – in particular, the communication role that he adopts, of informing, questioning, greeting, persuading, and the like. The interpersonal function thus subsumes both the expressive and the conative, which are not in fact distinct in the linguistic system: to give one example, the meanings 'I do not know' (expressive) and 'you tell me' (conative) are combined in a single semantic feature, that of question, typically expressed in the grammar by an interrogative; the interrogative is both expressive and conative at the same time. The set of communication roles is unique among social relations in that it is brought into being and maintained solely through language. But the interpersonal element in language extends beyond what we might think of as its rhetorical functions. In the wider context, language is required to serve in the establishment and maintenance of all human relationships; it is the means whereby social groups are integrated and the individual is identified and reinforced. It is, I think, significant for certain forms of literature that, since personality is dependent on interaction which is in turn mediated through language, the 'interpersonal' function in language is both interactional and personal: there is, in other words, a component in language which serves at one and the same time to express both the inner and the outer surfaces of the individual, as a single undifferentiated area of meaning potential that is personal in the broadest sense.[2]

These two functions, the ideational and the interpersonal, may seem sufficiently all-embracing; and in the context of an instrumental approach to language they are. But there is a third function which is in turn instrumental to these two, whereby language is, as it were, enabled to meet the demands that are made on it; I shall call this the *textual* function, since it is concerned with the creation of text. It is a function internal to language, and for this reason is not usually taken into account where the objects of investigation are extrinsic; but it came to be specifically associated with the term 'functional' in the work of the Prague scholars who developed Bühler's ideas within the framework of a linguistic theory (cf. their terms 'functional syntax', 'functional sentence perspective'). It is through this function that language makes links with itself and with the situation; and discourse becomes possible, because the speaker or writer can produce a text and the listener or reader can recognize one. A *text* is an operational unit of language, as a sentence is a syntactic unit; it may be spoken or written, long or short; and it includes as a special instance a literary text, whether haiku or Homeric epic. It is the text and not some super-sentence that is the relevant unit for stylistic studies; this is a functional-semantic concept and is not definable by size. And therefore the 'textual' function is not limited to the establishment of relations between sentences; it is concerned just as much with the internal organization of the sentence, with its meaning as a message both in itself and in relation to the context.

A tentative categorization of the principal elements of English syntax in terms of the above functions is given in Table 3.1. This table is intended to serve a twofold purpose. In the first place, it will help to make more concrete the present concept of a functional theory, by showing how the various functions are realized through the grammatical systems of the language, all of which are accounted for in this way. Not all the labels may be self-explanatory, nor is the framework so

Table 3.1

COHESION ("above the sentence": non-structural relations) reference; substitution & ellipsis; conjunction; lexical cohesion

rank:	function:	IDEATIONAL		INTERPERSONAL	TEXTUAL
		Experiential	Logical		
CLAUSE		TRANSITIVITY types of process participants and circumstances (identity clauses) (things, facts, and reports)	condition addition report / POLARITY	MOOD types of speech function modality (the WH-function)	THEME types of message (identity as text relation) (identification, predication, reference, substitution)
Verbal GROUP		TENSE (verb classes)	catenation secondary tense	PERSON ("marked" options)	VOICE ("constrastive" options)
Nominal GROUP		MODIFICATION epithet function enumeration (noun classes) (adjective classes)	classification sub-modification	ATTITUDE attitudinal modifiers intensifiers	DEIXIS determiners "phoric" elements (qualifiers) (definite article)
Adverbial (incl. prepositional GROUP)		"MINOR PROCESSES" prepositional relations (classes of circumstantial adjunct)	narrowing sub-modification	COMMENT (classes of comment adjunct)	CONJUNCTION (classes of discourse adjunct)
WORD (incl. lexical item)		LEXICAL "CONTENT" (taxonomic organization of vocabulary)	compounding derivation	LEXICAL "REGISTER" (expressive words) (stylistic organization of vocabulary)	COLLOCATION (collocational organization of vocabulary)
INFORMATION UNIT				TONE intonation systems	INFORMATION distribution and focus

PARATACTIC COMPLEXES (all ranks) coordination apposition

HYPOTACTIC COMPLEXES OF CLAUSE, GROUP, AND WORD

compartmental as in this bare outline it is made to seem: there is a high degree of indeterminacy in the fuller picture, representing the indeterminacy that is present throughout language, in its categories and its relations, its types and its tokens. Secondly it will bring out the fact that the syntax of a language is organized in such a way that it expresses as a whole the range of linguistic functions, but that the symptoms of functional diversity are not to be sought in single sentences or sentence types. In general, that is to say, we shall not find whole sentences or even smaller structures having just one function. Typically, each sentence embodies all functions, though one or another may be more prominent; and most constituents of sentences also embody more than one function, through their ability to combine two or more syntactic roles.

Let us introduce an example at this point. Here is a well-known passage from *Through the Looking-Glass, and What Alice Found There*:

> 'I don't understand you,' said Alice. 'It's dreadfully confusing!'
>
> 'That's the effect of living backwards,' the Queen said kindly: 'it always makes one a little giddy at first – '
>
> 'Living backwards!' Alice repeated in great astonishment. 'I never heard of such a thing!'
>
> ' – but there's one great advantage in it, that one's memory works both ways.'
>
> 'I'm sure *mine* only works one way,' Alice remarked. 'I can't remember things before they happen.'
>
> 'It's a poor sort of memory that only works backwards,' the Queen remarked.
>
> 'What sort of things do *you* remember best?' Alice ventured to ask.
>
> 'Oh, things that happened the week after next,' the Queen replied in a careless tone.

To illustrate the last point first, namely that most constituents of sentences embody more than one function, by combining different syntactic roles: the constituent *what sort of things* occupies simultaneously the syntactic roles of 'theme', of 'phenomenon' (that is, object of cognition, perception, etc.) and of 'interrogation point'. The theme represents a particular status in the message, and is thus an expression of 'textual' function: it is the speaker's point of departure. If the speaker is asking a question he usually, in English, takes the request for information as his theme, expressing this by putting the question phrase first; here, therefore, the same element is both theme and interrogation point – the latter being an expression of 'interpersonal' function since it defines the specific communication roles the speaker has chosen for himself and for the listener: the speaker is behaving as questioner. *What sort of things* is the phenomenon dependent on the mental process *remember*; and this concept of a mental phenomenon, as something that can be talked about, is an expression of the 'ideational' function of language – of language as content, relatable to the speaker's and the listener's experience. It should be emphasized that it is not, in fact, the syntactic role in isolation, but the structure of which it forms a part that is semantically significant: it is not the theme, for example, but the total theme-rheme structure which contributes to the texture of the discourse.

Thus the constituents themselves tend to be multivalent; which is another way of saying that the very notion of a constituent is itself rather too concrete to be of much help in a functional context. A constituent is a particular word or phrase in a particular place; but functionally the choice of an item may have one meaning, its repetition another, and its location in structure yet another – or many others, as we have seen. So, in the Queen's remark *it's a poor sort of memory that only works backwards*, the word *poor* is a 'modifier', and thus expresses a subclass of its head-word *memory* (ideational); while at the same time it is an 'epithet' expressing the Queen's attitude (interpersonal), and the choice of this word in this environment (as opposed to, say, *useful*) indicates more specifically that the attitude is one of disapproval. The words *it's ... that* have here no reference at all outside the sentence, but they structure the message in a particular way (textual), which represents the Queen's opinion as if it was an 'attribute' (ideational), and defines one class of *memory* as exclusively possessing this undesirable quality (ideational). The lexical repetition in *memory that only works backwards* relates the Queen's remark (textual) to *mine only works one way*, in which *mine* refers anaphorically, by ellipsis, to *memory* in the preceding sentence (textual) and also to *I* in Alice's expression of her own judgment *I'm sure* (interpersonal). Thus ideational content and personal interaction are woven together with, and by means of, the textual structure to form a coherent whole.

Taking a somewhat broader perspective, we again find the same interplay of functions. The ideational meaning of the passage is enshrined in the phrase *living backwards*; we have a general characterization of the nature of experience, in which *things that happened the week after next* turns out to be an acceptable sentence. (I am not suggesting it is serious, or offering a deep literary interpretation; I am merely using it to illustrate the nature of language.) On the interpersonal level the language expresses, through a pattern of question (or exclamation) and response, a basic relationship of seeker and guide, in interplay with various other paired functions such as yours and mine, for and against, child and adult, wonderment and judgment. The texture is that of dialogue in narrative, within which the Queen's complex thematic structures (e.g. *there's one great advantage to it, that*) contrast with the much simpler (i.e. linguistically unmarked) message patterns used by Alice.

A functional theory of language is a theory about meanings, not about words or constructions; we shall not attempt to assign a word or a construction directly to one function or another. Where then do we find the functions differentiated in language? They are differentiated semantically, as different areas of what I called the 'meaning potential'. Language is itself a potential: it is the totality of what the speaker can do. (By 'speaker' I mean always the language user, whether as speaker, listener, writer, or reader: *homo grammaticus*, in fact.) We are considering, as it were, the dynamics of the semantic strategies that are available to him. If we represent the language system in this way, as networks of inter-related options which define, as a whole, the resources for what the speaker wants to say, we find empirically that these options fall into a small number of fairly distinct sets. In the last resort, every option in language is related to every other; there are no completely independent choices. But the total network of meaning potential is actually composed of a number of smaller networks, each one highly complex in itself but related to the others in a way that is relatively simple: rather like an elaborate piece of circuitry made up of two or three complex blocks of wiring with fairly simple interconnections. Each of these blocks corresponds to one of the functions of language.

In Table 3.1, where the columns represent our linguistic functions, each column is one 'block' of options. These blocks are to be thought of as wired 'in parallel'. That is to say, the speaker does not first think of the content of what he wants to say and then go on to decide what kind of a message it is and where he himself comes into it – whether it will be statement or question, what modalities are involved and the like.[3] All these functions, the ideational, the interpersonal and the textual, are simultaneously embodied in his planning procedures. (If we pursue the metaphor, it is the rows of the table that are wired 'in series': they represent the hierarchy of constituents in the grammar, where the different functions come together. Each row is one constituent type, and is a point of intersection of options from the different columns.)

The linguistic differentiation among the ideational, interpersonal and textual functions is thus to be found in the way in which choices in meaning are interrelated to one another. Each function defines a set of options that is relatively – though only relatively – independent of the other sets. Dependence here refers to the degree of mutual determination: one part of the content of what one says tends to exert a considerable effect on other parts of the content, whereas one's attitudes and speech roles are relatively undetermined by it: the speaker is, by and large, free to associate any interpersonal meanings with any content. What I wish to stress here is that all types of option, from whatever function they are derived, are meaningful. At every point the speaker is selecting among a range of possibilities that differ in meaning; and if we attempt to separate meaning from choice we are turning a valuable distinction (between linguistic functions) into an arbitrary dichotomy (between 'meaningful' and 'meaningless' choices). All options are embedded in the language system: the system *is* a network of options, deriving from all the various functions of language. If we take the useful functional distinction of 'ideational' and 'interpersonal' and rewrite it, under the labels 'cognitive' and 'expressive', in such a way as sharply to separate the two, equating cognitive with meaning and expressive with style, we not only fail to recognize the experiential basis of many of our own intuitions about works of literature and their impact – style as the expression of what the thing is about, at some level (my own illustration in this paper is one example of this; cf. the discussion in Todorov 1971) – but we also attach the contrasting status of 'non-cognitive' (whatever this may mean) to precisely these options that seem best to embody our conception of a work of literature, those whereby the writer gives form to the discourse and expresses his own individuality.[4] Even if we are on our guard against the implication that the regions of language in which style resides are the ones which are linguistically non-significant, we are still drawing the wrong line. There are no regions of language in which style does not reside.

We should not in fact be drawing lines at all; the boundaries on our map consist only in shading and overlapping. Nevertheless they are there; and provided we are not forced into seeking an unreal distinction between the 'what' and the 'how', we can show, by reference to the generalized notion of linguistic functions, how such real contrasts as that of denotation and connotation relate to the functional map of language as a whole, and thus how they may be incorporated into the linguistic study of style. It is through this chain of reasoning that we may hope to establish criteria of relevance, and to demonstrate the connection between the syntactic observations which we make about a text and the nature of the impact which that text has upon us. If we can relate the linguistic patterns (grammatical, lexical, and even phonological) to the underlying functions of language, we have a criterion for eliminating what is trivial and for distinguishing true foregrounding from mere prominence of a statistical or an absolute kind.

Foregrounding, as I understand it, is prominence that is motivated. It is not difficult to find patterns of prominence in a poem or prose text, regularities in the sounds or words or structures that stand out in some way, or may be brought out by careful reading; and one may often be led in this way towards a new insight, through finding that such prominence contributes to the writer's total meaning. But unless it does, it will seem to lack motivation; a feature that is brought into prominence will be 'foregrounded' only if it relates to the meaning of the text as a whole. This relationship is a functional one: if a particular feature of the language contributes, by its prominence, to the total meaning of the work, it does so by virtue of and through the medium of its own value in the language – through the linguistic function from which its meaning is derived. Where that function is relevant to our interpretation of the work, the prominence will appear as motivated. I shall try to illustrate this by reference to *The Inheritors*. First, however, a few remarks about some points raised at the 1958 Style in Language Conference and in subsequent discussions, which I hope will make slightly more explicit the context within which Golding's work is being examined.

There are three questions I should like to touch on: is prominence to be regarded as a departure from or as the attainment of a norm? To what extent is prominence a quantitative effect, to be uncovered or at least stated by means of statistics? How real is the distinction between prominence that is due to subject-matter and prominence that is due to something else? All three questions are very familiar, and my justification for bringing them up once more is not that what I have to say about them is new but rather that some partial answers are needed if we are attempting an integrated approach to language and style, and that these answers will be pertinent to a consideration of our main question, which is that of criteria of relevance.

I have used the term *prominence* as a general name for the phenomenon of linguistic highlighting, whereby some feature of the language of a text stands out in some way. In choosing this term I hoped to avoid the assumption that a linguistic feature which is brought under attention will always be seen as a departure. It is quite natural to characterize such prominence as departure from a norm, since this explains why it is remarkable, especially if one is stressing the subjective nature of the highlighting effect; thus Leech, discussing what he refers to as 'schemes' ('foregrounded patterns ... in grammar or phonology'), writes 'It is ultimately a matter of subjective judgment whether ... the regularity seems remarkable enough to constitute a definite departure from the normal functions of language' (1965, p. 70). But at the same time it is often objected, not unreasonably, that the 'departure' view puts too high a value on oddness, and suggests that normal forms are of no interest in the study of style. Thus Wellek: 'The danger of linguistic stylistics is its focus on deviations from, and distortions of, the linguistic norm. We get a kind of counter-grammar, a science of discards. Normal stylistics is abandoned to the grammarian, and deviational stylistics is reserved for the student of literature. But often the most common-place, the most normal, linguistic elements are the constituents of literary structure' (1960, pp. 417–18).

Two kinds of answer have been given to this objection. One is that there are two types of prominence, only one of which is negative, a departure from a norm; the other is positive, and is the attainment or the establishment of a norm. The second is that departure may in any case be merely statistical: we are concerned not only with deviations, ungrammatical forms, but also with what we may call 'deflections', departures from some expected pattern of frequency.

The distinction between negative and positive prominence, or departures and regularities, is drawn by Leech, who contrasts foregrounding in the form of 'motivated deviation from linguistic, or other socially accepted norms' with foregrounding applied to 'the opposite circumstance, in which a writer temporarily renounces his permitted freedom of choice, introducing uniformity where there would normally be diversity' (1965, p. 69). Strictly speaking this is not an 'opposite circumstance', since if diversity is normal, then uniformity is a deviation. But where there is uniformity there is regularity; and this can be treated as a positive feature, as the establishment of a norm. Thus, to quote Hymes, 'in some sources, especially poets, style may not be deviation from but achievement of a norm' (1967, pp. 33–4).

However, this is not a distinction between two types of prominence; it is a distinction between two ways of looking at prominence, depending on the stand-point of the observer. There is no single universally relevant norm, no one set of expectancies to which all instances may be referred. On the one hand, there are differences of perspective. The text may be seen as 'part' of a larger 'whole', such as the author's complete works, or the tradition to which it belongs, so that what is globally a departure may be locally a norm. The expectancies may lie in 'the language as a whole', in a diatypic variety or register[5] characteristic of some situation type (Osgood's 'situational norms' [1960, p. 293]), in a genre or literary form, or in some special institution such as the Queen's Christmas message; we always have the choice of saying either 'this departs from a pattern' or 'this forms a pattern'. On the other hand, there are differences of attention. The text may be seen as 'this' in contrast with 'that', with another poem or another novel; stylistic studies are essentially comparative in nature, and either may be taken as the point of departure. As Hymes (1967) says, there are egalitarian universes, comprising sets of norms, and 'it would be arbitrary to choose one norm as a standard from which the others depart'. It may be more helpful to look at a given instance of prominence in one way rather than in another, sometimes as departure from a norm and sometimes as the attainment of a norm; but there is only one type of phenomenon here, not two.

There is perhaps a limiting case, the presence of one ungrammatical sentence in an entire poem or novel; presumably this could be viewed only as a departure. But in itself it would be unlikely to be of any interest. Deviation, the use of ungrammatical forms, has received a great deal of attention, and seems to be regarded, at times, as prominence *par excellence*. This is probably because it is a deterministic concept. Deviant forms are actually prohibited by the rules of whatever is taken to be the norm; or, to express it positively, the norm that is established by a set of deviant forms excludes all texts but the one in which they occur. But for this very reason deviation is of very limited interest in stylistics. It is rarely found; and when it is found, it is often not relevant. On the contrary, if we follow McIntosh (who finds it 'a chastening thought'), 'quite often ... the impact of an entire work may be enormous, yet word by word, phrase by phrase, clause by clause, sentence by sentence, there may seem to be nothing very unusual or arresting, in grammar or in vocabulary' (1965, p. 19).[6]

Hence the very reasonable supposition that prominence may be of a probabilistic kind, defined by Bloch (1953) as 'frequency distributions and transitional probabilities [which] differ from those ... in the language as a whole'. This is what we have referred to above as 'deflection'. It too may be viewed either as departure from a norm or as its attainment. If, for example, we meet seven occurrences of a rather specific grammatical pattern, such as that cited by Leech '*my* + noun + *you* + verb' (1965, p. 70), a norm has been set up and there is, or may be, a strong local expectancy that an eighth will follow; the probability of finding this pattern repeated in eight successive clauses is infinitesimally small, so that the same phenomenon constitutes a departure. It is fairly easy to see that the one always implies the other; the contravention of one expectation is, at the same time, the fulfillment of a different one. Either way, whether the prominence is said to consist in law-breaking or in law-making, we are dealing with a type of phenomenon that is expressible in quantitative terms, to which statistical concepts may be applied.

In the context of stylistic investigations, the term 'statistical' may refer to anything from a highly detailed measurement of the reactions of subjects to sets of linguistic variables, to the parenthetical insertion of figures of occurrences designed to explain why a particular feature is being singled out for discussion. What is common to all these is the assumption that numerical data on language may be stylistically significant; whatever subsequent operations are performed, there has nearly always been some counting of linguistic elements in the text, whether of phonological units or words or grammatical patterns, and the figures obtained are potentially an indication of prominence. The notion that prominence may be defined statistically is still not always accepted; there seem to be two main counterarguments, but whatever substance these may have as stated they are not, I think, valid objections to the point at issue. The first is essentially that, since style is a manifestation of the individual, it cannot be reduced to counting. This is true, but, as has often been said before, it misses the point. If there is such a thing as a recognizable style, whether of a work, an author, or an entire period or literary tradition, its distinctive quality can in the last analysis be stated in terms of relative frequencies, although the linguistic features that show significant variation may be simple and obvious or extremely subtle and complex. An example of how period styles may be revealed in this way will be found in Josephine Miles' 'Eras in English Poetry', in which she shows that different periods are characterized by a distinction in the dominant type of sentence structure, that between 'the sort which emphasizes substantival elements – the phrasal and co-ordinative modifications of subject and object – and the sort which emphasizes clausal co-ordination and complication of the predicate' (1967, pp. 175–6).

The second objection is that numbers of occurrences must be irrelevant to style because we are not aware of frequency in language and therefore cannot respond to it. This is almost certainly not true. We are probably rather sensitive to the relative frequency of different grammatical and lexical patterns, which is an aspect of 'meaning potential'; and our expectancies, as readers, are in part based on our awareness of the probabilities inherent in the language. This is what enables us to grasp the new probabilities of the text as local norm; our ability to perceive a statistical departure and restructure it as a norm is itself evidence of the essentially probabilistic nature of the language system. Our concern here, in any case, is not with psychological problems of the response to literature but with the linguistic options selected by the writer and their relation to the total meaning of the work. If in the selections he has made there is an unexpected pattern of frequency distributions, and this turns out to be motivated, it seems pointless to argue that such a phenomenon could not possibly be significant.

What cannot be expressed statistically is foregrounding: figures do not tell us whether a particular pattern has or has not 'value in the game' (cf. Miller 1960, p. 394). For this we need to know the rules. A distinctive frequency distribution is in itself no guarantee of stylistic relevance, as can be seen from authorship studies, where the diagnostic features are often, from a literary standpoint, very trivial ones.[7] Conversely, a linguistic feature that is stylistically very relevant may display a much less striking frequency pattern. But there is likely to be some quantitative turbulence, if a particular feature is felt to be prominent; and a few figures may be very suggestive. Counting, as Miller remarked, has many positive virtues. Ullmann offers a balanced view of these when he writes 'Yet even those who feel that detailed statistics are both unnecessary and unreliable [in a sphere where quality and context, aesthetic effects and suggestive overtones are of supreme importance] would probably agree that a rough indication of frequencies would often be helpful' (1965, p. 22). A rough indication of frequencies is often just what is needed: enough to suggest why we should accept the analyst's assertion that some feature is prominent in the text, and to allow us to check his statements. The figures, obviously, do not alone constitute an analysis, interpretation, or evaluation of the style.

But this is not, be it noted, a limitation on quantitative patterns as such; it is a limitation on the significance of prominence of any kind. Deviation is no more fundamental a phenomenon than statistical deflection: in fact there is no very clear line between the two, and in any given instance the most qualitatively deviant items may be among the least relevant. Thus if style cannot be reduced to counting, this is because it cannot be reduced to a simple question of prominence. An adequate characterization of an author's style is much more than an inventory of linguistic highlights. This is why linguists were so often reluctant to take up questions of criticism and evaluation, and tended to disclaim any contribution to the appraisal of what they were describing: they were very aware that statements about linguistic prominence by themselves offer no criterion of literary value. Nevertheless some values, or some aspects of value, must be expressed in linguistic terms. This is true, for example, of metrical patterns, which linguists have always considered their proper concern. The question is how far it is also true of patterns that are more directly related to meaning: what factors govern the relevance of 'effects' in grammar and vocabulary? The significance of rhythmic regularity has to be formulated linguistically, since it is a phonological phenomenon, although the ultimate value to which it relates is not 'given' by the language – that the sonnet is a highly valued pattern is not a linguistic fact, but the sonnet itself is (cf. Levin 1971). The sonnet form defines the relevance of certain types of phonological pattern. There may likewise be some linguistic factor involved in determining whether a syntactic or a lexical pattern is stylistically relevant or not.

Certainly there is no magic in unexpectedness; and one line of approach has been to attempt to state conditions under which the unexpected is *not* relevant – namely when it is not really unexpected. Prominence, in this view, is not significant if the linguistically unpredicted configuration is predictable on other grounds; specifically, by reference to subject-matter, the implication being that it would have been predicted if we had known beforehand what the passage was about. So, for example, Ullmann warns of the danger in the search for statistically defined key-words: 'One must carefully avoid what have been called contextual words whose frequency is due to the subject-matter rather than to any deep-seated stylistic or psychological tendency' (1965, p. 27). Ullmann's concern here is with words that serve as indices of a particular author, and he goes on to discuss the significance of recurrent imagery for style and personality, citing as an example the prominence of insect vocabulary in the writings of Sartre (Ullmann 1965, p. 29; see also Ullmann 1964, pp. 186–8); in this context we can see that, by contrast, the prevalence of such words in a treatise on entomology would be irrelevant. But it is less easy to see how this can be generalized, even in the realm of vocabulary; is lexical foregrounding entirely dependent on imagery?

Can we in fact dismiss, as irrelevant, prominence that is due to subject-matter? Can we even claim to identify it? This was the third and final question I asked earlier, and it is one which relates very closely to an interpretation of the style of *The Inheritors*. In *The Inheritors*, the features that come to our attention are largely syntactic, and we are in the realm of syntactic imagery, where the syntax, in Ohmann's words, 'serves [a] vision of things ... since there are innumerable kinds of deviance, we should expect that the ones elected by a poem or poet spring from particular semantic impulses, particular ways of looking at experience' (1967, p. 237). Ohmann is concerned primarily with 'syntactic irregularities', but syntax need not be deviant in order to serve a vision of things; a foregrounded selection of everyday syntactic options may be just as visionary, and perhaps more effective. The vision provides the motivation for their prominence; it makes them relevant, however ordinary they may be. The style of *The Inheritors* rests very much on foregrounding of this kind.

The prominence, in other words, is often due to the vision. But 'vision' and 'subject-matter' are merely the different levels of meaning which we expect to find in a literary work; and each of these, the inner as well as the outer, and any as it were intermediate layers, finds expression in the syntax. In Ruqaiya Hasan's words, 'Each utterance has a thesis: what it is talking about uniquely and instantially; and in addition to this, each utterance has a function in the internal organization of the text: in combination with other utterances of the text it realizes the theme, structure and other aspects' (1967, pp. 109–10; see also Hasan 1971). Patterns of syntactic prominence may reflect thesis or theme or 'other aspects' of the meaning of the work; every level is a potential source of motivation, a kind of semantic 'situational norm'. And since the role of syntax in language is to weave into a single fabric the different threads of meaning that derive from the variety of linguistic functions, one and the same syntactic feature is very likely to have at once both a deeper and a more immediate significance, like the participial structures in Milton as Chatman (1968) has interpreted them.

Thus we cannot really discount 'prominence due to subject-matter', at least as far as syntactic prominence is concerned; especially where vision and subject-matter are themselves as closely interwoven as they are in *The Inheritors*. Rather, perhaps, we might think of the choice of subject-matter as being itself a stylistic choice, in the sense that the subject-matter may be more or less relevant to the underlying themes of the work. To the extent that the subject-matter is an integral element in the total meaning – in the artistic unity, if you will – to that extent, prominence that is felt to be partly or wholly 'due to' the subject-matter, far from being irrelevant to the style, will turn out to be very clearly foregrounded.

To cite a small example that I have used elsewhere, the prominence of finite verbs in simple past tense in the well-known 'Return of Excalibur' lines in Tennyson's *Morte d'Arthur* relates immediately to the subject-matter: the passage is a direct narrative. But the choice of a story as subject-matter is itself related to the deeper preoccupations of the work – with heroism and, beyond that, with the *res gestae*, with deeds as the realization of the true spirit of a people, and with history and historicalism; the narrative register is an appropriate form of expression, one that is congruent with the total meaning, and so the verb forms that are characteristically associated with it are motivated at every level. Similarly, it is not irrelevant to the *style* of an entomological monograph (although we may not be very interested in its style) that it contains a lot of words for insects, if in fact it does. In stylistics we are concerned with language in relation to all the various levels of meaning that a work may have.

But while a given instance of syntactic or lexical prominence may be said to be 'motivated' either by the subject-matter or by some other level of the meaning, in the sense of deriving its relevance therefrom, it cannot really be said to be 'due to' it. Neither thesis nor theme imposes linguistic patterns. They may set up local expectancies, but these are by no means always fulfilled; there might actually be very few insect words in the work on entomology – and there are very few in Kafka.[8] There is always choice. In *The Inheritors*, Golding is offering a 'particular way of looking at experience', a vision of things which he ascribes to Neanderthal man; and he conveys this by syntactic prominence, by the frequency with which he selects certain key syntactic options. It is their frequency which establishes the clause types in question as prominent; but, as Ullmann has remarked, in stylistics we have *both* to count things *and* to look at them, one by one, and when we do this we find that the foregrounding effect is the product of two apparently opposed conditions of use. The foregrounded elements are certain clause types which display particular patterns of transitivity, as described in the next section; and in some instances the syntactic pattern is 'expected' in that it is the typical form of expression for the subject-matter – for the process, participants, and circumstances that make up the thesis of the clause. Elsewhere, however, the same syntactic elements are found precisely where they would not be expected, there being other, more likely ways of 'saying the same thing'.

Here we might be inclined to talk of semantic choice and syntactic choice: what the author chooses to say, and how he chooses to say it. But this is a misleading distinction; not only because it is unrealistic in application (most distinctions in language leave indeterminate instances, although here there would be suspiciously many) but more because the combined effect is cumulative: the one does not weaken or cut across the other but reinforces it. We have to do here with an interaction, not of meaning and form, but of two levels of meaning, both of which find expression in form, and through the same syntactic features. The immediate thesis and the underlying theme come together in the syntax; the choice of subject-matter is motivated by the deeper meaning, and the transitivity patterns realize both. This is the explanation of their powerful impact.

The foregrounding of certain patterns in syntax as the expression of an underlying theme is what we understand by 'syntactic imagery', and we assume that its effect will be striking. But in *The Inheritors* these same syntactic patterns also figure prominently in their 'literal' sense, as the expression of subject-matter; and their prominence here is doubly relevant, since the literal use not only is motivated in itself but also provides a context for the metaphorical – we accept the syntactic vision of things more readily because we can see that it coincides with, and is an extension of, the reality. *The Inheritors* provides a remarkable illustration of how grammar can convey levels of meaning in literature; and this relates closely to the notion of linguistic functions which I discussed at the beginning. The foregrounded patterns, in this instance, are ideational ones, whose meaning resides in the representation of experience; as such they express not only the content of the narrative but also the abstract structure of the reality through which that content is interpreted. Sometimes the interpretation matches our own, and at other times, as in the drawing of the bow in passage A below, it conflicts with it; these are the 'opposed conditions of use' referred to earlier. Yet each tells a part of the story. Language, because of the multiplicity of its functions, has a fugue-like quality in which a number of themes unfold simultaneously; each of these themes is apprehended in various settings, or perspectives, and each melodic line in the syntactic sequence has more than one value in the whole.

The Inheritors[9] is, in my opinion, a highly successful piece of imaginative prose writing; in the words of Kinkead-Weekes and Gregor, in their penetrating critical study (1967), it is a 'reaching out through the imagination into the unknown'. The persons of the story are a small band of Neanderthal people, initially eight strong, who refer to themselves as 'the people'; their world is then invaded by a group of more advanced stock, a fragment of a tribe, whom they call at first 'others' and later 'the new people'. This casual impact – casual, that is, from the tribe's point of view – proves to be the end of the people's world, and of the people themselves. At first, and for more than nine-tenths of the book (pp. 1–216), we share the life of the people and their view of the world, and also their view of the tribe: for a long passage (pp. 137–80) the principal character, Lok, is hidden in a tree watching the tribe in their work, their ritual and their play, and the account of their doings is confined within the limits of Lok's understanding, requiring at times a considerable effort of 'interpretation'. At the very end (pp. 216–38) the standpoint shifts to that of the tribe, the inheritors, and the world becomes recognizable as our own, or something very like it. I propose to examine an aspect of the linguistic resources as they are used first to characterize the people's world and then to effect the shift of world-view.

For this purpose I shall look closely at three passages taken from different parts of the book; these are reproduced in an Appendix to this chapter. Passage A is representative of the first, and longest, section, the narrative of the people; it is taken from the long account of Lok's vigil in the tree. Passage C is taken from the short final section, concerned with the tribe; while passage B spans the transition, the shift of standpoint occurring at the paragraph division within this passage. Linguistically, A and C differ in rather significant ways, while B is in certain respects transitional between them.

The clauses of passage A [56][10] are mainly clauses of action [21], location (including possession) [14], or mental process [16]; the remainder [5] are attributive.[11] Usually the process is expressed by a finite verb in simple past tense [46]. Almost all of the action clauses [19] describe simple movements (*turn, rise, hold, reach, throw forward*, etc.); and of these the majority [15] are intransitive; the exceptions are *the man was holding the stick, as though someone had clapped a hand over her mouth, he threw himself forward,* and *the echo of Liku's voice in his head sent him trembling at this perilous way of bushes towards the island.* The

Table 3.2 Frequencies of transitivity clause types

	ACTION				location/possession	mental process	attribution	other (equation, event)	
	intransitive movement	other	*transitive* movement	other					
A Process:									
human {people	9		1	1	1	12			24
human {tribe	2		1			1			4
part of body	2				1	3	2		8
inanimate	4		1		12		3		20
	17		3	1	14	16	5		56
B (i)									
human {people	4		1	3*	2	1			11
human {tribe	5		1	1	2				9
part of body									
inanimate	13	1	2		5			2	23
	22	1	4	4	9	1		2	43
B (ii)									
human {people	13	2	1		2	4			22
human {tribe									
part of body	3				1		2		6
inanimate	3	1	1	2	4		6	2	19
	19	3	2	2	7	4	8	2	47
C									
human {people	1		1	2		4			8
human {tribe	3	2	5	11	3	11	3	2	40
part of body	2	1					5		8
inanimate	2	1			3		4	1	11
	8	4	6	13	6	15	12	3	67

*Including two passives, which are also negative and in which the actor is not explicit: *The tree would not be cajoled or persuaded.*

typical pattern is exemplified by the first two clauses, *the bushes twitched again* and *Lok steadied by the tree*, and there is no clear line, here, between action and location: both types have some reference in space, and both have one participant only. The clauses of movement usually [16] also specify location, e.g. *the man turned sideways in the bushes, he rushed to the edge of the water*; and on the other hand, in addition to what is clearly movement, as in *a stick rose upright*, and what is clearly location, as in *there were hooks in the bone*, there is an intermediate type exemplified by *[the bushes] waded out*, where the verb is of the movement type but the subject is immobile.

The picture is one in which people act, but they do not act on things; they move, but they move only themselves, not other objects. Even such normally transitive verbs as *grab* occur intransitively: *he grabbed at the branches* is just another clause of movement (cf. *he smelled along the shaft of the twig*). Moreover a high proportion [exactly half] of the subjects are not people; they are either parts of the body [8] or inanimate objects [20], and of the human subjects half again [14] are found in clauses which are not clauses of action. Even among the four transitive action clauses, cited above, one has an inanimate subject and one is reflexive. There is a stress set up, a kind of syntactic counterpoint, between verbs of movement in their most active and dynamic form, that of finite verb in independent clause (cf. Halliday 1964, p. 29), in the simple past tense characteristic of the direct narrative of events in a time sequence, on the one hand, and on the other hand the preference for non-human subjects and the almost total absence of transitive clauses. It is particularly the lack of transitive clauses of action with human subjects (there are only two clauses in which a person acts on an external object) that creates an atmosphere of ineffectual activity: the scene is one of constant movement, but movement which is as much inanimate as human and in which only the mover is affected – nothing else changes. The syntactic tension expresses this combination of activity and helplessness.

No doubt this is a fair summary of the life of Neanderthal man. But Passage A is not a description of the people. The section from which it is taken is one in which Lok is observing and, to a certain extent, interacting with the tribe; they have captured one of the people, and it is for the most part their doings that are being described. And the tribe are not helpless. The transitivity patterns are not imposed by the subject-matter; they are the reflexion of the underlying theme, or rather of one of the underlying themes – the inherent limitations of understanding, whether cultural or biological, of Lok and his people, and their consequent inability to survive when confronted with beings at a higher stage of development. In terms of the processes and events as we would interpret them, and encode them in our grammar, there is no immediate justification for the predominance of intransitives; this is the result of their being expressed through the medium of the semantic structure of Lok's universe. In our interpretation, a goal-directed process (or, as I shall suggest below, an externally caused process) took place: someone held up a bow and drew it. In Lok's interpretation, the process was undirected (or, again, self-caused): *a stick rose upright* and *began to grow shorter at both ends*. (I would differ slightly here from Kinkead-Weekes and Gregor, who suggest, I think, that the form of Lok's vision is perception and no more. There may be very little processing, but there surely is some; Lok has a theory – as he must have, because he has language.)

Thus it is the syntax as such, rather than the syntactic reflection of the subject-matter, to which we are responding. This would not emerge if we had no account of the activities of the tribe, since elsewhere – in the description of the people's own doings, or of natural phenomena – the intransitiveness of the syntax would have been no more than a feature of the events themselves, and of the people's ineffectual manipulation of their environment. For this reason the vigil of Lok is a central element in the novel. We find, in its syntax, both levels of meaning side by side: Lok is now actor, now interpreter, and it is his potential in both these roles that is realized by the overall patterns of prominence that we have observed, the intransitives, the non-human subjects, and the like. This is the dominant mode of expression. At the same time, in passage A, among the clauses that have human subjects, there are just two in which the subject is acting on something external to himself, and in both these the subject is a member of the tribe; it is not Lok. There is no instance in which Lok's own actions extend beyond himself; but there is a brief hint that such extension is conceivable. The syntactic foregrounding, of which this passage provides a typical example, thus has a complex significance: the predominance of intransitives reflects, first, the limitations of the people's own actions; second, the people's world view, which in general cannot transcend these limitations – but within which there may arise, thirdly, a dim apprehension of the superior powers of the 'others', represented by the rare intrusion of a transitive clause such as *the man was holding the stick out to him.* Here the syntax leads us into a third level of meaning, Golding's concern with the nature of humanity; the intellectual and spiritual developments that contribute to the present human condition, and the conflicts that arise within it, are realized in the form of conflicts between the stages of that development – and, syntactically, between the types of transitivity.

Passage A is both text and sample. It is not only these particular sentences and their meanings that determine our response, but the fact that they are part of a general syntactic and semantic scheme. That this passage is representative in its transitivity patterns can be seen from comparison with other extracts.[12] It also exemplifies certain other relevant features of the language of this part of the book. We have seen that there is a strong preference for processes having only one participant: in general there is only one nominal element in the structure of the clause, which is therefore the subject. But while there are very few complements,[13] there is an abundance of adjuncts [44]; and most of these [40] have some spatial reference. Specifically, they are (a) static [25], of which most [21] are place adjuncts consisting of preposition plus noun, the noun being either an inanimate object of the immediate natural environment (e.g. *bush*) or a part of the body, the remainder [4] being localizers (*at their farthest, at the end,* etc.); and (b), dynamic [15], of which the majority [10] are of direction or non-terminal motion (*sideways, [rose] upright, at the branches, towards the island,* etc.) and the remainder [5] perception, or at least circumstantial to some process that is not a physical one (e.g. *[looked at Lok] along his shoulder, [shouted] at the green drifts*). Thus with the dynamic type, either the movement is purely perceptual or, if physical, it never reaches a goal: the nearest thing to terminal motion is *he rushed to the edge of the water* (which is followed by *and came back*!).

The restriction to a single participant also applies to mental process clauses [16]. This category includes perception, cognition, and reaction, as well as the rather distinct sub-category of verbalization; and such clauses in English typically contain a 'phenomenon', that which is seen, understood, liked, etc. Here however the phenomenon is often [8] either not expressed at all (e.g. *[Lok] gazed*) or expressed indirectly through a preposition, as in *he smelled along the shaft of the twig*; and sometimes [3] the subject is not a human being but a sense organ (*his nose examined this stuff and did not like it*). There is the same reluctance to envisage the 'whole man' (as distinct from a part of his body) participating in a process in which other entities are involved.

There is very little modification of nouns [10, out of about 100]; and all modifiers are non-defining (e.g. *green drifts, glittering water*) except where [2] the modifier is the only semantically significant element in the nominal, the head noun being a mere carrier demanded by the rules of English grammar (*white bone things, sticky brown stuff*). In terms of the immediate situation, things have defining attributes only if these attributes are their sole properties; at the more abstract level, in Lok's understanding the complex taxonomic ordering of natural phenomena that is implied by the use of defining modifiers is lacking, or is only rudimentary.

We can now formulate a description of a typical clause of what we may call 'Language A', the language in which the major part of the book is written and of which passage A is a sample, in terms of its process, participants and circumstances:

(1) There is one participant only, which is therefore subject; this is
      (a) actor in a non-directed action (action clauses are intransitive), or partici-
           pant in a mental process (the one who perceives, etc.), or simply the
           bearer of some attribute or some spatial property;
      (b) a person (*Lok, the man, he*, etc.), or a part of the body, or an inanimate
           object of the immediate and tangible natural environment (*bush, water,
           twig*, etc.);
      (c) unmodified, other than by a determiner which is either an anaphoric
           demonstrative (*this, that*) or, with parts of the body, a personal
           possessive (*his*, etc.).
(2) The process is
      (a) action (which is always movement in space), or location-possession
           (including e.g. *the man had white bone things above his eyes* = 'above the
           man's eyes there were ...'), or mental process (thinking and talking as
           well as seeing and feeling – a 'cunning brain'! — but often with a part
           of the body as subject);
      (b) active, non-modalized, finite, in simple past tense (one of a linear
           sequence of mutually independent processes).
(3) There are often other elements which are adjuncts, i.e. treated as circum-
      stances attendant on the process, not as participants in it; these are
      (a) static expressions of place (in the form of prepositional phrases), or, if
           dynamic, expressions of direction (adverbs only) or of non-terminal
           motion, or of directionality of perception (e.g. *peered at the stick*);
      (b) often obligatory, occurring in clauses which are purely locational (e.g.
           there were hooks in the bone).

A grammar of Language A would tell us not merely what clauses occurred in the text but also what clauses could occur in that language (cf. Thorne 1965). For example, as far as I know the clause *a branch curved downwards over the water* does not occur in the book; neither does *his hands felt along the base of the rock*.

But both of them could have. On the other hand, *he had very quickly broken off the lowest branches* breaks four rules: it has a human actor with a transitive verb, a tense other than simple past, a defining modifier, and a non-spatial adjunct. This is not to say that it could not occur. Each of these features is improbable, and their combination is very improbable; but they are not impossible. They are improbable in that they occur with significantly lower frequency than in other varieties of English (such as, for example, the final section of *The Inheritors*).

Before leaving this passage, let us briefly reconsider the transitivity features in the light of a somewhat different analysis of transitivity in English. I have suggested elsewhere that the most generalized pattern of transitivity in modern English, extending beyond action clauses to clauses of all types, those of mental process and those expressing attributive and other relations, is one that is based not on the notions of actor and goal but on those of cause and effect.[14] In any clause, there is one central and obligatory participant – let us call it the 'affected' participant – which is inherently involved in the process. This corresponds to the actor in an intransitive clause of action, to the goal in a transitive clause of action, and to the one who perceives, etc., in a clause of mental process; *Lok* has this function in all the following examples: *Lok turned away, Fa drew Lok away, Lok looked up at Fa, Lok was frightened, curiosity overcame Lok*. There may then be a second, optional participant, which is present only if the process is being regarded as brought about by some agency other than the participant affected by it: let us call this the 'agent'. This is the actor in a transitive clause of action and the initiator in the various types of causative; the function of *Tuami* in *Tuami waggled the paddle in the water* and *Tuami let the ivory drop from his hands*. As far as action clauses are concerned, an intransitive clause is one in which the roles of 'affected' and 'agent' are combined in the one participant; a transitive clause is one in which they are separated, the process being treated as one having an external cause.

In these terms, the entire transitivity structure of Language A can be summed up by saying that there is no cause and effect. More specifically: in this language, processes are seldom represented as resulting from an external cause; in those instances where they are, the 'agent' is seldom a human being; and where it is a human being, it is seldom one of the people. Whatever the type of process, there tends to be only one participant; any other entities are involved only indirectly, as circumstantial elements (syntactically, through the mediation of a preposition). It is as if doing was as passive as seeing, and things no more affected by actions than by perceptions: their role is as in clauses of mental process, where the object of perception is not in any sense 'acted on' – it is in fact the perceiver that is the 'affected' participant, not the thing perceived – and likewise tends to be expressed circumstantially (e.g. *Lok peered at the stick*). There is no effective relation between persons and objects: people do not bring about events in which anything other than they themselves, or parts of their bodies, are implicated.

There are, moreover, a great many, an excessive number, of these circumstantial elements; they are the objects in the natural environment, which as it were take the place of participants, and act as curbs and limitations on the process. People do not act on the things around them; they act within the limitations imposed by the things. The frustration of the struggle with the environment, of a life 'poised ... between the future and the past' (Kinkead-Weekes and Gregor 1967, p. 81), is embodied in the syntax: many of the intransitive clauses have potentially transitive verbs in them, but instead of a direct object there is a prepositional phrase. The feeling of frustration is perhaps further reinforced by the constant reference to complex mental activities of cognition and verbalization. Although there are very few abstract nouns, there are very many clauses of speaking, knowing and understanding (e.g. *Lok understood that the man was holding the stick out to him*); and a recurrent theme, an obsession almost, is the difficulty of communicating memories and images (*I cannot see this picture*) – of transmitting experience through language, the vital step towards that social learning which would be a precondition of their further advance.

Such are some of the characteristics of Language A, the language which tells the story of the people. There is no such thing as a 'Language B'. Passage B is simply the point of transition between the two parts of the book. There is a 'Language C': this is the language of the last sixteen pages of the novel, and it is exemplified by the extract shown as passage C below. But passage B is of interest because linguistically it is also to some extent transitional. There is no doubt that the first paragraph is basically in Language A and the second in Language C; moreover the switch is extremely sudden, being established in the first three words of B (ii), when Lok, with whom we have become closely identified, suddenly becomes *the red creature*. Nevertheless B (i) does provide some hints of the change to come.

There are a few instances [4] of a human 'agent' (actor in a transitive clause); not many, but one of them is Lok, in *Lok ... picked up Tanakil*. Here is Lok acting on his environment, and the object 'affected' is a human being, and one of the tribe! There are some non-spatial adjuncts, such as *with an agonized squealing, like the legs of a giant*. There are abstract nominals: *demoniac activity, its weight of branches*. And there are perhaps more modifiers and complex verb forms than usual. None of these features is occurring for the first time; we have had forward-looking flashes throughout, e.g. (p. 191) *He had a picture of Liku looking up with soft and adoring eyes at Tanakil, guessed how Ha had gone with a kind of eager fearfulness to meet his sudden death* and (pp. 212–3) '*Why did you not snatch the new one?*' and '*We will take Tanakil. Then they will give back the new one*', both spoken by the more intelligent Fa (when transitive action clauses do occur in Language A, they are often in the dialogue). But there is a greater concentration of them in B (i), a linguistic complexity that is also in harmony with the increased complexity of the events, which has been being built up ever since the tribe first impinged on the people with the mysterious disappearance of Ha (p. 65). The syntax expresses the climax of the gradual overwhelming of Lok's understanding by new things and events; and this coincides with the climax in the events themselves as, with the remainder of the people all killed or captured, Lok's last companion, Fa, is carried over the edge of the waterfall. Lok is alone; there are no more people, and the last trace of his humanity, his membership of a society, has gone. In that moment he belongs to the past.

Lok does not speak again, because there is no one to speak to. But for a while we follow him, as the tribe might have followed him, although they did not – or rather we follow *it*; there can be no *him* where there is no *you* and *me*. The language is now Language C, and the story is that of *homo sapiens*; but for a few paragraphs, beginning at B (ii), as we remain with Lok, the syntax harks back to the world of the people, just as in B (i) it was beginning to look forward. The transition has taken place; *it was a strange creature, smallish, and bowed* that we had come to know so well. But it is still the final, darkening traces of this creature's world that we are seeing, fleetingly as if in an escaping dream.

A brief sketch of B (ii): There are very few transitive clauses of action [4]; in only one of these is Lok the agent – and here the 'affected' entity is a part of his own body: *it put up a hand*. The others have *the water* and *the river* as agent. Yet nearly half [22] the total number of clauses [47] have Lok as subject; here, apart from a few [4] mental process clauses, the verb is again one of simple movement or posture, and intransitive (*turn, move, crouch*, etc.; but including for the first time some with a connotation of attitude like *sidle* and *trot*; cf. *broke into a queer, loping run*). The remaining subjects are inanimate objects [19] and parts of the body [6]. But there are differences in these subjects. The horizons have widened; in addition to *water* and *river* we now have *sun* and *green sky* – a reminder that the new people walk upright; cf. (p. 143) *they did not look at the earth but straight ahead*; and there are now also human evidences and artifacts: *path, rollers, ropes*. And the parts of the body no longer see or feel; they are subjects only of intransitive verbs of movement (e.g. *its long arms swinging*), and mainly in non-finite clauses, expressing the dependent nature of the processes in which they participate. A majority [32] of the finite verbs are still in simple past tense; but there is more variation in the remainder, as well as more non-finite verbs [8], reflecting a slightly increased proportion of dependent clauses that is also a characteristic of Language C. And while in many clauses [21] we still find spatial adjuncts, these tend to be more varied and more complex (e.g. *down the rocks beyond the terrace from the melting ice in the mountains*).

This is the world of the tribe; but it is still inhabited, for a brief moment of time, by Lok. Once again the theme is enunciated by the syntax. Nature is no longer totally impenetrable; yet Lok remains powerless, master of nothing but his own body. In passages A and B taken together, there are more than fifty clauses in which the subject is Lok; but only one of these has Lok as an agent acting on something external to himself, one that has already been mentioned: *Lok picked up Tanakil*. There is a double irony here. Of all the positive actions on his environment that Lok might have taken, the one he does take is the utterly improbable one of capturing a girl of the tribe – improbable in the event, at the level of subject-matter (let us call this 'level one'), and improbable also in the deeper context ('level two'), since Lok's newly awakened power manifests itself as power over the one element in the environment that is 'superior' to himself. It is at a still deeper 'level three' that the meaning becomes clear. The action gets him nowhere; but it is a syntactic hint that his people have played their part in the long trek towards the human condition.

By the time we reach passage C, the transition is complete. Here, for the first time, the majority of the clauses [48 out of 67] have a human subject; of these, more than half [25] are clauses of action, and most of these [19] are transitive. Leaving aside two in which the thing 'affected' is a part of the body, there is still a significant increase in the number of instances [17, contrasting with 5 in the whole of A and B together] in which a human agent is acting on an external object. The world of the inheritors is organized as ours is; or at least in a way that we can recognize. Among these are two clauses in which the subject is *they*, referring to the people ('the devils': e.g. *they have given me back a changeling*); in the tribe's scheme of things, the people are by no means powerless. There is a parallel here with the earlier part. In passage A the actions of the tribe are encoded in terms of the world-view of the people, so that the predominance of intransitive clauses is interpreted at what we called 'level two', although there is a partial reflection of 'level one' in the fact that they are marginally less predominant when the subject-matter concerns the tribe. Similarly, in passage C references to the people are encoded in terms of the world-view of the tribe, and transitive structures predominate; yet the only member of the people who is present – the only one to survive – is the captured baby, whose infant behaviour is described in largely intransitive terms (pp. 230–1). And the references to the people, in the dialogue, include such formulations as *'They cannot follow us, I tell you. They cannot pass over water'*, which is a 'level one' reassurance that, in a 'level two' world of cause and effect whose causes are often unseen and unknown, there are at least limits to the devils' power.

We can now see the full complementarity between the two 'languages', but it is not easy to state. In Language A there is a level-two theme, that of powerlessness. The momentary hints of potency that we are given at level one represent an antithetic variation which, however, has a significance at level three: the power is ascribed to the tribe but signifies Lok's own incipient awareness, the people's nascent understanding of the human potential. This has become a level-two theme in Language C; and in like fashion the level-two theme of Language A becomes in Language C a level-one variation, but again with a level-three significance. The people may be powerless, but the tribe's demand for explanations of things, born of their own more advanced state, leads them, while still fearfully insisting on the people's weakness in action, to ascribe to them supernatural powers.

While there are still inanimate subjects in the clause [11], as there always are in English, there is no single instance in passage C of an inanimate agent. In A and B we had *the echo of Liku's voice in his head sent him trembling, the branches took her, the water had scooped a bowl out of the rock*; in C we have only *the sail glowed, the sun was sitting in it, the hills grow less*. Likewise all clauses with parts of the body as subject [8] are now intransitive, and none of them is a clause of mental process. Parts of the body no longer feel or perceive; they have attributes ascribed to them (e.g. *his teeth were wolf's teeth*) or they move (*the lips parted, the mouth was opening and shutting*). The limbs may move and posture, but only the whole man perceives and reacts to his environment. Now, he also shapes his environment: his actions have become more varied – no longer simply move-ments; we find here *save, obey,* and *kiss* – and they produce results. Something, or someone, is affected by them.

Just as man's relation to his environment has altered, so his perception of it has changed; the environment has become enlarged. The objects in it are no longer the *twig, stick, bush, branch* of Language A, nor even the larger but still tangible *river, water, scars in the earth.* In passage B (ii) we already had *air* and *sun* and *sky* and *wind*; in C we have *the mountain ... full of golden light, the sun was blazing, the sand was swirling* (the last metaphorically); and also human artifacts: *the sail, the mast.* Nature is not tamed: the features of the natural environment may no longer be agents in the transitivity patterns, but neither are they direct objects. What has happened is that the horizons have broadened. Where the people were bounded by tree and river and rock, the tribe are bounded by sky and sea and mountain. Although they are not yet conquered, the features that surround them no longer circumscribe all action and all contemplation. Whereas Lok *rushed to the edge of the water and came back*, the new people *steer in towards the shore*, and *look across the water at the green hills*.

The Inheritors has provided a perspective for a linguistic inquiry of a kind whose relevance and significance is notoriously difficult to assess: an inquiry into the language of a full-length prose work. In this situation syntactic analysis is unlikely to offer anything in the way of new interpretations of particular sentences in terms of their subject-matter; the language as a whole is not deviant, and the difficulties of understanding are at the level of interpretation – or rather perhaps, in the present instance, re-interpretation, as when we insist on translating *the stick began to grow shorter at both ends* as 'the man drew the bow'. I have not, in this study, emphasized the use of linguistic analysis as a key; I doubt whether it has this function. What it can do is to establish certain regular patterns, on a comparative basis, in the form of differences which appear significant over a broad canvas. In *The Inheritors* these appear as differences within the text itself, between what we have called 'Language A' and 'Language C'. In terms of this novel, if either of these is to be regarded as a departure, it will be Language C, which appears only briefly at the very end; but in the context of modern English as a whole it is Language A which constitutes the departure and Language C the norm. There is thus a double shift of standpoint in the move from global to local norm, but one which brings us back to more or less where we started.

The focus of attention has been on language in general, on the language system and its relation to the meanings of a literary work. In the study of the text, we have examined instances where particular syntactic options have been selected with a greater than expected frequency, a selection that is partly but not wholly explained by reference to the subject-matter; and have suggested that, by considering how the meaning of these options, taken in the context of the ideational function of language as a whole, relates to an interpretation of the meaning of the work, one can show that they are relevant both as subject-matter and as underlying theme. Each sentence in the passages that were observed in detail is thus potentially of interest both in itself and as an instance of a general trend; and we have been able to ignore other differences, such as that between dialogue and narrative, although a study of these as subvarieties would almost certainly yield further points of interest. Within the present context, the prominence that we have observed can be said to be 'motivated'; it is reasonable to talk of foregrounding here, as an explanation of stylistic impact.

The establishment of a syntactic norm (for this is what it is) is thus a way of expressing one of the levels of meaning of the work: the fact that a particular pattern constitutes a norm *is* the meaning. The linguistic function of the pattern is therefore of some importance. The features that we have seen to be foregrounded in *The Inheritors* derive from the ideational component in the language system; hence they represent, at the level at which they constitute a norm, a world-view, a structuring of experience that is significant because there is no *a priori* reason why the experience should have been structured in this way rather than in another. More particularly, the foregrounded features were selections in transitivity. Transitivity is the set of options whereby the speaker encodes his experience of the processes of the external world, and of the internal world of his own consciousness, together with the participants in these processes and their attendant circumstances; and it embodies a very basic distinction of processes into two types, those that are regarded as due to an external cause, an agency other than the person or object involved, and those that are not. There are, in addition, many further categories and subtypes. Transitivity is really the cornerstone of the semantic organization of experience; and it is at one level what *The Inheritors* is about. The theme of the entire novel, in a sense, is transitivity: man's interpretation of his experience of the world, his understanding of its processes and of his own participation in them. This is the motivation for Golding's syntactic originality; it is because of this that the syntax is effective as a 'mode of meaning' (see Firth 1957). The particular transitivity patterns that stand out in the text contribute to the artistic whole through the functional significance, in the language system, of the semantic options which they express.

This is what we understand by 'relevance' – the notion that a linguistic feature 'belongs' in some way as part of the whole. The pursuit of prominence is not without significance for the understanding and evaluation of a literary work; but neither is it sufficient to be a rewarding activity in itself (cf. Fowler 1966). It has been said of phonological foregrounding that 'there must be appropriateness to the nexus of sound and meaning' (Hymes 1967, p. 53); and this is no less true of the syntactic and semantic levels, where, however, the relationship is not one of sound and meaning but one of meaning and meaning. Here 'relevance' implies a congruence with our interpretation of what the work is about, and hence the criteria of belonging are semantic ones. We might be tempted to express the relevance of syntactic patterns, such as we find in *The Inheritors*, as a 'unity of form and meaning', parallel to the 'sound and meaning' formulation above; but this would, I think, be a false parallel. The syntactic categories are *per se* the realizations of semantic options, and the relevance is the relevance of one set of meanings to another – a relationship among the levels of meaning of the work itself.

In *The Inheritors*, the syntax is part of the story. As readers, we are reacting to the whole of the writer's creative use of 'meaning potential'; and the nature of language is such that he can convey, in a line of print, a complex of simultaneous themes, reflecting the variety of functions that language is required to serve. And because the elements of the language, the words and phrases and syntactic structures, tend to have multiple values, any one theme may have more than one interpretation: in expressing some content, for example, the writer may invite us at the same time to interpret it in quite a different functional context – as a cry of despair, perhaps. It is the same property of language that enables us to react to hints, to take offence and do all the other things that display the rhetoric of everyday verbal interaction. A theme that is strongly foregrounded is especially likely to be interpreted at more than one level. In *The Inheritors* it is the linguistic representation of experience, through the syntactic resources of transitivity, that is especially brought into relief, although there may be other themes not mentioned here that stand out in the same way. Every work achieves a unique balance among the types and components of meaning, and embodies the writer's individual exploration of the functional diversity of language.

Appendix

Extracts from The Inheritors

A. (pp. 106–7)

The bushes twitched again. Lok steadied by the tree and gazed. A head and a chest faced him, half-hidden. There were white bone things behind the leaves and hair. The man had white bone things above his eyes and under the mouth so that his face was longer than a face should be. The man turned sideways in the bushes and looked at Lok along his shoulder. A stick rose upright and there was a lump of bone in the middle. Lok peered at the stick and the lump of bone and the small eyes in the bone things over the face. Suddenly Lok understood that the man was holding the stick out to him but neither he nor Lok could reach across the river. He would have laughed if it were not for the echo of the screaming in his head. The stick began to grow shorter at both ends. Then it shot out to full length again.

The dead tree by Lok's ear acquired a voice.

'Clop!'

His ears twitched and he turned to the tree. By his face there had grown a twig: a twig that smelt of other, and of goose, and of the bitter berries that Lok's stomach told him he must not eat. This twig had a white bone at the end. There were hooks in the bone and sticky brown stuff hung in the crooks. His nose examined this stuff and did not like it. He smelled along the shaft of the twig. The leaves on the twig were red feathers and reminded him of goose. He was lost in a generalized astonishment and excitement. He shouted at the green drifts across the glittering water and heard Liku crying out in answer but could not catch the words. They were cut off suddenly as though someone had clapped a hand over her mouth. He rushed to the edge of the water and came back. On either side of the open bank the bushes grew thickly in the flood; they waded out until at their farthest some of the leaves were opening under water; and these bushes leaned over.

The echo of Liku's voice in his head sent him trembling at this perilous way of bushes towards the island. He dashed at them where normally they would have been rooted on dry land and his feet splashed. He threw himself forward and grabbed at the branches with hands and feet. He shouted:

'I am coming!'

B. (pp. 215–17)

(i) Lok staggered to his feet, picked up Tanakil and ran after Fa along the terrace. There came a screaming from the figures by the hollow log and a loud bang from the jam. The tree began to move forward and the logs were lumbering about like the legs of a giant. The crumplefaced woman was struggling with Tuami on the rock by the hollow log; she burst free and came running towards Lok. There was movement everywhere, screaming, demoniac activity; the old man was coming across the tumbling logs. He threw something at Fa. Hunters were holding the hollow log against the terrace and the head of the tree with all its weight of branches and wet leaves was drawing along them. The fat woman was lying in the log, the crumpled woman was in it with Tanakil, the old man was tumbling into the back. The boughs crashed and drew along the rock with an agonized squealing. Fa was sitting by the water holding her head. The branches took her. She was moving with them out into the water and the hollow log was free of the rock and drawing away. The tree swung into the current with Fa sitting limply among the branches. Lok began to gibber again. He ran up and down on the terrace. The tree would not be cajoled or persuaded. It moved to the edge of the fall, it swung until it was lying along the lip. The water reared up over the trunk, pushing, the roots were over. The tree hung for a while with the head facing upstream. Slowly the root end sank and the head rose. Then it slid forward soundlessly and dropped over the fall.

(ii) The red creature stood on the edge of the terrace and did nothing. The hollow log was a dark spot on the water towards the place where the sun had gone down. The air in the gap was clear and blue and calm. There was no noise at all now except for the fall, for there was no wind and the green sky was clear. The red creature turned to the right and trotted slowly towards the far end of the terrace. Water was cascading down the rocks beyond the terrace from the melting ice in the mountains. The river was high and flat and drowned the edge of the terrace. There were long scars in the earth and rock where the branches of a tree had been dragged past by the water. The red creature came trotting back to a dark hollow in the side of the cliff where there was evidence of occupation. It looked at the other figure, dark now, that grinned down at it from the back of the hollow. Then it turned away and ran through the little passage that joined the terrace to the slope. It halted, peering down at the scars, the abandoned rollers and broken ropes. It turned again, sidled round a shoulder of rock, and stood on an almost imperceptible path that ran along the sheer rocks. It began to sidle along the path, crouch, its long arms swinging, touching, almost as firm a support as the legs. It was peering down into the thunderous waters but there was nothing to be seen but the columns of glimmering haze where the water had scooped a bowl out of the rock. It moved faster, broke into a queer loping run that made the head bob up and down and the forearms alternate like the legs of a horse. It stopped at the end of the path and looked down at the long streamers of weed that were moving backwards and forwards under the water. It put up a hand and scratched under its chinless mouth.

C. (pp. 228–9)

The sail glowed red-brown. Tuami glanced back at the gap through the mountain and saw that it was full of golden light and the sun was sitting in it. As if they were obeying some signal the people began to stir, to sit up and look across the water at the green hills. Twal bent over Tanakil and kissed her and murmured to her. Tanakil's lips parted. Her voice was harsh and came from far away in the night.

'Liku!'

Tuami heard Marlan whisper to him from by the mast.

'That is the devil's name. Only she may speak it.'

Now Vivani was really waking. They heard her huge, luxurious yawn and the bear skin was thrown off. She sat up, shook back her loose hair and looked first at Marlan then at Tuami. At once he was filled again with lust and hate. If she had been what she was, if Marlan, if her man, if she had saved her baby in the storm on the salt water –

'My breasts are paining me.'

If she had not wanted the child as a plaything, if I had not saved the other as a joke –

He began to talk high and fast.

'There are plains beyond those hills, Marlan, for they grow less; and there will be herds for hunting. Let us steer in towards the shore. Have we water – but of course we have water! Did the women bring the food? Did you bring the food, Twal?'

Twal lifted her face towards him and it was twisted with grief and hate.

'What have I to do with food, master? You and he gave my child to the devils and they have given me back a changeling who does not see or speak.'

The sand was swirling in Tuami's brain. He thought in panic: they have given me back a changed Tuami; what shall I do? Only Marlan is the same – smaller, weaker but the same. He peered forward to find the changeless one as something he could hold on to. The sun was blazing on the red sail and Marlan was red. His arms and legs were contracted, his hair stood out and his beard, his teeth were wolf's teeth and his eyes like blind stones. The mouth was opening and shutting.

'They cannot follow us, I tell you. They cannot pass over water.'

Notes

1 The results were presented in a paper read to the Conference of University Teachers of English, London (Bedford College), April 1965.

2 Paul Zumthor suggests (personal communication) that a particular literary tradition may be characterized by the emphasis and value placed on one particular function, a shift in emphasis being associated with a major break in the tradition. Cf. Zumthor (1971), showing the orientation of medieval lyric poetry towards a particular aspect of the interpersonal function of language.

3 Nor the other way round, at least in the typical instances. There are certain linguistic activities in which one or other function is prescribed and the speaker required to supply the remainder: 'language exercises' such as 'Now ask your neighbour a question' (in foreign language classes) and 'Write a sonnet' (in school).

4 Including those which specify types of communication role, or illocutionary force, which Ohmann (1971) proposes to use in a definition of literature.

5 On diatypic variation see Gregory (1967).

6 It is worth quoting further from the same paragraph: 'It is at least clear that any approach to this kind of problem which looks at anything less than the whole text as the ultimate unit has very little to contribute. Whatever it may be in linguistic analysis, the sentence is not the proper unit here. If there are any possibilities of progress, they must, I think, be on the lines of the old recognition, e.g. by the rhetoricians, of elements or strands of something or other which permeate long stretches of text and produce a gradual build-up of effect' (McIntosh 1965, p. 19).

7 See Milic (1971), in which he suggests that the diagnostic features of an author's style are generally to be found among the 'unconscious' elements.

8 'Metamorphosis' has, I believe, only two occurrences of an insect name, although 'crawl' is frequent.

9 William Golding, *The Inheritors* (London, 1955; paperback edition, 1961). The pagination is the same in both editions.

10 Figures in square brackets show numbers of occurrences. The most important of these are summarized in Table 3.2.

11 For a discussion of clause types see Halliday (1970).

12 The other extracts examined for comparison were three passages of similar length: p. 61 from *He remembered the old woman*; pp. 102–3 from *Then there was nothing more*; p. 166 from *At that the old man rushed forward*.

13 By 'complement' is understood all nominal elements other than the subject: direct object, indirect object, cognate object, and adjectival and nominal complement. 'Adjuncts' are non-nominal elements (adverbs and prepositional phrases).

14 For discussions of transitivity see Fillmore (1968), Halliday (1967 and 1967–8).

References

BLOCH, B. 1953: Linguistic structure and linguistic analysis. In Hill, A. A. (ed.), *Report of the fourth annual round table meeting on linguistics and language study*. Washington, DC: Georgetown University Press, 40–4.

BÜHLER, K. 1934: *Sprachtheorie*. Jena: Fischer.

CHATMAN, S. 1968: Milton's participial style. *Publications of the Modern Language Association of America* 83, 1386–99.

FILLMORE, C.J. 1968: The case for case. In Bach, E. and Harms, R. T. (eds), *Universals in linguistic theory*. New York: Holt Rinehart Winston, 1–88.

FIRTH, J. R. 1957(1951): Modes of meaning. In *Papers in linguistics 1934–1951*. London: Oxford University Press, 190–215.

FOWLER, R. 1966: Linguistic theory and the study of literature. In *Essays on style and language: Linguistic and critical approaches to literary style*. London: Routledge and Kegan Paul, 1–28.

GOLDING, W. 1961(1955): *The inheritors*. London: Faber.

GREGORY, M. 1967: Aspects of varieties differentiation. *Journal of Linguistics* 3, 177–98.

HALLIDAY, M. A. K. 1964: Descriptive linguistics in literary studies. In Duthie, A. (ed.), *English studies today*, third series. Edinburgh: Edinburgh University Press, 25–39.

—1967: *Grammar, society and the noun*. London: H. K. Lewis for University College London.

—1967–8: Notes on transitivity and theme in English (Parts 1 and 2). *Journal of Linguistics* 3 (1967), 37–81 and 4 (1968), 179–215.

—1970: Language structure and language function. In Lyons, J. (ed.), *New horizons in linguistics*. Harmondsworth: Penguin, 140–65.

HASAN, R. 1967: Linguistics and the study of literary texts. *Etudes de Linguistique Appliquée* 5: 106–21.

—1971: Rime and reason in literature. In Chatman, S. (ed.), *Literary style: A symposium*. London: Oxford University Press, 299–326.

HYMES, D. H. 1967: Phonological aspects of style: Some English sonnets. In Chatman, S. and Levin, S. (eds), *Essays on the language of literature*. Boston: Houghton Mifflin, 33–53.

KINKEAD-WEEKES, M. and GREGOR, I. 1967: *William Golding: A critical study*. London: Faber.

LEECH, G.N. 1965: 'This bread I break' – Language and interpretation. *A Review of English Literature* 6, 66–75.

LEVIN, S. R. 1971: The conventions of poetry. In Chatman, S. (ed.), *Literary style: A symposium*. London: Oxford University Press, 177–93.

McINTOSH, A. 1965: Saying. *A Review of English Literature* 6, 9–20.

MALINOWSKI, B. 1935: *Coral gardens and their magic*, Vol. 2. London: Allen & Unwin.

MILES, J. 1967: Eras in English poetry. In Chatman, S. and Levin, S. (eds), *Essays on the language of literature*. Boston: Houghton Mifflin, 175–96.

MILIC, L. 1971: Rhetorical choice and stylistic option. In Chatman, S. (ed.), *Literary style: A symposium*. London: Oxford University Press, 77–88.

MILLER, G. A. 1960: Closing statement (Retrospects and prospects from the viewpoint of psychology). In Sebeok, T. A. (ed.), *Style in language*. Cambridge, Mass.: MIT Press, 386–95.

OHMANN, R. 1967: Literature as sentences. In Chatman, S. and Levin, S. (eds), *Essays on the language of literature*. Boston: Houghton Mifflin, 231–8.

—1971: Speech, action, and style. In Chatman, S. (ed.), *Literary style: A symposium*. London: Oxford University Press, 241–54.

OSGOOD, C. E. 1960: Some effects of motivation on style of encoding. In Sebeok, T. A. (ed.), *Style in language*. Cambridge, Mass.: MIT Press, 293–306.

SINCLAIR, J. McH. 1965: Linguistic meaning in a literary text. Paper read to the Philological Society, Cambridge, March 1965.

THORNE, J. P. 1965: Stylistics and generative grammars. *Journal of Linguistics* 1, 49–59.

TODOROV, T. 1971: The place of style in the structure of the text. In Chatman, S. (ed.), *Literary style: A symposium*. London: Oxford University Press, 29–39.

ULLMANN, S. 1964: *Language and style*. Oxford: Blackwell.

—1965: Style and personality. *A Review of English Literature* 6, 20–5.

VACHEK, J. 1966: *The linguistic school of Prague*. Bloomington: Indiana University Press.

WELLEK, R. 1960: Closing statement (Retrospects and prospects from the viewpoint of literary criticism). In Sebeok, T. A. (ed.), *Style in language*. Cambridge, Mass.: MIT Press, 408–19.

ZUMTHOR, P. 1971: Style and expressive register in medieval poetry. In Chatman, S. (ed.), *Literary style: A symposium*. London: Oxford University Press, 263–77.

4

Recent trends in stylistics

Talbot J. Taylor *and* Michael Toolan

Despite a superficial appearance of intellectual ferment, stylistic theory has progressed little since the publication, in 1909, of Charles Bally's *Traité de Stylistique Française*. The aims and methods of contemporary stylistics are much the same as those originally proposed by Bally; and, not surprisingly, the problems his new discipline encountered then still perplex stylisticians today. Nevertheless, there are a few (albeit faint) signs of a fundamental change in the works, signalling a shift away from the structuralist principles of Bally. What is ironic about these new developments is that, from Bally's point of view, they might well be seen, not as progressive, but as regressive, incorporating a return to certain principles reminiscent of the prescriptive rhetorical theories which had preceded Bally's structuralism.

Like his mentor, F. de Saussure, Bally argued at great length against the prescriptivism inherent in earlier forms of grammar and rhetoric. They urged that the scientific study of the semiotic and the stylistic resources of language be set on firm, *descriptive* foundations. However, Bally's hopes have never been realized; wave after wave of new theories of descriptive stylistics have crashed on the same rocks where the rotting hulk of Bally's *système expressif* still lies. And yet, Bally would probably be less disturbed by the repeated failures of descriptive stylistics than by the signs today that stylistics is to return to an avowed prescriptivism. To be consoled, he would have to be convinced by recent philosophical and literary theoretical arguments to the effect that even his own descriptive enterprise had always, in fact, been covertly prescriptive.

If one glances through recent publications in stylistics, examples may be found both of the descriptivism of Bally's structuralist paradigm in its final throes as well as of the first tentative steps toward a new prescriptivism. The most interesting of the recent crop of stylistics books – Stanley Fish's *Is There A Text In This Class?* – is especially revealing because it includes an autobiographical account of the author's own gradual abandonment of the tenets of descriptivism for a new position which is avowedly prescriptive. Whereas the early Fish viewed himself as an empirical scientist, engaged in the task of describing the stylistic effects of literary texts, today Fish unabashedly accepts the authoritarian nature of his role as stylistician and literary critic. He now takes his task not to be that of describing how people actually read certain texts but to be one of persuading them to read as he sees fit. This, in turn, enables one to view the detailed, practical task of stylistic analysis from – at least within the context of twentieth-century language study – an entirely new perspective. Still, in order to present a clear sketch of these new developments in stylistic theory, we should begin not with Fish – who is in the *avant-garde* – but with the recent publications of stylisticians whose intellectual roots remain in the structuralist paradigm of Bally. But, before this, an outline of the divisions within contemporary structuralist stylistics is required.

Structural stylistics can meaningfully be viewed as split into two major camps: that holding an objectivist theory and that holding an affective theory of stylistic structure. More will be said later about affective stylistics (see chapters 5 and 6). Objectivist stylisticians believe style to be an inherent property of the text itself, taken as an utterance of the language. A further distinction must be made between two factions within the objectivist camp: between the formalists and the functionalists. Functionalists take the stylistic system of a language to be bi-planar, linking formal stylistic features with specific stylistic 'functions' (or 'effects', or 'values'). Consequently, the functionalist will only recognize as stylistically significant those linguistic features of a text which have a stylistic 'function' (much as the classical phonologist will recognize as phonological only those phonetic contrasts which are semantically significant). For instance, Bally urged the stylistician to determine whether an expression has stylistic potential by comparing it with one or more of its synonyms. Only if each of the synonyms conveyed a different communicative effect, revealed as supplementary to their semantic equivalence, could they be regarded as different forms within the stylistic *système expressif* of the language. Formalists, on the other hand, disregard the call for functional criteria in identifying stylistic forms. Much as distributional linguists had tried to avoid reference to meaning in identifying formal contrasts, the formalist stylisticians attempt to avoid the problems posed by functional criteria. Instead, they prefer purely formal criteria in identifying stylistic patterns and features. In general these formal criteria are borrowed from the dominant paradigms in the neighboring discipline of linguistics.

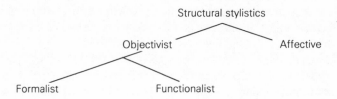

Figure 4.1

Within functionalist stylistics two recent books might well have won the approval of Bally. The first of these, *Style in Fiction* by Geoffrey Leech and Michael Short, is the long-awaited companion to Leech's *A Linguistic Guide to English Poetry* (Leech 1969). In the opening chapters the authors propose and illustrate a fairly traditional theory of functionalist stylistics. Much as Bally had (cf. Taylor 1981), they adopt a pluralistic view of language function (although they refer to the work of Michael Halliday, rather than that of Bally, as the source of their functional pluralism). Language is presumed to be structured to fulfil the functions for which it is required. Since language is needed to serve a variety of different interactional functions, it therefore must consist of a tissue of differing yet interwoven structural systems which enable it to fulfil these functions. Pluri-functionalism thus leads to pluri-structuralism. What this means for their theory of style is that the formal stylistic features and patterns of a text may be identified from any one of several differing functional perspectives. A further practical benefit of pluralism is that it allows the authors to borrow freely from different linguistic methodologies in constructing an eclectic method of stylistic analysis. Thus, one finds incorporated into their method ideas and techniques from such diverse fields as Gricean pragmatics, generative syntax, Prague school functionalism, quantitative stylistics, speech-act theory, structuralist poetics, discourse analysis, and French semiotics. It is perhaps this eclecticism which, in spite of its lack of methodological coherence, makes this book such a useful introduction textbook for students of stylistics.

Nevertheless, Leech and Short are not able to avoid what has always been the Achilles' heel of functionalist stylistics: the problem of criterial perspective. Although functionalist stylistics – whether dualistic or pluralistic – relies on a functional perspective from which to identify patterns and features of stylistic form, in practice no criteria are ever given with which one might identify the function (or functions) of an utterance. So the question will always arise: how is one to tell if this passage (utterance, word, etc.) has the same or a different function from another passage? Similarly, one may ask how it is possible to decide whether a particular passage does or does not have a particular function. When we recall that it is from the criterial perspective of function that the functionalist stylistician is obliged to identify features and patterns of stylistic form, it may be seen that the problem of first identifying functions is a crucial one. And yet, to date, no functionalist theory has been able to provide criteria for identifying the function (or 'stylistic effect', or 'value', etc.) of a passage. Indeed, the notion of ever producing such criteria becomes even more implausible when we ask ourselves whether one and the same passage (or utterance) can justifiably be assumed to have the same function (effect, significance, value, etc.) for each of its readers or whether function is not, to some degree, imposed upon the passage by those who read it. If the latter is the case, we see how misleading it would be to locate the structural source of stylistic functions in particular formal patterns of linguistic features in the text.

The difficulties of adopting function as a criterial perspective in identifying stylistic form are well known to many of the practitioners of functionalist stylistics. One of these, Roger Fowler, has in the last few years been working to remedy the problem with the aid of others currently or formerly at the University of East Anglia: Gareth Jones, Gunther Kress, Bob Hodge, and Tony Trew (see Hodge and Kress 1979, Taylor 1983, Fowler *et al.* 1979; see also chapter 11 in this volume). Many of the articles in his recent *Literature as Social Discourse* outline the principles which guide their research. Interestingly, like Bally, Fowler does not reserve a special place in stylistics (which he calls 'linguistic criticism') for the study of literary style. Instead, he and his colleagues aim to reveal the formal stylistic source in language for one particular function that all language – literary or non-literary – inevitably performs. Thus, Fowler quotes the functionalist's *credo*:

> The particular form taken by the grammatical system of language is closely related to the social and personal needs that language is required to serve.
>
> (Halliday 1970, quoted in Fowler 1981, p. 28)

The stylistic function in which Fowler and his colleagues are particularly interested is that which they call the 'ideological' function:

> we have been studying the meanings and functions of public discourse in a divided society, a society based on inequalities of power and opportunity: contemporary British society .... Given the nature of the society we live in, much communication is concerned with establishing and maintaining unequal power relationships between individuals, and between institutions and individuals. Our studies of various genres of discourse argue that this practice is carried out through a much wider variety of language usages and speech acts than just the rules and directives by which interpersonal control is obviously managed. Because language *must* continuously articulate ideology, and because ideology is simultaneously social product and social practice, all our language and that of others expresses theories of the way the world is organized, and the expression of these theories contributes to the legitimation of this theorized organization.
>
> (Fowler 1981, p. 29)

By taking the ideological function of style as their analytical target, Fowler and his colleagues both considerably reduce the focus of stylistics (to only one stylistic function) while at the same time greatly enlarging its domain (to all use of language).

Although they limit the focus of stylistics to the analysis of ideological function, they are not able to avoid the problem of identifying when a sentence or expression has a particular ideological function and when it has not. In practice, they seem to rely on a mixture of case analysis, pragmatics, and political intuition in identifying ideological functions. What they cannot do is to provide the would-be linguistic critic with a non-redundant method for identifying functions: that is, a method which does not simply take formal features themselves as the required criteria. It is, after all, from the perspective of function that the functionalist stylistician must identify stylistically significant formal features; thus, he may not, without being circular, identify functions from the perspective of formal criteria. Instead, what he needs is a criterial perspective from *outside* the bi-planar linking of form and function.

References

BALLY, C. 1951: *Traité de stylistique française*, 3rd ed. Paris: Klincksieck.
FISH, S. 1980: *Is there a text in this class? The authority of interpretive communities*. Cambridge, Mass.: Harvard University Press.
FOWLER, R. 1981: *Literature as social discourse: The practice of linguistic criticism*. London: Batsford Academic.

—HODGE, R., KRESS, G. and TREW, T. 1979: *Language and control*. London: Routledge and Kegan Paul.
HALLIDAY, M. A. K. 1970: Language structure and language function. In Lyons, J. (ed.), *New horizons in linguistics*. Harmondsworth: Penguin.
HODGE, R. and KRESS, G. 1979: *Language as ideology*. London: Routledge and Kegan Paul.
LEECH, G. 1969: *A linguistic guide to English poetry*. London: Longman.
—and SHORT, M. 1981: *Style in fiction: A linguistic introduction to English fictional prose*. London: Longman.
TAYLOR, T. J. 1981: *Linguistic theory and structural stylistics*. Oxford: Pergamon.
—1983: Review of Hodge and Kress *Language as ideology*. *Journal of Literary Semantics* 12, 92–5.

Part III

Affective stylistics

5

What is stylistics and why are they saying such terrible things about it?

Stanley E. Fish

The first of the questions in my title – what is stylistics? – has already been answered by the practitioners of the art. Stylistics was born of a reaction to the subjectivity and imprecision of literary studies. For the appreciative raptures of the impressionistic critic, stylisticians purport to substitute precise and rigorous linguistic descriptions, and to proceed from those descriptions to interpretations for which they can claim a measure of objectivity. Stylistics, in short, is an attempt to put criticism on a scientific basis. Answering my second question – why are they saying such terrible things about it? – will be the business of this essay, and I would like to begin (somewhat obliquely, I admit) by quoting from the *New York Times Book Review* of 23 April 1972. On pages 18 and 19 of that issue we find the publishing firm of Peter Wyden, Inc., proclaiming the merits of a new book by Tom Chetwynd. The book is entitled *How to Interpret Your Own Dreams (In One Minute or Less)*. The title appears on a reproduction of the book jacket and beneath it are the following descriptive claims: 'Your key to 583 Dream Subjects with 1442 Interpretations', 'An Encyclopedic Dictionary'. These claims are supported and extended by a report of the author's researches and by a portion of the index. 'What do *you* dream about?' the reader is asked, 'Angels (see page 171), Babies (page 150), Bells (page 40), Cars, Collisions, Cooking, Death, Dogs, Doors, Exams, Falling, Hands, Hats, Illness, Monsters, Mother, Nudity, Sex, Teeth, Travel ...' 'And these,' the blurb continues, 'are just a few of the 583 dream subjects covered.' 'To compile this book,' we are told, 'the author spent ten years analyzing the works of Freud, Jung, Adler and other dream authorities. Carefully indexed and cross indexed, each dream subject is rated in four ways: what it most likely means; what it could well mean; what it might mean; and what it might possibly mean .... This remarkable dream dictionary enables you to look up any dream instantly ... find complete clues to its meaning.' Finally, and with typographic aids, the claims underlying these claims are put forward: in italics, *it really works*, and in large white letters against a black bar background, BASED ON SOLID SCIENCE.

However amusing one finds this advertisement, it would be a mistake to underestimate the desire to which it appeals: the desire for an instant and automatic interpretive procedure based on an inventory of fixed relationships between observable data and meanings, meanings which do not vary with context and which can be read out independently of the analyst or observer who need only perform the operations specified by the 'key'. It is a desire as new as information theory and as old as the impulse to escape from the flux and variability of the human situation to the security and stability of a timeless formalism. It is also, I think, the desire behind stylistics, and in the first part of this paper I should like to examine some representative attempts to achieve it.

My first example is taken from the work of Louis Milic, author of *A Quantitative Approach to the Style of Jonathan Swift* (1967) and other statistical and computer studies. In an article written for *The Computer and Literary Style* (1966), Milic attempts to isolate the distinctive features of Swift's style. He is particularly interested in the Swiftian habit of piling up words in series and in Swift's preference for certain kinds of connectives. His method is to compare Swift, in these and other respects, with Macauley, Addison, Gibbon, and Johnson, and the results of his researches are presented in the form of tables: 'Word-Class Frequency Distribution of All the Whole Samples of Swift, with Computed Arithmetic Mean', 'Percentage of Initial Connectives in 2000-Sentence Samples of Addison, Johnson, Macauley, and Swift', 'Total Introductory Connectives and Total Introductory Determiners as Percentages of All Introductory Elements', 'Frequency of Occurrence of the Most Common Single Three-Word Pattern as a Percentage of Total Patterns', 'Total Number of Different Patterns per Sample'. It will not be my concern here to scrutinize the data-gathering methods of Milic or the other stylisticians (although some of them are challengeable even on their own terms), for my interest is primarily in what is done with the data after they have been gathered. This is also Milic's interest, and in the final paragraphs of his essay he poses the major question: 'What interpretive inferences can be drawn from the material?' (1966, p. 104). The answer comes in two parts and illustrates the two basic maneuvers executed by the stylisticians. The first is circular: 'The low frequency of initial determiners, taken together with the high frequency of initial connectives, makes [Swift] a writer who likes transitions and made much of connectives' (1966, p. 104). As the reader will no doubt have noticed, the two halves of this sentence present the same information in slightly different terms, even though its rhetoric suggests that something has been explained. Here is an example of what makes some people impatient with stylistics and its baggage. The machinery of categorization and classification merely provides momentary pigeonholes for the constituents of a text, constituents which are then retrieved and reassembled into exactly the form they previously had. There is in short no gain in understanding; the procedure has been executed, but it hasn't got you anywhere. Stylisticians, however, are *determined* to get somewhere, and exactly where they are determined to get is indicated by Milic's next sentence. '[Swift's] use of series argues [that is, is a sign of or means] a fertile and well stocked mind.' Here the procedure is not circular but arbitrary. The data are scrutinized and an interpretation is *asserted* for them; asserted rather than proven because there is nothing in the machinery Milic cranks up to authorize the leap (from the data to a specification of their value) he makes. What does authorize it is an unexamined and highly suspect assumption that one can read directly from the description of a text (however derived) to the shape or quality of its author's mind, in this case from the sheer quantity of verbal items to the largeness of the intelligence that produced them.

The counter-argument to this assumption is not that it can't be done (Milic, after all, has done it), but that it can be done all too easily, and in any direction one likes. One might conclude, for example, that Swift's use of series argues the presence of the contiguity disorder described by Roman Jakobson in *Fundamentals of Language* (Jakobson and Halle 1956, pp. 69–96); or that Swift's use of series argues an unwillingness to finish his sentences; or that Swift's use of series argues an anal-retentive personality; or that Swift's use of series argues a nominalist rather than a realist philosophy and is therefore evidence of a mind insufficiently stocked with abstract ideas. These conclusions are neither more nor less defensible than the conclusion Milic reaches, or reaches for (it is the enterprise and not any one of its results that should be challenged), and their availability points to a serious defect in the procedures of stylistics, the absence of any constraint on the way in which one moves from description to interpretation, with the result that any interpretation one puts forward is arbitrary.

Milic, for his part, is not unaware of the problem. In a concluding paragraph, he admits that relating devices of style to personality is 'risky' and 'the chance of error ... great' because 'no personality syntax paradigm is available ... neither syntactic stylistics nor personality theory is yet capable of making the leap' (1966, p. 105). Once again Milic provides a clear example of one of the basic maneuvers in the stylistics game: he acknowledges the dependence of his procedures on an unwarranted assumption, but then salvages both the assumption and the procedures by declaring that time and the collection of more data will give substance to the one and authorize the other. It is a remarkable *non sequitur* in which the suspect nature of his enterprise becomes a reason for continuing in it: a personality syntax paradigm may be currently unavailable or available in too many directions, but this only means that if we persist in our efforts to establish it, it will surely emerge. The more reasonable inference would be that the difficulty lies not with the present state of the art but with the art itself; and this is precisely what I shall finally argue, that the establishment of a syntax-personality or of any other paradigm is an impossible goal, which, because it is also an assumption, invalidates the procedures of the stylisticians before they begin, dooming them to successes that are meaningless because they are so easy.

Milic affords a particularly good perspective on what stylisticians do because his assumptions, along with their difficulties, are displayed so nakedly. A sentence like 'Swift's use of series argues a fertile and well stocked mind' doesn't come along very often. More typically, a stylistician will interpose a formidable apparatus between his descriptive and interpretive acts, thus obscuring the absence of any connection between them. For Richard Ohmann, that apparatus is transformational grammar and in 'Generative grammars and the concept of literary style' (1969a) he uses it to distinguish between the prose of Faulkner and Hemingway. Ohmann does this by demonstrating that Faulkner's style is no longer recognizable when 'the effects of three generalized transformations' – the relative clause transformation, the conjunction transformation, and the comparative transformation – are reversed. 'Denatured' of these transformations, a passage from 'The Bear', Ohmann says, retains 'virtually no traces of ... Faulkner's style' (1969a, p. 142). When the same denaturing is performed on Hemingway, however, 'the reduced passage still sounds very much like Hemingway. Nothing has been changed that seems crucial' (1969a, p. 144). From this, Ohmann declares, follow two conclusions: (1) Faulkner 'leans heavily upon a very small amount of grammatical apparatus' (1969a, p. 143); and (2) the 'stylistic difference ... between the Faulkner and Hemingway passages can be largely explained on the basis of [the] ... apparatus' (1969a, p. 145). To the first of these I would reply that it depends on what is meant by 'leans heavily upon'. Is this a statement about the apparatus or about the actual predilection of the author? (The confusion between the two is a hallmark of stylistic criticism.) To the second conclusion I would object strenuously, if by 'explained' Ohmann means anything more than made formalizable. That is, I am perfectly willing to admit that transformational grammar provides a better means of fingerprinting an author than would a measurement like the percentage of nouns or the mean length of sentences; for since the transformational model is able to deal not only with constituents but with their relationships, it can make distinctions at a structural, as opposed to a merely statistical, level. I am not willing, however, to give those distinctions an independent value, that is, to attach a fixed significance to the devices of the fingerprinting mechanism, any more than I would be willing to read from a man's actual fingerprint to his character or personality.

But this, as it turns out, is exactly what Ohmann wants to do. 'The move from formal description of styles to ... interpretation,' he asserts, 'should be the ultimate goal of stylistics,' and in the case of Faulkner, 'it seems reasonable to suppose that a writer whose style is so largely based on just these three semantically related transformations demonstrates in that style a certain conceptual orientation, a preferred way of organizing experience' (1969a, p. 143). But Faulkner's style can be said to be 'based on' these three transformations only in the sense that the submission of a Faulkner text to the transformational apparatus yields a description in which they dominate. In order to make anything more out of this, that is, in order to turn the description into a statement about Faulkner's conceptual orientation, Ohmann would have to do what Noam Chomsky so pointedly refrains from doing, assign a semantic value to the devices of his descriptive mechanism, so that rather than being neutral between the processes of production and reception, they are made directly to reflect them. In the course of this and other essays, Ohmann does just that, finding, for example, that Lawrence's heavy use of deletion transformations is responsible for the 'driving insistence one feels in reading' him (1969a, p. 148), and that Conrad's structures of chaining reflect his tendency to 'link one thing with another associatively' (1969b, p. 154), and that Dylan Thomas's breaking of selectional rules serves his 'vision of things' of 'the world as process, as interacting forces and repeating cycle' (1969b, p. 156); in short – and here I quote – 'that these syntactic preferences *correlate* with habits of meaning' (1969b, p. 154).

The distance between all of this and 'Swift's use of series argues a fertile and well stocked mind' is a matter only of methodological sophistication, not of substance, for both critics operate with the same assumptions and nominate the same goal, the establishing of an inventory in which formal items will be linked in a fixed relationship to semantic and psychological values. Like Milic, Ohmann admits that at this point his interpretive conclusions are speculative and tentative; but again, like Milic, he believes that it is only a matter of time before he can proceed more securely on the basis of a firm correlation between syntax and 'conceptual orientation', and the possibility of specifying such correlations, he declares, 'is one of the main justifications for studying style' (Ohmann 1969a, p. 143). If this is so, then the enterprise is in trouble, not because it will fail, but because it will, in every case, succeed. Ohmann will always be able to assert (although not to prove) a plausible connection between the 'conceptual orientation' he discerns in an author and the formal patterns his descriptive apparatus yields. But since there is no warrant for that connection in the grammar he appropriates, there is no constraint on the manner in which he makes it, and therefore his interpretations will be as arbitrary and unverifiable as those of the most impressionistic of critics.

The point will be clearer, I think, if we turn for a moment to the work of J. P. Thorne, another linguist of the generative persuasion. While Ohmann and Milic are interested in reading from syntax to personality, Thorne would like to move in the other direction, from syntax to either content or effect, but his procedures are similarly illegitimate. Thorne begins in the obligatory way, by deploring the presence in literary studies of 'impressionistic terms' (1970, p. 188; see also 1965 and 1969). Yet, he points out, these terms must be impressions of something, and what they are impressions of, he decides, 'are types of grammatical structures'. It follows from this that the task of stylistics is to construct a typology that would match up grammatical structures with the effects they invariably produce: 'If terms like "loose", or "terse" or "emphatic" have any significance ... – and surely they do – it must be because they relate to certain identifiable structural properties' (Thorne 1970, pp. 188–9). What follows is a series of analyses in which 'identifiable structural properties' are correlated with impressions and impressionistic terms. Thorne discovers, for example, that in Donne's 'A Nocturnal Upon St Lucie's Day' selectional rules are regularly broken. 'The poem has sentences which have inanimate nouns where one would usually expect to find animate nouns, and animate nouns ... where one would expect to find inanimate nouns.' 'It seems likely,' he concludes, 'that these linguistic facts underlie the sense of chaos and the breakdown of order which many literary critics have associated with the poem' (1970, p. 193). This is at once arbitrary and purposeful. The 'breakdown of order' exists only within his grammar's system of rules (and strange rules they are, since there is no penalty for breaking them); it is a formal, not a semantic fact (even though the rules are semantic), and there is no warrant at all for equating it with the 'sense' the poem supposedly conveys. That sense, however, has obviously been pre-selected by Thorne and the critics he cites, and is, in effect, responsible for its own discovery.

In other words, what Thorne has done is scrutinize his data until he discerns a 'structural property' which can be made to fit his preconceptions. The exercise is successful, but it is also circular.

It is not my intention flatly to deny any relationship between structure and sense, but to argue that if there is one, it is not to be explained by attributing an independent meaning to the linguistic facts, which will, in any case, mean differently in different circumstances. Indeed these same facts – animate nouns where one expects inanimate and inanimate where one expects animate – characterize much of Wordsworth's poetry, where the sense communicated is one of harmony rather than chaos. Of course, counter-examples of this kind do not prove that a critic is wrong (or right) in a particular case, but that the search for a paradigm of formal significances is a futile one. Those who are determined to pursue it, however, will find in transformational grammar the perfect vehicle; for since its formalisms operate independently of semantic and psychological processes (are neutral between production and reception) they can be assigned any semantic or psychological value one may wish them to carry. Thus Ohmann can determine that in one of Conrad's sentences the deep-structural subject 'secret sharer' appears thirteen times and conclude that the reader who understands the sentence must 'register' what is absent from its surface (1969b, pp. 152–3); while Roderick Jacobs and Peter Rosenbaum can, with equal plausibility, conclude that the presence of relative-clause reduction transformations in a story by John Updike results 'in a very careful suppression of any mention of individual beings' as agents (1971, pp. 103–6). In one analysis the grammatical machinery is translated into an activity the reader must perform; in the other it prevents him from performing that same activity. This is a game that is just too easy to play.

It is possible, I suppose, to salvage the game, at least temporarily, by making it more sophisticated, by contextualizing it. One could simply write a rule that allows for the different valuings of the same pattern by taking into account the features which surround it in context. But this would only lead to the bringing forward of further counter-examples and the continual and regressive rewriting of the rule. Eventually a point would be reached where a separate rule was required for each and every occurrence; and at that point the assumption that formal features *possess* meaning would no longer be tenable, and the enterprise of the stylisticians – at least as they conceive it – will have been abandoned.[1]

One can be certain, however, that it will not be abandoned, partly because the lure of 'solid science' and the promise of an automatic interpretive procedure is so great, and partly because apparent successes are so easy to come by. For a final and spectacular example I turn to Michael Halliday and an article entitled 'Linguistic function and literary style' (1971).[2] Halliday is the proprietor of what he calls a category-scale grammar, a grammar so complicated that a full explanation would take up more space than I have. Allow me, however, to introduce a few of the basic terms. The number of categories is four: unit, structure, class, and system. Two of these, unit and structure, are categories of chain; that is, they refer to the syntagmatic axis or axis of combination. The category of unit relates the linear constituents of discourse to one another as they combine; representative units are morpheme, word, group, clause, and sentence. The category of structure is concerned with the syntagmatic relationships within units: subject, complements, adjunct, and predicator are elements of structure. The other two categories are categories of choice, of the paradigmatic axis or the axis of selection. The category of class contains those items which can be substituted for one another at certain points in a unit; classes include nouns, verbs, and adjectives. The category of system refers to the systematic relationships between elements of structure, relationships of agreement and difference, such as singular and plural, active and passive. Together, these categories make it possible for the linguist to segment his text either horizontally or vertically; that is, they make possible an exhaustive taxonomy.

This, however, is only part of the story. In addition, Halliday introduces three scales of abstraction which link the categories to each other and to the language data. They are rank, exponence, and delicacy. The scale of rank refers to the operation of units within the structure of another unit: a clause, for example, may operate in the structure of another clause, or of a group, or even of a word, and these would be first, second, and third degree rank shifts, respectively. Exponence is the scale by which the abstractions of the system relate to the data: it allows you to trace your way back from any point in the descriptive act to the actual words of a text. And finally the scale of delicacy is the degree of depth at which the descriptive act is being performed. While in some instances one might be satisfied to specify at the level of a clause or a group, in a more delicate description one would want to describe the constituents and relationships within those units themselves.

If this were all, the apparatus would be formidable enough; but there is more. Halliday also adopts, with some modifications, Karl Bühler's tripartite division of language into three functions – the ideational function or the expression of content; the interpersonal function, the expression of the speaker's attitudes and evaluations, and of the relationships he sets up between himself and the listener; and the textual function, through which language makes links with itself and with the extralinguistic situation. Obviously these functions exist at a different level of abstraction from each other and from the taxonomic machinery of categories and scales, and just as obviously they create a whole new set of possible relationships between the items specified in that taxonomy; for as Halliday himself remarks, in a statement that boggles the mind with its mathematical implications, 'each sentence embodies all functions ... and most constituents of sentences also embody more than one function' (p. 61).

The result is that while the distinctions one can make with the grammar are minute and infinite, they are also meaningless, for they refer to nothing except the categories of the system that produced them, categories which are themselves unrelated to anything outside their circle except by an arbitrary act of assertion. It follows, then, that when this grammar is used to analyze a text, it can legitimately do nothing more than provide labels for its constituents, which is exactly what Halliday does to a sentence from *Through the Looking Glass*:

'It's a poor sort of memory that only works backwards.' Here is the analysis:

> The word *poor* is a 'modifier', and thus expresses a subclass of its head-word
> *memory* (ideational); while at the same time it is an 'epithet' expressing the
> Queen's attitude (interpersonal), and the choice of this word in this
> environment (as opposed to, say, *useful*) indicates more specifically that the
> attitude is one of disapproval. The words *it's ... that* have here no reference at
> all outside the sentence, but they structure the message in a particular way
> (textual), which represents the Queen's opinion as if it was an 'attribute'
> (ideational), and defines one class of *memory* as exclusively possessing this
> undesirable quality (ideational). The lexical repetition in *memory that only
> works backwards* relates the Queen's remark (textual) to *mine only works
> one way* in which *mine* refers anaphorically, by ellipsis, to *memory* in the
> preceding sentence (textual) and also to *I* in Alice's expression of her own
> judgment *I'm sure* (interpersonal). Thus ideational content and personal inter-
> action are woven together with, and by means of, the textual structure to form
> a coherent whole.
>
> (p. 62)

What, you might ask, is this coherent whole? The answer is, 'It's a poor sort of
memory that only works backwards.' But that, you object, is what we had at the
beginning. Exactly. When a text is run through Halliday's machine, its parts are
first disassembled, then labeled, and finally recombined into their original form.
The procedure is a complicated one, and it requires a great many operations,
but the critic who performs them has finally done nothing at all.

Halliday, however, is determined to do something, and what he is determined
to do is confer a value on the formal distinctions his machine reads out. His text
is William Golding's *The Inheritors*, a story of two prehistoric tribes one of which
supplants the other. The two tribes – the 'people' and the 'new people',
respectively – are distinguished not only by their activities but by their respective
languages, and these, in turn, are distinguishable from the language of the reader.
Language A, the language of the 'people', is, according to Halliday, dominant
for more than nine tenths of the novel. Here is a sample of it:

> The man turned sideways in the bushes and looked at Lok along his shoulder. A stick
> rose upright and there was a lump of bone in the middle. Lok peered at the stick and
> the lump of bone and the small eyes in the bone things over the face. Suddenly Lok
> understood that the man was holding the stick out to him but neither he nor Lok could
> reach across the river. He would have laughed if it were not for the echo of the
> screaming in his head. The stick began to grow shorter at both ends. Then it shot out
> to full length again.
> The dead tree by Lok's ear acquired a voice.
> 'Clop!'
> His ears twitched and he turned to the tree. By his face there had grown a twig.
>
> (quoted in Halliday, p. 82)

From this and other samples Halliday proceeds to a description of the people's
language, using the full apparatus of his category-scale grammar; but what begins
as a description turns very quickly into something else:

> The clauses of passage A ... are mainly clauses of action ... location ... or mental process ... the remainder are attributive ... Almost all of the action clauses ... describe simple movements ... and of these the majority ... are intransitive ... Even such normally transitive verbs as *grab* occur intransitively ... Moreover a high proportion ... of the subjects are not people; they are either parts of the body ... or inanimate objects ... and of the human subjects half again ... are found in clauses which are not clauses of action. Even among the four transitive action clauses ... one has an inanimate subject and one is reflexive. There is a stress set up, a kind of syntactic counterpoint, between verbs of movement in their most active and dynamic form ... and the preference for non-human subjects and the almost total absence of transitive clauses.
>
> (p. 71–3)

Here, of course, is where the sleight of hand begins. To label a verb 'active' is simply to locate it in a system of formal differences and relationships within a grammar; to call it 'dynamic' is to semanticize the label, and even, as we see when the description continues, to moralize it:

> It is particularly the lack of transitive clauses of action with human subjects ... that creates an atmosphere of ineffectual activity: the scene is one of constant movement, but movement which is as much inanimate as human and in which only the mover is affected ... The syntactic tension expresses this combination of activity and helplessness. No doubt this is a fair summary of the life of Neanderthal man.
>
> (p. 73)

This paragraph is a progression of illegitimate inferences. Halliday first gives his descriptive terms a value, and then he makes an ideogram of the patterns they yield. Moreover, the content of that ideogram – the Neanderthal mentality – is quite literally a fiction (one wonders where he got his information), and it is therefore impossible that these or any other forms should express it.

What happens next is predictable. The novel receives a Darwinian reading in which the grammatically impoverished 'people' are deservedly supplanted by the 'new people' whose fuller transitivity patterns are closer to our own: 'The transitivity patterns ... are the reflexion of the underlying theme ... the inherent limitations of understanding ... of Lok and his people, and their consequent inability to survive when confronted with beings at a higher stage of development' (p. 73). The remainder of the essay is full of statements like this; the verbal patterns 'reflect' the subject matter, are 'congruent' with it, 'express' it, 'embody' it, 'encode' it, and at one point even 'enshrine' it. The assumption is one we have met before – 'syntactic preferences correlate with habits of meaning' – but here it is put into practice on a much grander scale: 'The "people's" use of transitivity patterns argues a Neanderthal mind.'

In short, when Halliday does something with his apparatus, it is just as arbitrary as what Milic and Ohmann and Thorne do with theirs. But why, one might ask, is he arbitrary in this direction? Given the evidence, at least as he marshals it, the way seems equally open to an Edenic rather than a Darwinian reading of the novel, a reading in which the language of the 'people' reflects (or embodies or enshrines) a lost harmony between man and an animate nature. The triumph of the 'new people' would then be a disaster, the beginning of the end, of a decline into the taxonomic aridity of a mechanistic universe. There are two answers to this question, and the first should not surprise us. Halliday's interpretation precedes his gathering and evaluating of the data, and it, rather than any ability of the syntax to embody a conceptual orientation, is responsible for the way in which the data are read. There is some evidence that the interpretation is not his own (he refers with approval to the 'penetrating critical study' of Mark Kinkead-Weekes and Ian Gregor), but whatever its source – and this is the second answer to my question – its attraction is the opportunity it provides him to make his apparatus the hero of the novel. For in the reading Halliday offers, the deficiencies of the 'people' are measured by the inability of their language to fill out the categories of his grammar. Thus when he remarks that 'in Lok's understanding the complex taxonomic ordering of natural phenomena that is implied by the use of defining modifiers is lacking, or ... rudimentary' (p. 75), we see him sliding from an application of his system to a judgment on the descriptions it yields; and conversely, when the 'new people' win out, they do so in large part because they speak a language that requires for its analysis the full machinery of that system. Not only does Halliday go directly from formal categories to interpretation, but he goes to an interpretation which proclaims the superiority of his formal categories. The survival of the fittest tribe is coincidental with a step toward the emergence of the fittest grammar. Whether Golding knew it or not, it would seem that he was writing an allegory of the ultimate triumph of Neo-Firthian man.

Is there, then, no point to Halliday's exercise? Are the patterns he uncovers without meaning? Not at all. It is just that the explanation for that meaning is not the capacity of a syntax to express it, but the ability of a reader to confer it. Golding prefaces *The Inheritors* with an excerpt from H. G. Wells's discussion of Neanderthal Man. As a result, we enter the story expecting to encounter a people who differ from us in important respects, and we are predisposed to attach that difference to whatever in their behavior calls attention to itself. It is in this way that the language of the 'people' becomes significant, not because it is symbolic, but because it functions in a structure of expectations, and it is in the context of that structure that a reader is moved to assign it a value. The point is one that Halliday almost makes, but he throws it away, on two occasions; first when he remarks that the reader's entrance into the novel requires a 'considerable effort of interpretation' (p. 71), and later when he specifies the nature of that effort: 'the difficulties of understanding are at the level of interpretation – or rather ... re-interpretation, as when we insist on translating *the stick began to grow shorter at both ends* as "the man drew the bow" ' (p. 80). Here I would quarrel only with the phrase 'we insist'; for the decision to reinterpret is not made freely; it is inseparable from the activity of reading (the *text* insists), and the effort expended in the course of that activity becomes the measure and sign of the distance between us and the characters in the novel. In other words, the link between the language and any sense we have of Neanderthal Man is fashioned in response to the demands of the reading experience, it does not exist prior to that experience, and in the experience of another work it will not be fashioned, even if the work were to display the same formal features. In any number of contexts, the sentence 'the stick grew shorter at both ends' would present no difficulty for a reader; it would require no effort of reinterpretation, and therefore it would not take on the meaning which that effort *creates* in *The Inheritors*. Halliday's mistake is not to assert a value for his data but to locate that value in a paradigm and so bypass the context in which it is actually acquired.

This goes to the heart of my quarrel with the stylisticians: in their rush to establish an inventory of fixed significances, they bypass the activity in the course of which significances are, if only momentarily, fixed. I have said before that their procedures are arbitrary, and that they acknowledge no constraint on their interpretations of the data. The shape of the reader's experience is the constraint they decline to acknowledge. Were they to make that shape the focus of their analyses, it would lead them to the value conferred by its events. Instead they proceed in accordance with the rule laid down by Martin Joos (1961, p. 18): 'Text signals its own structure', treating the deposit of an activity as if it were the activity itself, as if meanings arose independently of human transactions. As a result, they are left with patterns and statistics that have been cut off from their animating source, banks of data that are unattached to anything but their own formal categories, and are therefore, quite literally, meaningless.

In this connection it is useful to turn to a distinction made by John Searle, between institutional facts – facts rooted in a recognition of human purposes, needs, and goals – and brute facts – facts that are merely quantifiable. 'Imagine', says Searle

> a group of highly trained observers describing a ... football game in statements only of brute facts. What could they say by way of description? Well, within certain areas a good deal could be said, and using statistical techniques certain 'laws' could even be formulated ... we can imagine that after a time our observers would discover the law of periodic clustering: at regular intervals organisms in like colored shirts cluster together in roughly circular fashion .... Furthermore, at equally regular intervals, circular clustering is followed by linear clustering ... and linear clustering is followed by the phenomenon of linear interpenetration .... But no matter how much data of this sort we imagine our observers to collect and no matter how many inductive generalizations we imagine them to make from the data, they still have not described football. What is missing from their description? What is missing are ... concepts such as touchdown, offside, game, points, first down, time out, etc ... The missing statements are precisely what describes the phenomenon on the field *as a game of football*. The other descriptions, the description of the brute facts can [only] be explained in terms of the institutional facts.
>
> (Searle 1969, p. 52)

In my argument the institutional facts are the events that are constitutive of the specifically human activity of reading, while the brute facts are the observable formal patterns that can be discerned in the traces or residue of that activity. The stylisticians are thus in the position of trying to do what Searle says cannot be done: explain the brute facts without reference to the institutional facts which give them value. They would specify the meaning of the moves in the game without taking into account the game itself. Paradoxically, however, this gap in their procedures does not hamper but free them; for while it is true, as Hubert Dreyfus has recently observed, that once the data have 'been taken out of context and stripped of all significance, it is not so easy to give it back' (1972, p. 200), the corollary is that it is *very* easy to replace it with whatever significance you wish to bring forward. The result is interpretations that are simultaneously fixed and arbitrary, fixed because they are specified apart from contexts, and arbitrary because they are fixed, because it is in contexts that meaning occurs.

The stylisticians, of course, have an alternative theory of meaning, and it is both the goal of, and the authorization for, their procedures. In that theory, meaning is located in the inventory of relationships they seek to specify, an inventory that exists independently of the activities of producers and consumers, who are reduced either to selecting items from its storehouse of significances or to recognizing the items that have been selected. As a theory, it is distinguished by what it does away with, and what it does away with are human beings, at least in so far as they are responsible for creating rather than simply exchanging meanings. This is why the stylisticians almost to a man identify meaning with either logic or message or information, because these entities are 'pure' and remain uninfluenced by the needs and purposes of those who traffic in them. I have been arguing all along that the goal of the stylisticians is impossible, but my larger objection is that it is unworthy, for it would deny to man the most remarkable of his abilities, the ability to give the world meaning rather than to extract a meaning that is already there.

This, however, is precisely what the stylisticians want to avoid, the protean and various significances which are attached, in context and by human beings, to any number of formal configurations. Behind their theory, which is reflected in their goal which authorizes their procedures, is a desire and a fear: the desire to be relieved of the burden of interpretation by handing it over to an algorithm, and the fear of being left alone with the self-renewing and unquantifiable power of human signifying. So strong is this fear that it rules their procedures even when they appear to be taking into account what I accuse them of ignoring. Michael Riffaterre is a case in point. In every way Mr Riffaterre seems to be on the right side. He criticizes descriptive techniques that fail to distinguish between merely linguistic patterns and patterns a reader could be expected to actualize (1959, p. 164). He rejects the attempts of other critics to endow 'formal ... categories ... with esthetic and ... ethical values' (1970, p. 197). He insists that the proper object of analysis is not the poem or message but the 'whole act of communication' (1970, p. 202). He argues for the necessity of 'following exactly the normal reading process' (1970, p. 203), and it is that process he seeks to describe when he asks readers, or as he calls them, informants, to report on their experiences. Once the process is described, however, Riffaterre does something very curious: he empties it of its content (1970; see also 1959, p. 164). That is, he discounts everything his readers tell him about what they were doing and retains only the points at which they were compelled to do it. The pattern that emerges, a pattern of contentless stresses and emphases, is then fleshed out by the interpretation he proceeds to educe.

In short, Riffaterre does exactly what the other stylisticians do, but he does it later: he cuts his data off from the source of value and is then free to confer any value he pleases. The explanation for this curious maneuver is to be found in his equation of meaning with message or information; for if the message is the meaning, a reader's activities can only be valued in so far as they contribute to its clear and firm reception; anything else is simply evidence of an unwanted subjectivity and must be discarded. While the reader is admitted into Riffaterre's procedures, there is no real place for him in the theory and he is sent away after he has performed the mechanical task of locating the field of analysis. In the end, Riffaterre is distinguished only by the nature of his diversionary machinery. Like the other stylisticians, he introduces a bulky apparatus which obscures the absence of any connection between his descriptive and interpretive acts; the difference is that his is precisely the apparatus that would supply the connection (it is not taxonomic but explanatory); but after introducing it, he eviscerates it.

Richard Ohmann performs somewhat the same operation on an entire school of philosophy. In his most recent work (1971a, 1971b, 1972a, 1972b, 1973), Ohmann has proposed literary applications to the speech-act theory of J. L. Austin (*How to Do Things with Words*) and John Searle, a theory that turns traditional philosophy around by denying the primacy and even the existence of pure or context-free statements. All utterances, argue Austin and Searle, are to be understood as instances of purposeful human actions which happen to require language for their performance. Some of these are promising, ordering, commanding, requesting, questioning, warning, stating, praising, greeting, etc. Even this abbreviated list should be enough to suggest the main contention of this school, which is captured in Searle's (1969, p. 25) declaration that propositional acts do not occur alone. What this means is that every utterance possesses an illocutionary force, an indication of the way it is to be taken (as a promise, threat, warning, etc.) and that no utterance is ever taken purely, without reference to an intention in a context. Thus, for example, the string of words 'I will come' may, in different circumstances, be a promise, a threat, a warning, a prediction; but it will always be one of these, and it will never be just a meaning unattached to a situation. What an older theory would have called the pure semantic value of the utterance is in this theory merely an abstraction, which, although it can be separated out for the sake of analysis, has no separate and independent status. The various illocutionary lives led by 'I will come' are not different handlings of the same meaning, they are different meanings. In speech-act theory, there is only one semantic level, not two; detached from its illocutionary force, a sentence is just a series of noises. Illocutionary force *is* meaning. (This is obvious in the paradigm instances where the illocutionary force marker is explicit, that is, a part of the utterance, which certainly cannot be detached from itself.)

It is not my intention here to embrace this theory (although I am attracted to it) but to explain some of its terms, terms which Ohmann appropriates. He also distorts them, in two predictable directions. First of all, he takes the slice of the speech act that Searle insists cannot stand alone and gives it an independent status. He calls it the locutionary act – a designation he borrows from Austin – and endows it with a force of its own, the semantic force of logical and grammatical structures (Ohmann 1971b, pp. 249–50). This locutionary act then becomes the basic level of a two-level system of significations. The second, and subsidiary, level is occupied by the inventory of illocutionary forces, which function more or less as a rhetoric of social conventions and intentions. Illocutionary force is thus dislodged from its primary position and reduced to a kind of *emphasis*, something that is added to a content which is detachable from it and survives its influence. Ohmann, in short, turns the major insight of the speech-act philosophers on its head, precisely undoing what they have so carefully done. It is in a way a remarkable feat: he manages to take a theory rooted in the recognition of human meaning and make it assert the primacy of a meaning that is specifiable apart from human activities. He succeeds, in the face of great odds, in preserving the context-free propositional core that is necessary if there is to be a rationale for the procedures of stylistics,[3] and it is only a measure of his success that he is then able to define literature impossibly as 'discourse without illocutionary force' (1971a, p. 13).[4]

I do not mean to suggest conscious intention on Ohmann's part, any more than I would argue that the stylisticians consciously perform illegitimate acts of interpretation which they then deliberately disguise. Indeed I take the performance of these acts as evidence of the extent to which they are unaware of their assumptions; for if they were true to their covert principles (as are, for example, the structuralists)[5] they would be content with the description of formal patterns and admit that the value-free operation of those patterns has always been their goal. But they are not so content and insist on leaping from those patterns to the human concerns their procedures exclude. The dehumanization of meaning may be the implication, as well as the result, of what they do; but it is not, I think, what they consciously *want* to do.

What we have then, is a confusion between methodology and intention, and it is a confusion that is difficult to discern in the midst of the pseudo-scientific paraphernalia the stylisticians bring to bear. I return to my opening paragraph and to a final paradox. While it is the program of stylistics to replace the subjectivity of literary studies with objective techniques of description and interpretation, its practitioners ignore what is *objectively* true – that meaning is not the property of a timeless formalism, but something acquired in the context of an activity – and therefore they are finally more subjective than the critics they would replace. For an open impressionism, they substitute the covert impressionism of anchorless statistics and self-referring categories. In the name of responsible procedures, they offer a methodized irresponsibility, and, as a result, they produce interpretations which are either circular – mechanical reshufflings of the data – or arbitrary – readings of the data that are unconstrained by anything in their machinery.

What makes this picture particularly disturbing is the unlikelihood of its changing; for among the favorite pronouncements of the stylisticians are two that protect them from confronting or even acknowledging the deficiencies of their operations. The first is: 'Stylistic studies are essentially comparative.' Properly understood, this article of faith is a covert admission of the charges I have been making. What the stylisticians compare are the statistics derived from applying their categories to a variety of texts; but since those categories are unattached to anything (are without meaning) the differences revealed by the statistics are purely formal, and the only thing one can legitimately do with them is compare them with each other. The weakness of the exercise is that it is without content, but this is also its strength, since it can be endlessly and satisfyingly repeated without hazarding assertions about meaning or value. It is when such assertions are hazarded that the stylisticians get into trouble, but at this point they are ready with a second article of faith: the apparent unreliability of our procedures is a condition of insufficient data. Thus while Lúbomir Doležel (to cite just one example) is forced to admit that 'there are surprising contradictions in the various interpretations of style characteristics', he manages to escape the implications of his admission by hanging everything on a future hope: 'All conclusions about the properties and nature of style characteristics, about the speaker type and text type, and about stylistic differences, are to be considered hypotheses that will be confirmed or refuted by the accumulation of vast empirical material' (Doležel 1969, p. 22). But the accumulation of empirical material will make a difference only if the ability of human beings to confer meaning is finite and circumscribable within a statistical formula; if it is not, then the resulting data will do nothing more than trace out more fully the past performance of that ability, rather than, as Doležel and others hope, make its future performances predictable. In other words, the statistics will never catch up with the phenomenon they seek to circumscribe. But one can avoid this realization simply by forever advancing the date when the availability of more data will make everything all right.[6] The failure of the basic assumption to prove itself is also the mechanism which assures its continuing life, and assures too that stylisticians will never come to terms with the theoretical difficulties of their enterprise.

If the enterprise is so troubled, if, in short, the things people say about stylistics aren't terrible enough, what is the remedy? What is the critic who is interested in verbal analysis to do? The answer to this question would be the substance of another essay, but it has been more than anticipated here, especially in my counter-analysis of *The Inheritors*. I do not, the reader will recall, deny that the formal distinctions Halliday uncovers are meaningful; but where he assumes that they *possess* meaning (as a consequence of a built-in relationship between formal features and cognitive capacities), I would argue that they *acquire* it, and that they acquire it by virtue of their position in a structure of experience. The structure with which the stylisticians are concerned is a structure of observable formal patterns, and while such patterns do exist they are themselves part of a larger pattern the description of which is necessary for a determination of their value. Thus, for example, while it is certainly possible (as Halliday demonstrates) to specify the properties of the languages spoken by the tribes in *The Inheritors*, the significance of those properties is a function of their reception and negotiation by a reader who comes upon them already oriented in the direction of specific concerns and possessed of (or by) certain expectations. These concerns and expectations themselves arise in the course of a consecutive activity engaged in by a finite consciousness; and it is my contention that a characterization of that activity must precede, and by preceding control, the characterization of the formal features which become part of *its* structure. In short, I am calling not for the end of stylistics but for a new stylistics, what I have termed elsewhere (Fish 1970, also 1967 and 1972) an 'affective' stylistics, in which the focus of attention is shifted from the spatial context of a page and its observable regularities to the temporal context of a mind and its experiences.

Does this mean a return to the dreaded impressionism? Quite the reverse. The demand for precision will be even greater because the object of analysis is a process whose shape is continually changing. In order to describe that shape, it will be necessary to make use of all the information that formal characterizations of language can provide, although that information will be viewed from a different perspective. Rather than regarding it as directly translatable into what a word or a pattern *means*, it will be used more exactly to specify what a reader, as he comes upon that word or pattern, is *doing*, what assumptions he is making, what conclusions he is reaching, what expectations he is forming, what attitudes he is entertaining, in short, what acts he is being moved to perform. When Milic (1970) observes that in Swift's prose connectives are often redundant and even contradictory – concessives cheek by jowl with causals – we can proceed from what he tells us to an account of what happens when a reader is alternately invited to anticipate a conclusion and asked to qualify it before it appears. When Ohmann declares that the syntactical deviance of Dylan Thomas's 'A Winter's Tale', 'breaks down categorical boundaries and converts juxtaposition into action' (1969b, p. 156), the boundaries, if they exist, take the form of a reader's expectations and their breaking down is an action *he* performs, thereby fashioning for himself the 'vision of things' which the critic would attribute to the language. And when Halliday demonstrates that in the language of the 'people' in Golding's *The Inheritors*, agency is given not to human but to inanimate subjects ('the stick grew shorter at both ends'), we can extrapolate from his evidence to the interpretive effort demanded of the reader who must negotiate it. In each case, a statement about the shape of the data is reformulated as a statement about the (necessary) shape of response, and in the kind of analysis I propose, a succession of such shapes would itself be given shape by the needs and concerns and abilities of a consciousness moving and working in time.

Information about language can be turned into information about response even when the formalizations are unattached to specific texts. Searle's analyses of questions, commands, promises, etc., in terms of the roles they involve, the obligations they institute, and the needs they presuppose, allow us, indeed oblige us, to include these things in any account of what a reader of a question or command or promise understands. Thus when Joan Didion begins *Play It As It Lays* with the sentence 'What makes Iago evil?', simply by taking the question in, the reader casts himself in the role of its answerer. Moreover, he is directed by the tense, aspect (frequentative), and semantic content of 'makes' to play that role in the context of a continuing and public literary debate about causality and motivation (how different would it be were the question 'Why is Iago evil?'); and he will respond, or so Miss Didion assumes, with one or more of the many explanations that have been offered for Iago's behavior.[7] That same reader, however, will be made a little less comfortable in his role by the second sentence: 'Some people ask.' The effect of 'some' is to divide the world into two groups, those who seek after reasons and causes and those who don't. The reader, of course, has already accepted the invitation extended by the prose to become a member of the first group, and, moreover, he has accepted it in assumed fellowship with the first-person voice. That fellowship is upset by the third sentence – 'I never ask' – which is also a judgment on what the reader has been (involuntarily) doing. Reader and narrator are now on different sides of the question originally introduced by the latter, and the tension between them gives point and direction to the experience of what follows.

Little of what I have said about this paragraph would emerge from a formal characterization of its components, but in my description of its experience I have been able to make use of formal characterizations – of a speech-act analysis of a question, of a logician's analysis of the properties of 'some', of a philosopher's analysis of making something happen – by regarding their content as cues for the reader to engage in activities. What is significant about these activities is that they are interpretive; for this means that a procedure in which their characterization is the first order of business avoids the chief theoretical deficiency of stylistics as it is now practiced. I have repeatedly objected to the absence in the work of the stylisticians of any connection between their descriptive and interpretive acts. In the kind of stylistics I propose, *interpretive acts are what is being described*; they, rather than verbal patterns arranging themselves in space, are the content of the analysis. This is more than a procedural distinction; for at its heart are different notions of what it is to read which are finally different notions of what it is to be human. Implicit in what the stylisticians do is the assumption that to read is to put together discrete bits of meaning until they form what a traditional grammar would call a complete thought. In this view, the world, or the world of the text, is already ordered and filled with significances and what the reader is required to do is get them out (hence the question, 'What did you get out of that?'). In short, the reader's job is to extract the meanings that formal patterns possess prior to, and independently of, his activities. In my view, these same activities are constitutive of a structure of concerns which is necessarily prior to any examination of meaningful patterns because it is itself the occasion of their coming into being. The stylisticians proceed as if there were observable facts that could first be described and then interpreted. What I am suggesting is that an interpreting entity, endowed with purposes and concerns, is, by virtue of its very operation, determining what counts as the facts to be observed,[8] and, moreover, that since this determining is not a neutral marking out of a valueless area, but the extension of an already existing field of interests, it *is* an interpretation.

The difference in the two views is enormous, for it amounts to no less than the difference between regarding human beings as passive and disinterested comprehenders of a knowledge external to them (that is, of an *objective* knowledge) and regarding human beings as at every moment creating the experiential spaces into which a personal knowledge flows. It is also a difference in methodological responsibility and rigor, between a procedure which is from the very beginning organizing itself in terms of what is significant, and a procedure which has no obligatory point of origin or rest. That is, if one sets out to describe in the absence of that which marks out the field of description, there is no way of deciding either where to begin or where to stop, because there is no way of deciding what counts. In such a situation, one either goes on at random and forever (here we might cite the monumental aridity of Jakobson's analyses of Baudelaire and Shakespeare) or one stops when the accumulated data can be made to fit a preconceived interpretive thesis. It has seemed to many that these are the only alternatives, and that, as Roger Fowler (1971, pp. 38–9) has declared, the choice is between 'mere description' or description performed at the direction of a preformulated literary hunch. I have been arguing for a third way, one which neither begs the question of meaning nor pre-decides it arbitrarily, but takes as its point of departure the interpretive activity (experience) by virtue of which meanings occur.

This, then, is the way to repair the ruins of stylistics, not by linking the descriptive and interpretive acts, but by making them one.[9] It is hardly necessary to say that this kind of analysis is not without problems, and the problems are for the most part a direct consequence of its assumptions about what it means to be human. It can have no rules in the sense of discovery procedures, since the contextualizing ability that characterizes being human is not circumscribed by its previous performances, performances which, while they constitute the history of that ability, do not constitute its limits. Thus the value a formal feature may acquire in the context of a reader's concerns and expectations is local and temporary; and there is no guarantee that the value-formal feature correlation that obtains once will obtain again (although an awareness that it has obtained once is not without interest or usefulness). All you have when you begin is a sense of this finite but infinitely flexible ability and a personal knowledge of what it means to have it. You then attempt to project the course that ability would take in its interaction with a specific text, using as the basis of your projection what you know, and at the same time adding to what you know by the very effort to make analytical use of it. There are other things that can help. Formal linguistic characterizations can help, if, as I have said, one views their content as potential cues for the performing acts. Literary history can help, if one views its conventions in the same way; a description of a genre, for example, can and should be seen as a prediction of the shape of response. Other minds can help, because they know what you know, but with the same lack of distance between themselves and their knowledge which makes the effort so difficult. Analyses of perceptual strategy can help (e.g. Bever 1972), because they acquaint us with the past performances of the ability we are trying to know. (Our trying is itself just such a performance.) Finally, however, you are left only with yourself and with the impossible enterprise of understanding understanding; impossible because it is endless, endless because to have reached an end is to have performed an operation that once again extends it beyond your reach. In short, this way lacks the satisfaction of a closed system of demonstration and is unable ever to prove anything, although, paradoxically, this makes rigor and precision more, not less, necessary; but these very deficiencies are the reverse side of its greatest virtue (in both the modern and Renaissance sense): the recognition that meaning is human.

Notes

1 My argument here has affinities with Hubert Dreyfus's explanation of the impasse at which programmers of artificial intelligence find themselves. 'The programmer must either claim that some features are intrinsically relevant and have a fixed meaning regardless of content ... or the programmer will be faced with an infinite regress of contexts' (1972, p. 133). Dreyfus's conclusion anticipates the proposal I will offer at the end of this essay for the reform of stylistics. 'Human beings seem to embody a third possibility which would offer a way out of this dilemma. Instead of a hierarchy of contexts, the present situation is recognized as a continuation or modification of the present one. Thus we carry over from the immediate past a set of anticipations based on what was relevant and important a moment ago. This carry-over gives us certain predispositions as to what is worth noticing' (1972, p.134).

2 Halliday's paper is reprinted in chapter 3 of this volume. Page references to Halliday's paper as it appears in chapter 3 will be given in the text.
See also Halliday (1961, 1964, 1967–8, 1970a, 1970b). For an exposition of Halliday's grammar and its application to literary analysis, see Spencer and Gregory (1964, pp. 59–105). For a critique of the tradition in which Halliday works, see Langendoen (1968).

3 That is to say, stylistics requires that there be two separate systems – one of content or message, the other of everything else – which it is the stylistician's job to match up or correlate. Otherwise, they complain, there would be nothing for them to do. Ohmann is consistent in his dualism from his earliest writings – when his grammar was structural – to his 'middle period' – when the deep-surface distinction of Transformational Grammar seemed to give new authorization to the form-content split – to the present day – when the illocutionary force–propositional content distinction serves the same need. See Ohmann (1972b, p.4, MS paging): '[In] the distinction between the unactivated meaning and the fully launched illocutionary act we have the kind of split required for style to exist.'

4 The definition is impossible because discourse without illocutionary force would be discourse unrelated to the conventions of everyday speech and therefore discourse that was unintelligible (just a series of noises). To put it another way, the language of literature would be wholly discontinuous with the language we

ordinarily speak, and in order to read it one would have to learn it from scratch. (Of course, there are special poetic vocabularies, for example, silver-age Latin, but these are always precisely parallel to, that is, parasitic on, everyday usage.) Ohmann seems aware of this difficulty in his definition, since he modifies it on the very next page, admitting that a literary work has illocutionary force, but declaring that it is 'mimetic'. These mimetic speech acts, however, turn out to be just like real ones, and it seems that this strange class has been instituted only to remedy the deficiency of the original definition.

5 That is, like the stylisticians, the structuralists dislodge man from his privileged position as the originator of meanings, and locate meaning instead in the self-sufficient operation of a timeless formalism. The difference is that they do consciously what the stylisticians do inadvertently; they deliberately raise the implied antihumanism of other formalist methodologies to a principle. The parallel holds too in the matter of interpretation. Since the structuralists' goal is the system of signifiers – intelligibility rather than what is made intelligible – they either decline interpretation or perform it in such a way as to make its arbitrary contingent nature inescapable (for example, Barthes 1975). Again the similarity with what the stylisticians do is less important than the self-consciousness with which it is done. One may disagree with the assumptions impelling the structuralists' enterprise, but one cannot accuse them of being unaware of those assumptions.

6 Indeed the stylisticians often make incredibly damaging admissions and then walk away from them as if their entire program were still intact. Two examples from the work of Manfred Bierwisch will have to suffice. In Bierwisch (1970a, p. 183), he points out that a semantic theory will have to be able 'to explain how one of the several meanings associated with a particular word or sentence is selected in accordance with a particular universe of discourse'. He then admits that at the present time there seems no way precisely to formalize (i.e. make predictable) the process by which, for example, the various meanings of the word 'group' are selected; but he can still conclude (with no warrant whatsoever) that 'although little progress has yet been made in the systematic treatment of these problems, they do not seem to pose difficulties of principle' (1970a, p. 184). In another of his articles, the problem is not an unsupported conclusion but a conclusion he fails to make. The article is 'Poetics and linguistics' (Bierwisch 1970b), and at the close of it Bierwisch points out that references in poems to other poems or to other universes of discourse (e.g. art history) 'can never be expressed in an exhaustive linguistic semantics and ... thus mark ... the boundaries of a complete theory of poetic effect and style' (1970b, p. 112). The conclusion that he doesn't reach (although it seems inescapable) is that a theory with those limitations is of questionable value.

7 Let me take the opportunity this example offers to clarify what I mean by *the* reader or, as I have elsewhere termed him, the 'informed' reader. There are at least four potential readers of this sentence: (a) the reader for whom the name Iago means nothing; (b) the reader who knows that Iago is a character in a play by Shakespeare; (c) the reader who has read the play; (d) the reader who is aware that the question has its own history, that everyone has had a whack at answering it, and that it has become a paradigm question for the philosophical-moral problem of motivation. Now each of these readers will assume the role of answerer because each of them (presumably) is a native speaker of English

who knows what is involved in a felicitous question. (His knowledge is the content of Searle's formalizations.) But the precision with which that role is played will be a function of the reader's particular knowledge of Iago. That is, the reader who is a member of my fourth class will not only recognize that he is being asked to perform the activity of answering but will perform it in a very specific direction (and consequently the speaker's withdrawal from that direction will be felt by him all the more sharply). He will be my informed reader and I would want to say that his experience of the sentence will not only be different from, but better than, his less-informed fellows. Note that this is not a distinction between real and ideal readers; all the readers are real, as are all their experiences. Nor do I assume a uniformity of attitude and opinion among informed readers. Some readers may believe that Iago is motivated by jealousy, others that he is motiveless, still others that he is not evil but heroic. It is the ability of the reader to have an opinion (or even to know that having an opinion is what is called for), and not the opinion he has, which makes him informed in my sense; for then, no matter what opinion he has, he will have committed himself to considering the issues of motivation and agency. That commitment will be the *content* of his experience and it will not be the content of the experience of readers less informed than he.

8 Again my argument intersects with that of Dreyfus (1972, p. 136): 'There must be some way of avoiding the self-contradictory regress of contexts, or the incomprehensible notion of recognizing an ultimate context, as the only way of giving significance to independent, neutral facts. The only way out seems to be to deny the separation of fact and situation ... to give up the independence of the facts and understand them as a product of the situation. This would amount to arguing that only in terms of situationally determined relevance are there any facts at all.'

9 The resulting 'single-shot' procedure also spells the end of another distinction, the distinction between style and meaning. This distinction depends on the primacy of propositional content (that which it is the reader's job to extract), but in an analysis which has as its object the structure of the reader's experience, the achieving of propositional clarity is only one among many activities, and there is no warrant for making it the privileged center in relation to which all other activities are either appendages or excrescences. Rather than the traditional dichotomy between process and product (the how and the what), everything becomes process and nothing is granted the stability that would lead to its being designated 'content'. Thus there is only style, or, if you prefer, there is only meaning, and what the philosophers have traditionally called meaning becomes an abstraction from the total meaning experience. Describing that experience becomes the goal of analysis and the resulting shape is both the form and the content of the description. (This is a 'monism' not open to the usual objection that it leaves you with nothing to do.)

References

AUSTIN, J. L. 1965: *How to do things with words*. New York: Oxford University Press.

BARTHES, R. 1975: *S/Z*, trans. R. Miller. London: Cape.

BEVER, T. G 1972: Perceptions, thought, and language. In Freedle, R. O. and Carroll, J. B. (eds), *Language comprehension and the acquisition of knowledge*. New York: Halsted Press, 99–112.

BIERWISCH, M. 1970a: Semantics. In Lyons, J. (ed.), *New horizons in linguistics*. Baltimore: Penguin, 166–84.

—1970b: Poetics and linguistics. In Freeman, D. C. (ed.), *Linguistics and literary style*. New York: Holt Rinehart Winston, 96–115.

DOLEŽEL, L. 1969: A framework for the statistical analysis of style. In Doležel, L. and Bailey, R. M. (eds), *Statistics and style*. New York: Elsevier, 10–25.

DREYFUS, H. 1972: *What computers can't do*. New York: Harper.

FISH, S. 1967: *Surprised by sin: The reader in Paradise Lost*. New York: St Martins.

—1970: Literature in the reader: affective stylistics. *New Literary History* 2, 123–62.

—1972: *Self-consuming artifacts*. Berkeley: University of California Press.

FOWLER, R. 1971: *The languages of literature: Some linguistic contributions to criticism*. London: Routledge and Kegan Paul.

HALLIDAY, M. A. K. 1961: Categories of the theory of grammar. *Word* 17, 241–92.

—1964: The linguistic study of literary texts. In Lunt, H. (ed.), *Proceedings of the Ninth International Congress of Linguists*. The Hague: Mouton, 302–7.

—1967–8: Notes on transitivity and theme in English. *Journal of Linguistics* 3 (1967), 37–81, 199–244, and 4 (1968), 179–215.

—1970a: Descriptive linguistics in literary studies. In Freeman, D. C. (ed.), *Linguistics and literary style*. New York: Holt Rinehart Winston, 57–72.

—1970b: Language structure and language function. In Lyons, J. (ed.), *New horizons in linguistics*. Baltimore: Penguin, 140–65.

—1971: Linguistic function and literary style. In Chatman, S. (ed.), *Literary style: A symposium*. New York: Oxford University Press, 330–65.

JACOBS, R. A. and ROSENBAUM, P.S. 1971: *Transformations, style and meaning*. Waltham, Mass.: Ginn.

JAKOBSON, R. and HALLE, M. 1956: *Fundamentals of language*. The Hague: Mouton.

JOOS, M. 1961: Linguistic prospects in the United States. In Mohrmann, C. (ed.), *Trends in European and American linguistics 1930–1960*. Utrecht: Spectrum, 11–20.

KINKEAD-WEEKES, M. and GREGOR, I. 1967: *William Golding: A critical study*. London: Faber.

LANGENDOEN, D. T. 1968: *The London school of linguistics*. Cambridge, Mass.: MIT Press.

MILIC, L. 1966: Unconscious ordering in the prose of Swift. In Leed, J. (ed.), *The computer and literary style*. Kent, Ohio: Kent State University Press, 79–106.

—1967: *A quantitative approach to the style of Jonathan Swift*. The Hague: Mouton.

—1970: Connectives in Swift's prose style. In Freeman, D. C. (ed.), *Linguistics and literary style*. New York: Holt Rinehart Winston, 243–57.

OHMANN, R. 1969a: Generative grammars and the concept of literary style. In Love, G. A. and Payne, M. (eds), *Contemporary essays on style*. Glenview, Ill.: Scott Foresman, 133–48.

—1969b: Literature as sentences. In Love, G. A. and Payne, M. (eds), *Contemporary essays on style*. Glenview, Ill.: Scott Foresman, 149–57.

—1971a: Speech acts and the definition of literature. *Philosophy and Rhetoric* 4, 1–19.

—1971b: Speech, action, and style. In Chatman, S. (ed.), *Literary style: A symposium*. New York: Oxford University Press, 241–59.

—1972a: Speech, literature, and the space between. *New Literary History* 4, 47–64.

—1972b: Instrumental style: Notes on the theory of speech as action. In Kachru, B. B. and Stahlke, F. W. (eds), *Current trends in stylistics*. Edmonton: Linguistic Research, 115–42.

—1973: Literature as act. In Chatman, S. (ed.), *Approaches to poetics*. New York: Columbia University Press, 81–108.

RIFFATERRE, M. 1959: Criteria for style analysis. *Word* 15, 154–74.

—1970: Describing poetic structures. In Ehrmann, J. (ed.), *Structuralism*. New York: Anchor Books.

SEARLE, J. 1969: *Speech acts: An essay in the philosophy of language*. Cambridge: Cambridge University Press.

SPENCER, J. and GREGORY, M. J. 1964: An approach to the study of style. In Enkvist, N. E., Spencer, J. and Gregory, M. *Linguistics and style*. London: Oxford University Press, 59–105.

THORNE, J. P. 1965: Stylistics and generative grammars. *Journal of Linguistics* 1, 49–59.

—1969: Poetry, stylistics and imaginary grammars. *Journal of Linguistics* 5, 147–50.

—1970: Generative grammar and stylistic analysis. In Lyons, J. (ed.), *New horizons in linguistics*. Baltimore: Penguin, 185–97.

6

Stylistics and its discontents; or, getting off the Fish 'hook'

Michael Toolan

6.1 Style and literary linguistics

The concept of style has had a troubled history in the modern period. Both within and outside literary study, it has commonly been argued that we use the term 'style' without knowing its meaning. Most of us have little difficulty in using words like 'style' and 'stylish' in everyday discourse, to refer to some characteristic of a person or thing which we find distinctive and pleasing. But the status of the judgement usually remains unexamined. When we speak of style in Milton – or McEnroe – are we merely spontaneously asserting the presence of some quality which is subjectively perceived and unanalysable, that is, making a purely arbitrary personal evaluation or 'witnessing'? In this chapter I want to sketch the wider background of orthodox literary and linguistic studies, particularly as these bear on influential theorizations of such key notions as style, stylistics, literature, and linguistics.

By way of a beginning, we might consider a question that arises with regard to the specific domain of *literary* style, namely whether style is a linguistic topic, part of the linguistic description of a text, or chiefly a topic in literary criticism and appreciation of a text, hence largely subjective.

It may be a clarification rather than a distortion to posit two such divergent responses to style, for such deep-seated conflict underlies much of the wrangling between linguists and critics in their various contributions to this controversial question during the last twenty years. Too many of the contributors have preferred, for whatever reason, to adopt a combative stance in the face of their alleged antagonists, and have indulged in a destructively extreme dialecticalism of debate. Too few have noted, as Roger Fowler did long ago (Fowler 1971), the considerable community of interests of style students, whether from the literary or linguistic camp, and their common intellectual and cultural ancestry in nineteenth- and twentieth-century philology.

However, in the last fifteen years or so a new polyphony of contending approaches, subdisciplines, and agendas – a renewed sense of lost or multiple directions, the sceptic might suggest – has emerged. So many formerly cast-iron and irrefutable distinctions, in both linguistic and literary criticism, are now acknowledged to be disconcertingly vulnerable to challenge (see, for example, McLain 1977). After Derrida, it seems, every binary categorization one cares to think of is vulnerable to deconstruction: speech versus writing; poem versus novel; dialogue versus narrative; character versus incident; and, perhaps, linguistics versus literary criticism. In the domain of linguistics, the Chomskyan generativist epoch promoted the claims of a number of universalizable characteristics of language and, more important, promised that the theory might eventually provide a full description of a native language-user's competence. But linguists now increasingly acknowledge both the narrowness, in practice, of the microlinguistic turn that generativism took, and the theoretical uncertainty of even such fundamental distinctions as that between competence and performance (early critics included Gross 1979; Koerner 1983). There is renewed debate about what constitutes a language, and how linguistics relates to communication (Harris 1980; Pateman 1983; Itkonen 1984). Many of the post-Saussurean categories of linguistic theory, supposedly fundamental, are now seen to contain quite arbitrary suppositions. Perhaps the most notorious of these are those surrounding Chomsky's idealized conceptualization of the homogeneous speech community whose members know their language perfectly. The stronger objection to this is not that it is an idealization – all theory idealizes in some respects – but that it presents, as a workable conceptualization, a construct which stipulates homogeneity and perfect knowledge of a phenomenon which, definitionally, needs to be characterized in terms of heterogeneity and difference. As Love (1981) has suggested, Chomsky's idealization may be no more useful than the concept of a square circle (on these issues, see also Love 1988). Many recent studies argue quite explicitly for the need to attend anew to the observed phenomena of linguistic behaviour, in all their seemingly chaotic diversity, and notwithstanding the difficulties for modelling and description that this involves (see Harris 1981, 1987; Milroy 1981; Le Page and Tabouret-Keller 1985; Romaine 1983, 1988; Hudson 1980).

The crisis in literary studies is as acute. Many literary scholars continue to assert that artistic literature is different in kind from 'ordinary' language, and that there is a sharp divide between the two types of discourse. This view is often held in conjunction with the familiar New Critical verdict on form and content: in ordinary language form and content are separable, statements are often synonymous and paraphrasable, but in verbal art content is never paraphrasable, nor separable from form.

To anyone with a vocational interest in literature it is difficult to resist some of the pull of New Criticism, which both mystifies the production of artistic literature and makes the poem itself a sacred mystery. New Criticism is, technically, utterly defunct, universally dismissed as a theoretical dinosaur; but the kinds of critical practice that it privileged are still widely adhered to, and the preoccupation, in theory, with Lacan, Lyotard, Foucault, Bakhtin, etc., has done little to shift that adherence. Like high priests of former times, a special elect group with apparently sole rights to approach and interpret the venerated texts for and to the common faithful, New Critics were instrumental in clearing and occupying a particular space in the sociocultural terrain. Theirs was perhaps the first professionalization of literary study; and the chief benefit of this professionalization was that, for a time at least, there was renewed consciousness, in some sections of the societies affected, that literature was important. Of the problems that arose, one was the familiar characteristic of a profession to become hidebound in its thinking, self-perpetuating, swift to close ranks in the face of criticism, resistant to consideration of fundamental premises. I have cited two of these – that literature is essentially different from ordinary language use, and that it is non-paraphrasable. Neither of these can be plausibly defended today without substantial reformulation (for various arguments against seeing literary language as a special language, see Pratt 1977; Lodge 1977; Fish 1980).

In place of the unmaintainable absolutes of the linguistics and literary criticism of a generation ago, new relativist tendencies have emerged. Linguistics may be a science, in that it pursues knowledge which may be formalized and generalized about the way people have and use language, but it is much more a social science than a pure one. The generative linguists' pursuit of rules and representations of competence, expressible in abstract terms akin to those of mathematics, has often been conducted to the neglect of many of the most interesting characteristics of language (see Gross 1979; Koerner 1983). Among some linguists at least, there has latterly been a noticeable redirection of attention away from narrow abstractions and towards the actual dynamics of language as our chief resource in the achievement of interpersonal communication and the negotiation of individual goals. Even those uncritical of the theoretical assumptions and idealizations of generative linguistics widely recognize that in the contemporary world there are many other applications of linguistic expertise, of pressing concern, to make demands on linguists' intellectual energy: 'language universals in government and binding theory' must accept 'complex-sentence comprehension in the very old' and 'pragmalinguistic guidelines for the questions formulated by immigration officers' as equally legitimate research topics.

In light of these changes in theory and practice, a recent paper by Mary Louise Pratt, surveying the unreally utopian nature of contemporary linguistic idealizations and modellings, is of particular interest. Over and over again, she argues, problematic phenomena, heterogeneity, and difference are marginalized or silenced altogether by prevailing models of egalitarian homogeneity: 'Disorders ... are almost automatically seen as failures or breakdowns not to be accounted for within the system' (Pratt 1987, p. 51). Instead, models of 'imagined communities' are constructed, 'speech communities with their own boundaries, sovereignty, fraternity and authenticity' (1987, p. 56). This has persisted even in sociolinguistics, Pratt argues, despite the 'empowering' effect of, for example, Labov's imagined community of black English vernacular speakers, or early feminist accounts of 'women's language'. These have value as far as they go, she concedes, but adds:

> What the 'subcommunity' approach does not do, however, is see the dominated and dominant *in their relations with each other* – this is the limitation imposed by the imaginings of community .... Social difference is seen as constituted by distance and separation rather than by ongoing contact and structured relations in a shared social space. Language is seen as a nexus of social identity, but not as a site of social struggle or a producer of social relations.
>
> (Pratt 1987, p. 56)

In the cases of both Labov and Bernstein, for example, though the former is utopian and the latter dystopian in their view of the community dialects they examine (so that black English vernacular is presented as no problem, British working-class verbal culture as nothing but a problem), the upshot of both treatments is to legitimize the assimilationist practices of the dominant culture: in both cases, via bidialectalism, the out-group code can be learned and maintained alongside the already acquired one. As Harris notes of Bernstein (Harris 1980, p. 96) – and this reflects the non-conflictual nature of most such modellings – one thing Bernstein is concerned to deny is that, for instance, middle-class English children and working-class English children speak different languages. For Bernstein the codes relate to linguistic performance only, and not to linguistic competence. In making this compromise in support of the idealized community of potential homogeneity, as Harris notes, much of the force of Bernstein's theory is dissipated: difference is asserted, but only surface difference.

While there is much in Pratt's proposal for a 'linguistics of contact' that one might accept, certain questions remain open. First, she does not demonstrate – although she clearly implies it – that analyses which highlight 'the hierarchical and conflictive web of social relations' shaping any encounter between individuals (subjects) in a divided and stratified society *cannot* be produced using the linguistics of community. In fact, it is hard to image how a linguistics of contact itself, a linguistics focused on conflict, contrast, and difference, can operate without a linguistics that models community in some way. Conflict, contrast, and difference are – clearly – relational terms that cannot signify without their implicit counterparts: harmony, identity, and sameness. One 'unravelling' of the speech-community notion that may be attractive is that proposed by Milroy (1981), who argues for a sociolinguistic modelling that captures the intricate, intersecting, and overlapping networks of cultural and linguistic relation which individual speakers construct, in the process making diverse acts of identity (see Le Page and Tabouret-Keller 1985) with a spectrum of other speakers. But for those concerned to emphasize the workings of 'gross' categorizations, such as class or gender domination, the social-networks model may be unattractive, since it does less to dramatize the effects of such larger factors.

If linguistics has begun to embrace a much broader field of enquiry, beyond abstract rule formulations, literary criticism has also developed along lines other than the indirect reinforcement of normative values (criticism as refined and 'improving' conversation; for an ingenious but controversial revaluation of the notion of 'conversation' in humanistic discourse, see Rorty 1982). Influential critics are those who acknowledge and analyse the cultural conventions and conditions affecting what a society admits as artistic literature, the intricate network of (often binary) categorizations, privileging one, excluding or marginalizing the other, investing with voice here, silencing there – the complex but substantial (shifting) system of values and significations on the basis of which meanings and evaluations are made. Artistic literature is thus newly attended to, in such studies, as continuous with all other language uses, even while lacking the immediate communicational function or illocutionary force of most language use.

At the same time, however, it seems clear that in some ways literature does remain unlike much everyday language use – not just in its high status within a society, but in such features of construction as the degree of revision that writers apply to their texts. Following Ochs's distinctions between various types of planned and unplanned discourse (Ochs 1979), literature might be treated as 'written to be read, then rewritten to be read'. The writing of literature is often highly self-conscious, and this reflexivity may reach a point where there can be said to be a focus on the message for the message's own sake (Jakobson 1960). But such radical reflexivity is a potential rather than a necessary condition. Lodge's important amendments to Jakobson's claims are worth holding in mind: thoroughly message-focused literature is literary language at its most material and metaphorical, but a great deal of literature is (read as) less thoroughly self-focused, more other-focused, more conventionally referential, communicative, and, to use the Jakobsonian term, metonymical. Mention may be made here of Attridge's excellent reassessment of Jakobson's seminal 'Closing statement: linguistics and poetics', and the commitment therein to 'objective' linguistic explanations of poetic language (Attridge 1987).[1] As Attridge shows, Jakobson's own orientation towards objectivist analysis of the palpable form (Jakobson refers to the latter as the 'message', although 'text' would be a more usual label) means that his 'functions' and functionalism are of a severely attenuated kind:

> [The] avoidance of any appeal to the reader, and to the values or expectations he or she brings to the text, is part of a wider elision of the cultural determination of literature itself, in its many changing and differently interpreted forms, though the word 'function' remains like the ghost of these excluded possibilities.
>
> (p. 40–1)

6.2 Style and the bi-planar model of language

Whatever the degree of metaphoricality of a particular literary text, the standard treatment of that text's style has fitted well with the equally standard model of language as a fixed bi-planar system mapping forms on to meanings. This theory, reinvigorated by Saussure in the twentieth century, propounds that two essential levels in language production and description are those of surface linguistic forms (morphological/phonological) and underlying semantic contents. A general principle is asserted, namely that surface forms are systematically and predictably relatable to underlying abstract semantic contents.

This bi-planar model has long presented itself as an irrefutable foundation of western linguistic study, with the consequence that many of the discussions of linguistic topics I shall draw on have themselves been shaped and coloured by at least latent bi-planar assumptions. Indeed, the 'new' twentieth-century science of linguistics is bi-planar to its Saussurean roots and is only now experiencing, in any widespread and consequential way, a painful, resisted process of demythologizing (see especially Harris 1981 and 1987; Taylor 1980). There are many facets to Harris's critique of orthodox bi-planar linguistic theorizing, and it would be perilous to attempt a summary here. What follows are brief descriptive remarks on Harris's objections, and on some features of his contrasting, 'integrationalist', perspective. For Harris the two interrelated assumptions of the contemporary language myth are that language is telementational in function (that words convey speaker A's thoughts, along the linguistic channel, to hearer B), and that this telementation is guaranteed by the fact that a language is a fixed code (the thoughts in the various heads of members of a language community are firmly linked to the verbal symbols in use, thanks to a fixed, collective code). Such a scenario of determinate telementation has been instrumental to the spread of the idea that human linguistic activity is machine-like, made possible by complex cerebral mechanisms, and eventually open to mechanical replication, when sufficiently intelligent computers are designed. Such assumptions, however, run counter to the whole purpose of language and our everyday experience of its situated unpredictability. Over and against bi-planar decontextualizations and mechanicalities, Harris insists upon the routine unexpectedness of language use, its everyday creativity (not the impoverished sense of creativity – rule-bound rearrangements of predetermined units – allowed in standard approaches), and the cotemporal integratedness of verbal and non-verbal activity. Some representative extracts from Harris (1981) are offered below:

> The basic principle which an integrational linguistics will be concerned to give adequate expression to is that language is continuously created by the interaction of individuals in specific communication situations. It is this interaction which confers relevance upon the participants' past experience with words; and not, as orthodox linguistics would have us believe, past experience (that is to say, mastery of 'the language') which determines the communicational possibilities of their present interaction.
>
> (Harris 1981, p. 167)

> The central indeterminacy of all communication is indeterminacy of what is meant. ... Insofar as what is meant is determinate, it can be only a provisional determinacy, relativised to a particular interactional situation.
>
> (1981, p. 167)

> If language is a game at all, it is a game we mostly make up as we go along. It is a communication game in which there is no referee, and the only rule that cannot be bent says that players shall improvise as best they can. ... An integrational linguistics would be concerned with the analysis of this improvisation as a function, simultaneously, of relevant past experience and a current communication situation. It would, however, give priority to the latter. ... What is important from an integrational perspective is not so much the fund of past linguistic experience as the individual's adaptive use of it to meet the communication requirements of the present.
>
> (1981, p. 187)

The limitations of stylistic theory predicated upon a conception of language as determinate telementation are amply exposed in Taylor (1980). There it is persuasively argued that the entire enterprise of structural stylistics, from Bally onwards, has been built on the flimsy foundations of bi-planar linguistics, and has accordingly been doomed to repeat the contradictions and arbitrary analytical moves first perpetrated by Bally. In a thorough critical review of work in structural stylistics from Bally through Jakobson and Riffaterre to the generativist stylisticians, Taylor concludes: 'The guiding principle throughout the development of structural stylistics has been linguistic reductionism. This principle holds that the effects produced in verbal communication have their causal source in observable features of the expression-plane' (1980, p. 104). Furthermore, Taylor notes, these produced stylistic effects are claimed to be shared uniformly by all readers:

> The assumption that stylistic content is inter-subjective has surfaced in every new specification. This is the assumption that a message communicates the same content to each of its addressees. The content actually *belongs* to the message ... Were this not to be true – so the argument goes – there would be no sense in speaking of a message *communicating* at all.
>
> (Taylor 1980, pp. 104–5; original emphases)

Taylor charts the failures of successive models to specify these proposed stylistic effects, arguing that, ignoring the disabling theoretical assumptions of bi-planar identical telementation which undermined their work from the outset, each theoretician in turn has claimed some sort of privileged access to unobservable mental events. In practice, such theorists were simply developing new ways of talking about mental experience, rather than properly characterizing mental experience:

> The result is a rather curious cause-effect study where the cause is supposed to be observable, but the identification of the effect remains a question of guesswork, tradition, and some rather autocratic theory-making. The empirical study of how language 'gives' us what we 'get' in communication continues to be frustrated by the impossibility of analysing just what it is we all do indeed 'get'.
>
> (Taylor 1980, p. 106)

Taylor urges that stylisticians – and linguisticians – adopt a new concept of communication, which would hold that in our perception and interpretation of speech events we are, individually, 'heavily influenced by situational, experiential, emotional, and social factors' (1980, p. 107).

A theme of such critiques of the fixed-code telementational orthodoxy in linguistic theorizing is that all models which claim to identify and predict fixed correlations between form and meaning in language behaviour tend towards error. We have no independent grounds for predicting meanings: these are always, from an integrationalist perspective, context-bound, individual-bound, and provisional. Analysts may therefore need to be content with reporting and understanding (apparent) uses. Relatedly, any stylistic theory of reading is doomed if it claims to capture, prescribe, or predict on the basis of what a particular stylistician 'does and thinks'. (The latter formulation echoes Sapir's succinct early definition of culture as what a society does and thinks, and seeks to emphasize that stylistics itself is a cultural activity and a culture-bound practice.) A stylistics model is a way of reading, a particular stylistician's preferred way of reading, and is as partial or contingent as any written grammar or dictionary. The latter, like objectivist stylistics, tend to invoke the protection and authority of 'impartial description' and 'educated usage'; but they are ultimately shaped by particular individuals and particular interests.

With those preliminary orientations in view, what is meant by 'a stylistic reading of a particular literary work'? What is the status of this process and product; and what might be the justification – linguistic or literary? To the extent that these questions are premised on a view of linguistics as a scientific study of a fixed bi-planar structural system, and on the received orthodoxy of literary criticism that it is the sensitive open-minded pursuit of *the* richest interpretation of the work as well-wrought icon of significations (an interpretation which is somehow the inalienable property of the text rather than of the reader), the questions may be misleading. Conventional – prevailing – linguistics and criticism have both miscast the relations between the individual and the community. Linguistics has assumed that meanings and interpretations are or can be shared, just as words seem to be. And professional criticism, while paying lip-service to the facts of private individual reading and interpretation, typically proceeds – through teaching, examinations, and publishing – to disallow much of the rich variety of proffered readings, to foster in readers a self-censorship of the 'eccentric' reading, and to privilege one (perhaps two or three, if it's a classic text) allegedly rich and widely accepted interpretation. Both enterprises suppress the active role of the individual addressee in verbal communication. A stylistics that does not face and challenge these facts about the disciplines which spawned it will simply be furnishing orthodox critical practice with another instrument (linguistics) with which to enforce its authoritarian and repressive readings of literature.

So as to resist both the objectivist and fixed-code tendencies of linguistic analysis and the discounting of variant interpretation practised by traditional criticism, I propose that stylistics be viewed as a way rather than a method – a confessedly partial or oriented act of intervention, a reading which is strategic, as all readings necessarily are. The attraction of the 'way' of stylistics lies in its attempt at public-ness, even as it acknowledges private-ness, unpredictability. If that is an unhappy compromise, it is not easy – from this perspective – to conceive of a happier one or a less compromised happiness. If we reject the privileging of undecidability of the wilder deconstructionists (Derrida himself seems not to be of their number), engaged in their private revels of pure textuality, we must inevitably grapple with (though we may avoid succumbing to) what Norris (1982, p. 113) has called 'the normative constraints of effective communication'. Be she never so radical in her reading, the critic's published interpretation of a text is necessarily norm-shaping, norm-creating. The acts of publication, inviting readers to read your views, entail struggling to compel or persuade readers to privilege your reading of a work over theirs – or at least to engage with your reading and (too often) submit to it through exhaustion, inertia, pressure of other demands. Hence the professionals' double-bind: damned if they do not publish, by effecting little intervention in their intellectual communities (to say nothing of the pressure to publish or cease to be professionally engaged), they are damned if they do publish, vulnerable to the complaint that their writing is authoritarian and prescriptive, coercive of readers and students.

In the circumstances, what is essential is a renewed self-critical awareness of the provisionality of one's reading, of the roots of description in rhetorical persuasion, and of the heterogeneity of cultural myths and tastes that contribute to the constitution of 'the literary' and the academic discipline of literature. Those cultural myths and tastes should not be characterized as arbitrary in the sense of random or beyond explanation (in the way that the arbitrary matching of the utterance of the sounds in [dag] in American English, with the concept 'dog', is beyond explanation). Rather they are undoubtedly motivated, but by a background of contingent circumstances rather than logical factors or timeless essentials of the human condition. Renewed awareness of the provisionality of interpretations, held up – but also held, trapped – in a complex net of contingently motivated assumptions and discriminations, should bring with it a renewed recognition that behind the bland nominalization 'the literary profession', a term without a referent, stands the reality of a process, an activity maintained in innumerable ways around the world: professing literature.

A stylistic reading is, in part, an artefact shaped by the adopted model and theory; but there is no alternative to this. There is no absolute or essential reading of a particular literary work, since there are no absolute context-free models or theories. Interpretation and persuasion are always at work. Paul B. Armstrong has put the case with admirable succinctness:

> The presuppositions of any interpretive method are both enabling and limiting. They give us a vantage point from which to construe the work – a specific place of observation, without which knowing would be impossible. They also furnish a set of expectations with which to pose questions to a work that would otherwise remain silent, and they provide guidance and inspiration as we begin to make guesses. But presuppositions are at the same time limiting because in opening up a work in a particular way they close off other potential modes of access. Every interpretive approach reveals something only by disguising something else that a competing method with different assumptions might disclose.
>
> (Armstrong 1983, p. 343)

Interestingly, both Fish (1980) and Armstrong (the latter explicitly following C. S. Peirce) appeal to the notion of the 'interpretive community' and communal agreement, as a ground for justifying continued adherence to particular interpretative presuppositions. For Fish, discussed more fully in the next section, interpretations derive from, and are validated and sustained by, particular communities of interpreters: groups of indefinite extent from whom derives and in whom resides the authority (provisional, local, community-bound) for such readings. That, says Fish, is all the authority ye have or need to have.

This clearly rejects one dominant set of myths in traditional western modes of literature study, namely that authorial intentions are crucial, the major goal of study, and that there is an ideal, 'full' reading of any text, like a Platonic form, in relation to which the dissonant versions of contending critics are only approximations. But the alternative position Fish sketches (Fish 1980) is in need of much more presentation and critique. It is never made clear just what these 'interpretive communities' are, where they are, how they are constituted, influenced, and changed. If one thinks of groups in the world to which one might readily attach the label 'community' – the community of Latter-Day Saints, Bristol's West Indian community, the European Economic Community – each such grouping is bound together, in the public imagination, by nominal adherence to a public and retrievable set of shared commitments, practices, and experiences. The world at large is well aware that these communities exist in some sense, and is aware that members of such communities manifest (freely or under duress) a preference for certain values or practices rather than others. Consequently, erstwhile members of these communities can opt out, explicitly and publicly withdraw from such affiliations, and the communities themselves may dissolve or divide under the pressure of conflicting interests: class, gender, nationality, and so on. Whether Fish's 'interpretive communities' exist at all, simply in the sense that, by standards of public accounting, the 'Bristol West Indian community' may be said to exist, remains to be demonstrated. There are perspectives from sociolinguistics, social theory, and cultural criticism that may be helpful here, including the following: Goffman (1971, 1981), Halliday (1978), Berger and Luckmann (1967), Said (1982), Foucault (1972), Giddens (1979), and Anderson (1983).

Those sceptical of Fish's notions that the authority of interpretations rests with communities and that interpretation is all, often ask what these acts of interpreting are interpretations *of*. For those wedded to a goal of comprehensive description of the 'interpretative competence' of an interpretative community, there is the awful prospect of an infinite regress (the loadedness of the word 'regress' here should not be ignored), of reading as entering the abyss. Once a belief is unpicked, its interpretative roots specified (to the extent that this is possible), it ceases to be the *fons et origo* of one's interpretative practices – those identified roots now are, instead. In the view of Knapp and Michaels (1982) this points to the irrelevance of theory to practice; for practice is guided by true belief, and that, they argue, cannot be held and unpicked at the same time. Similarly, Armstrong (1983, p. 348) has written, probably with intentional understatement: 'There is something a priori about accepting any set of presuppositions as our hermeneutic point of departure.' Countering Knapp and Michaels, Walter Davis (1984) has argued that a degree of reflexive critique of one's interpretative groundings is both possible and relevant. One wonders if the dispute does not hinge on what is felt to be useful and relevant critique: while, with Knapp and Michaels, we might accept that we cannot 'do' critical interpretation and simultaneously reflect on its grounds, yet, with Davis, we might hold that a subsequent interrogation of the principles, rationales, and strategies we appeared to be guided by in our critical practice is possible, and that such a diachronic perspective is useful, in that we learn the logic of the lessons of our past interpretative practice.

What, then, of stylistics, and its interpretative foundations in language description? Cannot language description, like any other descriptive-cum-interpretative base, be unpicked, analysed, dissolved? In principle, yes; but not in practice, if we continue to want to see poems as a public discourse that can be in some sense and to some degree shared by diverse readers. The pull of convention, collectivity, normativity, social cohesion, and accommodation interacts dialectically with individualism and consciousness of self.

6.3 Literary linguistics and its critics

Literary linguistics, or linguistic criticism – the gathering of linguistic information about a literary text, and the use of that information in critical interpretation of the text – has aims and practices related to those of many stylisticians. But it is to be contrasted with some of the stylistics of the 1960s, and Jakobsonian poetics, in the relative modesty of its programme and expectations. The weaknesses of earlier versions of stylistics have been amply noted in recent years (e.g. in Fowler 1975 and 1979). What is newly clear is that close study of the language features of a text may often be valuable to the literary critic, but that such study can never supplant interpretation and criticism more broadly conceived (not least because stylistics itself entails various interpretative and critical assumptions, which too often pass unnoted). In this study I want to demonstrate in addition that familiar procedures such as simple frequency counts, comparisons with norms (chiefly those derived from the text's own 'economy'), and so on are also of value, so long as those norms are not canonized as absolutes, and so long as the linguistic statistician remains mindful of all the contextual variations and influences affecting the textual form. Earlier studies that might be claimed to lie within such a tradition include Spitzer (1948), Halliday (1964, 1971), and Bronzwaer (1970).

During the past twenty years, in the field of linguistics applied to literature, a story of frustration seems to have predominated, a showing and telling of what stylistics cannot do. In the more recent past the story has seemed in danger of final resolution, with stylisticians caught helplessly on the Fish 'hook' – the accounts, reprinted in Fish (1980), of how more-objective-than-thou stylisticians have traded shamelessly on unexamined and indefensible assumptions, assumptions without which the attractions of stylistics are, to say the least, considerably diminished.

In 'What is stylistics and why are they saying such terrible things about it?'[2] Fish criticizes the work of Milic (1967), Ohmann (1971, 1972), and Thorne (1965, 1970) for its fondness for mentalist and interpretative leaps. Transformational grammar, Fish argues, is particularly conducive of bad stylistics: 'For since its formalisms operate independently of semantic and psychological processes (are neutral between production and reception) they can be assigned any semantic or psychological value one may wish them to carry' (p. 99). He sees no comfort in contextualization: that way leads only to a geometric expansion of rules to the point of chaos. He turns to Halliday's influential article (1971) on transitivity and agency in the language(s) of Golding's *The Inheritors* to argue that in Halliday, just as in Milic and others, there are the same unproven assumptions that 'syntactic preferences correlate with habits of meaning' (p. 102) and that the yoking of grammar to interpretation is not arbitrary. By way of refutation of these allegedly suspect moves, Fish suggests that, instead of what he sees as Halliday's Darwinian interpretation of the supplanting of the primitive people by the more sophisticated tribe within the novel, there could be an Edenic view of the innocent non-manipulative state of the former group.

To this, however, one might assent enthusiastically, arguing that both interpretations are supported by the grammatical contrasts Halliday notes. By prevailing conventions and community preference, the potential infinity of possible interpretations is discounted by most readers, constrained by a desire for sharedness of literary experience. With that constraint at work, along with many other socially sustained conventions and evaluations, certain interpretations may, with or without dialectical negotiation, be arrived at and sanctioned by a particular community occupying a particular sociohistorical position. In the western liberal-humanist academic communities to which Fish and Halliday both belong, the Edenic and Darwinian 'approaches' to *The Inheritors* are elements in the two major perspectives on this novel. Literary linguistics does not adopt the assumption that *the* meaning is in the syntax, as Fish portrays it as doing, but rather makes the assumption that syntactic (and lexical) characteristics (a less ambiguous term than 'preferences') themselves often carry meanings. And the rationale for these meanings can often be corroborated independently. Fish's general case, however, against any totalizing stylistic account or characterization of a text remains persuasive; and he rightly emphasizes that different contexts yield different meanings.

One wonders, however, whether Fish would still take the sceptical line concerning stylistics that he formerly adopted towards Halliday and others. More recent writings point to his conceding that stylistics, like any other constraining set of interpretative strategies, proceeds on assumptions that are not merely unproven but unprovable. Unless one adopts the early Chomskyan view that syntax is independent of meaning, autonomous of semantics, there is nothing to stop the analyst assuming that variations in syntax, like variations in lexis or pronunciation or clothes, may convey an intended meaning from an addresser to an addressee. I doubt that Fish would any longer question this. But what he might and I must question is whether a particular syntactic variation, in general or on a particular occasion, will necessarily convey an identical import to all readers. If we reject the identical-import assumption, then the interpretative or explanatory power of syntactic stylistics seems to be nil. There is some restoration of power, however, if, maintaining our distrust of the facile reductivism of the identical-import assumption, we yet counterpose to it the recognition that syntax like lexis is a part of a necessarily public enterprise, language, necessarily sustained by means of habitual and conventional imports for its syntax, lexis, and so on.

Fish's view is that the reader is always 'already oriented in the direction of specific concerns and ... expectations': in a characteristically bald assertion of the reader's alleged omnipotence, and temporarily blind to the dialectical practice in which the reader's assumptions and those of the text interact, he declares that the reader manipulates the text, and never the reverse. With such premises, the need for an 'affective stylistics' specifying the reader's assumptions, expectations, and so on, in the face of any particular word or verbal pattern, is quite clear.

But even this affective-stylistic model carries with it its own arbitrarily privileged method and presuppositions, as Fish lucidly exposes in his book, *Is There a Text in this Class?: The Authority of Interpretive Communities* (1980). By gathering together, in sequence, his major articles over the previous ten years, the book presents a clear picture of Fish's marked shift in critical emphasis away from the 'self-sufficient' text, in favour of the reader's experience of the text, as a developing, temporally extended process of actualizing meanings. It is also a shift away from treating the reader as mere instrument, a key for unlocking text-bound meanings, towards revaluing that reader as in dynamic relation to the text, bringing to it his or her own expectations, which in turn enter into the reader's construction of text-related meanings. Fish's reader is thus engaged, active, and responsible.

Much of this is most sharply set forth in the introduction to the book. Here Fish grapples again with formalism, concluding that a critic's interpretative principles (e.g. that readers are performers of interpretation) are too often self-fulfilling prophecies, inducing a particular focus on certain formal features which can then, by a sleight of hand, be named as the 'true and initial' source of the produced interpretation. It is interpretative strategies which give texts their shape, but such strategies are not individual (as might lead to an anarchic pluralism of readings) but 'community property' (1980, p. 14). They are sustained or authorized by 'interpretive communities', made up of 'those who share interpretive strategies not for reading but for writing texts, for constituting their properties' (1980, p. 14). Reader-response criticism itself, then, is more accurately a rewriting (by readers) of texts, on the basis of a shared interpretative orientation. Steven Mailloux articulates the shift in his own thinking, as well as that of Fish, from an 'innocent' reader-response criticism to an 'aware' focus on interpretation, when he summarizes thus:

> It is true that reader-response criticism claims to approximate closely the content of reading experiences that are always assumed to pre-exist the critical performance. But what in fact takes place is quite different: the critical performance fills those reading experiences with its own interpretive moves. Like all critical approaches, reader-response criticism is a set of interpretive conventions that constitutes what it claims to describe.
>
> (Mailloux 1979, p. 107)

Although Fish does not state this explicitly, his thesis appears to be analogous to one model of how a natural language works. All competent users of a language, it is often thought, share a remarkably complex interrelated and interdependent set of interpretative conventions for expressing and constituting their shared world (not truly a code, since there is no 'message' prior to this 'code'). This is the grammar that no grammar or linguistics book has ever adequately captured. So far so good, but the picture is perhaps more complicated than it has been painted to be by Fish and others. For there is plenty of evidence to call into question both the idea of language communities as discrete, sharply bounded groups, and the idea that competence is 'full' and largely guided by innate predispositions. Competence in a language, in actuality, is often noticeably differential, subject to various constraints on its full acquisition; and the assumption that there is an evident and necessary arrival at shared usage, conventionally agreed patterns of interpretation and signification, all by some marvellously egalitarian process of induction, also seems far from the truth. As in life, so in language in general, so also in the language activity of literary criticism in particular, we have differential access to the formulation and invocation of interpretative strategies.

What Fish's *Is There a Text in this Class?* signally lacks is the extended discussion of the nature of interpretative communities which his theory requires. Members of the same community will necessarily maintain stability of interpretations 'because they will see (and by seeing, make) everything in relation to that community's assumed purposes and goals' (1980, p. 15). There is not so much an individualized literary competence (as in Culler 1975) as a normative perspective and a shared, communal competence. The term 'community' is an attractive one, connoting a cohesive, caring fraternity of equals. But is it an accurate description of the sort of group which confirms and sustains any critical reading? More specifically, do all communities merit approval (presumably not), and how do they change or become changed? Or would the theory claim that communities do not change, rather that new communities come into existence? The same difficulty emerges here as in the Saussurean idealized community sharing a common *langue*: no account is advanced as to how the evident changes in community and in *langue* actually occur – a silence that fosters the suspicion that any such accounting would expose the inadequacy of the prior conceptualizations of *langue* and community. We need much more information about the several roles played by readers, authors, and texts in the shaping and changing of interpretative communities. It seems too naive to suppose that all community members are equally free to lobby for revisions in interpretations, since there is ample evidence that hierarchies of power, influence, patronage, intelligence, access to the channels of dissemination of views, and adeptness at and interest in persuasion exist. It is easier to rehearse such general observations than to assess in detail the different factors involved, but a necessary beginning is an acknowledgement that diverse and opposed interests are involved, that criticism involves intellectual resistance and struggle. The objection to Fish that comes from Cain (1981, p. 86) is along such lines: 'His theory lacks a politically charged vocabulary, which would reveal "interpretation" to be a system of difficult, even violent, exchanges, with forced entrances of new communities and exclusions of old ones.' The analysis might well benefit from an orientation which was receptive to recent arguments in sociology for a 'conflict methodology'. On the other hand perhaps too much is made of the idea of interpretative conflict amounting to 'violent exchange'. Personalities apart, interpretations themselves and the whole tenor of literary discourse seem far more typically characterized by a spirit of polite and co-operative negotiation.

In short, Fish's book has been an invaluable corrective to the objectivist mentalist tendencies that stylistics had long nurtured (since Bally), tendencies which came to maturity in work of the 1960s. Introducing the second of the book's two chapters on stylistics, Fish writes: 'Here I assert that the act of description is itself interpretive and that therefore at no point is the stylistician even within hailing distance of a fact that has been independently (that is, objectively) specified' (1980, p. 246). Most stylisticians, it seems, are now quite prepared to renounce claims to any such 'objective specification of facts', so that the impact of the reproof is considerably reduced. However, looking again at Fish's formulation, it may be worth reflecting upon whether, as Fish assumes, *independent* specification and *objective* specification amount to the same thing. For a conception of stylistics such as my own does persist in the fond hope that independent specification of linguistic forms and communicative functions, as suggested (certainly not ordained) by preferred, habitual, and conventional usage, is some guide to both formulaic conformity and creative departure in verbal art. As soon as the word 'independently' is used, we must ask, 'independently of what?', since the claim of independence is necessarily made in relation to certain interests or factors rather than others, these others often effecting veiled determinations of description. In the case of stylistics, the *dependence* on the analyst's linguistic descriptive system, and the dependence of this upon the analyst's understanding of what a language is and does, are the declared, public, and – perhaps – corrigible groundings.

From his literary perspective Fish attacks the 'strong theory' stylistics of Jakobson, Riffaterre, and Ohmann which Taylor (1980) has challenged from a linguistic one. One objection is to various claims that the phonology of particular poems is mimetic of their sense – stylistic games which are said to be just too easy to play. For such passages alone the book should be recommended reading for anyone contemplating linguistic study of literary texts. Fish rightly argues that the stylistician's focus on a particular phonological or syntactical pattern in a text is itself an interpretative act. As I hope to have suggested, this in itself does not constitute an overwhelming argument to stop doing stylistics unless (a) that interpretative act is shown to be incoherent or ill grounded, or (b) more coherent interpretative acts are presented, and preferably both.

No such moves are made in the book under discussion. We are reminded that any description we offer is an imposed interpretation, that responses are occasioned by interpretative frameworks which themselves are products, not 'real', objective *ur*-sources, because there are no such things. No more than Archimedes can we find one firm spot on which to stand so as to move the earth. To the troubled question 'What, then, is interpretation an interpretation of?' Fish cheerfully assures us we cannot finally know the answer: we must (will, inevitably) carry on, not quite as before, more aware that we are necessarily interpreting interpreting.

The question of interpretative groundings that Fish raises is also approached by Dillon, from a Whorfian perspective. Dillon argues that stylisticians make a claim which roughly parallels a Whorfian one, namely that 'analyzing the structure of a literary work can yield insight into the way the work conceptualizes experience (or "the world of the poem")' (Dillon 1982, p. 73). The crucial issue in such a claim, he notes, concerns what kind of knowledge such formal analysis is taken to yield. The first thing Dillon emphasizes is that neither Whorfianism nor stylistics is so mechanical or arbitrary a procedure as Fish pretends. All such analysts are intent on grasping a 'fashion of speaking' (of a culture, or an author), the linguistic patterning when viewed as comprehensively as possible, no matter how atomic the intermediate stages of analysis – the focusing on forms and elements – may appear. Intrinsic to this effort of generalization will be varying conclusions due to varying interpretative assumptions:

> The characterization of the unique fashion of speaking is as much a product of the interpreter's art as the characterization of the culture's world view. This art in both instances is largely intuitive and cannot be reduced to a method.
>
> (Dillon, 1982, p. 74)

Dillon rightly dismisses the idea that stylistics can be a discovery procedure for finding interpretations or a means of validating an interpretation, and suggests that such imagined scientific purposes – discovery, validation – should not be applied to this activity.

> One engages in formal analysis to specify and articulate one's own response and perhaps to share it with others. ... The proper response to a successful piece of stylistic analysis would be 'I see' and not 'You've proved your point'.
>
> (Dillon, 1982, p. 75)

Ironically, by contrast with this innocent reliance on the interpreter's touch, there is much shrewd calculation, even method, in Fish's version of the business of criticism. That business is 'to establish by political and persuasive means ... the set of interpretive assumptions from the vantage of which the evidence (and the facts and the intentions and everything else) will hereafter be specifiable' (Fish 1980, p. 16). Again, it is striking that Fish writes of a 'vantage', that Armstrong – in the passage quoted above – writes of an interpretative 'vantage point', and that others speak of a *point d'appui*: all recognize that the given perspective or frame is both advantageous and a taking advantage. Determining our interpretative codes seems to be the project Culler has in mind when he writes of a 'systematic poetics' or 'a semiotics of reading' (Culler 1981). Such a semiotics of reading has not emerged, he complains, because time and time again, from Frye to Mailloux, writers have slipped – or retreated – from reading theory back to traditional interpretative criticism (see also the valuable recent survey of reader-response criticism and theory in Freund 1987). The former is descriptive and systematic, the latter attempts to adjudicate and persuade. Of course Fish would be eager to remind those who claim such a distinction that every description is an interpretative strategy of persuasion. However, as I have tried to argue earlier, that game is just too easy to play. It is keeping the politics of interpretation at a removed level where, in the words of Mitchell, 'the infinite regress of understanding can be contemplated the way abysses usually are – as thrilling landscapes of the sublime' (1982, p. vi). It is itself the adoption of a particular interpretative strategy, in which a strictly limited reflexivity and self-criticism are adduced.

If Fish has by and large declined to explore the groundings we adduce from our interpretative codes, many others, it should be emphasized, have begun that work, from a perspective that is semiotic in a broad sense. Emphases vary greatly, but contributions that range from the cultural semiotics of Barthes and Eco, through the work of Culler, Mailloux, Foucault, and Lotman, and, from a linguistic perspective, Halliday, may be noted. Particularly innovative has been feminist criticism and its uncovering of interpretative groundings (see, for example, Gilbert and Gubar 1979; Moi 1985; Modleski 1982).

Notes

1 Attridge's paper is reprinted in chapter 2 of this volume. Page references to Attridge's paper as it appears in chapter 2 will be given in the text.
2 Page references are to Fish's paper as it appears in chapter 5 of this volume.

References

ANDERSON, B. 1983: *Imagined communities*. London: Verso.

ARMSTRONG, P. B. 1983: The conflict of interpretations and the limits of pluralism. *Publications of the Modern Language Association of America* 98, 341–52.

ATTRIDGE, D. 1987: Closing statement: Linguistics and poetics in retrospect. In Fabb, N., Attridge, D., Durant, A. and MacCabe, C. (eds), *The linguistics of writing*. New York: Methuen, 15–32.

BERGER, P. and LUCKMANN, T. 1967: *The social construction of reality*. Harmondsworth: Penguin.

BRONZWAER, W. J. M. 1970: *Tense in the novel*. Groningen: Wolters Noordhoff.

CAIN, W. 1981: Constraints and politics in the literary theory of Stanley Fish. *Bucknell Review* 26, 75–88.

CULLER, J. 1975: *Structuralist poetics*. London: Routledge and Kegan Paul.

—1981: *The pursuit of signs*. London: Routledge and Kegan Paul.

DAVIS, W. 1984: Offending the profession. *Critical Inquiry* 10, 706–18.

DILLON, G. 1982: Whorfian stylistics. *Journal of Literary Semantics* 11, 73–7.

FISH, S. 1980: *Is there a text in this class?* Cambridge, Mass.: Harvard University Press.

FOUCAULT, M. 1972: *The archaeology of knowledge*. London: Tavistock.

FOWLER, R. 1971: *The languages of literature*. London: Routledge and Kegan Paul.

—(ed.) 1975: *Style and structure in literature*. Oxford: Blackwell.

—1979: Linguistics and, and versus, poetics. *Journal of Literary Semantics* 8, 3–21.

FREUND, E. 1987: *The return of the reader*. London: Methuen.

GIDDENS, A. 1979: *Central problems in social theory*. Berkeley: University of California Press.

GILBERT, S. and GUBAR, S. 1979: *The madwoman in the attic: The woman writer and the nineteenth century literary imagination*. New Haven: Yale University Press.

GOFFMAN, E. 1971: *Relations in public*. New York: Harper and Row.
—1981: *Forms of talk*. Philadelphia: University of Pennsylvania Press.
GROSS, M. 1979: On the failure of generative grammar. *Language* 55, 859–95.
HALLIDAY, M. A. K. 1964: Descriptive linguistics in literary studies. *English Studies Today* 3, 25–39.
—1971: Linguistic function and literary style: An inquiry into the language of William Golding's *The Inheritors*. In Chatman, S. (ed.), *Literary style: A symposium*. London: Oxford University Press, 330–68.
—1978: *Language as social semiotic*. London: Edward Arnold.
HARRIS, R. 1980: *The language makers*. London: Duckworth.
—1981: *The language myth*. London: Duckworth.
—1987: *The language machine*. London: Duckworth.
HUDSON, R. 1980: *Sociolinguistics*. Cambridge: Cambridge University Press.
ITKONEN, E. 1984: Concerning the ontological question in linguistics. *Language and Communication* 4, 241–6.
JAKOBSON, R. 1960: Closing statement: Linguistics and poetics. In Sebeok, T. (ed.), *Style in language*. Cambridge, Mass.: MIT Press, 350–77.
KNAPP, S. and MICHAELS, W. 1982: Against theory. *Critical Inquiry* 8, 723–42.
KOERNER, K. 1983: The Chomskyan 'revolution' and its historiography: A few critical remarks. *Language and Communication* 3, 147–69.
LABOV, W. 1972: *Language in the inner city*. Philadelphia: University of Pennsylvania Press.
LE PAGE, R. and TABOURET-KELLER, A. 1985: *Acts of identity*. Cambridge: Cambridge University Press.
LODGE, D. 1977: *The modes of modern writing*. London: Edward Arnold.
LOVE, N. 1981: Making sense of Chomsky's revolution. *Language and Communication* 1, 275–87.
—1988: Ideal linguistics. *Language and Communication* 8, 69–84.
McLAIN, R. 1977: The problem of 'style'. *Language and Style* 10, 52–65.
MAILLOUX, S. 1979: Learning to read: Interpretation and reader-response criticism. *Studies in the Literary Imagination* 12, 93–108.
MILIC, L. T. 1967: *A quantitative approach to the style of Jonathan Swift*. The Hague: Mouton.
MILROY, L. 1981: *Language and social networks*. Oxford: Blackwell.
MITCHELL, W. J. T. 1982: Editor's introduction: The politics of interpretation. *Critical Inquiry* 9,1, iii–viii.
MODLESKI, T. 1982: *Loving with a vengeance: Mass-produced fantasies for women*. Hamden: Archon Books.
MOI, T. 1985: *Sexual/textual politics*. London: Methuen.
NORRIS, C. 1982: *Deconstruction: Theory and practice*. London: Methuen.
OCHS, E. 1979: Planned and unplanned discourse. In Givón, T. (ed.), *Syntax and semantics* Vol. 12. New York: Academic Press, 51–80.
OHMANN, R. 1971: Speech, action and style. In Chatman, S. (ed.), *Literary style: A symposium*. London: Oxford University Press, 241–54.
—1972: Instrumental style: Notes on the theory of speech as action. In Kachru, B. and Stahlke, H. (eds.), *Current trends in stylistics*. Edmonton: Linguistic Research Inc., 115–41.
PATEMAN, T. 1983: What is a language? *Language and Communication* 3, 101–27.

PRATT, M. L. 1977: *Toward a speech-act theory of literary discourse*. Bloomington: Indiana University Press.

—1987: Linguistic utopias. In Fabb, N., Attridge, D., Durant, A. and MacCabe, C. (eds.), *The linguistics of writing*. New York: Methuen, 48–66.

ROMAINE, S. 1983: Variable rules, OK? Or can there be sociolinguistic grammars? *Language and Communication* 5, 53–67.

—1988: *Pidgin and creole languages*. London: Longman.

RORTY, R. 1982: *Consequences of pragmatism*. Minnesota: University of Minnesota Press.

SAID, E. 1982: *The world, the text, and the critic*. London: Faber.

SPITZER, L. 1948: *Linguistics and literary history*. Princeton: Princeton University Press.

TAYLOR, T. 1980: *Linguistic theory and structural stylistics*. Oxford: Pergamon Press.

THORNE, J. P. 1965: Stylistics and generative grammars. *Journal of Linguistics* 1, 49–59.

—1970: Generative grammar and stylistic analysis. In Lyons, J. (ed.), *New horizons in linguistics*. Harmondsworth: Penguin, 185–97.

Part IV

Pedagogical stylistics

7

Stylistics: An approach to stylistic analysis

H. G. Widdowson

The purpose of stylistic analysis is to investigate how the resources of a language code are put to use in the production of actual messages. It is concerned with patterns of use in given texts.

The user of a language acquires two kinds of knowledge: knowledge of the rules of the code and knowledge of the conventions which regulate the use of these rules in the production of messages. The first kind ensures that what he or she says is grammatical, and the second kind ensures that what he or she says is appropriate. Both kinds of knowledge are essential if the user of the language is to enter into effective communication with his fellows. Together they provide language with what is generally recognized as its unique feature: its creativity. It has often been wondered at that human beings continually generate utterances which they have never spoken or heard before; what is equally to be wondered at is the fact that these novel utterances are understood. The reason for this is that though they are novel as manifestations of code, they are familiar as messages. The user of a language is creative because the novel linguistic forms he generates function as familiar units of communication: if they did not, he would only generate gibberish.

The impression is sometimes given that only code is systematic, so that the task of textual analysis is to count the occurrence of tokens of the types of unit discovered in the code. But it is clear that messages are produced in accordance with systems of social convention, otherwise they would not be understood; so that units of the message are not simply tokens but types in their own right definable in terms of social communication. Stylistics is concerned with such message types; its purpose is to discover what linguistic units count as in communication and how the effects of different conventions reveal themselves in the way messages are organized in texts.

Stylistics, then, is the study of the social function of language and is a branch of what has come to be called sociolinguistics. It aims to characterize texts as pieces of communication. It is not part of its purpose to provide a means of discovering the different social functions of language: it is technological rather than scientific in that it works on data provided by others. Texts are assumed to be given.

In this chapter we shall confine the scope of stylistics even further to a consideration of literary texts. This should not be taken as an indication of the limited applicability of stylistic analysis, but as an indication of the limited applications that have so far been made. There is as yet no satisfactory heuristic that can be used to extend stylistics to a consideration of all 'varieties' of language, though tentative beginnings have been made. Meanwhile, we focus our attention on literature.

There are two reasons why it is fitting that stylistics should first concern itself with literary texts: one is methodological and relates to the nature of literature as such, and the other is pedagogical and relates to the value stylistic analysis has for the teaching of language.

To take the first reason first: there are certain features about literature as a mode of communication which are unique and which simplify the task of stylistics. In the first place, it does not fit into any conventional communication situation. In all other forms of language use, we have a sender of the message and a receiver, the addresser and the addressee grammatically marked as the first and second person respectively. The third person is incorporated, as it were, as reference within the message itself. Both first and second persons are necessary in the communication situation: whenever we use language we assume a receiver. Now in literature we constantly find that the normal indivisible amalgam of sender/first person and receiver/second person has been split up. Thus the writer is separated from the addresser and the reader from the addressee. As a consequence of this, all kinds of curious participants enter into the communication situation: among addressers for example we find insects (in Gray) a brook (in Tennyson) and among addressees innumerable aspects of nature: mountains, rivers, flowers, birds and so on, as well as a Grecian urn (in Keats) and, of course, McGonagall's immortal 'railway bridge over the silvry Tay'. The first and second person then has, along with the third person, become incorporated into the text. This points to the essential difference between literary and other uses of language: in literature, the message is text-contained, and presupposes no wider context so that everything necessary for its interpretation is to be found within the message itself. All other uses of language on the other hand find some place in the general social matrix; they develop from antecedent events and presuppose consequent events; they are contextualized in a social continuity. Clearly, to characterize the messages in a conventional text, some account must be taken of its social environment. It is this which complicates matters and makes stylistic analysis difficult. With literary texts, this problem does not cause such difficulties; generally speaking we can concentrate on the text itself without worrying about distracting social appendages. This is not to say, of course, that there are no problems. As we shall see there are plenty: most of them are corollaries of the unique feature of literature which has just been pointed out. But before turning to these, we must briefly mention the pedagogical reason which lends support to the concentration of stylistics on literary texts. This is important because it justifies the inclusion of stylistics within applied linguistics seen as an area of enquiry which brings the findings of linguistics to bear on the practical problems of language teaching.

By tradition, the study of literature has been regarded as a branch of aesthetics. As such it has been concerned with the total effect of literary texts as artistic wholes. Description has been by reference to artistic value, and the implication is that there are certain 'universals' of art which find expression in different ways according to media but which can be described in the same terms. Thus a poem, a painting and a piano concerto are different arrangements of universal artistic features realized in different media. Though this is not made explicit, literary criticism of the traditional kind makes appeal to a theory of aesthetics which postulates artistic universals. Unfortunately, the absence of explicitness is crucial. If, as seems on the face of it to be likely, it is possible to describe literature by reference to artistic universals, then it would seem to be essential to establish just what these universals are and to devise a metalanguage for their description. Meanwhile, the literary critic assumes that the artistic value of a work is available to intuitive awareness, and he makes use of an impressionistic terminology to communicate this awareness to others. The difficulty with this procedure is that it makes appeal to intuitions which the reader may not share with the critic. This is generally the case with language learners whose knowledge of the language has not reached the point at which they have an intuitive sense of the subtlety of language use. In this case the critic's impressionistic description can find no response. This is where stylistics can make its contribution. Its concern is with the patterning of language in texts and it makes no presupposition as to artistic value. By investigating the way language is used in a text, it can make apparent those linguistic patterns upon which an intuitive awareness of artistic values ultimately depend. It provides a basis for aesthetic appreciation by bringing to the level of conscious awareness features of the text otherwise only accessible to trained intuition. In brief, stylistics takes the language as primary and artistic values are regarded as incidental to linguistic description: literary criticism, on the other hand, takes artistic values as primary and refers to language in so far as it serves as evidence for aesthetic assessments. Stylistics renders an essential service to language learning in that even if the learner does not develop an appreciation of literature as literature, he will have acquired an awareness of the way language functions in at least this form of communication: he will have developed an awareness of literature as language. This indicates how the study of literary texts can be correlated with the study of texts exemplifying other forms of social communication and suggests a means of co-ordinating the teaching of language and the teaching of literature (at present so often undertaken in mutual isolation) in a way which would be beneficial to both.

These then are two reasons which excuse, if they do not justify, the present restriction of stylistic analysis to literary texts. We can now proceed with outlining an approach to the characterization of such texts. We have already noted certain unique features of literary writing. In the following discussion we will follow up the implications of this observation and see where they lead us.

The irregular realization of the addresser/addressee relationship in literary writing is symptomatic of a general non-conformity with normal conventions of communication. As has already been pointed out literary messages do not find a place in the social matrix as do other messages: they presuppose no preceding events and anticipate no future action. They are complete in themselves, and their significance is accordingly enclosed within the limits of the form they take. On the other hand, the significance of normal messages derives in large part from external circumstances, from the social situations in which they occur. But literary messages are not only notable for their somewhat cavalier treatment of context, but also for their idiosyncratic deployment of the resources of the code. It has been frequently pointed out that literature, and in particular poetry, contains a good deal of language which is grammatically and semantically deviant. Furthermore, poetry makes use of one phonological unit – the metrical line – which occurs in no other use of language. Since the forms that literary messages take do not wholly conform to either the conventions of use or the rules of the code, the question arises: how do they manage to convey any meaning at all? And even if they do manage to convey meaning, what kind of meaning is it? The two questions are closely related, and in considering them we shall be defining the task which stylistic analysis must undertake.

Literary messages manage to convey meaning because they organize their deviations from the code into patterns which are discernible in the texts themselves. What happens is that the writer in breaking the rules of the code diminishes the meaning of language and then proceeds to make up for the deficiency by placing the deviant item in a pattern whereby it acquires meaning by relation with other items within the internal context of the message. Thus the relations set up within a text constitute a secondary language system which combines, and so replaces, the separate functions of what would conventionally be distinguished as code and context.

The interpretation of any text involves the recognition of two sets of relations: extra-textual relations between language items and the code from which they derive and intra-textual relations between language items within the context itself. What is unique about literary texts is that typically the two sets of relations do not converge to form one unit of meaning which represents a projection, as it were, from code into context. Instead, they overlap to create a unit of meaning which belongs to neither one nor the other: a hybrid unit which derives from both code and context and yet is a unit of neither of them. An illustration will help to clarify this.

R. B. Lees (1960) points out that the nouns in a language code, as recorded in a dictionary, do not, numerous as they are, supply all our needs for names. We cannot, for instance, simply utter the word 'coffee' on every occasion we wish to refer to this substance. In order to produce appropriate referring expressions we make use of rules in the code which permit us to combine this noun with other language items. Using such rules, we are able to compose phrases like 'The cup of coffee you left in the kitchen', 'A cup of black coffee' and so on, which refer to particular instances or manifestations of the substance coffee. Combinations of words as such, like 'A cup of black coffee', do not, of course, appear in the code: they are composed to meet the contingencies of the context. What we have to notice is that the 'projection' of items in the code into specific contexts involves no change of reference. The occurrences of the noun 'coffee' in the above phrases are instances of the general reference as registered in the code; instances which have been contextually particularized as units of the message. The change in the environment of a noun which enables it to play its part in contextual reference does not involve a change in its referential meaning, which is bestowed upon it by the code. Recognizing the contextual implications of a word does not involve a revision of the dictionary.

In literary writing, on the other hand, the case is often different. Consider the occurrence of the word 'coffee' in these lines of Alexander Pope:

> She went, to plain-work, and to purling brooks,
> Old fashioned halls, dull aunts, and croaking rooks:
> She went from opera, park, assembly, play,
> To morning walks, and prayers three hours a day;
> To part her time 'twixt reading and bohea;
> To muse, and spill her solitary tea;
> Or o'er cold coffee trifle with the spoon,
> Count the slow clock, and dine exact at noon
>> (Epistle to Miss Blount, on her leaving the town after the coronation.)

Now the context in which the word occurs makes it clear that it is meant to count as something more than a particular instance of a general reference. 'Cold coffee' here has a significance over and above that which is recoverable from the code. Trifling with a spoon over cold coffee is represented as a similar activity to counting the slow clock and dining exact at noon. Cold coffee is a sign of boredom. This is borne out further by the phonological relations between 'cold', 'coffee', 'spoon', and 'count', 'slow', 'clock' which associate all these words in a pattern, and by the words immediately preceding 'cold coffee' which are the onomatopoeic representation of a yawn. The intra-textual relations which are set up between the item 'coffee' and the other items in its immediate vicinity create a significance, then, beyond that which the item carries in the code. The recognition of the contextual implications of the word do involve a revision of its dictionary meaning, in this case in the form of an extension.

It might be thought that all that we are illustrating here is the familiar distinction between connotation and denotation, and that the preceding discussion simply amounts to saying that literature is characteristically connotative. The point is, however, that literature characteristically effaces the distinction between these two different types of meaning. Connotative meaning is generally taken to be a matter of personal associations, essentially idiosyncratic, and unsystematizable. But as we have seen, contextual meaning within literary texts is a result of the setting of linguistic items in a system of intra-textual relations. While one may regard it, therefore, as connotative with reference to the code, one must regard it as denotative with reference to the secondary language system established by the regularities of the context. The meaning of 'coffee' in Pope's lines is both connotative and denotative in a sense; and in a sense, of course, neither.

Let us look at another example from Pope:

Here files of pins extend their shining rows,
Puffs, powders, patches, bibles, billet-doux.

(The Rape of the Lock)

Here, 'bibles' acquires an additional significance in that it is made a member of the same class of objects as puffs and powders and other accoutrements of female vanity. As before, the association of the item in question with the other items in its environment is strengthened by phonological relations: we note the identical syllabic structure of the immediately preceding items and the fact that their initial consonants differ only in their absence of voice from the initial consonant of 'bibles'. The effect of all this, then, is to attribute to the word an additional significance derived entirely from the context in which it appears. This combines with the significance it has as an item in the code to create a hybrid unit of meaning. Clearly this is not recoverable from the code alone: no dictionary will include cosmetics among the defining features in an entry for 'bible'. Nor is it recoverable from the context alone – if we did not know the established referent for 'bible', of course, the ironic force of the line would be entirely lost. As a result we have objects littering Belinda's dressing table which are bibles, and yet not bibles; recognizably holy writ but somehow the same sort of thing as the trivia of female vanity at the same time.

We have seen how poetry tends to destroy the distinction between denotation and connotation to create hybrid meanings. We might note also that it has a way of blurring another well-established linguistic distinction: that which is commonly referred to as double articulation or duality of patterning. By this it is meant that language is structured on two different planes: that of phonology and that of syntax. But as we have seen from our consideration of Pope's lines, phonological structure can, in poetry, operate directly in establishing relations between different words; in this way it takes on some of the function which is normally the prerogative of syntax. It is by compounding linguistic distinctions in this way that literary language is able to express meanings other than those which are communicable by conventional means.

These are, then, very simple illustrations of how literary messages convey meaning, but before we move on to more complex examples we must consider the second and related question: what kind of meaning does a literary message convey?

We can begin by following the implications of the fact that language is essentially a social phenomenon. It serves a social purpose, and to put the matter simply, it does so by codifying those aspects of reality which a society wishes in some way to control. Language, then, can be regarded as a socially sanctioned representation of the external world. Without such a representation, the external world is a chaos beyond human control. In the beginning was the Word. The members of a society accept the codification which their language provides because it gives them a necessary sense of security. Reality is under control because they share a common attitude towards it by sharing a common means of communication. Communication can only take place if there are conventionally accepted ways of looking at the world. But now we come to the important point: because people as members of a society accept a conventional view of reality as a social convenience, it does not follow that as individuals they are not aware of reality beyond that which their language represents. Indeed, the existence of religion and art is evidence that they are very much aware of reality beyond the bounds of common communication and social sanction. Social conventions supply people's needs insofar as they are members of society, but they have needs as individuals which such conventions by their very nature are incapable of satisfying. Every society has some form of art and some form of religion, and these serve as a necessary outlet for individual attitudes whose expression would otherwise disrupt the ordered pattern of reality which society promotes and upon which its survival depends. Art and religion are a recognition that there is other reality apart from that which is, as it were, officially recommended. What, then, is the nature of this reality?

The first thing to notice is that it is both a part of conventional reality and yet apart from it. This will be clear from a brief consideration of religion, which deals in such contradictions on a large scale. Thus gods have human attributes and are both human and non-human at the same time, omnipresent and yet incarnate in particular animate forms: immortal, yet affected by mortal longings: conceived without benefit of natural processes and dying only to be reborn. This other reality, then, is related to that which is conventionally recognized in the same way as literary language is related to the conventional code. What literature, and indeed all art, does is to create patterns out of deviations from normality and these patterns then represent a different reality from that represented by the conventional code. In so doing, literature gives formal expression to the individual's awareness of a world beyond the reach of communal communication.

Having indicated how literary language conveys meanings, and what kinds of meanings they are which are conveyed, we can now have a closer look at some of the kinds of patterning which occur in literary texts and at the meanings they convey. We shall do this by analysing a poem. The reason why a poem has been chosen and not a piece of prose is that it is important for our purposes that we should investigate intra-textual relations within one complete message unit and exigencies of space rule complete prose texts out. It is obvious that patterns in a text can only be recognized as such when they are seen as parts of a whole. It is true that there is often a hierarchical arrangement of patterns, smaller ones functioning as constituents in larger ones and so on up to the total complex of patterns which constitute the whole, so it would be possible to exemplify types of patterns by selecting from different constituent levels. But such a procedure would be likely to be a somewhat arid academic exercise, and for an important reason. As will by now be apparent the unique mode of language organization to be found in literary texts is indistinguishable from the significance these texts have as messages. Since the texts create their own systems of language they inevitably create a different reality, and our awareness of one necessarily entails our awareness of the other. No purpose can be served in attempting to distinguish form from meaning. What we shall be concerned with, therefore, is not the exemplification of constituent patterns but the interpretation of complete textual units, that is to say, with messages as units of meaning.

Futility

Move him into the sun –
Gently its touch awoke him once,
At home, whispering of fields unsown.
Always it woke him, even in France,
Until this morning and this snow.
If anything might rouse him now
The kind old sun will know.

Think how it wakes the seeds –
Woke, once, the clays of a cold star.
Are limbs, so dear-achieved, are sides
Full-nerved – still warm – too hard to stir?
Was it for this the clay grew tall?
– O what made fatuous sunbeams toil
To break earth's sleep at all?

Wilfred Owen

How do we first set about discovering the patterns of language and reality which are presented in this poem? There is no rigid order of procedure; the technique is to pick on features in the text which appeal to first impression as unusual or striking in some way and then explore their ramifications.

Here we may begin by noticing that 'sun', an inanimate noun in the code, has been given the attributes of animacy in the context, and more particularly of humanness. Thus it is represented as touching the living sleeper to wake him up and as whispering in his ear. Further, its occurrence in the environment 'The kind old ... will know' suggests that it is to be equated with 'man' or 'woman' which would be normal collocates here. But we must notice that although the context confers human qualities on the sun, at the same time the word retains the quality of inanimacy which accompanies it from the code. The pronouns, we note, are inanimate. So we have here an example of a hybrid unit created by the overlap of extra-textual relations which link the word with the code and intra-textual relations which link the word with other items of language in the context. The sun here is both inanimate and human, and yet, of course, at the same time, neither. Having made this observation, we may now proceed to investigate how it relates to the rest of the text.

We may notice next that a recurrent theme in the text is the ability of the sun to awaken things – people, seeds, the earth; and that this theme runs throughout the poem, 'awoke', 'woke' and 'rouse' occurring in the first verse, and 'wakes', 'woke', 'stir', 'break ... sleep' in the second. Since we have established that the sun has both human and inanimate features, we might reasonably ask whether it is in its human or in its inanimate capacity that it performs the action of waking.

At this point we notice that the word 'wake' is used in three different senses in the poem. In the first place, it is used to refer to the action of rousing an already living human being from sleep and here the sun acts in a human capacity. Secondly, it is used to refer to the action of triggering off, as it were, the dormant life of seeds. Here the sun is the inanimate catalyst which stimulates seasonal growth. Thirdly, it is used to refer to the action of actual creation, and here the sun is represented as the elemental life-force which engenders life from the primeval clay. The first of these meanings relates to the diurnal cycle of night and day, the second to the seasonal cycle and the third to the cycle of creation. The three are, of course, commonly conceived as analogues, which accounts for the multiple meanings conventionally attributed to the words 'wake' and 'sleep'.

Now it is clear that the poet is attempting to conflate these different senses: his argument is that since the sun has the capacity to wake, there should be no difficulty in its exercising this capacity on a corpse. But the futility of this argument lies in the fact that the sun as an elemental life-giver has already done its work: the clay has been activated into life already – it is indeed still warm, which is proof of the fact and therefore a reason for the very reverse of hope. If the sun is regarded as a life-force, it has already fulfilled its function: if it is regarded as a kind old person, on the other hand, it has no function to fulfil since it is not a matter of rousing the living sleeper. The sun in its capacity as a stimulant to dormant life is irrelevant since we are concerned with something which has already grown.

What has happened here is that the composite meaning of the hybrid unit 'sun' develops into an internecine conflict between its constituent features of meaning because the word 'wake' and its semantic adherents like 'stir' and 'sleep', with which 'sun' is intra-textually associated, represent three meanings, each of which remains distinct. We can see in the text an attempt to develop a rational argument to counter the facts of reality which gradually assert themselves on the poet's awareness as the poem progresses. The patterns of imposed logic cannot be sustained, but this failure creates other patterns which represent the reality of the poet's experience, and which provide the text with its essential unity. It is to these patterns that we now turn.

The poem begins with an imperative in the first line and this is matched by an imperative in the first line of the second verse. Syntactically the two lines are, on one level, equivalent, and represent a pattern which relates the two verses. The illocutionary force of these two lines, however, is quite different: the first is an order, the second an appeal. Whereas the similarity of these lines links the two verses, the difference between them marks a transition from the confident command of the first to the somewhat wistful appeal of the second. The similarity serves to draw attention to the difference.

This transition can be said to reflect the realization that rationalization will not work, and the reasoning takes on a desperate note as the second verse develops. But this realization is anticipated in the first verse. Consider the line:

Until this morning and this snow.

Here the word 'snow' acquires a contextual significance over and above that which it has in the code by its association with 'morning', appearing as it does in an identical syntactic environment. 'Until this morning' and '(until) this snow' are syntactically equivalent and both function as temporal locatives. The effect of this is to bring 'snow' and 'morning' into semantic association. But in another respect they are diametrically opposed semantically. Extra-textually, 'snow' is related to 'winter' and both extra and intra-textually it is related to 'clays' and 'cold star' by virtue of the common semantic feature of coldness. Now 'winter' corresponds in the seasonal cycle to 'clays of a cold star' in the cycle of creation: both represent lifelessness. 'Morning', on the other hand, represents life in the diurnal cycle. Thus by bringing 'morning' and 'snow' together in a relation of equivalence, the poet realizes the very contradiction upon which his argument founders. What is true of one cycle is not necessarily true of another: morning and snow can co-exist so that waking in one sense does not entail waking in another sense.

The awareness of the futility of reasoning develops through the second verse. After the initial appeal, the second line produces an echo of the second line of the first verse: 'awoke him once' and 'woke, once', but again the similarity which serves to link these two expressions also draws attention to their difference. The word 'once' is ambiguous and can refer to recurrent or non-recurrent action. 'Awoke him once' might mean 'used to wake him' or 'woke him once and only once' but the context makes the former more likely, and the fourth line, which is again related to it by the occurrence of 'woke', with its placing of 'Always' in initial position and its distinct reveille rhythm, confirms us in this interpretation:

Always it woke him, even in France.

The initial placing of 'Always', in fact has the effect of deliberately – perhaps too deliberately – dispelling any possibility of an alternative interpretation. The second occurrence of 'once', on the other hand, really admits only of the second interpretation; it is more or less imposed upon us by the fact that it is enclosed in commas and contrasts with 'wakes' in the first line, whose tense carries the meaning of recurrent action. All of this suggests that the poet is aware of the ambiguity of the word and is becoming aware of the implications of this in his use of the word with which 'once' is in close association. 'Once' referring to recurrent action necessarily makes 'awoke' in the first verse recurrent too: 'once' referring to non-recurrent action similarly makes 'woke' in the second verse non-recurrent. The two words, for all their similarity of form, do not mean the same thing. The argument now takes on a more desperate tone as if in reaction to this realization.

The last three sentences of the text are interrogative in form and are, therefore, in some degree of syntactic equivalence. As with the two imperative forms we have already discussed, however, their similarity of form disguises a considerable difference in illocutionary force. The first is a genuine question in that it presupposes the possibility of a reply, though it must be added that the question is framed in such a way as to suggest what the reply must be: it is, in fact, a leading question and carries something of the force of an expression like

'Surely these limbs are not too hard to stir'. The second sentence is somewhat different: in fact it is not really so much a question as a challenge or an accusation. It suggests an attitude which might be alternatively expressed as something like: 'So that's all the flesh grew tall for!' The increase in frustration is reflected in the expression 'the clay grew tall', which recalls the reference to seeds in the first line of the verse and represents a convergence of the seasonal and creative cycles referred to in the first and second lines respectively, again bringing out the contradiction which makes the argument essentially futile. This futility is most fully realized in the third interrogative sentence in this verse, which is different again from the other two and has even less of the force of a normal question: it is rather a cry of despair which carries with it the assumption that there can be no answer.

Two final observations might be made about this movement towards despair which is developed through these last three sentences. Firstly, we may notice the syntactic complexity of the holophrastic expressions 'dear-achieved' and 'full-nerved' which are in marked contrast to the simple attributives in the rest of the text. Their compressed complexity might be said to suggest an emotional intensity and a definite shift from the rationally controlled simplicity of the preceding lines. Secondly, the representation of the sun as both a human and an inanimate entity recurs in the last sentence and links the end of the poem with the beginning. The logical inconsistency that is entailed by the concept of an inanimate-human sun does not lead the poet to abandon the concept, but to recognize different implications in it. The sun even in its role as elemental life force in the form of inanimate sunbeams is humanly fatuous and toils to fulfil its primeval task like humans working in 'fields unsown'.

Reference

LEES, R. B. 1960: *The grammar of English nominalization*. Bloomington: Indiana University Research Center in Anthropology, Folklore and Linguistics.

8

Study strategies in the teaching of literature to foreign students

Ronald Carter

8.1 Introduction

The main aim of this chapter is to argue that in the teaching of a foreign language, opportunities should be sought for more extensive and integrated study of language and literature than is commonly the case at present. The chapter discusses some language-based *study skills* which I consider important preliminary activities to reading literature. Although the study skills I discuss are language-based, I am not claiming that understanding the language is the same as understanding the literature. For this reason, I stress that these skills/ activities are preliminary and pre-literary.

Other related aims of this chapter are as follows. It is suggested that for students of a foreign literature pre-literary linguistic activities can:

(a) aid recognition of and sensitivity to the nature of *language organization* in related discourse types in the target language;
(b) lay a basis for *interpretation* of texts by analysing closely key structural features of the language of that text;
(c) explain the literary *character* of particular texts (in this instance, narrative style in a short story);
(d) point to features of *literariness* in texts by simultaneous application of relevant models to non-literary texts *and* to texts conventionally considered literary;
(e) promote *learner-centred language activities* which are useful in their own right.

8.2 Language teaching strategies

In this section a number of teaching strategies are proposed. They have no special claim to originality; indeed, language teachers will probably recognize them as part of their everyday tools of the trade. They are employed in the belief that they can assist the preliminary or pre-literary process of understanding and appreciating the text in question. It is clear that another text may require different strategies and also that any adequate teaching of a literary text goes beyond language teaching techniques, however widely used and principled they may be. However, it is claimed in the case of short narratives like Somerset Maugham's 'The Man with the Scar' that the strategies are broadly generalizable. The opening paragraph of the story is printed at the end of the chapter.

8.2.1 Prediction: What comes next?

This requires careful preparation before the story is read in class. The technique is for the teacher to stop the reading at key points and to elicit predictions of how the narrative will develop. In the case of 'The Man with the Scar' a number of stopping places can be suggested.

(a) The title can be omitted and, after the story has been read, students can be invited to predict what it should be.
(b) At the end of the first paragraph, students might be asked to predict, on the basis of the information supplied about the man, what the story is going to be about. This can be an important stage in sensitizing students to the function of the opening of the story in an interpretation of the whole. This opening bears an interestingly oblique relation to the rest of the text.

This is not the place to discuss in detail the nature of predictions made. Each class will produce its own varied responses. The teaching point to underline is that a heightened degree of attentiveness to the story can be brought about by prediction. There is increased involvement from the natural desire of seeing one's own expectations fulfilled or contravened.

Features of the structure of the story can be highlighted for subsequent discussion. A firm basis is laid for discussing such questions as: why did the man do what he did?; was he right or wrong in so doing?; did the general torture him more by allowing him to live? Prediction exercises lend themselves particularly to work in pairs or small groups, with individuals being invited to justify their own or the group's verbal prediction by close reference to the foregoing text and to their own individual experiences of human behaviour. Some groups persist in their preferences for outcomes alternative to those given by the writer, and they can be encouraged in this so long as evidence and support is forthcoming. Such activities can be a basis for stimulating and motivating class oral work and discussion. There is no reason why in some cases this should not be done in the students' own language, but the target language should be used wherever feasible.

In the face of 'gaps' (see Rimmon-Kenan 1983, pp. 125–7) in the narrative, such as some conclusion or evaluation of the behaviour of the man with the scar on the part of the first narrator, then prediction serves the function of allowing that gap to be filled by the reader. However, it must be said that prediction activities should be used sparingly. Not all texts lend themselves to this kind of macro-stylistic work. Most lyric poems, for example, or texts where descriptive states are evoked do not benefit. But texts with a strong plot component, where the next step in the action can be significant, do force readers to predict. And the best narratives will contain the seeds of their own development, so that readers have to read back as well as project forward. This is the case, I want to assert, with 'The Man with the Scar', where an additional advantage of prediction exercises is that they draw attention to the dual narrative structure of the story.

8.2.2 Cloze procedure

This is, as many language teachers know, a form of prediction. The focus is on individual words or sequences of words, rather than on stretches of text. There is also an inevitable concentration on micro-stylistic effects which can be of a subtle and complex kind in some stories. Teachers will need to give careful attention to the number of words deleted, to the relative multivalency of the chosen items, to the linguistic competence of a group, and, perhaps, to preparatory activities on non-literary texts in order to give practice in contexts where a greater degree of predictability may obtain (though predictability is not the exclusive preserve of the non-literary text – indeed, 'literary' effects can be produced by predictable *and* unpredictable elements). Items which might be deleted from this story include:

(a) from the title: 'The Man with — —' (e.g. *a* scar; lottery tickets; a grudge?)
(b) from the first paragraph: 'strolling leisurely round the bar offer — for sale'

and so on.

Lexical prediction can be made during a reading or after the story has been read, and preferably after some preliminary discussion. It can be used as well as, or instead of, structural prediction. Reasonable and supportable predictions require students to be alert both to the overall pattern of the story and to the immediate verbal context in which the deleted word occurs. Some students are assisted if the first letter of the word is given or if a list of words – from which an appropriate choice is to be made – is supplied by the teacher. For example, if students are asked to choose from a list of words as follows:

'It was a — gesture,' he said at last.
brave noble foolhardy futile ignoble

then they are being asked to focus on words which have resonances across the whole story. To justify and account for their decisions they are being asked to demonstrate careful and close reading of the story.

As with structural prediction, such 'lexical' prediction can lead to the kind of individual and group involvement with the text as well as to the kind of oral language practice which are not usually engendered by exposition from the teacher. Structural and lexical prediction can be employed jointly, and interesting oral and group language can emerge from asking students to delete words for other classes to predict. (For an interesting history of cloze methods in language teaching, some with obvious possibilities of transfer to the literature class, see Soudek and Soudek 1983.)

8.2.3 Summary: What's it all about?

A strategy designed to focus attention on the overall point or meaning of the story is to ask students to produce summaries of the text. Indiscriminate use of summary has its dangers, and instructions need to be fairly precisely formulated, because otherwise there is a danger of committing the heresy of paraphrase by suggesting that there *is* a paraphrasable meaning to the story. The technique should be seen rather as an enabling device for students in their personal process of interpretation or engagement with the text.

It is useful to impose a word limit for the summary (in a range, say, 25–40 words, in the case of a story as short as 'The Man with the Scar'), and to ask initially for a summary which is not an interpretation of the story but rather an account of *what happens*. The reasons for this are mainly threefold:

(a) An imposed word limit makes the exercise a useful one linguistically. Much syntactic re-structuring, deletion, and lexical re-shaping goes into meeting the word limit. The teacher can do much here to foster integrated language and literature work.

(b) A word limit enforces selection of what is significant. Does the summary, for example, include reference to the 'scar' or to the man's run of bad luck at cards prior to the execution? Is the story's political background brought into the foreground? Students learn that even a summary of what happens is in one sense an interpretive act.

(c) Students come to see that a summary of what happens is not a reason for valuing our reading of short stories by writers such as Maugham. There is, of course, more to it than this. But they should also come to understand the difference between plot and theme, evaluate the role of plot in a story like this, discuss why there appears to be no clear indication that we are to read this as any more than an account of what happens. That is, the title (in one sense a summary) is strangely oblique and there is minimal thematic pointing by the two narrators – especially in their dialogue at the close of the story. Summarizing the story means that attention can be focused on *how* it is narrated as well as on what is narrated, and questions can be generated about the structure and shape of this kind of narrative.

A related linguistic and literary exercise is to invite students to compare and criticize alternative summaries. Here are three recently produced in my own class (structured limits were not always met, but the effort to conform is valuable for all):

A man with a scar now lives a life of misery because, when facing an execution, he killed the woman he loved and was pardoned.

A man received a scar from a burst ginger-beer bottle. He was a general and was to be executed but is now a lottery ticket seller.

A political exile from Nicaragua ensures his own survival by murdering his wife in a sufficiently 'noble' way. He impresses his executioners but becomes emotionally scarred.

Note that summaries can also be supplied by the teacher for comparison. (See also discussion in Nash 1986 and Widdowson 1986.)

8.2.4 Forum: Debating opposing viewpoints

One advantage of a story such as 'The Man with the Scar' is that it is a relatively open text, sufficiently inexplicit in its meanings to allow for students to be asked to debate opposing propositions.

(a) *The man calculated that to murder his wife was the only way he could survive execution. He deserved the scar he got, but life is a lottery.*

(b) *The man was so devoted to his wife that he knew their life could not be lived alone. He thought they should both die together. The scar is the surface sign of a deep emotional wounding at his loss. He did not deserve this kind of scar, but life is a lottery.*

'Forum' is not a technical term but suggests the inherent potentiality of literature to mobilize among students discussion and debate with each other. The exercise is one which lends itself to small group-based activity with groups being allocated to defence of either one of the propositions, even if this may not be their own personal view. The group (and then its spokesman/woman) adduces evidence from a combination of world knowledge and the text in question to support points relevant to the 'argument'. The other groups listen and try to provide counter-examples. Either the whole class can participate or a section of the class can be assigned the task of judging and then voting for which propositions they consider to have been most persuasively argued. The whole exercise is a stimulus to oral language work through role play and can be prepared for accordingly; from a specifically literary-textual viewpoint students learn that texts *of any kind* do not easily allow of singular or unitary interpretation.

8.2.5 Guided re-writing

Guided re-writing is another widely employed language teaching strategy. It is aimed at helping students to recognize the broader discoursal patterns of texts and the styles appropriate to them. It involves the student in re-writing stretches of discourse to change its communicative value. As Johnson (1983) puts it:

> In such an approach, the starting point for a production exercise is pieces of discourse which the student is asked to do operations on.

In the case of communicative language teaching this can involve re-writing a set of instructions as a description, or turning a lecture transcript into academic prose. The basis for the strategy is to provide practice at expressing intents within contexts according to clearly specified information about audiences and purposes. In the case of a literary text it is, of course, much less easy to specify such parameters, but it is claimed that, as a general rule, it can be productive to focus re-writing exercises at the beginnings of texts, since it is here that the kind of 'information' conveyed can have most impact on readers. It is also claimed that the re-writing of one style into another should help students to get inside a writer's intended communicative effects and to explore the connections between styles and meanings: furthermore, such investigation can be especially illuminating when openings to literary and non-literary texts are juxtaposed.

The following re-writing exercise would be designed to sensitize students to the different ways in which information is structured for readers in different texts:

> Re-write the opening paragraph of 'The Man with the Scar', including as many details as you can invent about the man, his name, age, where he is from, how he got his scar, why he is selling lottery tickets in this bar, and so on.

Teachers will doubtless be able to construct for themselves numerous related activities. A more technical linguistic discussion can be found in Harweg (1980).

What can students and teachers hope to gain from this kind of examination? It is to be hoped that the following learning takes place:

(a) Students begin to manipulate or, at least, practise manipulating bits of English text. This is a linguistically-based, language improvement exercise, but it is useful to consider such activities in the light of an article by Brazil (1983) where he concludes:

> Possibly the best way of fostering a pupil's sensitivity to literature is not by feeding him more and more literature but by encouraging him to see literary language as continuous with, and deriving its power to move from, his total language experience.

For example, here is an 'alternative' re-written opening to 'The Man with the Scar', produced by a small group of German students of English. It is based on the exercise given above:

> Emmanuel Montes was always noticed on account of a broad, red scar which ran in a great crescent from his temple to his chin. He was 42 years of age and widowed. He frequented the 'Palace Hotel' in Guatemala City where he tried to sell lottery tickets to the guests although he was an exile from Nicaragua and not really at home here. He often looked miserable and indeed his life had been a sad one. He had been subjected to the kind of absurd quirks of fate that made the selling of lottery tickets somehow appropriate. For example, his scar was caused when a ginger beer bottle accidentally burst open at the bar. However, he was a noble and dignified figure and I learned from an acquaintance of mine a story which well illustrated both his loving devotion to his former wife and his sense of self-sacrifice if fate demanded it.

(b) Students learn that different texts have different communicative values based, in part at least, on the different ways in which readers are expected to go about making sense of what information they are given.

In a literary text the only place the reader can turn for the resolution of background information is the text itself, or at the very least to the other texts to which this text might allude. Such allusiveness or 'intertextuality' takes two main forms: either there is reference to other works which the reader may be expected to know, or the writer assumes that the reader is conversant with certain literary conventions which govern how the story is to be read (for example, in a 'whodunnit' we do not know the motivation for the murder, but we know that the immediate suspect is unlikely to be the person named as the killer in the final act of the drama). It is predominantly the case, therefore, that unlike other sources, *literariness* is marked by the extent to which the material is read as largely self-referential. Seeking the reason why the man is selling lottery tickets or has the kind of scar he has is an active interpretative process which involves the reader in constructing the necessary 'information' from the story itself.

However, another significant marker of literariness can be the way in which the omission of certain expected propositions or background information is assigned thematic significance. For example, we consider a number of ways to interpret 'scar' when the 'normal' explanation is not forthcoming, or we start to equate the absence of names and defined places in the text with an anonymous, featureless scenario for the story. We begin to question the constant repetition of the word 'lottery' and the references to the man's luck. This text, in particular, seems to require to be read with an additional semantic overlay in these sorts of key places. The author does not allow his narrators much overt comment and the reader is made to infer more. Literary texts differ in the degree of information supplied to a reader. In a non-literary text, however, information omitted is not generally assumed to be relevant.[1]

Appendix

The Man with the Scar

It was on account of the scar that I first noticed him, for it ran, broad and red, in a great crescent from his temple to his chin. It must have been due to a formidable wound and I wondered whether this had been caused by a sabre or by a fragment of shell. It was unexpected on that fat, round and good-humoured face. He had small and undistinguished features and his expression was artless. His face went oddly with his corpulent body. He was a powerful man of more than common height. I never saw him in anything but a very shabby grey suit, a khaki shirt and a battered sombrero. He was far from clean. He used to come into the Palace Hotel at Guatemala City every day at cocktail time and strolling leisurely round the bar offer lottery tickets for sale. If this was the way he made his living it must have been a poor one for I never saw anyone buy, but now and then I saw him offered a drink. He never refused it. He threaded his way among the tables with a sort of rolling walk as though he were accustomed to traverse long distances on foot, paused at each table, with a little smile mentioned the numbers he had for sale and then, when no notice was taken of him, with the same smile passed on. I think he was for the most part a trifle the worse for liquor.

(Maugham 1977, p. 183)

Note

1 This chapter is an abridged version of a much longer paper by Ronald Carter entitled 'Linguistic Models, Language, and Literariness: Study strategies in the teaching of literature to foreign students' and published in C. J. Brumfit and R. A. Carter (eds) *Literature and Language Teaching* (Oxford University Press, 1986) [Ed.].

References

BRAZIL, D. C. 1983: Kinds of English: spoken, written, literary. In Stubbs, M. W. and Hillier, H. (eds), *Readings on language, schools and classrooms*. London: Methuen.

HARWEG, R. 1980: Beginning a text. *Discourse Processes* 3.

JOHNSON, K. 1983: Communicative writing practice and Aristotelian rhetoric. In Freedman, A., Pringle, I. and Yalden, J. (eds), *Learning to write: First language/ second language*. London: Longman.

MAUGHAM, W. S. 1977: The man with the scar. In *Collected short stories*, Vol. 2. Harmondsworth: Penguin, 183–6.

NASH, W. 1986: The possibilities of paraphrase in the teaching of literary idiom. In Brumfit, C. J. and Carter, R. A. (eds), *Literature and language teaching*. Oxford: Oxford University Press, 70–88.

RIMMON-KENAN, S. 1983: *Narrative fiction: Contemporary poetics*. London: Methuen.

SOUDEK, M. and SOUDEK, L. 1983: Cloze after 30 years: New uses in language teaching. *ELT Journal* 37, 335–40.

WIDDOWSON, H. G. 1986: The untrodden ways. In Brumfit, C. J. and Carter, R. A. (eds), *Literature and language teaching*. Oxford: Oxford University Press, 133–9.

Part V

Pragmatic stylistics

9

Discourse analysis and the analysis of drama

Mick Short

9.1 Background remarks

It has become a commonplace of dramatic criticism over the past ten years or so to suggest that the only adequate analysis of drama must be the analysis of performance. In the first part of this chapter I argue that this view is incorrect and that critics should concentrate on dramatic texts. I also argue that this erroneous view has come about partly because of the inability of practical criticism (including traditional stylistic analysis, which has concerned itself mainly with deviation and textual pattern) to cope with the meanings which are produced by dramatic texts. During the whole of this chapter I shall be limiting myself to matters of *interpretation* only. Those critics who have argued over what the object of dramatic criticism should be have concerned themselves with interpretation and effects on the audience, sometimes without discriminating sufficiently between these aspects. It is my view that the position that I argue with respect to the interpretation of plays holds good for many audience effects as well; but the substantiation of this position would require separate argumentation, something which is beyond the scope of the present chapter.

9.2 What should we study – text or performance?

Dramatic criticism of the 1940s, 1950s and 1960s was a text-based study which treated plays rather like poems, analysing metaphors, strands of imagery and so on, often lifting parts of plays (for example, soliloquies) out of context in order to treat them more or less as poems in their own right. It is not surprising that such a criticism arose when we remember that the analysis of poetry was (and still is) the most developed of the Anglo-American critical apparatus. Until very recently there have been no ways of analysing in texts what is commonly held to be the stuff of drama, namely the meanings which are said to be implied behind the words that the characters speak, and which are often made apparent to the audience in a theatre by the use of gesture, tone of voice and so on. Necessarily, therefore, these features have only been observable in performance, and this has led many recent critics to suggest that plays can only be properly understood and evaluated on the stage. Hence J. D. Styan tells us that:

> The worst difficulty in thinking about a play is simply to remember that, given words for demonstration on a stage, there is no other *completely* valid means of judging their

efficiency and value except within their own terms. Leave your armchair throne of judgement, says Granville-Barker, submit for the while to be tossed to and fro in the action of the play: drama's first aim is to subdue us.

(Styan 1960, p. 65)

He, like many other critics, distinguished between complete appreciation, which can only go on in the theatre, and a by definition impoverished literary analysis.[1] Talking of Ibsen's *Rosmersholm* he says:

A 'literary' analysis will tend to confine itself to comments on the theme of the play, and perhaps to a statement about Rebecca's realization of the position she has reached in her understanding of the household. On the stage Ibsen gives us a much larger statement.

(Styan 1960, p. 18)

The problems which bringing the theatrical experience into the realm of criticism raises are twofold. First, plays have to be treated in a *radically* different way from other literary works. This means that there can be no coherent discipline called criticism. Second, the object of dramatic criticism becomes infinitely variable. Both meanings and value will change not just from one production to another but also from one performance of a particular production to another. There then becomes no play to criticize. Instead we will have to talk about 'X's production of *Hamlet* performed in theatre Y on the evening of Z', and critical discussion becomes impossible unless the two critics concerned have both seen and are arguing about exactly the same performance.

Luckily there are a number of considerations which suggest that the object of dramatic criticism should not be the theatrical performance:

(a) Teachers and students have traditionally read plays without necessarily seeing them performed and have still managed to understand them and argue about them.

(b) A special case of this is the dramatic producer, who must be able to read and understand a play in order to decide how to produce it. Such a decision is also crucial because a production of a play is in effect a play plus an interpretation of it, in just the same way that a reading (performance) of a poem must select one of a number of possible interpretations.

(c) There is a logical and terminological distinction between a play and a performance of it. Coming out of the theatre, people can be heard making comments of the form 'that was a good/bad production of a good/bad play'. Moreover, this distinction works not just for value judgments about plays and performances but also in terms of whether or not a particular production of a play was a *faithful* one. After a performance of *Hamlet* I once heard one academic tell another that what he had seen was 'good theatre but bad Shakespeare'. In this case, then, both the play and the performance were deemed to be good but the latter was not thought of as being an accurate rendering of the former.

All this does not suggest that critics should never go to the theatre. After all, general knowledge of theatrical conventions is part of the equipment that we have to possess in order to be able to understand this particular universe of discourse; but it does indicate that going to a performance of such and such a play is not a *necessary* condition for understanding it and responding to it sensitively. In other words, we must, as Styan and others have done, distinguish between literary and theatrical analysis but not so that one is deemed to be the poor relation of the other. Literary criticism should take the text as its object of investigation and develop techniques of textual analysis able to cope with the implied aspects of meaning mentioned earlier. Theatrical criticism on the other hand has a perfectly valid area of interest in, for example, comparing different ways of performing the same scene (a) in terms of its theatrical effect and (b) in terms of its faithfulness to the dramatic text. Literary criticism and theatre studies are distinct areas of study which have overlapping boundaries. Hence the critical analysis of a dramatic text is likely to produce suggestions for performance which would have to be tested in the theatre, and a new performance of a play might well suggest an interpretation which no critic had ever thought of but which could only be evaluated by checking it against the text.

Such a distinction entails a decision not to merge wilfully the contribution of playwright, producer and actor, as some have done. Stanley Wells, for example:

> But no matter how detailed the instructions a playwright may give – let him not only be the writer of the play but also the producer, the designer of the sets and costumes, the composer of the music, the choreographer – he remains a participant in an essentially collaborative act. The hints that he gives have to be transmitted to the audience by people other than himself. Other human beings come between his creative effort and the experience of the audience. They may dull it, or they may sharpen it. They may be inefficient transmitters, or they may themselves bring to their roles a creative capacity, making it impossible for us to distinguish between the achievements of the writer and of the actor.
>
> (Wells 1970, p. 7)

Wells produces a number of examples of the kind of merger that he is talking about. What is interesting, however, is that in describing them he is forced to do what he claims is impossible, namely to distinguish between the playwright's and the actor's contribution. For example, he analyses a contemporary account of Irving's utterance of the word 'exactly' while playing Mathias in L. Lewis's *The Bells*. While claiming that the contributions of the various people involved are intermingled inextricably, he describes what is very obviously Irving's contribution alone, and concludes by saying:

> When we have said that with Irving as Mathias it was successful we have acknowledged that the writer is only one of the team that is necessary to make a good play. We have admitted that Leopold Lewis wrote a script that, with a genius in the main role, provided an absorbing theatrical experience. We have not suggested that what he wrote has any literary value, or that it should have any intrinsic interest for later generations. It happened that Irving came upon a script that suited his talents peculiarly well; and the result has passed into theatrical history.
>
> (Wells 1970, pp. 16–17)

It is quite apparent that the latter part of this quotation belies the first. Although it takes a team to perform a play, it takes only one person to write it.

I suspect that many readers will by now have decided that I have given the game away by my constant reference to the dramatic *text*, and that the problem with textual analysis is that it does not get at many of the meanings that people perceive in plays. No amount of textual analysis will enable one to capture the significance felt in the theatre when Hamlet produces his crushing reply to Polonius:

Polonius: What do you read, my lord?
Hamlet: Words, words, words.

(II.ii.190–1)

It is precisely this kind of meaning which must be accounted for, and it can only be done by regarding the text in a less impoverished light than that in which it has previously been held.

Much of the blame here must lie at the door of the New Critics, who have tended to make us all believe that texts are merely verbal objects. But it should be apparent on reflection that no text can be just this. To understand the meaning of a word in a poem one needs to know its normal meaning, the significance of its particular position in its syntactic construction and so on. In other words a text can only be understood as an object embedded within a set of linguistic (and other – for example, sociological, literary) conventions. One of the most important sets of linguistic conventions for interpretation are those which govern language use. For instance, we generally assume that one should answer questions relevantly and with a degree of information appropriate to one's interlocutor. Thus, if my young daughter comes into my study while I am writing a lecture and asks me how to make butter, I might reasonably reply by telling her to put some cream into a bottle and shake it until it solidifies. If I reply 'buy a cow' I am giving insufficient and non-relevant information and will probably be interpreted as being offhand. She may well therefore conclude that I don't want to be disturbed. Similar kinds of consideration apply to the quotation from Hamlet above. Hamlet answers Polonius's question by stating the obvious. He has therefore not given the old man an appropriate reply, and, given our experience of the play so far, we are likely to conclude that Hamlet is being rude to Polonius in order to get rid of him, or that he is trying to feign madness. Further contextual considerations will then have to be taken into account to enable us to choose between the possible alternatives. This in effect means treating the text as a series of communicative acts, not just as a configuration of phonetic, syntactic and lexical patterns. This is what I suggest that the sensitive reader does when he reads a play in any case. It is only by applying such criteria that he can judge the significance of Hamlet's reply to Polonius. The important point to note is that we do not have to see the play in order to understand Hamlet's words and their significance. But what dramatic criticism does need is a way of explaining how these meanings are arrived at. And it is recent developments within discourse analysis, I would claim, that allow one to begin to do just this, hence rescuing dramatic criticism from the variability of performance analysis on the one hand and the inadequacy of traditional textual analysis on the other.

9.3 Discourse analysis and its application to dramatic texts

Recent developments in discourse analysis are now fairly familiar, and as the main aim of what follows is to show how that analysis can be applied to dramatic texts the description of each type of analysis will be relatively brief and informal. For those not familiar with a particular approach, references to more expanded treatments are given at appropriate points in the text.

9.3.1 Speech acts

The theory of speech acts (Austin 1962; Searle 1965, 1969) has drawn attention to the fact that when we produce various utterances we actually *do* things. Thus when A says to B 'I promise to bring it tomorrow', under normal circumstances A actually makes a promise. In this case the action is made obvious by the presence of the performative verb 'promise'. However, 'I will bring it tomorrow' can also be a promise, given the right contextual circumstances. The introduction of context is important because it is this (what Searle [1969, ch. 3] calls *preparatory and sincerity conditions*) which helps us to capture the important observation that the same sentence may in different circumstances perform different acts. Thus 'I will bring it tomorrow' is a promise when the action mentioned is beneficial to B and when A knows this. If it is obviously not of benefit then the speech-act status changes to that of a threat or warning – where it is a court summons, for example. Given general knowledge about the world, it is often possible to deduce the speech act status from the utterance alone. Hence 'I'll kick your face in' and 'I'll bring you tea in bed' are unlikely to be thought of as having the same speech act status (although they *could*, of course, given knowledge of very special contextual circumstances). This is dramatically important at the beginnings of plays and when new characters are introduced, as it allows us immediately to grasp important social relations. Thus when Jonson's *The Alchemist* opens with:

Face:	Believ't I will.
Subtle:	Thy worst. I fart at thee.
Dol Common:	Ha' you your wits? Why, gentlemen! for love –
Face:	Sirrah, I'll strip you –

(I.i.1–4)

it is quite apparent, even without the stage direction that tells us so, that Face and Subtle are quarrelling, because they are abusing and threatening each other. On stage the actors would have to produce appropriate actions and tone of voice, which might be actualized in a number of different ways. But the intended meaning and effect are clear from the text and general knowledge alone (for example, that being stripped is usually unpleasant). The fact that Face and Subtle are threatening each other also allows us to deduce that they are of roughly equal social status. A servant cannot, given normal circumstances, threaten a master. If he does so in a play, it signals a change in their relationship.

Commands, like threats, are not accessible to all of the participants in a particular speech situation and therefore also mark clear social relationships. One of the most obvious examples is the first entrance of Lucky and Pozzo in Beckett's *Waiting for Godot*, where the master-servant relationship is marked before Pozzo even appears on the stage:

> *Enter Pozzo and Lucky, Pozzo drives Lucky by means of a rope passed round his neck, so that Lucky is the first to appear, followed by the rope which is long enough to allow him to reach the middle of the stage before Pozzo appears. Lucky carries a heavy bag, a folding stool, picnic basket and a greatcoat. Pozzo a whip.*
> Pozzo: (*Off.*) On! (*Crack of whip. Pozzo appears.*)

(Beckett 1965, pp. 21–2)

This is also a good example of the prescribed visual and verbal aspects supporting each other to reinforce the significance of the deduction that one makes.

The felicity conditions that have been explored so far have all concerned factors prior to the speech event. But Searle notes that post-conditions also apply. Thus, if you make a promise and then fail to carry it out, you have broken that promise (unless outside circumstances have prevented you). At the end of each act of *Waiting for Godot* Vladimir and Estragon make an agreement, which on both occasions they fail to carry out:

> *Vladimir*:   Well, shall we go?
> *Estragon*:   Yes, let's go.
>   (*They do not move*)

(p. 94)

It is the fact that they agree to go and then do not which the critic has to explain. Presumably they either wilfully break agreements, in which case the value of agreeing in their world is different from ours, or they are prevented from doing what they want by some unknown internal or external force. Which way one jumps interpretatively will depend upon other information. For example, the fact that Pozzo also has difficulty in leaving when he apparently intends to is likely to incline us to the second of the two types of possibility outlined above. What is important to note here is that it is our knowledge of the normal production of speech acts which allows us to deduce contextual information when that production is apparently normal and which also allows us to perceive deviant speech act production and interpret it. (For a discussion of the status of speech acts in fiction, see Searle 1975a.)

9.3.2 Presuppositions

The work on presuppositions within both linguistics and philosophy is assuming voluminous proportions, and there is considerable dispute as to how to analyse and categorize them. See, for example, Keenan (1971), Kempson (1975) and

Leech (1974). It will be noted that presuppositions often form part of the preconditions for the felicitous production of speech acts. Here I wish to discuss three overlapping kinds of presupposition: existential, linguistic and pragmatic. They are distinguished as useful categories for textual analysis rather than because they are theoretically distinct. Debate on the kinds of presupposition is still inconclusive. For Kempson (1975) and Wilson (1975), for example, all presuppositions are pragmatic.

The notion of *existential presupposition* was first developed by Strawson (1952) to cope with the philosophical question whether statements like 'The present king of France is wise' could be deemed to be true or false. He claimed that such a sentence presupposed that the king of France existed and therefore could only have a truth value when the presupposition was true. In fictions there are of course many sentences which have false presuppositions; while we experience such fictions, we conventionally assume that such presuppositions are true, and it is this convention amongst others that allows us to 'enter into' the world of the novel or play. Thus when, at the beginning of Marlowe's play, Faustus says:

> How I am glutted with conceit of this!
> Shall I make spirits fetch me what I please,
> Resolve me of all ambiguities,
> Perform what desperate enterprise I will?
> I'll have them fly to India for gold
>
> (*Doctor Faustus*, I.i.77–81)

we conventionally enter into a world where spirits exist, in spite of the fact that we may not believe in such things at all. 'Spirits' in this quotation can be interpreted as non-referential, as it is generic and occurs in an interrogative sentence. But 'them' in the last line of the quotation does have definite reference, and co-refers to 'spirits'.

Once the world of the play is established we expect to see and hear things consistent with that world. Inconsistencies produce a jarring which the critic is likely to explain either by ascribing demerit to the work or by changing his mind as to the kind of work in front of him. Arguably, the first obvious indication of the absurd nature of *Waiting for Godot* involves a clash between the existential presuppositions held by us and those held by one of the characters. On the first page, Vladimir turns to Estragon saying 'So there you are again', and Estragon replies by asking 'Am I?' Here Estragon challenges a presupposition, namely that he exists, that we assume he must hold.[2]

The distinction which Strawson makes between what a sentence asserts and what it presupposes is useful for explaining the communicative effect of much embedded material in English sentences. Thus the sentence 'The man that I met yesterday is ill' 'contains' two propositions:

(a) I met a man yesterday
(b) The man that I met yesterday is ill.

The sentence presupposes (a) and asserts (b). These clauses or phrases which are embedded in sentences in this manner may be said to contain *linguistic presuppositions*. There are, of course, other presuppositions in the sentence besides 'I met a man yesterday', for example, that the man exists. Indeed in theoretical terms existential presuppositions are probably best treated as a subset of linguistic presuppositions. I have treated them as a separate category above because of their interesting role in the establishment of fictions. Because the information structure of sentences is arranged so that one is invited to challenge what a sentence asserts rather than what it presupposes, writers of persuasive prose sometimes place rather dubious propositions in the presupposed parts of sentences (for example, in nominalized or relative clauses) in order to dupe their audience into accepting them without thinking. In plays such presuppositions are often used to establish the world of the play, and in absurd drama much of the absurdity can come from a clash between presuppositions held by the characters and those held by the audience. Hence, in N. F. Simpson's *One Way Pendulum*, Mrs Groomkirby says:

> If you were to do your proper share of the eating between you, instead of leaving it all to me, I shouldn't have to have Mrs Gantry in anything like so often. (*Pause*) Paying out good money all the time. (*Pause*) If it weren't for your father's parking meters we just shouldn't be able to run it. Then we should *have* to get it eaten ourselves.
>
> (Simpson 1960, p. 24)

Mrs Groomkirby's third sentence presupposes that her husband owns a string of parking meters from which he gains revenue. Her assumption goes unchallenged by the other characters and therefore is presumably shared by them. However, it is obviously at odds with the presuppositions which we as onlookers hold. In our world parking meters are only owned by town councils and the like. But perhaps the most astounding feature of this quotation is Mrs Groomkirby's remarks about eating. The noun phrase 'your proper share of the eating' presupposes that eating is a chore to be shared by the whole family. This presupposition in concert with other assumptions allows us to take part in a complex and crazy chain of inference whereby we deduce that all food has to be eaten, and that you have to pay a professional to finish up what you cannot finish. Presumably, without Mr Groomkirby's parking meters they would not have been able to buy the food that they have to get rid of, let alone pay Mrs Gantry to eat it!

The term 'pragmatic' is usually reserved for presuppositions relating to immediate context and immediate social relations. Hence a command like 'shut the door' presuppposes that the speaker is in a social relation to the hearer such that he is able to order him to do things. The preconditions for the production of the threats in the extract from *The Alchemist* discussed above are obvious examples of *pragmatic presuppositions*. Another interesting example comes from the first scene of *King Lear*, where Lear as king is in an obvious position of authority. Kent continually tries to intercede on Cordelia's behalf, thus using his status as adviser. Lear slaps him down on each occasion, forcing Kent to produce more and more obvious intercessions, ranging from mere vocatives like 'good my liege' through questions and opposing statements and finally to the very explicit commands and warnings which provoke his banishment:

> *Kent*:   Revoke thy gift,
> Or, whilst I can vent clamour from my throat
> I'll tell thee thou dost evil.
> *Lear*:   Hear me recreant
> ... if, on the tenth day following
> Thy banish'd trunk be found in our dominions,
> The moment is thy death
>
> (I.i.164–78)

Each time Kent tries to protect Cordelia he is prevented. This forces him to use speech acts carrying pragmatic presuppositions (reinforced by the insulting use of *thee*) which assume social relations more and more at odds with those that in fact exist, until the role relations become apparently almost reversed. It is at this point that Lear finally banishes him.

9.3.3 General discourse relations

The canonical form of a communicative event is one in which one person addresses and gives information to another (see Figure 9.1).

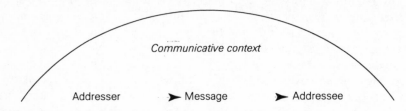

Figure 9.1

In a conversation the two participants continually exchange roles, and it is easy to think of situations which deviate from this basic form in some way. For example the addresser and addressee may be the same (a diary), there might be one addresser and many addressees (a lecture), the addresser and addressees may be physically and temporally separated (a recorded party political broadcast) and so on. However, these situations are all variations in some way on the basic format. Drama shares this base form, but like many texts it has a structure whereby one level of discourse is embedded in another. Sometimes one is tempted to characterize play-going as a situation in which we 'overhear' the talk between the characters. But the situation of drama is unlike that of eavesdropping because it is arranged to be overheard on purpose (see Fig. 9.2).

Character speaks to character, and this discourse is part of what the playwright 'tells' the audience. Any play will consist of a series of such embedded discourses,

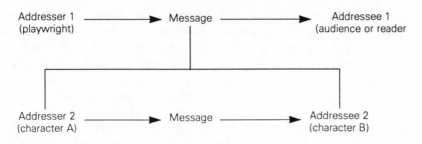

Figure 9.2

and there can be even more layers, as when one character reports to another the words of a third. But the important thing to notice is the general *embedded* nature of drama, because features which, for example, mark social relations between two people at the character level become messages *about* the characters at the level of discourse which pertains between author and reader/audience. Hence the ability of Pozzo to command Lucky is something which is taken as given between them but is important information *about* them for the critic. When relations change, as in the Kent/Lear example, there is a message conveyed between the two characters, namely that Kent is challenging Lear's authority, and this message is the same at the author/reader level. The assumptions which the characters share in *One Way Pendulum* are presumably not thought of as odd by the characters. But the fact that they clash with our assumptions in a play world which at first sight appears to be isomorphic with our own itself constitutes one of a number of accumulated messages which Simpson is giving us about the world in which his characters live. It should be apparent that this embedded model of discourse has been tacitly assumed in the discussion so far. It becomes even more obviously relevant when one examines Grice's notion of the co-operative principle.

9.3.4 The co-operative principle in conversation

Grice (1975) is one of the first attempts to account for meaning as it develops in conversation. To this end he distinguishes between what a sentence means and what someone means by uttering that sentence. Hence in the following possible dialogue:

A: Did you enjoy the play?
B: Well, I thought the ice creams they sold in the interval were good.

it is quite apparent that B is saying in an indirect and therefore relatively polite way that he did not enjoy the play, even though he does not actually say so. In ordinary language terms we might say that B implied that he did not like the play even though he did not say so. In order to avoid confusion over the term 'imply', which has a more technical use within philosophical logic, Grice coins the term 'implicature' for this kind of indirect, context-determined meaning. Hence, in the above example, B *implicates* that he did not enjoy the play.

Grice distinguishes first between what he calls *conventional* and *conversational* implicature. Conventional implicature has to do with the conventional as opposed to the logical meaning of certain words, particularly connectors. Hence, if someone says 'She comes from Oxford, so she must be a snob', the word *so* apparently marks an implicative relation between coming from Oxford and being a snob, in spite of the fact that when asked the speaker is hardly likely to want to say that *everyone* from Oxford is a snob.

An interesting example of the use of conventional implicature comes from Act III of Oscar Wilde's *The Importance of Being Earnest*. Jack is trying to persuade Lady Bracknell of the eligibility of Cecily Cardew:

Jack: Miss Cardew's family solicitors are Messrs. Markby, Markby and Markby.

Lady Bracknell: Markby, Markby and Markby? A firm of the very highest position in their profession. Indeed I am told that one of the Mr Markbys is occasionally to be seen at dinner parties. So far I am satisfied.

(III.139–44)

The sentence relating one of the Mr Markby's presence at dinner parties is obviously meant to be a reason for suggesting that the firm is 'of the very highest in their profession'. This is apparent from Lady Bracknell's use of the adverb 'indeed'. For *her*, someone's professional reputation can be judged by which table he sits at. However, this is unlikely to be the case for the audience and the use of 'indeed' points up the ironic contrast between us and her.

The distinction between what one says and what one means is also apparent in conversational implicature, where inferred interpretations cannot be ascribed to the conventional meanings of words like *so* and *indeed*. In explanation of this kind of meaning Grice claims that people entering into conversation with each other tacitly agree to co-operate towards mutual communicative ends, thus obeying the co-operative principle and its regulative conventions. He calls these conventions maxims, and has suggested that at least the following four obtain:

1. *the maxim of quantity*: make your contribution as informative as is required – don't give too much or too little information;
2. *the maxim of quality*: make your contribution one that you believe to be true;
3. *the maxim of relation*: be relevant;
4. *the maxim of manner*: avoid unnecessary prolixity, obscurity of expression and ambiguity, and be orderly.

Maxims are not, however, as strongly regulative as grammatical rules, and are therefore broken quite often. Grice outlines four such cases:

(a) A speaker may unostentatiously *violate* a maxim; this accounts for lies and deceits.
(b) He may *opt out* of the co-operative principle, as, for example, members of government do when they refuse to answer questions on the ground that the information required is classified.

(c) He may be faced with a *clash*, and will have therefore to break one maxim or another.

(d) He may ostentatiously *flout* a maxim, so that it is apparent to his interlocutors.

It is under the final specification that conversational implicature occurs. Hence in the dialogue between A and B cited above, where maxims (1), (3) and (4) are broken, it is quite apparent to A that B could answer directly, relevantly and more economically whether or not he enjoyed the play. A assumes that B is still obeying the co-operative principle and that B knows that he will assume this. Given this set of assumptions, A then works out the implicature, namely that B did not enjoy the play but does not want to say so in a direct and relatively impolite way.

At this stage in the development of the theory it is by no means clear how much conversational meaning can be accounted for in this way, or how it fits in exactly with linguistic theory as a whole. Searle's (1975b) suggestion that the rules for conversational implicature form merely a subset of a set of rules and procedures for the specification of what he calls 'indirect speech acts' looks promising. Both Grice and Searle insist that implicatures must be derivable from an informal set of step-by-step inferences, and there appears to be much conversational meaning which cannot yet be adequately accounted for in this way. But it should be apparent that even the initial work in this area has considerable relevance for the study of literary texts in general and dramatic texts in particular (for other initial suggestions in this area see Tanaka 1972; Pratt 1977, chs 4 and 5). Hamlet's reply of 'Words, words, words' to Polonius is an obvious flouting of the maxim of quantity, as it merely gives Polonius information which he patently already possesses. The flouting of the maxim of quantity often seems to be rude, as can be seen from the first scene of *Romeo and Juliet*, where Gregory and Sampson are picking a quarrel with Abraham and Balthasar:

> *Abraham*: Do you bite your thumb at us, sir?
> *Sampson*: I do bite my thumb, sir.

(I.i.43–4)

It is arguable that Sampson's reply breaks the maxim of relation as well, and the repetition and parallelism also help mark the aggression. But what is important to notice here is that Shakespeare exploits the co-operative principle to help establish very quickly indeed the state of near war between the Capulets and Montagues. Incidentally, Shakespeare uses a similar tactic later on in the scene to mark the offhand way in which Romeo treats Benvolio's anxious inquiries about him:

> *Benvolio*: Tell me in sadness, who is it that you love
> ...
> *Romeo*: In sadness cousin, I do love a woman.

(I.i.203, 207)

As Grice (1975, p. 52) himself says, one obvious kind of example of the breaking of the maxim of quality is the phenomenon of metaphor:

Romeo:	If I profane with my unworthiest hand
	This holy shrine, the gentle sin is this:
	My lips, two blushing pilgrims, ready stand
	To smooth that rough touch with a tender kiss.

(I.v.95–8)

Juliet's hand is self-evidently not a holy shrine; but, by stating that it is, Romeo can implicate his respect and devotion. Similarly his lips are not two blushing pilgrims, but Juliet and the audience can easily infer his intention to reinforce his statement of quasi-religious love.

An example of the breaking of the maxim of relation can be seen in Tom Stoppard's *Enter a Free Man*:

Riley: (*sharply*)	Give me that tape.
Brown:	I haven't got one!
Riley:	My patience is not inexhaustible!

(Stoppard 1968, p. 26)

Brown explicitly rejects the presupposition contained in Riley's first utterance that he has got a tape. Riley interprets this as being an avoidance strategy, and in effect threatens him when he says: 'My patience is not inexhaustible'. We infer that this is a threat because Riley's statement about his patience, although not strictly relevant to the conversation at this point, can be interpreted as an indication that an important pre-condition for violent action on his part, namely the losing of his temper, is about to be fulfilled. Riley's statement also breaks the maxim of manner because of its indirect, double negative form. Interestingly enough, if the *indeed* was removed from the Oscar Wilde example quoted above, the ironic contrast between the workings of our world and Lady Bracknell's would still be apparent. It is thus possible that Grice's category of conventional implicature is really a special, explicit case of the maxim of relation. This maxim is also problematical in other ways, because it is sometimes difficult to determine if it is broken when a speaker tries to change the topic of a conversation. Consider, for example, the following interchange in Act I of Robert Bolt's *A Man For All Seasons*. More and his daughter are talking just after the exit of Roper:

Margaret:	You're very gay. Did he talk about the divorce?
More:	Mm? You know I think we've been on the wrong track with Will – It's no good arguing with a Roper –
Margaret:	Father, did he?
More:	*Old* Roper was just the same. Now let him think he's going *with* the swim and he'll turn around and start swimming in the opposite direction.

(Bolt 1960, p. 18)

It is quite apparent that More wants to change the subject in order not to talk about the royal divorce and hence refuses to answer Margaret's questions. She, on the other hand, is anxious to know what happened, and therefore makes her second question unrelatable to his utterance by echoing her first question. More avoids it. Do implicatures pass *between the characters* here, are they just ignoring each other's contribution in order to gain topic control, or are both of these things happening? The possible ambiguity arises partly because of the embedded nature of dramatic discourse. What is an implicature for us, the audience, is not necessarily one for More's addressee. Does More want Margaret to realize his intention or not? Conversational structures where one or more participants more or less ignore each other's contributions have been noted by Sacks, for example. In the extract below, Roger and Jim are battling for control of the topic of conversation by relating their utterances not to the immediately previous one but to the last but one. It is not at all obvious, in spite of the fact that some of the utterances are not relevant to the previous one, that implicatures are being passed:

> *Roger*: Isn't the New Pike depressing?
> *Ken*: Hh. The Pike?
> *Roger*: Yeah! Oh the place is disgusting. Any day of the week
> *Jim*: I think that P.O.P. is depressing it's just –
> *Roger*: But you go – you go – take
> *Jim*: Those guys are losing money.
> *Roger*: But you go down-dow, down to the New Pike.
>
> (quoted by Coulthard 1977, p. 78)

This phenomenon, which it is claimed is fairly common in ordinary conversation, has been termed 'skip connecting' (see Coulthard 1977, pp. 78–9).

For some reason it is fairly difficult to find clear examples of the flouting of the maxim of manner, especially in isolation. Another extract from *A Man For All Seasons* is particularly interesting, however. Norfolk is quizzing Rich in Act II about the cup which More gave to Rich in Act I, and which Cromwell wants to use as evidence of More accepting bribes:

> *Norfolk*: When did Thomas give you this thing?
> *Rich*: I don't exactly remember.
> *Norfolk*: Well, make an effort. Wait! I can tell you! I can tell you – it was that Spring – it was that night we were there together. You had a cup with you when we left; was that it?
> *(Rich looks to Cromwell for guidance but gets none.)*
> *Rich*: It may have been.
> *Norfolk*: Did he often give you cups?
> *Rich*: I don't suppose so, Your Grace.
>
> (p. 60)

First, it should be noted that this text contains examples of someone unostentatiously breaking the maxim of quality. Rich does not want to admit the details of the gift to Norfolk. But his replies are also more indirect than they need be. The modification of 'I don't remember' by 'exactly' and the use of 'I don't suppose so' are obvious examples. Rich's purpose in breaking the maxim of manner is not to convey implicatures to Norfolk. Quite the contrary. But at the higher level of discourse Bolt demonstrates to his audience/reader Rich's discomfiture in attempting to conceal the truth.

9.3.5 More general discourse relations

A number of categories discussed so far (for example, speech acts and pragmatic presuppositions) are relevant to the explication of social relations, which is of much importance to the study of drama. Another fruitful area is the socio-linguistic study of status and terms of address. As is pointed out in Brown and Gilman (1960, pp. 253–60), the 'T/V distinction' (for example, *tu/vous* in French) is used not just to account for singular and plural but also to indicate nearness or remoteness in social relations. This then gives rise to the possibility of productive stylistic use of such categories to indicate swift variation of attitude along the closeness/remoteness scale. Interesting early examples of the discussion of such variation (using *thee* and *thou*) in Shakespeare can be found in Mulholland (1967) and Quirk (1974).

Closely related to the use of the pronoun system is the exploitation of the naming system. The sociolinguistic use of terms of address in American English has been ably described by Ervin-Tripp (1969). The rules for British English are slightly different and just as complex. But some simple examples will suffice here. Title plus last name and *Sir* plus first name can be used by people of inferior status when addressing social superiors. Last name alone is used by superiors to inferiors who are not well known. First name alone is used by close equals or by people of superior status to well known inferiors. In fact the situation is rather more complex than the above description suggests, but this general level of analysis will be sufficient to show how the social relations between More and the steward are marked at the beginning of *A Man For All Seasons*:

> *More*:   The wine, please, Matthew.
> *Steward*: It's there, Sir Thomas.
>
> (p. 2)

It is also interesting to note in this respect that Lady Britomart, when talking to her son at the beginning of Shaw's *Major Barbara*, uses the first-name vocative 'Stephen' in eight out of her first nine utterances and 'my dear boy' in the other. This consistent usage in conjunction with other features, such as the frequent use of commands, demonstrates the complete dominance of Lady Britomart over her son, and contributes markedly to the comedy when she says a few lines later 'Stephen, may I ask you how soon you intend to realise that you are a grown-up man, and that I am only a woman?' (Shaw 1965, p. 52). Other factors which indicate the dominance relation at the beginning of *Major Barbara* are who speaks first, and hence initiates the exchanges, and who speaks the most.

One strange use of the pronoun system in English is the reference to people present in the speech situation by the third-person pronoun. This occurs where it is assumed by the interlocutors that some other person is of such an inferior status as to debar him from making a reasonable contribution. One example is the way in which many parents talk over their children; another is where interlocutors talk about people with disabilities as if they were not there, even in situations where the disability involved may not actually impair the ability to contribute to the conversation at all. This rather bizarre usage has been ably demonstrated by the ironic title of a radio series for the blind on BBC Radio 4, *Does He Take Sugar?* Productive use of this kind of feature is also made in *Romeo and Juliet*, when Capulet indicates his anger at his daughter's refusal to marry Paris by asking questions about her as if she were not there:

Capulet:	Soft! Take me with you, take me with you, wife.
	How will she none? Doth she not give us thanks?
	Is she not proud? Doth she not count her blest,
	Unworthy as she is, that we have wrought
	So worthy a gentleman to be her bridegroom?

(III.v.141–5)

An interesting preliminary attempt to apply general discourse analysis to Shakespeare is Coulthard's discussion (1977, pp. 170–81) of *Othello*.

9.4 'Trouble in the Works'

So far in this chapter I have given illustrative examples of the ways in which discourse analysis can help explain meanings which we intuitively perceive in dramatic texts. However, a better sense of its use can be gained from a more extended analysis. To this end I now turn to an examination of a complete short text, a sketch by Harold Pinter called *Trouble in the Works*. For ease of reference the full text is given below along with sentence numbering. Given the limitations of space, my treatment of the text can only be relatively superficial. A full analysis would have to be more systematic than that which appears below, and would need to be supplemented by a full stylistic analysis of the more traditional kind.

(*An office in a factory.*(1) *Mr Fibbs at the desk.*(2) *A knock at the door.*(3) *Enter Mr Wills.*(4))

Fibbs:	Ah, Wills.(5) Good.(6) Come in.(7) Sit down, will you?(8)
Wills:	Thanks, Mr Fibbs.(9)
Fibbs:	You got my message?(10)
Wills:	I just got it.(11)
Fibbs:	Good.(12) Good.(13)
	(*Pause.*(14))
	Good.(15) Well now ...(16) Have a cigar?(17)
Wills:	No, thanks, not for me, Mr Fibbs.(18)
Fibbs:	Well, now, Wills, I hear there's been a little trouble in the factory.(19)
Wills:	Yes, I ... I suppose you could call it that, Mr Fibbs.(20)
Fibbs:	Well, what in heaven's name is it all about?(21)
Wills:	Well, I don't exactly know how to put it, Mr Fibbs.(22)
Fibbs:	Now come on, Wills, I've got to know what it is, before I can do anything about it.(23)
Wills:	Well, Mr Fibbs, it's simply a matter that the men have ... well, they seem to have taken a turn against some of the products.(24)
Fibbs:	Taken a turn?(25)
Wills:	They just don't seem to like them much any more.(26)

Fibbs: Don't like them?(27) But we've got the reputation of having the finest machine part turnover in the country.(28) They're the best paid men in the industry.(29) We've got the cheapest canteen in Yorkshire.(30) No two menus are alike.(31) We've got a billiard hall, haven't we, on the premises, we've got a swimming pool for the use of staff.(32) And what about the long-playing record room?(33) And you tell me they're dissatisfied?(34)

Wills: Oh, the men are very grateful for all the amenities, sir.(35) They just don't like the products.(36)

Fibbs: But they're beautiful products.(37) I've been in this business a lifetime.(38) I've never seen such beautiful products.(39)

Wills: There it is, sir.(40)

Fibbs: Which ones don't they like?(41)

Wills: Well, there's the brass pet cock, for instance.(42)

Fibbs: The brass pet cock?(43) What's the matter with the brass pet cock?(44)

Wills: They just don't seem to like it any more.(45)

Fibbs: But what exactly don't they like about it?(46)

Wills: Perhaps it's just the look of it.(47)

Fibbs: That brass pet cock?(48) But I tell you it's perfection.(49) Nothing short of perfection.(50)

Wills: They've just gone right off it.(51)

Fibbs: Well, I'm flabbergasted.(52)

Wills: It's not only the brass pet cock, Mr Fibbs.(53)

Fibbs: What else?(54)

Wills: There's the hemi unibal spherical rod end.(55)

Fibbs: The hemi unibal spherical rod end?(56) But where could you find a finer rod end?(57)

Wills: There are rod ends and rod ends, Mr Fibbs.(58)

Fibbs: I know there are rod ends and rod ends.(59) But where could you find a finer hemi unibal spherical rod end?(60)

Wills: They just don't want to have anything more to do with it.(61)

Fibbs: This is shattering.(62) Shattering.(63) What else?(64) Come on, Wills.(65) There's no point in hiding anything from me.(66)

Wills: Well, I hate to say it, but they've gone very vicious about the high speed taper shank spiral flute reamers.(67)

Fibbs: The high speed taper shank spiral flute reamers.(68) But that's absolutely ridiculous!(69) What could they possibly have against the high speed taper shank spiral flute reamers?(70)

Wills: All I can say is they're in a state of very bad agitation about them.(71) And then there's the gunmetal side outlet relief with handwheel.(72)

Fibbs: What!(73)

Wills: There's the nippled connector and the nippled adaptor and the vertical mechanical comparator.(74)

Fibbs: No!(75)

Wills: And the one they can't speak about without trembling is the jaw for Jacob's chuck for use on portable drill.(76)

Fibbs: My own Jacob's chuck?(77) Not my very own Jacob's chuck?(78)

Wills: They've just taken a turn against the whole lot of them, I tell you.(79) Male elbow adaptors, tubing nuts, grub screws, internal fan washers, dog points, half dog points, white metal bushes – (80)

Fibbs:	But not, surely not, my lovely parallel male stud couplings.(81)
Wills:	They hate and detest your lovely parallel male stud couplings, and the straight flange pump connectors, and back nuts, and front nuts, *and* the bronzedraw off cock with handwheel and the bronzedraw off cock without handwheel!(82)
Fibbs:	Not the bronzedraw off cock with handwheel?(83)
Wills:	And without handwheel.(84)
Fibbs:	Without handwheel?(85)
Wills:	And with handwheel.(86)
Fibbs:	Not with handwheel?(87)
Wills:	And without handwheel.(88)
Fibbs:	Without handwheel?(89)
Wills:	With handwheel *and* without handwheel.(90)
Fibbs:	With handwheel *and* without handwheel?(91)
Wills:	With or without!(92)
	(*Pause*.(93))
Fibbs:	(*Broken*) Tell me.(94) What do they want to make in its place?(95)
Wills:	Brandy balls.(96)

(Pinter 1977, pp. 241–3)

I once saw this sketch performed by a student group. At the beginning of the scene Fibbs, the manager, was seated in a swivel chair at a large desk on a raised dais and dressed in a three-piece suit. When Wills sat down it was on a small chair in front of the desk and below the dais. As the sketch progressed the two men got up and moved clockwise round the desk, so that at the end Fibbs was in Wills's seat and vice versa. This aspect of the staging was obviously designed to bring out one of the sketch's main characteristics, namely that by the end the role relations which have been established at the beginning of the piece, and which normally pertain between employer and worker, have been reversed. This in turn contributes to the second characteristic which I intend to explicate, the sketch's patently absurd nature.

The role relations of the two characters will be marked on stage by their dress, seating position, etc. But even on a reading of the sketch, they are easily perceived from the beginning. First, they are indicated by the vocatives. Fibbs always uses last name only, whereas Wills uses either title plus last name or 'sir'. In the first part of the sketch Fibbs speaks first and initiates the conversational exchanges (see Coulthard 1977, pp. 95–6). He also uses the speech acts of commanding and questioning, which correlate with the pragmatic presupposition that he is socially superior to Wills. Wills, for his part, at the beginning of the piece answers the questions exactly, producing no extra comments of his own, uses lexical items introduced by Fibbs rather than bringing in his own, and does not initiate new topics (cf. the pregnant pause (14)).

When Fibbs asks Wills the cause of the trouble it is quite apparent that Wills is distinctly uneasy about telling his boss:

Fibbs:	Well, now, Wills, I hear there's been a little trouble in the factory.(19)
Wills:	Yes, I ... I suppose you could call it that, Mr Fibbs.(20)
Fibbs:	Well, what in heaven's name is it all about?(21)
Wills:	Well, I don't exactly know how to put it, Mr Fibbs.(22)

> *Fibbs:*   Now come on, Wills, I've got to know what it is, before I can do anything about it.(23)
>
> *Wills:*   Well, Mr Fibbs, it's simply a matter that the men have ... well, they seem to have taken a turn against some of the products.(24)

Wills's unease is indicated largely by his flouting of the maxim of manner. In sentence 20 he might have replied with 'Yes', but that would have broken the maxim of quality, as there has obviously been more than a little trouble. Instead, he uses the modal verb 'could' (which allows the possibility of *couldn't*) embedded under the non-factive 'suppose'. In 22 he breaks both manner and relation. In 24 he hesitates and has to reformulate his sentence, and then gives the essential information that the men have 'taken a turn' against some of the products, embedded under another non-factive, 'seem'. This circumlocution allied to the use of 'seem' is also used in 26 and 45.

The turn-around in relations in the sketch occurs as Fibbs discovers how intransigent the men are towards the products he is so attached to. This takes place gradually in the middle of the sketch. I therefore want to suggest a division of the text into three main sections, corresponding approximately to the following sentence numbers: I = 1–35; II = 36–71; III = 72–96. In terms of numbers of sentences these sections are roughly equal. The first shows Fibbs dominant over Wills and exhibits all of the features outlined above, the third shows Wills dominant over Fibbs, and the second provides the mediation for the change. I have selected sentence 36 as the hinge point between sections I and II because it is here that Wills initiates a conversational exchange for the first time in the sketch. First he replies to Fibbs's question and then he adds a new comment, taking the subject back to that of his previous utterance (26). In so doing, he also denies the presupposition in Fibbs's question, namely that employees cannot be dissatisfied if they have good amenities. Section II shows the two men exchanging control of the conversation. Fibbs takes back the initiative in 41, Wills attempts to take control in 53, Fibbs takes it back in 54, and so on. Section III, on the other hand, is marked by the fact that from the point at which Wills takes back the initiative in 72 he never loses it. As the sketch progresses through this last section Wills's lexis also becomes dominant, so that at the end, in the sequence about the bronzedraw off cock with and without handwheel, Fibbs, in his disbelief, merely repeats the main part of Wills's previous utterance. The last section is also completely denuded of vocatives marking their 'official' status relations. If we compare the density of status-marking vocatives in sections I and II we find that in section I there are five instances of 'Mr Fibbs', one occasion where Wills calls Fibbs 'sir', and three occasions where Fibbs uses 'Wills' – i.e. there is a status-marking vocative once every three and a half sentences. In section II there are two instances of 'Mr Fibbs', one of 'sir' and none of 'Wills' – i.e. one every ten sentences. Section III has none at all. We have already noticed that the conversational initiative changes hands relatively often only in the middle section. Hence there is a fairly gradual change in the relations exhibited between the two men. It is also interesting to note in this respect that as the middle section develops Wills breaks the maxim of manner less and less, becoming more and more direct in his replies. The battle for dominance can be neatly illustrated in sentences 55–61:

Wills: There's the hemi unibal spherical rod end.(55)
Fibbs: The hemi unibal spherical rod end?(56) Where could you find a finer rod end?(57)
Wills: There are rod ends and rod ends, Mr Fibbs.(58)
Fibbs: I know there are rod ends and rod ends.(59) But where could you find a finer hemi unibal spherical rod end?(60)
Wills: They just don't want to have anything more to do with it.(61)

In 58 Wills breaks the maxim of relation by not directly answering Fibbs's question, and the maxim of quantity by producing a near tautology. The implicature is that Fibbs's rod ends are not superior after all. Fibbs still keeps the initiative in the conversation with his next question, but Wills immediately counters by breaking the relation maxim in 61.

By now the linguistic basis for the turn-around in the situation should be clear. This leads to the absurd position whereby the manager at the end of the sketch is at the mercy of his shop steward. But this is not the only thing which makes the sketch unreal. It is also the case that there is a series of existential presuppositional clashes between characters and audience. Wills and Fibbs spend their time discussing items about whose existence we must have considerable doubt. A good example is 'high speed taper shank spiral flute reamers'. Like the other products in the sketch they are referred to partly by the use of a noun–noun sequence, this time an extremely long one. Noun–noun sequences in English are difficult for foreign learners because they exhibit few surface relational markers but can cover a wide range of semantic relations:

bath mat – mat for being placed by the side of a bath
armchair – chair with arms to it
desk drawer – drawer in a desk
can opener – product designed to open cans.

Because of the wide range of semantic relations associated with such sequences, the longer they get the more uninterpretable they become. Even 'spiral flute reamer' would present problems. Is it something spiral which reams flutes, or a reamer with a spiral flute? And so on. This problem of interpretability is made worse by the use of technical terms like 'comparator', 'flange' and 'bronzedraw', and the fact that a good few of the words and phrases carry overt sexual connotations, for example, 'parallel male stud couplings', 'off cock', 'pet cock'. Given the difficulty of interpreting the sequences and their bizarre connotations, I suggest that most people would infer that Pinter had made them up (in fact I am informed that they all exist; it would be interesting in this respect to know whether a group of workers from appropriate factories would find the sketch so absurd). We thus have a situation where the two men are becoming very heated over items whose existence we doubt. This is made even worse by the fact that both men presuppose that these objects are to be evaluated not in terms of utility but aesthetically and emotionally (cf. 'beautiful products' (37, 39), 'perfection' (49, 50), 'lovely parallel male stud couplings' (81, 82) and 'my ... own Jacob's chuck' (77, 80) and Wills's explanation that 'perhaps it's just the look of it' (47)).

This analysis has not used all of the categories outlined in the previous section of this chapter. It is, after all, only tentative and incomplete, and in any case it is unlikely that one short sketch would exhibit all the features discussed earlier. But it should be apparent that discourse analysis can be usefully applied in this example to account for much of the sketch's absurdity and 'dramatic' nature, a quality which is quite apparent even if one has never seen the piece enacted.

9.5 Conclusion

There are of course problems in using the kind of analyses outlined above.[3] Not least is the fact that the linguistic theory used for analysis is still open to discussion and modification. In spite of initial work by Searle (1975b) it is by no means clear how conversational implicature fits in exactly with the more general notion of indirect speech acts. Moreover, because the original categorization, although not as informal as my treatment, is still relatively informal, it is difficult in some cases to know whether a particular maxim is broken or not (cf. the discussion in subsection 9.3.4 above of the relation maxim), or whether a 'meaning' of which one is intuitively aware can be explained by the implicature theory. A related problem is that of the relative uncontrollability of speaker intention in what has sometimes been called a communication-intention theory of meaning. A speaker might break the maxim of manner, for example, either to implicate something or to try to disguise something from his interlocutor, as Rich does in the example from *A Man For All Seasons* in subsection 9.3.4 above. A complete theory will need to determine which case applies where. The maxim of quality often appears to be broken in casual conversation, where people quite frequently repeat what has already been said in another form. But the 'meaning' of such behaviour is more likely to be part of the general expression of social cohesion than implicature-like in type. Ordinary conversation is also more meandering than the strict application of the maxim of relation would allow. These two features of 'man-in-the-street-speak' can be observed in some dramatic dialogues, for example Pinter's sketch, *Last To Go* (for discussion of this work in sociolinguistic terms see Burton 1980, ch. 1), where the implicatures that arise pass not from character to character but from Pinter to his audience. The problem as to what level of discourse implicatures operate at is a good indication of the need for a fuller and more formal account; and to count as a reasonable and observable analysis almost all the passages I have looked at would require more detailed and explicit treatment. Another question which arises is 'How many maxims are there?' Grice suggests the possibility of a politeness maxim, for example, a notion which has been expanded in Leech (1983, *passim*), and which I have not really touched on at all.

What holds for implicatures also often applies to speech acts and presuppositions. It is not clear how many speech acts there are, or if they can be defined so that each is distinguishable from one another, particularly when we seem to be able to subdivide within speech act types – cf. requesting, begging, pleading etc. Do all speech acts have to have names already existing in our vocabulary? What speech act is performed by the normal utterance of 'Here's your tea, dear'? There are also problems in distinguishing presupposition from logical implication, and the types of presupposition that I have discussed do not seem to be discrete categories any more than those for speech act analysis are. But in a sense these are questions which always dog the stylistician. There will always be arguments over how detailed and explicit critical analysis should be. And as no area of linguistic analysis can ever really be said to be complete, the stylistician has always to take the analysis he applies partly on trust. Otherwise he would never begin his work at all.[4]

Notes

1 In fact the text v. performance controversy is a long-standing one, going back to at least Renaissance times (cf. Dessen 1977).
2 It is possible to treat Estragon's question as having to do with location rather than existence; but existence presumably depends upon spatio-temporal location in any case. Either way, Estragon's question is absurd.
3 For an 'opening out' of many of the above questions from within the domain of semiotics, see Elam (1981).
4 Many people have read this chapter for me. In particular I should like to thank Malcolm Coulthard, Geoffrey Leech, John Sinclair, Katie Wales, Richard Dutton and Henry Widdo.vson for their helpful comments.

References

AUSTIN, J. L. 1962: *How to do things with words*. Oxford: Oxford University Press.
BECKETT, S. 1965: *Waiting for Godot*, 2nd edn. London: Faber.
BOLT, R. 1960: *A man for all seasons*, with notes by E. R. Wood. London: Heinemann Educational.
BROWN, R. and GILMAN, A. 1960: The pronouns of power and solidarity. In Sebeok, T. A. (ed.), *Style in language*. Cambridge, Mass: MIT Press, 253–76.
BURTON, D. 1980: *Dialogue and discourse: A sociolinguistic approach to modern drama dialogue and naturally occurring conversation*. London: Routledge and Kegan Paul.
COULTHARD, R. M. 1977: *An introduction to discourse analysis*. London: Longman.
DESSEN, A. C. 1977: *Elizabethan drama and the viewer's eye*. Chapel Hill, NC: North Carolina University Press.
ELAM, K. 1981: *The semiotics of theatre and drama*. London: Methuen.
ERVIN-TRIPP, S. M. 1969: Sociolinguistic rules of address. In Berkowitz, L. (ed.), *Advances in experimental social psychology*, Vol. 4. New York: Academic Press, 93–107.
GRICE, H. P. 1975: Logic and conversation. In Cole, P. and Morgan, J. (eds), *Syntax and semantics*, Vol. 3, *Speech acts*. New York: Academic Press, 41–58.
KEENAN, E. L. 1971: Two kinds of presupposition in natural language. In Fillmore, C. J. and Langendoen, D. T. (eds), *Studies in linguistic semantics*. New York: Holt Rinehart Winston, 45–54.

KEMPSON, R. M. 1975: *Presupposition and the delimitation of semantics*. Cambridge: Cambridge University Press.

LEECH, G. N. 1974: *Semantics*. Harmondsworth: Penguin.

—1983: *Principles of pragmatics*. London: Longman.

MULHOLLAND, J. 1967: 'Thou' and 'You' in Shakespeare: A study in the second person pronoun. *English Studies* 48, 34–43.

PINTER, H. 1977: Trouble in the works. In *Plays: Two*. London: Methuen, 241–3.

PRATT, M. L. 1977: *Toward a speech act theory of literary discourse*. Bloomington: Indiana University Press.

QUIRK, R. 1974: Shakespeare and the English language. In *The linguist and the English language*. London: Edward Arnold, 46–64.

SEARLE, J. R. 1965: What is a speech act? In Black, M. (ed.), *Philosophy in America*. London: Allen & Unwin, 221–39.

—1969: *Speech acts: An essay in the philosophy of language*. Cambridge: Cambridge University Press.

—1975a: The logical status of fictional discourse. *New Literary History* 6, 319–32.

—1975b: Indirect speech acts. In Cole, P. and Morgan, J. (eds), *Syntax and semantics*, Vol. 3, *Speech acts*. New York: Academic Press, 59–82.

SHAW, G. B. 1965: *Major Barbara*. Harmondsworth: Penguin.

SIMPSON, N. F. 1960: *One way pendulum*. London: Faber.

STOPPARD, T. 1968: *Enter a free man*. London: Faber.

STRAWSON, P. 1952: *Introduction to logical theory*. London: Methuen.

STYAN, J. D. 1960: *The elements of drama*. Cambridge: Cambridge University Press.

TANAKA, R. 1972: Action and meaning in literary theory. *Journal of Literary Semantics* 1, 41–56.

WELLS, S. 1970: *Literature and drama*. London: Routledge and Kegan Paul.

WILSON, D. 1975: *Presuppositions and non-truth-conditional semantics*. London: Academic Press.

10

Ideology and speech-act theory

Mary Louise Pratt

A few years ago, assessing the impact of the Chomskyan revolution on linguistics, Michael Halliday said:

> For much of the past twenty years linguistics has been dominated by an individualistic ideology, having as one of its articles of faith the astonishing dictum, first enunciated by Katz and Fodor, in a treatise on semantics which explicitly banished all reference to the social context of language, that 'nearly every sentence is uttered for the first time'. Only in a very special kind of social context could such a claim be taken seriously – that of a highly intellectual and individual conception of language in which the object of study was the idealized sentence of an equally idealized speaker.
>
> (1978, p. 4)

Halliday is making an observation many scholars would wish to overlook: that linguistic theories encode social values; that they are, among other things, ideologically determined. These ideological determinants are observable in the assumptions theories make about what are the most basic and significant characteristics of language and its subjects; in claims about what kind of language is unmarked or 'normal'; in conceptions of what the project of linguistics is; in the content of idealizations. As Halliday suggests, linguistic theories often reproduce ideologies that hold in the social milieu of the people doing the linguistics: academic elites make theories in their own image. Through dialogue, people adopting different approaches to language can bring each other's ideological determinants into relief and make them available for recognition, acceptance, or critique. The impact such mutual demystification can have is suggested by the extent to which it tends to be avoided in contemporary linguistic debate.

Speech-act theory has been seen as a corrective to the abstract, individualized concept of language criticized by Halliday. It has offered many people, in linguistics, philosophy, criticism, psychology, even law, a way to move out of the realm of language as autonomous, self-contained grammatical system into the realm of language as social practice. This was the move that followed from Austin's original insight that not all utterances could be accounted for by truth-conditional logic. Some have adopted speech-act theory as a complement to autonomous linguistics, sort of a guest wing added to the house of Chomsky, and often labelled communicative competence (Hymes 1972). Others see it as part of a theory of communication distinct from the theory of language (Bierwisch 1980); yet others see it as a replacement for autonomous linguistics, arguing that social practice must be the point of departure of linguistic inquiry (cf. Halliday: 'language is as it is because of the functions it has evolved to serve in people's lives' [1978, p. 4]).

Speech-act philosophers tend to be very skeptical, however, about the theory's potential for characterizing language as social practice. While often acknowledging the theory's dependence on undeveloped assumptions about social interaction, they argue that it is impossible to develop these assumptions in any satisfactory way. Manfred Bierwisch, for instance, acknowledges that felicity conditions and Gricean maxims of cooperation represent scraps of an unarticulated theory of social interaction on which speech-act theory ultimately rests, but he argues that we are unequipped to begin working out this theory. Relatedly, Searle has observed that 'the literal meaning of a sentence only determines a set of truth conditions (or other sorts of conditions of satisfaction) against a background of assumptions and practices' (1980, p. 231), but he argues that trying to spell out that background can only lead to infinite regress, and should therefore not be attempted. Here we see speech-act theory working as a component of, rather than an alternative to, an autonomous linguistics. Thus, despite Austin's original thrust away from logic, much work in speech-act theory today is focused on exploring the logical properties of individual sentences. The fact that sentences are social interactions enters the picture as a rule only when a discrepancy exists between a sentence's literal meaning and its potential uses, as for example when someone says, 'Why don't you call Bill?' and the addressee, instead of answering the question, calls Bill.

Whether it is operating inside or outside autonomous linguistics, however, some of the ideological dimensions of speech-act theory remain constant. It is my purpose to examine some of these constants here, especially as they determine the view of literature that has followed from speech-act theory. Above all it is the normalizing and naturalizing work of ideology that I am looking at here, that is, its action of specifying within a discourse what is given or normal or natural, and what is problematic or abnormal or unnatural. It is perhaps helpful here to recall Catherine Belsey's characterization of ideology's capacity 'to present the position of the subject as fixed and unchangeable, an element in a given system of differences which is human nature and the world of human experience, and to show possible action as an endless repetition of "normal" familiar action' (1982, p. 90).

Like most contemporary linguistics, speech-act theory implicitly adopts one-to-one speech as the norm or unmarked case for language use. Examples and descriptions of speech acts always refer to THE speaker and THE hearer, and questions of intention and inference are always formulated in terms of only these two presences. Now it is true that private one-to-one interaction does characterize certain highly valued, and highly privileged contexts in this society, such as lovemaking, psychiatry, private tennis instruction or dental hygiene. But one needs to be skeptical about this case as representing any kind of natural norm. Certainly there is no reason to think of it as a quantitative norm, in this society or in any other. In addition to speech situations involving multiple participants with multiple intentions toward one another, people have myriad encounters each day with utterances directed at a mass addressee – radio, television, labels on packages, instruction sheets, and so many others. Even most of the two-party interaction that does take place is systematically shaped by the presence of other people, be they hearers, as in coffee shops and buses, or listeners as in talk shows and debates, or potential speakers, such as fellow participants in a meal. In short, not all communicative activity is as privatized as the speech-act model might suggest. It is argued that mass and multiple participant speech situations can always be analyzed as variants of or complex combinations of one-to-one inter-actions. The question I am now posing is not whether this can be done, but whether it should be, and why.

The one to one norm has been internalized to a fairly high degree by speech-act approaches to literature too, so the literary speech situation tends to be viewed as a one-to-one private interaction between THE reader and THE text (with the text substituting for THE author because she or he is not actually there). Such a model fosters talk of THE role of THE reader, but not talk about readerships, kinds of readers, and kinds of readings; or differentiations, for example, between reading as professionals (which is what professors do) and reading as apprentices (which is what students do), or between reading as a leisure activity and reading as work. It does not foster discussion of how texts are constructed to address mass and multiple readerships, or to place a single reading subject in multiple roles at once. This model makes it easy to overlook the fact that, though literary production and reception often take place in private settings, literary works are public speech acts (in the sense that they are institutional, and have no personalized addressee), and people are playing generalized social roles when they participate in them. Again, it is only fair to point out that much literary theory shares the one-to-one model of the literary speech situation.

Then, too, these lone pairs of speakers and hearers are generally taken in speech-act theory to be strikingly monolithic entities. In fact, the speakers and hearers of traditional speech-act theory are clear instances of the notorious unified subject, a villainous creature now being hounded out of France, and seeking refuge in corners of England and North America. Speech-act theory, in at least some of its dominant versions, supposes the existence behind every normal speech act of an authentic, self-consistent, essential subject, a 'true self,' which does or does not want to know the answer to the question, does or does not hold the intention that the other is supposed to recognize, does or does not have evidence for the truth of p, and so forth. It is to these selves, in other words, that illocutionary intentions and felicity conditions ultimately attach. The content of linguistic interaction is determined by the intentions these individuals form towards each other, and the quality of interaction depends on personal qualities, like rationality, sincerity, self-consistency, of the individuals involved. It is all a matter, as Austin loved to say, of a man's (*sic*) word being his bond. The idea is of an authentic self, fully realized through speech, and of speech fully adequate to the self-speech from the heart. Derrida's (1977) critique of speech-act theory addresses this aspect of the theory, as does a more recent critique by anthropologist Michelle Rosaldo (1982), who points out, among other things, the ethnocentrism of emphasizing sincerity and intentionality. Using data from her field work among the Ilongots, Rosaldo argues that these categories, and Searle's taxonomy of speech acts as well, cannot be extended to societies where the concept of self is different from our own. As Rosaldo observes, the focus on promising in speech-act theory is symptomatic of its commitment to a unified subject. More than perhaps any other speech act, promises (when felicitous) confirm the continuity of the individual over time – the beliefs, intentions, abilities, and desires that are here today will still be there a month or a year from now when the promise falls due.

One superficial but revealing consequence of the emphasis on individual beliefs, desires, intentions, and responsibilities is that speech situations in which people speak for or through other people look like marked or abnormal cases. These would include such examples as a person passing on a message, reporting on a meeting, newscasting, representing a client, being a spokesperson for a group, and many others. In fact, it might strictly include speaking in any institutionalized or ritual role that exists apart from the particular person who occupies it, because for any such role the intentions, beliefs, etc. behind the speech act attach to the office and not the particular speakers. Yet I can see no convincing reason to treat such situations as being odd in any way – they are so only with respect to an excessively privatized view of language.

In fact, once you set aside the notion of speech acts as normally anchored in a unified, essential subject, it becomes apparent that people always speak from and in a socially constituted position, a position that is, moreover, constantly shifting, and defined in a speech situation by the intersection of many different forces. On this view, speaking 'for oneself', 'from the heart' names only one position among the many from which a person might speak in the course of her or his everyday life. At other points, that person will be speaking, for instance, as a member of some collective, or as a rank in a hierarchy, and so forth. Nor is there any guarantee that these positions will be internally consistent or consistent with each other. Everyone has had the experience of being situated among complex and contradictory forces, as, for example, press secretaries stationed between the revelation demanded by their addressees and the concealment demanded by those for whom they speak, or the underling required on the one hand never to correct superiors so that they will not look stupid, and required on the other hand always to correct superiors so that they will not look stupid.

On this view of the non-essential, socially constituted speaking subject, context is not just the backdrop against which a person speaks; rather, the context and the subject mutually determine each other ongoingly. Beliefs, desires, and intentions are seen not as arising out of and attaching to an authentic, monolithic self, but rather as forces that are in play in the situation. Within the ideology of sincerity, when Lawrence Welk appears on a television advertisement and says, 'Buy these polka records. You'll love them. I know I do', he poses a problem: one should 'normally' be able to attach such statements and commands to some real Lawrence Welk speaking from the heart, but one suspects instead that the real Lawrence Welk is just doing it for the money. The advertisement is thus a violation of 'normal' communication. But once you step outside the ideology of sincerity, once you stop privileging the privatized individual or the concept of the personal, there is no one real Lawrence Welk – a hard idea to give up, I concede – there is only a subject (and in this case only an image) which in a given encounter is positioned in a certain way. At this point it is possible to characterize the situation beyond simply labelling it as deviant.

The usual argument in speech-act theory as regards the subject is to say that the actual complexity of a subject's position or inner state is irrelevant. What counts in the game of talk are the beliefs, intentions, knowledge, desires, and so on that the subject *takes responsibility for having* in making the speech act. But I think this will not solve the difficulty. It has for example been a matter of legal debate what (legal) subjects take responsibility for in making advertisements like the Lawrence Welk one. Moreover, people constructing grammars have to deal with the fact that complex and contradictory subjective states obviously have an impact on what actually gets said. The most familiar example is indirect speech acts. These can be analysed precisely as acts which mediate and express complex intentional states, such as wanting to get people to do things as if it were they who wanted to do those things.

In literature, the concept of a unified, personalized speaking subject has had a conspicuous effect on the way the role of author has been understood. For literary texts can manifestly not be taken as involving a private, individualized, monolithic self addressing another such self, sincerely, straight from the heart. To mediate these discrepancies, theoreticians have invented a special entity called the implied author, a voice or position abstracted away from the 'real' author who produced the text but who cannot exist 'personally' for recipients of the text. I believe this mediation is the only motive there is for postulating an implied author. If you stop privileging the category of the 'personal', and abandon the search for a monolithic authentic, 'real author' out there somewhere, the special, literary category of implied author becomes unnecessary. 'Authorship' becomes a certain position occupied by a speaking subject and endowed with certain characteristics and certain relationships to other dimensions of that subject. Alternatively, one could say that an implied author exists equally in all speech acts – an author is implied in a text only in the same way subjects are implied in any speech act they perform. In either view, authorship is no more, and no less, than another of the many ways a subject realizes itself through speech.

So far I have tried to show how one-to-one interaction and a unified, personalized subject are normalized by speech-act theory. Now when these pairs of unified subjects get together to talk, what exactly is it that they do? The speech-act answer, implied or explicit, is that they cooperate. Speech-act theory stresses language as essentially a cooperative form of behavior, in which participants work together rationally to achieve shared or common goals. These basic tenets emerge most explicitly in Paul Grice's well-known Cooperative Principle and conversational maxims. The Cooperative Principle, it will be recalled, is in

Grice's words, 'a rough general principle which participants in a speech exchange will be expected (ceteris paribus) to observe' and which says 'Make your contribution such as is required, at the stage at which it occurs, by the accepted purpose or direction of the talk-exchange in which you are engaged.' Grice elaborates this principle with four maxims: the maxim of quantity (say as much and no more than is required); maxim of quality (do not say things you believe are false or for which you lack adequate evidence); maxim of relation (be relevant); and maxim of manner (be clear, unambiguous, orderly, and so on). There is a clear supposition by Grice that cooperativeness is based on rationality, and that both are, to use a loaded but accurate term, human nature. To quote Grice, 'My avowed aim is to see talking as a special case or variety of purposive, indeed rational behavior. I would like to be able to think of the standard type of conversational practice not merely as something which all or most do in fact follow, but as something it is *reasonable* for us to follow' (Grice 1975, pp. 46–8).

Many speech-act theoreticians dissociate themselves from Grice's formulations either because of their informality or their value-ladenness. Richard Thomason bestows his kiss of death on them when he says they 'have more in common with the best and most rigorous literary criticism than with mathematical logic' (quoted in Gazdar 1979, p. 7). One frequent claim is that Grice's rules are regulative rules, rather than the constitutive ones speech-act theory is properly concerned with. Yet it is clear that much of the material stated in Grice's maxims is shared by the (constitutive) felicity conditions laid out by Austin and Searle. Sincerity conditions, for example, are analogues of Grice's maxim of quality; non-obviousness conditions are analogues of the maxim of quantity; and some of the preparatory conditions are analogues of the maxim of relation. Perhaps these parallels further the case for questioning the regulative/constitutive distinction.

In his own writing, Grice is careful to point out another limitation on his maxims, namely that they are formulated only to apply to language used for the 'maximally efficient exchange of information', and that they would have to be modified to apply to other situations. Such an elaboration has never taken place, however, and Grice's formulations now function widely in literature on the subject as the norm for non-literary verbal interaction (e.g. Gazdar 1979; Smith 1978). This despite the fact that people are surrounded all the time by speech events that are principled ways, not cooperative, not exchanges, not efficient, and where truthfulness, proportion, relevance, and informativeness are systematically absent or mitigated.

Several ideological parameters converge in this normalizing of the 'maximally efficient exchange of information'. The efficiency criterion represents speech as a form of production to be rationalized along the same lines as all production in industrial societies. Efficiency is taken as a natural or normal objective. The construct of exchange represents speech as a product or commodity being marketed by a speaker in a competitive but metaphorical arena often called the linguistic marketplace. What needs or desires motivate exchange here remains obscure (more on this below). The commodity being exchanged is named, however; it is information, a category associated above all with positivist science and mass communications. In normalizing information, the Gricean model normalizes what Foucault has referred to as the 'discourse of truth and falsehood'. In this respect it expresses the legacy of Russell's dictum that 'the essential business of language is to assert or deny facts'. Industrial production, commerce, science, mass media – these are the most powerful determinants of social and material life in the world of Grice and his audience, and his view of language is designed in their image. No wonder the Gricean view makes such a familiar and comfortable 'ideological *vraisemblable*' (as Coward and Ellis 1977 put it), meeting with such ready acceptance. Indeed, there has even been some research into child language undertaken to show that the Cooperative Principle is innate.

It has apparently been 'reasonable', however, to question the Gricean maxims in relation to other cultures. In an excellent early paper, anthropologist Elinor Keenan showed the inadequacy of the maxims for explaining the way knowledge circulated in the Madagascar community she worked in. Years later, this paper is still routinely quoted as the only living counterexample to Grice. For instance, here is Gerald Gazdar in his book on pragmatics and presupposition. The quotation is from a section revealingly entitled 'Some residual issues':

> If one could show that there are language communities which do not obey some or all of the maxims, but are nevertheless reasonable and rational, then Grice's strong claim about the nature of the maxims could not be sustained. One such community is discussed in Keenan (1976) ... where she shows that Malagasy speakers make their contributions as uninformative as possible. For example, if asked where somebody is they may typically reply with a disjunction even though they know, and are known to know, which disjunct is true. Likewise they normally may use syntactic constructions which delete the agent in order to conceal the identity of the person responsible for the action described. Also they use indefinites or common nouns even to refer to close relatives. This last mentioned practice is in direct contravention of a special case of Grice's quantity maxim ... Keenan's findings imply that Grice's maxims are only 'reasonable' and 'rational' relative to a given culture, community, or state of affairs. They cannot be defended as universal principles of conversation.
>
> (Gazdar 1979, pp. 54–5)

The astonishing revelation that the maxims are not universal could of course have been reached by examining almost any press conference, board meeting, classroom, or family room in the country, where the exotic and perverse practices that Keenan found among the Malagasy are likewise routine. Gazdar's conclusion that 'If Keenan is correct, then certain kinds of presupposition suspension, for example, that in disjunction, will not take place in Malagasy' (1979, p. 55) is revealing. It relates the oddities back to the logical structure of the Malagasy language, rather than to the sociolinguistic practices of the speech community in question. Speech-act theory is once again reclaimed by formal grammar, aimed away from its socio- and ethno-linguistic potential.

At this point, everyone's linguistic training compels them to object: 'But wait. The fact that Grice's maxims are not fulfilled in actual interactions is irrelevant. They are the rules that underlie interaction, and they are in practice honored as often in the breach as in the observance. That is the relation between the grammar and performance.' But the fact that a grammar is not an account of performance does not mean that the grammar has no relation to performance whatsoever. On the one hand, the grammar is in part an extrapolation from performance. On the other, the grammar does imply analytical statements about specific utterances. At the very least, it labels them as being either breaches or observances with respect to the grammar. This is what the normalizing potential of grammar mainly consists in. Obviously it matters a great deal where these normalizing lines are drawn. Minimally, analysing a phenomenon as a breach or a violation means according it a different theoretical status from phenomena that do not count as violations. It makes a difference whether repetitiveness in advertising, say, is analysed negatively as a violation of the Cooperative Principle or positively as an observance of some other principle that stands in the grammar on a par with the Cooperative Principle. As the example suggests, these lines are bound in some measure to be value-laden, to be ideological.

If one wanted to outline what is systematically missing in the Gricean cooperative account, and the less explicit Searlean account, one could start with three factors: affective relations, power relations, and the question of shared goals. First, affective relations among participants – degrees of hostility, intimacy, mutual concern, and so on – have a radical impact not just on what people do, but also on what rules they operate by in a situation. Take quarrels, for example. There is an obvious sense in which quarreling is cooperative. People quarreling do listen to each other, take turns yelling, maintain a degree of coherence, and so forth. But one would also have to recognize the operation of a logic of hostility which would give rise to different principles of interaction, such as a maxim of quality that says 'exaggerate the other person's faults' or a maxim of quantity that says 'try to get in the last word'. At the other end of the affective scale, we are equally uncooperative, in Gricean terms, with those we care about most. Consider the amount of sheer repetition that goes on among intimates, to say nothing of different standards of truthfulness and relevance. The Gricean sincerity-and-cooperativeness account expresses only a limited range of affective settings. Specifically, the account embodies the norms of emotive distancing, and commitment to efficiency and factualness that hold for predominantly male, professional, especially intellectual, discourse (such as this essay, for example). It is far from clear that these should be adopted as the unmarked case for all interaction.

Second, power relations. The Cooperative Principle refers to 'talk exchange', suggesting interactions in which all parties have an equal part. But it is equally common for one person or group to be calling the shots for others, for one person or group to be defining the purpose of an encounter, determining what quantity is enough, what topics are relevant, what counts as truth and adequate evidence, who gets to speak at all. Think of your last interaction with a police officer, or your employer. It would be incorrect to think of speech roles as always or even normally a matter of choice, of cooperation as always or normally voluntary, of non-cooperation as always or normally irrational. For hierarchical speech situations, to do so is often to define things only from the viewpoint of the most powerful party.

More generally, the notion of language as exchange brings before us the persistent and terribly misleading metaphor of the linguistic marketplace, a kind of verbal utopia where a mythical free enterprise of words prevails, all voices vying equally to be heard. An account of linguistic interaction based on the idea of exchange glosses over the very basic facts that, to put it crudely, some people get to do more talking than others, some are supposed to do more listening, and not everybody's words are worth the same. In addition to the commercial metaphor, one cannot help recognizing in this formulation the values of the academy with its vision of free exchange of ideas among peers untrammeled by hierarchy, where the production and distribution of true statements is seen as a self-motivating *sui generis* activity directed only by the intrinsic value of the products offered.

Speech-act theory thus tends uncritically to reproduce the norms of 'assertive discourse', the discourse of truth and falsehood now being examined from an ideological viewpoint by many writers, including Foucault, Derrida, Greimas, Fowler, Kress, Coward, Ellis, Silverman and Torode. An essay by George Alexander indicates the direction this critique has been taking: 'A certain kind of function is given to language in assertive discourse which is mined with difficulties: language is seen as representation and intentional, and therefore the position of the subject who signifies (judges, and affirms, and then goes on to legislate) remains unchallenged ... the tactics of assertion bring into play an either/or logic essential to the production of the discourses of truth and falsity, which function as effects of power' (1978, p. 25).

Third and following from the last two points, only some speech situations are characterized by shared objectives among participants. Clearly it is at least as common for speakers to have divergent goals and interests in a situation. Indeed, one of the most conspicuous and most systematic examples is the language of the real marketplace. When you step out of the dressing room in a clothing store in a pair of ghastly, ill-fitting pants and the clerk remarks 'Those look nice', the remark in quantity, quality, relation and manner makes sense only in connection with the interests attaching to the clerk's position, and these run partly counter to your own. There may be no good reason at all to think of shared goals as representing any kind of natural norm in verbal interaction. Jean Baudrillard says, 'This "scientific" construction institutes communication in a simulating model from which reciprocity, antagonism of partners, or ambivalence of their exchange are excluded right away' (in Foss and Morris 1978, p. 91). This is a part of what Baudrillard refers to as 'the terrorism of the code'. Presumably, Baudrillard would be equally terrorized by the Cooperative Principle or felicity conditions.

Several maneuvers are available to deal with the many cases where the standard account of verbal cooperativeness, sincerity, non-obviousness, and so on, does not fully apply. One is to uphold the standard account and say that all these other instances are violations of it; that quarreling, gossiping, flattery, exaggeration, bargaining, advertising, and so on involve deviant, infelicitous, or otherwise non-normal kinds of language use. In a Chomskyan model, such instances are referred, for instance, to the domain of performance theory. In their book on speech acts, Bach and Harnish (1979) use a similar maneuver. They set up a category called 'collateral acts' to contain a disparate set of supposedly deviant practices, including jokes, kidding around, punning, mimicking, reciting, circumlocution, changing the subject, small talk, ambiguity, and something they call 'sneaky presupposition'. These 'collateral acts', they argue, are not illocutionary acts, but acts which 'can be performed in conjunction with or in lieu of illocutionary acts' (1979, pp. 97ff).

No social meaning is supposed to attach to the words 'deviant', 'infelicitous', or 'collateral' in these formulations of course. They are merely supposed to mean that the instance in question falls outside the system accounted for by the grammar and must be dealt with at a different theoretical level, outside the grammar proper. At the same time, as I suggested earlier, these lines of normalization are ideologically laden. Among the cases systematically marked as deviant, one invariably finds all ludic kinds of expression (language as play rather than productive work); some forms of expression primarily associated with women, such as gossip, small talk, or euphemism; and other forms like circumlocution, indirectness, or deliberate ambiguity, that are associated with communication across hierarchy and across lines of conflict. The 'normalized' forms of expression invoke a harmonious and homogeneous social world that is quite different from any known social formation.

Most of the speech acts listed as falling outside the cooperativeness analysis are extremely commonplace and conventional. There are good reasons to be dissatisfied with a theory that designates much of what people do linguistically as lying outside the norms of their language. A second option is to expand the theory so that it is descriptively adequate to the status quo. In Gricean terms, this could mean adding some new principles of interaction, for example, a Coercive Principle, a Conflictive Principle, a Subversive Principle, a Submissive Principle. (It is far from clear that the Gricean model is the best one to pursue, however.) A third possibility is explicitly to declare the value-ladenness of the linguistic norms one is postulating, so that grammar-building becomes an avowedly utopian project. This is the move Jürgen Habermas makes in his work with speech-act theory. Habermas's ideal speech act (which has a number of features in common with the Gricean sincerity/cooperativeness ideal) is postulated as the basis for a social critique: to the extent that people's actual activities diverge from the norms of the grammar, those activities are seen as distorted – 'systematically distorted', in Habermas's terms, by malformations of their society (Habermas 1979, 1984; McCarthy 1978).

Questioning the norms of sincerity and cooperativeness has some clear repercussions for the analysis of literature. At present, the speech-act view of the pact between the reader and author is one of rational cooperation toward shared objectives. But just as one must question the notion of cooperation in other contexts, so one must do for literature. One must be able to talk about reader/text/author relations that are coercive, subversive, conflictive, submissive, as well as cooperative, and about relations that are some or all of these simultaneously or at different points in a text. Such developments would considerably enrich the speech-act account of avant garde texts, and of 'resisting readings' (Fetterley 1978) of the sort discussed by many feminist critics.

Let me turn finally to the literary question to which speech-act theory has been summoned most, namely the question of fictivity. Speech-act theory uses what Roy Harris in *The Language Makers* (1980) calls a 'surrogationalist' view of representative discourse. That is, it views representative (or constative or assertive) speech acts as language that stands for the world, as verbal undertakings to fit words to the world (see, for example, Searle 1975). Thus as I suggested before, the making of true assertions tends to be treated as a transparent, sui generis activity by speech-act theory. Perhaps because literary critics know so well the inadequacies of such a view, they have been happy to see literature excepted from it. Speech-act theory has so far produced a characterization of fictional discourse as a domain of verbal activity where the normal rules for speech acts are violated or suspended. This is a negative characterization: fictional speech acts are described in terms of what they are not, but little progress has been made in characterizing what they are. People say, 'Well, what they involve is pretending.' But as far as I can tell, pretending never gets defined as anything more than *not* doing the real thing – and there you are back where you started.

Now one can perhaps imagine why philosophers might be satisfied with dropping the matter there. Fictional representations, after all, are not their main concern. But it is a little more puzzling why literary critics, if they are interested in speech action at all, would settle for such a marginalization. Literary critics are perhaps better placed than linguists to recognize how misleading it is to think of representative discourse as only a matter of language molding itself to the world, and to think that true-false are adequate parameters for characterizing such discourse.

What is needed is a theory of linguistic representation which acknowledges that representative discourse is always engaged in both fitting words to world and fitting world to words; that language and linguistic institutions in part construct or constitute the world for people in speech communities, rather than merely depicting it. Representative discourses, fictional or non-fictional, must be treated as simultaneously world-creating, world-describing, and world-changing undertakings. For fiction, one must talk not only about assertions that stand in negative relation to actual worlds, but about utterances which place fictional states of affairs in some, but complex, but positively specifiable, relation to actual worlds. As this formulation implies, I believe the problem of how fictional discourses relate to actual worlds will not be solved by an attempt to find referential assertions embedded in fictional texts, as some have proposed (e.g. Graff 1979, pp. 41–58; Woodmansee 1978). It is just too simplistic to reduce all the signifying practices involved in representation to the production of true or false assertions. The irony is this: re-examining the norm of assertive discourse promises to open better ways of talking about fiction; at the same time it calls into question the very discourse to which linguistics and criticism aspire. Nevertheless, there is no doubt as to how to proceed. If there is going to be a serious linguistic criticism, there must also be a seriously critical linguistics.

References

ALEXANDER, G. 1978: Introduction to *Language, sexuality, and subversion*, ed. by P. Foss and M. Morris. Darlington, Australia: Feral Publications, 7–16.

BACH, K. and HARNISH, R. M. 1979: *Linguistic communication and speech acts.* Cambridge, Mass.: MIT Press.

BAUDRILLARD, J. 1977: *Le miroir de la production*. Paris: Casterman.

BELSEY, C. 1982: *Critical practice*. London: Methuen.

BIERWISCH, M. 1980: Semantic structure and illocutionary force. In Searle, J., Kiefer, F. and Bierwisch, M. (eds.), *Speech-act theory and pragmatics*. Dordrecht: D. Reidel, 1–36.

COWARD, R. and ELLIS, J. 1977: *Language and materialism*. London: Routledge and Kegan Paul.

DERRIDA, J. 1977: Signature, event context. *Glyph* 1, 172–97.

FETTERLEY, J. 1978: *The resisting reader*. Bloomington: Indiana University Press.

FOSS, P. and MORRIS, M. 1978: *Language, sexuality, and subversion*. Darlington, Australia: Feral Publications.

FOUCAULT, M. 1972(1969): *The archaeology of knowledge and the discourse on language*, trans. A. M. Sheridan Smith. New York: Harper and Row.

FOWLER, R., HODGE, B., KRESS, G. and TREW, T. 1979 *Language and control*. London: Routledge and Kegan Paul.

GAZDAR, G. 1979: *Pragmatics: Implicature, presupposition, and logical form*. New York: Academic Press.

GRAFF, G. 1979: *Literature against itself*. Chicago: University of Chicago Press.

GRICE, P. 1975: Logic and conversation. In Cole, P. and Morgan, J. (eds), *Syntax and semantics*, Vol. 3, *Speech acts*. New York: Academic Press, 41–58.

HABERMAS, J. 1979: What is universal pragmatics? In *Communication and the evolution of society*, trans. T. McCarthy. Boston: Beacon Press, 1–68.

—1984(1981): *The theory of communicative action*, Vol. 1, trans. T. McCarthy. Boston: Beacon Press.

HALLIDAY, M. A. K. 1978: *Language as social semiotic*. London: Edward Arnold.

HARRIS, R. 1980: *The language makers*. Ithaca: Cornell University Press.

HYMES, D. 1972: Models of the interaction of language and social life. In Gumperz, J. and Hymes, D. (eds.), *Directions in sociolinguistics: The ethnography of communication*. New York: Holt Rinehart Winston, 35–71.

KEENAN, E. O. 1976: On the universality of conversational implicatures. *Language in Society* 5, 67–80.

McCARTHY, T. 1978: *The critical theory of Jürgen Habermas*. Cambridge, Mass.: Harvard University Press.

PRATT, M. L. 1977: *Toward a speech-act theory of literary discourse*. Bloomington: Indiana University Press.

ROSALDO, M. Z. 1982: The things we do with words. *Language in Society* 11, 203–38.

SEARLE, J. 1975: The logical status of fictional discourse. *New Literary History* 6, 319–32.

—1976: A classification of illocutionary acts. *Language in Society* 5, 1–23.

—1980: The background of meaning. In Searle, J., Kiefer, F. and Bierwisch, M. (eds.), *Speech-act theory and pragmatics*. Dordrecht: D. Reidel, 221–32.

SILVERMAN, D. and TORODE, B. 1980: *The material word*. London: Routledge and Kegan Paul.

SMITH, B. H. 1978: *On the margins of discourse*. Chicago: University of Chicago Press.

WOODMANSEE, M. 1978: Speech-act theory and the perpetuation of the dogma of literary autonomy. *Centrum* 6, 75–89.

Part VI

Critical stylistics

11

Studying literature as language

Roger Fowler

For the past twenty-five years or so, there has been a running dispute between literary critics and linguists on the question of whether it is appropriate to apply linguistic methods – that is to say, methods derived from the discipline of linguistics – to the study of literature. There has been almost universal confidence among the linguists that this activity is entirely justified; and almost universal resistance by the critics, who have regarded the exercise with almost moral indignation. In this unyielding dispute, the claims and denials on both sides have been voiced with great force and passion. Here is Roman Jakobson (1960) putting the linguist's case:

> Poetics deals with problems of verbal structure, just as the analysis of painting is concerned with pictorial structure. Since linguistics is the global science of verbal structure, poetics may be regarded as an integral part of linguistics.
>
> (p. 10)[1]

But the critics will not have this. In a long, bitter controversy between the late F. W. Bateson and myself in 1967, the counter-argument against linguistics was based essentially on an allegation of unfitness. Linguistics is a science, claims Bateson, but literature has what he calls an 'ineradicable subjective core' which is inaccessible to science. Again, linguistic processing is only a preliminary to literary response, so the linguist is incapable of taking us far enough in an account of literary form and experience.

Finally, here is a dismissive opposition formulated by David Lodge, which is really saying that never the twain shall meet:

> One still feels obliged to assert that the discipline of linguistics will never *replace* literary criticism, or radically change the bases of its claims to be a useful and meaningful form of human inquiry. It is the essential characteristic of modern linguistics that it claims to be a science. It is the essential characteristic of literature that it concerns values. And values are not amenable to scientific method.
>
> (Lodge 1966, p. 57)

The opposition between science and values is at the heart of the refusal to agree; it manifests itself in different specific forms in many distinct arguments among protagonists for the two cases. What I would like you to note in this contribution by Lodge is the way in which the key terms, 'science' and 'values', are felt to be self-explanatory and conclusive. Lodge, like most of the debaters on both sides, requires us to take the central terms on trust, to accept them in their commonsense meanings with their ordinary values presupposed. In effect, Lodge is perceiving the two disciplines in terms of stereotypes, rather than analysing carefully the terms and concepts involved in the comparison. I do not say that Lodge is especially culpable, merely that this statement of his is characteristic of this habit, in the debate, of relying on undefined and stereotypical terms. Both sides are guilty of this.

I realized a long time ago that I must stop adding fuel to this dispute; since the confrontation was conducted in conditions of quite inadequate theorization, it was impossible to participate in it as a reasoned debate. Without getting involved in the controversy again, I would like to merely mention some common failures of theorization which render it impossible to deal sensibly with a question so naively formulated as 'Can linguistics be applied to literature?'.

1. A major difficulty, on both sides, is a completely uncritical understanding of what is meant by 'linguistics'. The literary critics make no allowance for the fact that there exist different linguistic theories with quite distinct characteristics. While it might be true of linguistic model 'A' that it can or cannot carry out some particular function of criticism, the same might not be true of model 'B' which has a different scope or different manner of proceeding. If the critics are not well enough informed to discriminate between models, the linguists do not acknowledge the distinctions; a linguist will work on literature in terms of the theory s/he happens to uphold as the 'correct' theory. Such is the competitiveness of the schools of linguistics that a devotee of one theory will not acknowledge that a rival might have some advantages for the task in hand.

2. A second persistent fallacy about linguistics, again represented on both sides, concerns the analytic *modus operandi* of linguistic method. It will be clear from what I have just said that different models have quite diverse aims, and procedures towards those aims. One model may have the purpose of accounting for the structure of particular texts; another may focus on sociolinguistic variation; another may be concerned to increase our knowledge about linguistic universals; and so on.

But there is a common misconception that linguistics – any linguistics – is a kind of automatic analysing device which, fed a text, will output a description without human intervention. (The critics of course regard this as a soullessly destructive process, a cruelty to poems, but that is simply an emotional over-reaction based on a misconception.) Now whatever differences there are between contemporary linguistic theories, I think they would all agree with Chomsky's insistence that linguistics is *not* a discovery procedure. Linguistic analysis works only in relation to what speakers know already, or what linguists hypothesize in advance. So the whole range of objections to linguistics on the grounds that it is merely a mechanical procedure can be dismissed; linguistic analysis is a flexible, directed operation completely under the control of its users, who can direct it towards any goals which are within the scope of the model being used. Complete human control is possible if you carefully theorize the nature of your objective, and the nature of the object you are studying.

Which leads me to mention a second set of deficiencies in the way linguistic criticism is theorized, and then to the more positive part of my argument.

Even if critics and linguists positively acknowledge that language is of fundamental importance to the structure of the literary text, there is no guarantee that they will present language in a realistic and illuminating way. There are three representations of language that I regard as particularly unhelpful, and I will briefly instance them by reference to the work of scholars whose commitment to language is undoubted and substantial.

1. The first problematic attitude is that which regards language in literature as an *object*. This position is implicit throughout the work of Roman Jakobson (see Fowler 1979a and 1979b). Jakobson's 'poetic function' claims that the important thing about literature is the way in which structure is organized to foreground the substantive elements of text – in particular, phonology and syntax. The patterns of parallelism and equivalence which he finds in his poems, at these levels of language, bulk out the formal structure, e.g. metrical and stanzaic structure, so that the text is re-presented as if its main mode of existence were perceptible physical form. The cost of this imaginary process is minimization of what we might call communicative and interpersonal – in a word, *pragmatic* – functions of the text. As I shall show in a moment, it is exactly these pragmatic dimensions which give the richest significance for critical studies. It is a pity that this 'objective' theory of language in literature should have been given currency by such a brilliant and influential linguist as Jakobson.

2. A second unhelpful attitude to language is that which treats it as a *medium* through which literature is transmitted. Here I quote David Lodge again: 'The novelist's medium is language: whatever he does, *qua* novelist, he does in and through language' (1966, p. ix). Presumably language as a medium is analogous to paint, bronze or celluloid for other arts. But the metaphor easily comes to mean 'only a medium': the real thing is the novel (or poem, etc.) which is conveyed 'in and through' the medium. Thus the substance of literature is shifted into some obscure, undefined, sphere of existence which is somehow beyond language. But for linguistics, literature *is* language, to be theorized just like any other discourse; it makes no sense to degrade the language to a mere medium, since the meanings, themes, larger structures of a text, 'literary' or not, are uniquely constructed by the text in its interrelation with social and other contexts.

This position is difficult for literary critics to swallow, because it appears to remove the claimed special status (and value) of literature, to reduce it to the level of the language of the market-place. But this levelling is essential to linguistic criticism if the whole range of insights about language provided by linguistics is to be made available. We want to show that a novel or a poem is a complexly structured text; that its structural form, by social semiotic processes, constitutes a representation of a world, characterized by activities and states and values; that this text is a communicative interaction between its producer and its consumers, within relevant social and institutional contexts. Now these characteristics of the novel or poem are no more than what functional linguistics is looking for in studying, say, conversations or letters or official documents. Perhaps this is a richer and thus more acceptable characterization of the aims of linguistic analysis than literary critics usually expect. But for me at any rate, this is what theorization as language involves. No abstract literary properties 'beyond' the medium need to be postulated, for the rhetorical and semiotic properties in question should appear within an ordinary linguistic characterization, unless linguistics is conceived in too restricted a way.

3. Implicit in what I have just said is my reluctance to accept one further assumption about language which is widespread in stylistics and criticism. This is the belief that there is a distinct difference between poetic or literary language on the one hand and ordinary language on the other. Critics generally take for granted some version of this distinction; and some linguists have attempted to demonstrate it: we find strong arguments to this effect in the writings of, for example, Jakobson and Mukařovský. But these arguments are not empirically legitimate, and they are a serious obstacle to a linguistic criticism which attempts to allow to literature the communicative fullness that is a common property of language.

I have given some reasons why the apparently simple question 'Can linguistics be applied to literature?' is unlikely to be satisfactorily answered. Because I believe that linguistics *can* very appropriately and revealingly be applied to literature, I want to re-orient the issue, in different terms. The solution is, it seems to me, to simply theorize literature *as* language, and to do this using the richest and most suitable linguistic model.

To be adequate to this task, a linguistic model should possess the following broad characteristics. It should be *comprehensive* in accounting for the whole range of dimensions of linguistic structure, particularly pragmatic dimensions. It should be capable of providing an account of the *functions* of given linguistic constructions (in real texts), particularly the thought-shaping (Halliday's 'ideational') function. It should acknowledge the *social* basis of the formation of meanings (Halliday's 'social semiotic'; see Halliday 1978 and Kress 1976).

The requisite linguistics for our purpose, unlike most other, artificially restricted, forms of linguistics, should aim to be comprehensive in offering a complete account of language structure and usage at all levels: semantics, the organization of meanings within a language; syntax, the processes and orderings which arrange signs into the sentences of a language; phonology and phonetics, respectively the classification and ordering, and the actual articulation, of the sounds of speech; text-grammar, the sequencing of sentences in coherent extended discourse; and pragmatics, the conventional relationships between linguistic constructions and the users and uses of language.

Pragmatics is a part of linguistics which is still very much subject to debate and development (see Leech 1983), but it is clear that it includes roughly the following topics: the interpersonal and social acts that speakers perform by speaking and writing; thus, the structure of not only conversation but also of all other sorts of linguistic communication as *interaction*; the diverse relationships between language use and its different types of context; particularly the relationships with social contexts and their historical development; and fundamentally, the systems of shared knowledge within communities, and between speakers, which make communication possible – this is where pragmatics and semantics overlap. In various writings (Fowler 1981) I have stressed the need in linguistic criticism to mend the neglect of the interactional facets of 'literary' texts: the rhetorical relationships between addresser and addressee, the dynamics of construction of fictional characters, and the sociolinguistic relationships between the producers and consumers of literature (see Fowler 1981). The second strand of pragmatics, concerning linguistic structure and systems of knowledge, will enrich linguistic criticism even more, and bring it into positive collaboration with literary criticism.

A 'functional' model of language works on the premise that linguistic structures are not arbitrary, nor, as Chomsky claims, broadly constrained by universal properties of mind. Rather, particular language structures assume the forms they do in response to the communicative uses to which they are put, within a speech community. Halliday proposes three categories of 'function': ideational, interpersonal, and textual. The ideational function is a key concept in linguistic criticism. The experience of individuals, and, around them, their communities, is encoded in the language they use as sets of ideas; and the ideational will differ as the dominant ideas of speakers differ. A simple example would be the operational concepts of a science, coded for the relevant speakers in a technical terminology; for these speakers, the terminology is one part of the linguistic organization of their experience: though this is a specialized part of the ideational, a technical terminology is only an obvious instance of a general principle, namely that language structure, in its ideational function, is constitutive of a speaker's experience of reality.

And of a community's experience; this is what 'social semiotic' means. Although, undoubtedly, some of the meanings encoded in language are natural in origin, reflecting the kind of organism we are (e.g. basic colour, shape and direction terms; see Clark and Clark 1977, ch. 14), most meanings are social: the dominant preoccupations, theories or ideologies of a community are coded in its language, so that the semantic structure is a map of the community's knowledge and its organization. An important development of this principle follows from the fact that communities are ideologically diverse: the existence of complex and competing sets of ideas gives rise to diverse styles, registers or varieties carrying semiotically distinct versions of reality according to the distinct views of individuals and of subcommunities. For the critics, this is linguistic support for the traditional assumption (formulated by Leo Spitzer but implicit much more widely) that a style embodies a view of the world. The advance in Halliday's and my formulation is that the availability of a formal method of linguistic analysis facilitates the unpicking of relationships between style and the representation of experience.

I want now to look at a textual example; for economy of exposition, a very familiar passage. This will not 'prove the theory', but it will suggest the directions in which this theory of language might take us. The extract is the opening of William Faulkner's *The Sound and the Fury*, a familiar but striking example of the way in which language structure gives form to a view of the world:

> Through the fence, between the curling flower spaces, I could see them hitting. They were coming towards where the flag was and I went along the fence. Luster was hunting in the grass by the flower tree. They took the flag out, and they were hitting. Then they

put the flag back and they went to the table, and he hit and the other hit. Then they went on, and I went along the fence. Luster came away from the flower tree and we went along the fence and they stopped and we stopped and I looked through the fence while Luster was hunting in the grass.

'Here, caddie.' He hit. They went across the pasture. I held to the fence and watched them going away.

'Listen at you, now,' Luster said. 'Ain't you something, thirty-three years old, going on that way. After I done went all the way to town to buy you that cake. Hush up that moaning. Ain't you going to help me find that quarter so I can go to the show tonight?'

They were hitting little, across the pasture. I went back along the fence to where the flag was. It flapped on the bright grass and trees.

(Faulkner 1972, p. 11)

The character from whose point of view this part of the narrative is told is Benjy, a 33-year-old man with the mind of a young child. It is obvious that Faulkner has designed this language to suggest the limitations of Benjy's grasp of the world around him. But how does the reader arrive at this almost instinctive realization? There are some linguistic clues, and these are very suggestive, but by themselves they do not answer the question of how we give the passage the interpretation I have assigned to it.

Starting with the language: although it is deviant, it is not disintegrated in a haphazard fashion, but systematically patterned in certain areas of structure. Two observations are relevant here. First, random deviance or self-consistent deviance were options for Faulkner; they could be considered different models of mental deficiency. Second, certain types of structure, through repetition, are 'foregrounded' (a process well known to stylisticians): foregrounding implies perceptual salience for readers, a pointer to areas of significance.

Most striking is a consistent oddity in what linguists call *transitivity*: the linguistic structuring of actions and events. In this passage there are almost no transitive verbs; instead, a preponderance of intransitives ('coming', 'went', 'hunting', etc.) and one transitive ('hit') used repeatedly without an object, as if it were intransitive. It is implied that Benjy has little sense of actions and their effects on objects: a restricted notion of causation.

Second, Benjy has no names for certain concepts which are crucial to his understanding of what he is witnessing. In certain cases the word is suppressed entirely: notably, the word 'golf'; in others he uses circumlocutions to designate objects for which he lacks a term: 'the curling flower spaces', 'where the flag was', 'the flower tree'. The implication of this is that he has command of only a part of his society's classification of objects.

Third, he uses personal pronouns in an odd way – look at the sequence 'them ... they ... They ... they ... they ... he ... the other'. He uses these pronouns without identifying who he is referring to and with little variation in the pronoun forms themselves. It is suggested by this that Benjy does not appreciate what is needed if one wishes to specify to another person an object which one knows about but the other person does not. This would obviously be a severe communicative handicap.

Fourth, there is a problem with Benjy's *deictic* terms: the words used to point to and orient objects and actions. There are plenty of these deictics in the passage: 'Through ... between ... coming toward where ... went along', etc. But these words do not add up to a consistent and comprehensible picture of the positions and movements of Benjy himself, his companion Luster, and the golfers whom they are watching. Try drawing diagrams of the sequence of positions and movements. Benjy is literally disoriented, with little sense of his location and of others' relationships with him within a context. The deictic inconsistency produces, for the reader, a sense of incoherence in the narrating, a feeling of being in the presence of a story-teller whose perceptions are disjointed.

In each of the above four paragraphs, I have first noted a recurrent linguistic construction, and then added an interpretative comment. The question arises (or ought to) of what is the authority for these comments. Let us be clear that there are no mimetic considerations involved, and no question of objective criteria for fidelity of representation: what reader could say 'I recognize this as an accurate rendering of the story-telling style of a person with such-and-such a cognitive disability'? and wouldn't this response anyway miss the point that language constructs fictions rather than models reality? But it might be argued, on the 'fiction-constructing' premise, that what happens here is precisely that the specific language of this text somehow creates Benjy's consciousness *ab initio*. This kind of argument, common in literary criticism, has never seemed to me very plausible; since linguistic forms come to the writer already loaded with significances, it is unlikely that words and sentences could be used to create new meanings autonomously in a particular text. It is probable, then, that the significances here are conventional, but having said that, it is necessary to define more precisely what is going on in the interaction between text, reader, and culture. At this stage of research, I cannot be absolutely exact, but can indicate something of the complexity of the processes.

Functional grammar maintains that linguistic constructions are selected according to the communicative purposes that they serve. It can be assumed that the total linguistic resources available to a speaker have been cumulatively formed by the communicative practices of the society into which s/he is born, and then by the practices in which s/he participates during socialization. On this theory, an explanation of my phrase 'loaded with significances' above would be that the linguistic units and structures available to an individual signify their associated functions: e.g. the word 'photosynthesis', in addition to its dictionary meaning of a certain botanical life-process, has the association of a scientific register of language; 'once upon a time' signifies narrative for children; and so on. If it were as simple as this, each individual would possess, in addition to his/her semantic and syntactic and phonological competence, a kind of 'pragmatic dictionary' in which the communicative and social significances of forms were reliably stored. This would, of course, differ from individual to individual depending on their communicative roles within society, but with very substantial overlap.

The catch with this model is that linguistic forms may be pragmatically, as well as semantically, ambiguous. There is not an invariant relationship between form and function. So the linguistic critic, like the ordinary reader or hearer, cannot just recognize the linguistic structure and, consulting his pragmatic competence, assign a significance to it. A more realistic view of linguistic interaction is that we process text as *discourse*, that is, as a unified whole of text and context – rather than as structure with function attached. We approach the text with a hypothesis about a relevant context, based on our previous experiences of relevant discourse, and relevant contexts: this hypothesis helps us to point to an interpretation, to assign significances, which are confirmed or disconfirmed or modified as the discourse proceeds. In the case of face-to-face interaction in conversation, feedback occurs to assist the refining of the hypothesis; with written texts, we are reliant on our existing familiarity with relevant modes of discourse and on our skill (developed in literary education and in other conscious studies of discourse, e.g. sociolinguistics) at bringing appropriate discourse models to bear. As critics know, the reader's realization of a literary text as discourse takes reading and re-reading, on the basis of the maximum possible previous experience of the canon of literature and of other relevant discourse; to assist this process and to firm up our hypotheses, discussion with other experienced readers of literature is invaluable.

I am not an expert on Faulkner, and can only suggest the direction in which the analysis might go. The features noted can be traced in other texts which characterize various limitations of cognitive ability or of experience. For example, similar peculiarities of transitivity have been noted by Halliday (1971) in the language which depicts the thought-processes of William Golding's Neanderthal Man Lok in his novel *The Inheritors*, and he has interpreted them, as I have done here, as suggestions of a weak grasp of causation. Circumlocutions like Benjy's 'the flower tree' are examples of a process called *underlexicalization* which is common in the characterization of naive, inexperienced people; cf. my comments on Kingsley Amis's treatment of his provincial heroine Jenny Bunn in *Take a Girl like You* (Fowler 1983, pp. 101–3). The use of personal pronouns without specifying their referents, according to the sociologist Basil Bernstein (1971, pp. 178–9), is a sign of an excessive dependence on context characteristic of working-class speakers of 'restricted code'; interestingly, this suggestion is based not on empirical evidence but on an example fabricated by a co-researcher: thus Bernstein is operating with an essentially fictional model.

The fact that the three texts I have referred to all come many years *after* the publication of *The Sound and the Fury* is not especially damaging: I am not, in this paper, discussing sources and influences, direct historical influence of one specific text upon another. I could readily find earlier instances of all four constructions with comparable cognitive significances (in older Gothic, naive poetry, diaries and letters of poorly educated people, etc.), but the point is to show that there exist for the modern reader established modes of discourse for the characterization of naive consciousness and which guide her/him towards the interpretations which I have suggested. This is the only basis on which the contemporary critic can begin to read a text. Later stages of critical practice can, and perhaps ought to be, more strictly historical. Faulkner is building a specific model of idiocy, as in the other sections of the novel, he is constituting other types of consciousness. The moral relationships between these points of view are of course the central concern of the fiction: Faulkner is juxtaposing modes of discourse to involve readers in a practice of evaluation. What literary, psychological and sociological discourses went to mould and articulate his models of deviant personalities is a question in historical sociolinguistics and pragmatics which I am not competent to answer without a great deal of research. But the research would be a kind of historical criticism of discourse and values. Critics may find it comforting that such research is compatible with the present theory of language – though of course not with previous formalist conceptions of linguistic stylistics.

Let me add a brief pedagogical and methodological conclusion. The theory of literature as language as I have articulated it is congruent with the elementary observation that students' critical performance, ability to 'read' in the sense of realizing text as significant discourse, is very much dependent on how much and what they have read. Because reading and criticism depend on knowledge of discourse, not ability to dissect text structurally, it should not be expected that teaching formal linguistic analysis to beginning literature students will in itself produce any great advance in critical aptitude. However, linguistics of the kind indicated in this paper, with sociolinguistics, discourse analysis and pragmatics, in the context of a literature course of decent length – in our case three years – is very effective. In this type of course students mature gradually in their command of modes of literary discourse, simultaneously gaining a theoretical knowledge of language and its use, and an analytic method and terminology with which to describe the relationships between linguistic structures and their functions in 'literary' discourses. Finally, since knowledge is formed for the individual in *social* structure, this approach is best taught and discussed in seminar groups rather than lectures and tutorials: thus experience of discourse can be shared.

Underlying these comments on linguistic criticism in literary education are my answers to some basic methodological – or meta-methodological – questions which were implicit in my opening discussion. These have to do with whether linguistic criticism is *objective*. The linguistic description of structures in text is certainly objective, particularly at the levels of syntax and phonology (semantic description produces less agreement among linguists). But it is clear that the assignment of functions or significances is not an objective process, because of the noted lack of co-variation of form and function. This does not mean that interpretation is a purely subjective, individual practice (a desperate and anarchic position into which those critics who stress the primacy of individual experience argue themselves). Criticism is an *intersubjective* practice. The significances which an individual critic assigns are the product of social constitution; cultural meanings coded in the discourses in which the critic is competent. It is understandable, then, that critical interpretation is a matter of public discussion and debate; linguistic description, allowing clear descriptions of structures and a theory of social semiotic, is of fundamental importance in ensuring a clear grasp of the objective and intersubjective elements of texts under discussion.

Note

1 The page reference is to Jakobson's paper as it appears in chapter 1 of this volume.

References

BERNSTEIN, B. 1971: *Class, codes and control*, Vol. 1. London: Routledge and Kegan Paul.
CLARK, H. H. and CLARK, E. V. 1977: *Psychology and language*. New York: Harcourt Brace Jovanovich.
FAULKNER, W. 1972(1931): *The sound and the fury*. Harmondsworth: Penguin.
FOWLER, R. 1979a: Linguistics and, and versus, poetics. *Journal of Literary Semantics* 8, 3–21.
—1979b: Preliminaries to a sociolinguistic theory of literary discourse. *Poetics* 8, 531–56.
—1981: *Literature as social discourse*. London: Batsford.
—1983: *Linguistics and the novel*, 2nd edn. London: Methuen.
HALLIDAY, M. A. K. 1971: Linguistic function and literary style: An inquiry into the language of William Golding's *The Inheritors*. In Chatman, S. (ed.), *Literary style: A symposium*. London: Oxford University Press, 330–65.
—1978: *Language as social semiotic*. London: Edward Arnold.
JAKOBSON, R. 1960: Concluding statement: Linguistics and poetics. In Sebeok, T. A. (ed.), *Style in language*. Cambridge, Mass.: MIT Press, 350–77.
KRESS, G. (ed.) 1976: *Halliday: System and function in language*. London: Oxford University Press.
LEECH, G. N. 1983: *Principles of pragmatics*. London: Longman.
LODGE, D. 1966: *Language of fiction*. London: Routledge and Kegan Paul.

12

'Working effects with words' – whose words?: Stylistics and reader intertextuality

David Birch

The starting point for interpretation processes has to be the language of the text. The question, of course, is 'Whose language? Whose words?' The writer's? The reader's? Can we, as readers, 'access' a text – any text – if we are concerned only with the language of the writer? Can we 'get' to that language without using 'our own'? Can we 'get' to the text without constructing it with our own inter-textuality? When we talk about style and stylistic effects, whose are they? 'Ours' as readers, or 'theirs' as writers? Neither literary nor stylistic analysis (if indeed one can make that separation at all) is just a matter of discussing such effects of language in a text, but is, as Deirdre Burton has suggested, 'a powerful method for understanding the ways in which all sorts of *realities* are constructed through language' (p. 230).[1] But what realities? Whose realities? The writers' or the readers'? Or that of the worlds they variously belong to – including the academic? Statements made by the critic only gain significance when the forms of the text are related to textual functions in one or more of those (and other) contexts. Understanding and articulating that context, I would suggest, requires rather close attention to be paid to the reader's intertextuality.

Deirdre Burton has posed the following question:

> And where do you go from here? You've taken some poem or conveniently sized piece of prose. You've spent time and effort mastering a sensible descriptive grammar of English. You've meshed understanding and knowledge of both to produce a rigorous analysis of the language used to construct your text, together with a relevant sensitive interpretation. You have talked about 'effects', 'foregrounded features', 'overall impressions', and so on. Very nice. Very satisfying. But what are you going to *do* with it. What now?
>
> (p. 224)

The question, I would suggest, is the wrong way round. The analysis should not come *before* the question 'where do you go from here?'; the *where* needs to be determined by the *why*? and *so what*? of the analysis. And that is determined, it seems to me, by readers, and articulated *through* their recognition of what it is that makes them read a text in a particular way, i.e. *intertextuality*. Analysis therefore provides the means for you as reader to relate the text to your own experience of language and reality by actually constructing the text through and with your intertextual experiences.

October 1997

ARNOLD
338 Euston Road
London NW1 3BH
tel: 0171 873 6000
fax: 0171 873 6325

Dear Lecturer,

I am pleased to present our new literary linguistics textbook, **Language in Literature - An Introduction to Stylistics**, by Michael Toolan, Professor of English, University of Birmingham, UK.

An activity-based introduction to stylistics, this textbook explains some of the topics in literary linguistics and assists students in the analysis of written texts. **Language in Literature** examines the ways in which language is organised to create particular meanings or effects. By covering a range of topics - naming patterns, modality and evaluation, the structure of simple narratives, the recording of character speech and thought, the dynamics of dialogue, presuppositions and textual revision - the reader learns about the structuring principles within the English language. Activities and end-of-chapter commentaries encourage a 'learning by doing' approach, teaching the student the main linguistic terms necessary for the analysis of literary and non-literary texts.

ORDER FORM

Please return to: Humanities, Marketing Department, Arnold, 338 Euston Road, London, NW1 3BH, UK

Tel:+44 (0)171 873 6355   Fax: +44 (0)171 873 6325   E-mail: arnold@hodder.co.uk

Language in Literature - An Introduction to Stylistics, by Michael Toolan
Published   December 1997   c.320pp

A Student's Dictionary of Language and Linguistics, by R L Trask
Published   April 1997   320pp

○ Please send me the following **on inspection** (paperback only):

○ I would like to **purchase** the following:

Qty	Title	Author	ISBN	Price
___	Language in Literature - An introduction to Stylistics (PB)	Toolan	0 340 66214 X	c.£14.99
___	Language in Literature - An introduction to Stylistics (HB)	Toolan	0 340 66213 1	c.£40.00
___	A Student's Dictionary of Language and Linguistics, 320pp (PB)	Trask	0 340 65266 7	£13.99
___	A Student's Dictionary of Language and Linguistics, 320pp (HB)	Trask	0 340 65267 5	£40.00

Subtotal _____
Postage* _____
Total _____

*Postage: UK - Please add £2.50 to orders.
Overseas - Please add £3.50 to the total order.

Method of payment

○ I enclose a cheque/Eurocheque payable to **Bookpoint Ltd** (cheques must be drawn on a UK bank)

○ Please charge my credit/debit card (please specify type) _____

Card no. _____ Expiry date _____

If the registered address of the cardholder differs from the address given below please supply registered address.

Name _____

Department _____

Institution _____

Street _____

Town _____

County _____

Postcode _____

Country _____

Telephone no. _____ Fax no. _____

E-mail no. _____

Signature _____ Date _____

VAT Registration no. _____

(for all customers who are registered for VAT in EC countries)

MEH70907   A   B

- **Contains a wide range of literary and non-literary samples**
- **Gradually introduces the principles of linguistic analysis of text**

Contents: Getting started / Cohesion / Modality and generic sentences / Processes and participants / Recorded speech and thought / Narrative structure / A few well-chosen words / Talking: acts of give and take / Presuppositions.

Readership: Undergraduate students of linguistics, literature, applied linguistics and sylistics.

Also available is R L Trask's ***A Student's Dictionary of Language and Linguistics.*** It provides accessible and authoritative explanations of the terms and concepts currently in use in all the major areas of language and linguistics, as well as in the study of the social, anthropological, psychological and neurological aspects of language. There are entries for the names of major language families, and there are also brief biographies of the major figures in the field, past and present.

- **Offers clear, concise explanations with a minimum of jargon**
- **Includes an extensive cross-referencing system**
- **An invaluable aid throughout the student's course and for revision**

If you would like to receive an inspection copy of either title, or both, please complete and return the order form overleaf.

Yours faithfully,

Milly Neate

Milly Neate
Product Manager - Humanities

But is that all? I would suggest not. We need to add that construction and consequent articulation of your understanding *how* and *why* you read in the way you did cannot be done in a non-committed, apolitical, neutral way. 'Language use is not merely an effect or reflex of social organisation and processes, it is a *part* of social process. It constitutes social meanings and thus social practices' (Fowler *et al.* 1979, p. 2). All language use is value-laden, but the quest for scientificness of language study has resulted in a discipline that is not prepared to make any judgements about its results, nor prepared to apply those judgements to the society in which the so-called 'science' operates.

Linguistic structures can and are used to 'systematise, transform and often obscure analyses of reality; to regulate the ideas and behaviour of others; to classify and rank people, events and objects in order to assert institutional or personal status' (Fowler *et al.* 1979, p. 2). It is naive to suppose that literature is any different from any other language in use in this respect. A critical linguistics, in this light, is therefore an alternative to a mainstream linguistics which has failed to 'serve as a tool for the reformation of society' (Jonz 1982, p. 176). As part of this politicizing of linguistic stylistics, linguistic analysis and the experiences of the reader should *determine* the analysis and interpretation from the very beginning.

The Cartesian legacy of self, free from context, is no longer tenable in linguistics (see Quinn 1982, p. 34). And the myth of 'self' as writer, and 'self' as reader functioning as separate, unrelated entities becomes equally untenable.

Linguistic structure is not arbitrary (see Pécheux 1982). It is determined by the functions it performs. Linguistics, for whatever use, must therefore be reoriented. This is happening, and, as it happens, more and more information is going to be made available for mapping the networks of meaning and significance which mediate between the structure and representations of reality. Probably one of the most common reactions to the earlier Jakobsonian analyses of texts, and their reluctance to engage in such discussions of meaning, has been a stylistics which is close to traditional literary analysis and concerns, and, of course, to traditional literary ideologies about the status of the text and its language within the canon.

Where discussions of meaning have been drawn from linguistics, the emphasis has tended to rest almost exclusively at an ideational level, resulting in a stylistics that seeks more and more to relate literary effect to linguistic forms within a *single* text. Rarely does this stylistics move beyond the boundaries of this text. The result tends, then, to be little more than a linguistically oriented practical criticism, with the ideologies of a literature discipline determining the theoretical direction of the stylistics (and all that means in terms of a privileging discourse and critical elite) and not the ideologies of a linguistic discipline that sees, for example, language as social semiotic.

But too much work has been done, it seems to me, in both literary and linguistic theory for stylistics to continue, as it seems to be doing, underpinned with a theoretical assumption that the text is sufficient unto itself. Single-text analyses dominate almost exclusively (but see Threadgold 1987). Intertextuality – the consequent alternative to analyses determined by a 'text in itself' ideology – has never been effectively tackled within literary stylistics, not that it has actually moved very far from its theoretical base into practical literary studies either. The consequence of this inactivity is a stylistics which continues to support the primacy of the writer and to interpret the linguistic struggles of the writer, not the struggles of readers, to produce dynamic meanings. A stylistics predominantly concerned with static interpretation spends its time *recovering* meaning by close analysis of interrelated linguistic levels. This is an argument in support of maintaining the primacy of the writer (and the mythical static meaning supposedly encoded into the text by the writer), and as a consequence, in support of the whole literature discipline and literature machinery that judges what should and should not be read (but see Hyland 1986). Such a stylistics produces some valuable insights, but they are insights related to a theoretical base which is, for me at any rate, wholly unsatisfactory. I prefer to work with a stylistics that is more focused on the semiotics of the production of meanings in social discourse, of which a text, determined by whatever means to be literary, is just a part, not the whole; a stylistics, then, which is rather more concerned with reading processes; a stylistics which is intertextual, instead of treating the text as an autonomous artefact labelled as intrinsically special by literary ideologues. This does not mean that this stylistics is simply a study of register, but that it is concerned with understanding literariness and intertextuality as *a process of reading*, and with demythologizing notions of autonomy of text and 'poetic language' and that language, style, literary form and critic are innocent, disinterested and transparent vehicles for the expressing of meaning.

As a way of moving towards that, I look here at a tiny segment of the literary work of Edwin Thumboo, Professor of English Literature in the National University of Singapore, critic, academic, 'blooded' dissenter against British colonial rule in the 1950s, and now member of one of the higher echelons of the Singapore establishment. These are important things to mention, because this knowledge and the fact that I worked with him for four and a half years determine the way I read his work, both poetry and criticism.

I am interested here in a short poem called 'Steel', written very early in Thumboo's career as a poet (1954), and published in his first collection of poems *Rib of the Earth* (Thumboo 1956):

Steel

They gave me subterraneous thoughts
How to work effects with words; for sauce
I gamed with alphabet,
Marshalling sense into the line
Till cunning showed beneath the verbs, cunningly.

Till mind, my mind, grew slanting
With habitations of the past.
Bowels of the soul congested, cough
In a current of fixed sounds.

How can others know my tongue-fire
Agony deprived of action?

O Abel, Rima's chords are lost:
The serpent bites,
Green Mansions, a scarecrow of steel
To hang our automatic greetings.

I chose this poem because it struck me as being an interesting statement about the dilemma faced by a writer as a radical under colonial domination (Singapore gained independence in 1965) – a dilemma which stands at odds with my image of Edwin Thumboo as a conservative, establishment figure in contemporary Singapore. This analysis is a way of me trying to sort out these different images I have as a reader of Edwin Thumboo. To get that far I have made certain assumptions: (a) that the 'me' of the poem is a writer, Edwin Thumboo, (b) that the 'they' of the poem represents a colonial presence; and (c) that the relation between these two creates a dilemma for one, but not necessarily for the other.

Beginning, then, with the first line, I immediately need to know who the 'they' are and who the 'me' is. What I know is that the 'they' gave 'subterraneous thoughts' to the 'me'. I wonder immediately about what is happening here. Can thoughts actually be given from one agent to another? The nominal 'subterraneous thoughts' is a surface realization for an underlying relational. That relational is a judgemental statement. What I do not know, though, is who is making that judgement. Is it the 'they' or is it the 'me'? The answer is important because, as 'subterraneous' denotes something underground, and possibly connotes 'dissent' when collocated with 'thoughts', who determines the dissent is presumably of importance. If it is the 'they' who are the cause of the dissent, then the 'they' might well refer to some organization intent on dissent. If it is the 'me', then presumably the dissent rests with the individual, and it is dissent quite possibly against the 'they'. The nominal does not tell me, but looking at it in this way can raise some interesting questions and more importantly fix the stylistics into an analytic methodology that questions every underlying assumption – a methodology that never assumes we have a shared vocabulary and understanding of texts. Is the 'me' the subject of the following verb group 'to work effects', or is it the 'they'? If it is the 'me', and the 'me' is the source of the dissent, then presumably the working of effects with words is tangible evidence of the dissent. One cannot work an effect without making the words public. I do not know, of course, whether the words are made public, what those words are even. If it is dissent that is being talked about here, though, it is tentative, uncommitted. I read it like that because of the following clause: 'sauce' connotes for me, in tandem with the idea of dissent, a sort of 'cheekiness' that may dissent but does so in a sort of tag-game way, a brief touch, not a full-blooded grasp and dissent against an issue. The verb 'gamed' seems to support this reading; it connotes, for me, the idea of playing, of toying with something. What that something is is the alphabet. What alphabet it is the poem does not reveal – is it for English? Malay? It is not Chinese. Is it the language of the 'they' as well as the 'me'?

Presumably it is the language of the people that effects are being worked for, but whether that is the same as the 'they' is not given. This, presumably, would be needed information if I were reading 'dissent' as one of the meanings in this poem. The 'me' is presumably the subject of the following verb 'marshalling', which connotes an opposite for me of the idea of playing. But just how does one marshal sense into a line? The image is military, it seems to me, one of bringing language under control, on the one hand, and of bringing, perhaps, people in a line under control as well. It may be different, of course, for other readers. Perhaps a reading that would contrast the control of the 'me' by the 'they' with the control of the language by the 'me' might work for me here? But of course I have made quite a large assumption in doing that. 'Sense' denotes both the idea of meaning and the idea of common-sense. Perhaps this refers to both the sense required to argue against control by someone and the sense required to recognize that one should dissent against such control. Either way, the manner in which such sense can be marshalled is not tackled, but a result is given which suggests that 'cunning showed beneath the verbs cunningly'. 'Cunning' connotes for me both the idea of dissent and the idea of knowledge. Both suggest the idea of power. Whose power, and what type of power, is not given. What is the agent for the verb 'showed'? 'Cunning' is the subject, but someone – an agent – needed to put it where it was so that it could be seen. The agent is not made clear here, and as a consequence the activity looks rather mysterious, as if it just happens naturally. Things, of course, do not work like that.

What I am reading here is a set of assumptions. One is that language can be controlled as an instrument of dissent, another is that the agent of that dissent is somehow 'outside' that language once meaning or sense has been marshalled into a line; 'cunning' shows all by itself, but it was put there 'cunningly', in other words 'knowingly' as one reading of 'cunning', and as a sort of sleight of hand, as another way of reading 'cunning'. The 'sleight of hand' reading would seem to be supported by 'sauce', 'gamed' and indeed 'alphabet', with its connotations of the nursery/playroom. The 'knowingly' reading would seem to be supported by the 'to work effects' and 'marshalling', where material supervention processes connote a rather more serious agentive control, one that looks outside the playroom and into the big nasty world where dissent is a political and dangerous activity. I do not think, though, that it is an either/or reading here. Agentive control is exercised both in playing a game and in controlling dissent. The question here is 'Who is the agent, and who put that agent into this position?' The nursery/playroom image is useful here, I think, in helping me understand my reading. Nurseries are where minds are shaped by people – usually parents or guardians. Perhaps that is what is actually happening here. The following line suggests this, 'Till mind, my mind, grew slanting'. Of course 'my mind' may be a grammatical subject of the verb 'grew slanting', but it is certainly not the agent. Who or what is? 'Slanting' connotes both deviation and conformity. Deviation from what? Conformity to what? Whatever the 'what' is, the supervention process suggests a mysteriousness, as if it is perfectly natural for minds to grow in a particular direction. But of course this is not the case. Someone or something determines that direction. Presumably the 'they' of this poem. If it is the 'they', then the 'they' are the nursery guardians, to keep that image going for the moment, and the 'me' the occupant of that nursery. In other words the 'me' is under the control of the 'they', not just in an ability to put words together in a particular way but controlled to the extent that thinking processes are controlled; they have been slanted with 'habitations of the past'. This is not such an innocent nominal as might at first appear. I would suggest that it is a complicated realization of several processes conflated together, the result of which is to make unclear whose habitations are being talked about, and whose past is being talked about. The chances are it is the habitation of the 'they', the guardians, and the past of the 'they' as well. In other words the 'me' is shaped and directed towards a particular way of thinking, and that thinking is located in a past that belongs not to the 'me' but to an unnamed 'they'.

My reading so far is that someone, the 'me', is under control. That control is in the hands of a 'they' who do not simply control innocent activity but also determine thought. That thought is the early, shaping, cultural thought of early life, and also a thought that recognizes this determinism as an activity unescapable though undesirable. The effect, I would suggest, is a dilemma of identity. People are what they are, yet, given certain changing circumstances, what they are may not be the appropriate identity. The result: one uses what one is, to determine what one ought to be. In the light of this poem, and the reading so far, I would suggest that this is the dilemma of the English-educated anglophile conscious of a past and an identity rooted in the colonial power but mindful of the need to break away from that colonial power and strike out on one's own. The child, if you like, is ready to break away from the family, i.e. the colonized country is ready to break away from the colonial power, but the break is difficult because emotions are pulled in both ways. The phenomenon is very interesting in a South-East Asian context, because the image of the child breaking away is a product of the colonial value-system, not the Asian one, rooted in the notion of an undivided family. This is the dilemma in 'Steel' it seems to me, written by an English-educated Thumboo in 1954 when calls for breaking away from Britain came strong and fast. It was not a dilemma that the Chinese-educated faced; the colonial power was never the guardian that shaped their thoughts in the nursery.

I have, of course, from the very beginning been reading 'beyond the text itself', and am, in effect, using the text as a surface on which to combine a variety of intertextual sources of my previous reading knowledge. So far these sources have remained unnamed. But I need to incorporate some of my reading history into my analysis of my reading of 'Steel'. Compare, for example, the following:

Singapore Writing in English:
A Need for Commitment

Despite being a residue of colonialism, English turned out to have blessings the more practical of which are too well known to repeat. At least three ASEAN nations are among the beneficiaries. Such is the rate of change nowadays that 25 years of gathering direction ought to suffice for a language to steady its literary nerves. If one had to hazard a date for so subtle a matter as a shift in attitudes to a language, I would suggest 1950 as the time by which English, which had arrived more than a century earlier, ceased to lie outside the imagination, the aesthetics of those using it. What marginally creative writing that had hitherto emerged, sporadically, remained so precisely because writers did not see themselves as Singaporean or Malayan. Their literary conscious-ness, the idiom they employed or approved in others were appendages of metropoli-tan traditions represented by England and America. They lacked an informing vision, and even were there semblance of one, fragmented and dim, its ingredients were not drawn from the real-politik of life under colonial dispensation. Borrowed visions, however potent, tempting and fructifying originally, do not take root in colonised hearts.

(Thumboo 1978, pp. 20–1)

This is an academic article written by Professor Thumboo and published in 1978, more than twenty years, at least, after the writing of 'Steel'. It is not disinterested, it is not the innocent, neutral comments of an objective academic: such things do not exist.

There are a number of assumptions here of interest for me:

1. English, a residue of colonialism, has blessings.
2. A language can steady its literary nerves.
3. After 1950 English did not lie outside the imagination of those using it.
4. Creative writing in English would not have been 'marginal' if the writers before 1950 had had an 'informing vision'.
5. A shift took place from English as a descriptive medium to English as a creative medium.
6. This shift was crucial to the growth of literature.
7. This literature was specifically Singaporean/Malayan.
8. The shift was created by those who rose against colonial power.

The opening clause, with its nominal 'a residue of colonialism', followed by the noun 'English' acting in apposition to the first clause and as subject of the second clause, avoids actually stating the underlying relational: 'English is a resi-due of colonialism'. This is a fairly bold judgemental statement about how one sees the role of English. 'Residue of colonialism' is a pejorative, and, as one half of a relational, English would presumably also be a pejorative. This is avoided by giving theme prominence to the adverbial 'despite' in the first clause, and not to 'English', which is as far away as it could possibly be from a theme position in the first clause, by using the progressive aspect of the verb; and by making 'English' the subject and theme of the second clause. 'English', which is actually understood to be a pejorative, is kept quite far away from that judgement in the surface of the text. Instead, 'English' 'turned out' to have blessings. Just what exactly is the agent of the verb 'turned'? Certainly not 'English', because English itself cannot be the agent of a material action or supervention clause. But, by making 'English' the subject of this verb and giving it thematic prominence, the writer makes it look as if 'English' is actually the agent as well. What does not actually get said is who did the turning. In other words just who exactly is it who decided that 'English' 'turned out' to have blessings? It certainly did not happen by itself, though it is made to look as if this was a perfectly natural phenomenon.

I then read that it has 'blessings' which, following the clausal patterning of the first and second clause, has an appositional nominal following – 'the more practical of which' – which acts as subject and theme of the third clause. What happens here is that the nominal actually realizes conflated relationals: 'there are blessings'; 'some blessings are practical'; 'some blessings are not practical'. Thematic prominence is given to the 'practical' not the unpractical blessings. In other words the emphasis is again on the positive side of English, even though it is a residue of colonialism. That positive side is reflected in the use of the nominal 'beneficiaries', which realizes something like 'X receives benefits'. The nominal actually conceals the process involved in the idea of receiving benefits – someone gives the benefits. The nominal here focuses attention away from that 'someone'. The 'someone' presumably would be the 'owners' of English, i.e. the colonial power, but the nominal makes it appear as if receiving benefits is just something that happens naturally, or, because the theme position in the clause is taken up by the nominal 'At least three ASEAN nations', that it is actually these nations and not the colonial power who are the agents beneath the nominal 'beneficiaries'.

Information that I am lacking at the moment, then, is just what are the blessings and who actually discovered them?

Being told that 'they are too well known to repeat' begs the question. Who are they too well known to? The readers of a journal devoted to English literature and thus with a vested interest in ensuring that English as a residue of colonialism is made to appear valuable in a country that actually rejected that colonialism and is made up of a population very few of whom could claim English as a mother tongue?

I get into the third sentence with a number of assumptions already made about the status of English, though none of them adequately explained. The explanation for accepting this 'residue of colonialism' starts to be made in this third sentence. The explanation rests on the nominal 'the rate of change', which assumes that the rate at which things change is a natural activity, that no one is actually responsible for that rate of change, yet is a realization of a verbal process that would require there to be an agent. Using the nominal removes the agent and hence the people responsible for the act of change. This is true also of the following nominal '25 years of gathering direction'. The verbal process of directing is removed by using the nominal. Who determines the direction? What exactly is that direction? Directions do not 'gather' on their own. People are behind this – who are these people? Who controls the rate at which the direction 'gathers'? Who decides how fast or slow it goes? The nominal makes it look as if directions just 'gather' mysteriously on their own, but this is not the reality. The reality is that there are people with vested interests in the direction something takes. In this case, that something is the status of a language which is the 'residue of colonialism'. Hence, the people with the vested interests are the people who wish to keep that residue of colonialism, rather than rejecting it with the rest of colonialism.

The distancing of these agents continues in this same sentence. What is the 'real' agent behind the process of the language steadying its literary nerves? Languages do not steady. People steady. So who are these people who have decided that 25 years is a long enough time for English to 'steady its literary nerves'? Because it certainly is not a natural process, as it is made to appear here. Likewise, the nominal in the following sentence, 'a shift in attitudes to a language'. Here I seem to have moved from a point where time was the mysterious and innocent agent involved in making English acceptable, to a position where it is assumed that time created the shift in attitudes. I do not read who the agents are of the process realized by the nominal 'a shift', yet shift implies a supervention process which in turn requires an agent. It is not given, and again the whole process of accepting English is seen to be one without agents; without people with vested interests involved; as if it is simply a natural, uncontrollable event. It is not.

I read that 1950 might usefully be suggested as the time when English 'ceased to lie outside the imagination, the aesthetics of those using it'. The point of pinpointing the actual date is to show at which time the 'literary nerves' of English had settled. Again, the verbal process realized by the nominal 'literary nerves' (a relational) is disguised in the nominal, and as a consequence so are the agents of that process. The relational, 'nerves are literary' or some such equivalent, is a judgement made by someone, not a natural phenomenon. In other words 1950 is a point in time when someone made a judgement about the ability of English to be used for writing literature. But what had it been used for before then? Was it incapable of producing literature before 1950? Well, it was a residue of colonialism, so presumably before 1950, when it was not capable of literature, it was capable of colonialism. In other words English equals colonialism but not literature before 1950, and because it can be used for literature after 1950 it is no longer equatable with colonialism. The logic involved here seems to be a little skewed towards a vested interest in maintaining English as a language for writing in, even though it represents in 'real' terms – though not in the terms of Thumboo's article – colonialism. It could be used for literature after 1950 because before then it did 'lie outside the imagination, the aesthetics of those using it' but by 1950, because of the *mysterious* agency of time, it did not.

Just what does this mean? First of all it looks as if one of the blessings that English had was that it could lie outside the imagination. But of course this makes it appear as if 'English' could cease of its own volition to lie outside the imagination, when in fact there had to be agents involved in that process. Who are the agents who decided that English could cease to lie outside the imagination?

Obviously, in these terms, one of the 'practical blessings' of English is therefore its ability to cease to lie outside the imagination, and thus be usable for writing literature. But of course this is a decision that has been made by an agent, not by language or time, as is made to appear the case here. In other words by an agent with a vested interest in promulgating English as a vehicle for writing literature in a country that had rejected colonialism, and all that that meant for the status of writing in English.

The next nominal to follow is 'what marginally creative writing', which is a conflated nominal for a series of processes something like: 'there is creative writing'; 'creative writing is marginal'; 'creative writing is not marginal'. In other words in the relationals underlying this nominal a judgement is being made; this judgement is not something that is 'natural', something that is innocent, it is a judgement made by an agent. Again, I do not read who that agent is in this text. It appears as if everything here is part of the natural, not culturally created, order. Further, the notion of marginal is not something that is related to the natural order of things. Again, someone has to decide what marginal means, what it is relative to. I read that marginal is relative to whether or not the writer was a Singaporean or Malayan. In other words creative writing was marginal before 1950 because it was produced with a language that was colonial and by writers for whom the language did lie outside their imagination and aesthetic. In other words those writers who did not identify themselves as anti-colonial produced marginally creative writing in English. Those who claimed themselves to be anti-colonial in and after 1950 produced non-marginally creative writing – presumably.

I further read with another nominal that 'the literary consciousness', etc. of these writers who did not proclaim themselves as anti-colonial were 'appendages of metropolitan traditions'. The traditions belonged to England or America, and so therefore did the consciousness of the writer who had not declared an anti-colonial interest. How then did that consciousness become Singaporean or Malayan? I read this in another nominal – with 'an informing vision'. Of course, the nominal realizes an underlying process, the agent of which is not clearly seen or stated in this article. Who decides on what constitutes 'informing'? Who does this actual informing? It is assumed, again, that it is a natural, innocent operation. It is not, of course; people with vested interests are the agents. What I read is that the informing vision would come 'from the real-politik of life under colonial dispensation' – in other words, unpacking the nominal and the processes it realizes, *dissent* would inform the vision. Those visions which are borrowed from colonialism 'do not take root', but visions cannot take root, they can be put into place, though, by people.

What I have tried to show so far is that the position Edwin Thumboo takes up in this article informs the way I read his poem 'Steel'. It does not mean, of course, that this is at all relevant to Edwin Thumboo's reading of this poem. I am not trying to psychologize readings for Thumboo; I am not trying to uncover meanings in the poem that say anything about him. It is *my* reading I am trying to understand and explain, not Thumboo's intended meanings.

I suggested in that reading that identity was a central issue for me. The critical article supports my reading to the extent of showing that a writer like Edwin Thumboo inevitably has a vested interest in his English-educated roots, though this needed to be unpacked in this article. Further understanding might perhaps be had by comparing two other poems by Thumboo, 'May 1954', a poem written, as far as I can tell, at pretty much the same time as 'Steel', and 'Fifteen Years After', dedicated to Shamus Frazer, Edwin Thumboo's English literature teacher in Singapore and written many years after 'Steel'.

May 1954

We do not merely ask
No more, no less, this much:
That you white man,
Boasting of many parts,
Some talk of Alexander, some of Hercules
Some broken not long ago
By little yellow soldiers
Out of the Rising Sun ...
We ask you see
The bitter, curving tide of history,
See well enough relinquish,
Restore this place, this sun
To us ... and the waiting generations.

Depart white man.

Your minions riot among
Our young in Penang Road
Their officers, un-Britannic,
Full of service, look
Angry and short of breath.

You whored on milk and honey.
Tried our spirit, spent our muscle,
Extracted from our earth;
Gave yourselves superior ways
At our expense, in our midst.

Depart:
You knew when to come;
Surely know when to go.

Do not ignore, dismiss,
Pretending we are foolish;
Harbour contempt in eloquence.
We know your language.

My father felt his master's voice,
Obeyed but hid his grievous, wounded self.
I have learnt:
There is an Asian tide
That sings such power
Into my dreaming side:
My father's anger turns my cause.

Gently, with ceremony;
We may still be friends,
Even love you ... from a distance.

Fifteen years after

That day when you left,
Taking for the safe keeping of us,
My figure from Bali,
Smooth, beckoning goddess
Urged to serenity by the lotus she stood on,
You too were poised in the brittle afternoon ...
That day of incense I have kept to this.

You died recently. They say you died.

But no matter,
Image and breath persist,
Grow as I grow, would not suffer the mind's quip.
Your beard, dubious, smelling of cheese and beer,
Affectionate, still presides; your voice pursues,
Sweet or harsh, but ever itself.
Many sit in their rooms, remembering how
You took us through Christabel, Sohrab and Rustum,
Death's Jest-Book, The Raven,
Brought new worlds to meet our own.
You lived – beautiful, precarious
Feeding us irrevocably on your self
While other gods shed their skin, withdrew,
Taking their notes with them.

But teacher and friend, white man,
What are they doing to you.
They, who come after?

Smaller, paler, full of themselves,
Suave, sideburned, tousled? Setting up trade
In principle, freedom, intellectual honesties?

They are eloquent,
These revivers of cliches, these late comers,
Who strike a neat phrase, write letters to the press.

Old Shamus,
Your image and breath slip.
You are dying now,
When I need you most to live.

'May 1954' shows mostly in the modals and the qualifications, the dilemma that exists between the 'they' and 'me' of 'Steel', i.e., in my reading, between the colonial and the English-educated 'anti-colonist' torn between independence of nation and independence (or lack of it) of thought. The contrast in 'May 1954' is expressed as existing between the 'we' and the 'you white man'. Dissent is open: the moods of the verbs are imperatives; the agent of those imperatives is the 'we', the goal the 'white man'. The language is no longer seen as belonging to the 'we', as it was in 'Steel' and as it was in the critical article; here it belongs to the white man. What belongs to the 'we' is the land, 'this place', 'the sun', peaceful streets, natural resources, self-respect, national identity, Asian identity. The only thing that belongs to the white man is the language. 'May 1954' represents one side of that dilemma, then: the need to demonstrate solidarity with a cause against colonialism. The modal 'may' in the line near the end of the poem 'We may still be friends' could well be expressing a willingness to remain friends, or it may well be a way of showing that the power now rests in the hands of the 'we' not the 'white man'. The modal shows that a decision has to be taken, and that decision lies in the hands of the ones ordering the white man to leave. Identity in this poem, though, rests with a return to non-colonial roots, in other words the ones not talked about in 'Steel'. The nominal 'waiting generations' is a realization for an underlying relational which is a judgement based on an assumption that future generations are (a) waiting to be born and (b) waiting for the white man to depart. The contrast is made throughout between the 'we' and the 'white man'; it is 'your minions' versus 'our young', 'our spirit', 'our earth', 'our expense', 'our midst'; and it is these that will be the heritage of those 'waiting generations', not the colonials who whore, who are short of breath, who riot, who adversely influence the young by such rioting, who try the spirits of others, who make their muscles tired, who extract things from the earth that is not theirs, who give themselves superior ways. The agents are out in the open, and it is clear, it seems to me, that identity in this case rests not so much in a positive vision of the future – that occurs nowhere in my reading of this text – but in a rejection of what is considered to be negative.

The other side of the dilemma, it seems to me, can be read in Thumboo's poem 'Fifteen Years After'. Here the actual heritage is a heritage rooted not in a father's anger 'turning a cause', as in 'May 1954', but in an English education which shaped a young mind. This mind expresses itself in a language which, if indigenized, could create a literature within which a national identity could be located. Potentially, it is a language which, if Singaporeanized, would be a mark of colonialism no longer. But the roots go deep. The English literature teacher – a white man, a colonist – is not treated as the white men of 'May 1954' are. It is interesting that 'Fifteen Years After' was not included in *Rib of Earth*, Edwin Thumboo's collection of poems which was dedicated to Shamus Frazer and contained 'Steel'. The white man of 'Fifteen Years After' is compared, like the anti-colonialists and the 'white man' of 'May 1954', with the new white men of post-colonial Singapore – the expatriates who 'come after'. I note the agent deletion here: the expatriates do not mysteriously 'come' to Singapore, they are invited and paid for doing a job, which, if it could be, would be done by a Singaporean. These expatriates, like the colonials in 'May 1954', are negatively contrasted in the poem. Shamus Frazer had a sweet voice, not harsh, 'ever itself', which connotes for me the idea of honesty. He 'brought new worlds', he 'lived – beautiful, precarious', he fed his students with his self. He was a teacher and friend; he was also a colonialist and all that meant in 'May 1954', but none of this is mentioned. Shamus Frazer belongs to the nursery; he is one of the guardians I posited in my reading of 'Steel', who helped to slant the mind, to shape the subterraneous thoughts, to show how to work effects with words, to marshal sense into a line. He was part of the 'habitations of the past', and he is uncriticized in 'Fifteen Years After'. He, I would suggest, is the other half of the identity dilemma. The expatriates in 'Fifteen Years After' are the necessary scapegoat for the sycophantic presentation of English education in the poem. They are used to offer a post-colonial, ideologically acceptable view of a Singaporean identity which in 'May 1954' came with a rejection of the colonials, and which in the critical article came with what looked like a rejection of colonialism but, once unpacked stylistically, turned out to be an embrace of it. The expatriates in this poem are like the colonials in 'May 1954'; they are small, pale, 'full of themselves', which I presume to connote 'arrogance'; they are suave, sideburned and tousled. They revive cliches and write letters to the press. In other words they show themselves to be disrespectful of the new order; they upset the kindly face of English colonialist humanism which was held so dear in 'Steel', in the critical article and in the figure of Shamus Frazer in 'Fifteen Years After', whose image is dying and being damaged by the white men who came 'after'.

The dilemma is very apparent. English, the residue of colonialism, was what shaped the 'me' of 'Steel'; it belonged to kindly old men like Shamus Frazer, who helped to shape the mind of the 'me' in 'Steel'. English as a language shaped the heritage of the 'me'; that heritage is inescapable and cannot be lost or shaken off, neither could the actual languages, the critical article made clear. Solution: suggest arguments about national identity and so on that are based on the reshaping of English as the property no longer of the colonial but now of the Singaporean/Malayan. The second paragraph of the critical article opens with the following line:

The shift from descriptive to creative modes, which turned English into an instrument meeting the expanding psyches, themselves evolving, was crucial to the growth of literature.

(Thumboo 1978)

What caused this shift? This is not mentioned. Shifts do not happen by themselves, they are created and controlled by people – people with vested interests. If your heritage, your mind, was shaped by English, as suggested in 'Steel', then you have a vested interest. If you are a Professor of English Literature in a country that rejected colonialism and have been writing only in English, you have a vested interest. If you have argued that English is now a property of Singaporean identity, then you are going to condemn expatriates who come to Singapore and use that language to 'revive cliches' and write letters to the press, because you are disturbing the carefully constructed order that has been designed (it did not happen naturally) by the people with the vested interests in maintaining the controlling power of English.

This, then, is the sort of analysis I would offer in an alternative, intertextual stylistics designed to explain readings. It is not disinterested; it is motivated from a position that is interested in understanding a text as a surface upon which meanings can be produced – meanings created by readers, not meanings supposedly encoded in a text by a writer. Whether they are 'in there' is not the issue. Something has 'allowed' me to read 'Steel' in that way, and I have tried to show some of the ways in which that has happened. I have tried to understand some of the relations that I feel obtain amongst my readings of a number of texts (a very limited number for the purposes of this chapter). More delicate analyses could take place amongst these texts and more stylistic comparisons be made at more sophisticated, more detailed levels than I have undertaken here. Further texts could be added.[2] My message is that an interested, intertextual reader's stylistics will necessarily be open-ended; it will be discursive and will not be specifically designed to articulate, as its sole purpose, connections between linguistic levels and literary effects, but will be as concerned with the reader's connections amongst texts as well. Intertextual approaches argue against seeing a text as an end in itself, and argue against explanations of reactions and responses to texts by intralinguistic means only.[3]

Notes

1 Page references are to Burton's paper as it appears in chapter 13 of this volume.
2 In this paper I concentrate on the criticism and poetry of Edwin Thumboo, but see Birch (1986, pp. 171–90) for a much wider selection of texts by other writers which form a part of my reading intertextuality for 'Steel'.
3 A version of this essay was delivered to the 23rd AULLA Congress, Melbourne, February 1985, and appeared as Birch (1986). I have also included some of Birch (1984), given the difficulty of obtaining that volume.

References

ALEXANDER, G. 1982: Politics of the pronoun in the literature of the English revolution. In Carter, R. (ed.), *Language and literature*. London: Allen and Unwin, pp. 217–35.

BIRCH, D. 1984: Style, structure and criticism: Introduction. *Indian Journal of Applied Linguistics* 20, 1–8.

—1986: Cunning beneath the verbs: Demythologising Singapore English poetry. In Hyland, P. (ed.), *Discharging the canon: Cross-cultural readings in literature*. Singapore: Singapore University Press, 147–90.

BURTON, D. 1982: Through glass darkly: Through dark glasses. In Carter, R. (ed.), *Language and literature*. London: Allen and Unwin, 195–214.

DURKIN, K. 1983: Review of Kress and Hodge (1979). *Journal of Pragmatics* 7, 101–4.

FOWLER, R. (ed.) 1975: *Style and structure in literature: Essays in the new stylistics*. Oxford: Blackwell.

—1980: Linguistic criticism. *University of East Anglia Papers in Linguistics* 11, 1–26.

—, HODGE, R., KRESS, G. and TREW, T. 1979: *Language and control*. London: Routledge and Kegan Paul.

HODGE, R. 1977: Literacy and society: Some consequences of linguistic modes of production. *University of East Anglia Papers in Linguistics* 4, 1–17.

—and KRESS, G. 1974: Transformations, models, and processes: Towards a more usable linguistics. *Journal of Literary Semantics* 3, 5–21.

HYLAND, P. (ed.) 1986: *Discharging the canon: Cross-cultural readings in literature*. Singapore: Singapore University Press.

JONZ, J. 1982: Review of Fowler *et al*. (1979). *Applied Linguistics* 3, 176–8.

KRESS, G. and HODGE, R. 1979: *Language as ideology*. London: Routledge and Kegan Paul.

NORRIS, C. 1976: Theory of language and the language of literature. *Journal of Literary Semantics* 5, 90–7.

PECHEUX, M. 1982: *Language, semantics, ideology*, trans. H. Nagpal. London: Macmillan.

QUINN, Jr. C. J. 1982: 'Literary' language: Is it different? *University of Michigan Papers in Linguistics* 4, 29–56.

THREADGOLD, T. 1986: Introduction to Threadgold, T., Grosz, E. A., Kress, G. and Halliday, M. A. K. (eds), *Language, semiotics, ideology*. Sydney Studies in Society and Culture 3. Sydney: University of Sydney, 15–60.

—1987: Stories of race and gender: An unbounded discourse. In Birch, D. and O'Toole, M. (eds), *Functions of style*. London: Frances Pinter, 169–204.

THUMBOO, E. 1956: *Rib of earth*. Singapore: privately published.

—1970: *The flowering tree*. Singapore: Educational Publication Bureau.

—(ed.) 1973: *Seven poets: Singapore and Malaysia*. Singapore: Singapore University Press.

—(ed.) 1976: *The second tongue: An anthology of poetry from Malaysia and Singapore*. Singapore: Heinemann.

—1977: *Gods can die*. Singapore: Heinemann.

—1978: Singapore writing in English: A need for commitment. *Commentary* (Singapore) 2, 20–5.

—1979: *Ulysses by the Merlion*. Singapore: Heinemann.

Part VII

Feminist stylistics

13

Through glass darkly: Through dark glasses

On stylistics and political commitment – via a study of a passage from Sylvia Plath's The Bell Jar

Deirdre Burton

13.1 Introduction

And where do you go from here? You've taken some poem or conveniently sized piece of prose. You've spent time and effort mastering a sensible descriptive grammar of English. You've meshed understanding and knowledge of both to produce a rigorous analysis of the language used to construct your text, together with a 'relevant' sensitive interpretation. You have talked about 'effects', 'foregrounded features', 'overall impressions', and so on. Very nice. Very satisfying. But what are you going to *do* with it? What now?

Don't misunderstand me. I am not, in any way, suggesting that I see no value in this sort of analytical method *as far as it goes*. Certainly, given, say, the shamefully scant attention generally paid to analytical skills in English language work in secondary education in Britain at the moment, I can see very good reasons for teaching explicit and rigorous methods for analysing the linguistic structures in texts. This can be seen as extremely useful preparatory material for worthwhile intellectual work in both literary studies and linguistics. On the one hand, it means that all students have, at the very least, a 'way in' to articulating their understanding, interpretations, or confusions about *any* literary text. This seems to me to be a considerable advance on the vague and slippery, 'competitive sensitivity' approach that often passes as a method of text explication in English literature classes, and which disenables many a bewildered student, who would love to do good work if only he or she could work out the rules of the game. On the other hand, an awareness of the fascinating complexity and organization of linguistic structure available as the meaning potential[1] of the language, together with a certain degree of confidence in recognizing and being articulate about structural choices and their resultant meanings, opens up the way to a substantial number of nice areas of study in linguistics *per se*; both the standard core elements in theories of language-and-mind and language-in-use, and the various interdisciplines like psycholinguistics, sociolinguistics, language-in-education, computational linguistics, and so on.

However, while all this is very much to the good in first-order pedagogic terms, it is some of the taken-for-granted, pretheoretical notions of practising stylisticians with which I wish to take issue here. To put my main point simply (and crudely), I am unhappy with the tacit assumption behind almost all the work in this field, that presumes that it is the legitimate task of the stylistician to observe and describe phenomena in a 'neutral'[2] and 'objective' way. More particularly still, I wish to take issue with the assumption that any such work *can* be done in a politically neutral way.

Historically, it is easy to see why stylistics has gone overboard on the 'objective', 'scientific', 'simple descriptive' approach to text. As an antidote to the extreme, élitist, elusive and determinedly dogged 'subjectivity' of traditional literary criticism in the twentieth century, recourse to the precise technicalities available within linguistics – an exciting, promising and challenging discipline available to many a discontented (and puzzled) modern languages graduate – was a welcome release from the vagueness and precarious lucky chance of insightful reactions to literature available in other models of debate. However, while linguistic models clearly do concern themselves with the precise organization of phenomena, and the relationships of generalization and abstraction to particulars, as well as the intricacies of the networks between theory and data, it is only the epistemologically naive who could believe that all this bears any simple relationship to 'objectivity'. There is no space here to rehearse the relevant arguments in the philosophy of science (and interested readers should refer to the following at least: Popper 1977, 1979; Kuhn 1962, 1967; Lakatos 1970, 1976; Feyerabend 1975, 1978; Tarski 1956; Davidson 1967), but I take it as axiomatic that *all* observation, let alone description, *must* take place within an already constructed theoretical framework of socially, ideologically and linguistically constructed reality, whether the observer/describer of observati.... is articulately aware of that framework or not. (For further discussion, see Burton 1981; see also Lakoff and Johnson 1980, who offer a very neat discussion of 'rational subjectivity' as a possible mediation between the artificially constructed contradictions in the subjective/objective dichotomy.) I also take it that any work which does not explicitly acknowledge its theoretical boundaries is open to analysis for its theoretical presuppositions, and *cannot avoid* demonstrating such presuppositions in some way.

This brings me to the question of 'political neutrality'. Again, I take it as unquestionable that there is no conceivable 'a-political' work in this, or any other, society. By which I do not mean that it is always easy to perceive or discuss or explain the precise and delicate relationships that obtain between any instance of work and its political status or political inference. Again, given that the focus of this chapter must – in time, dear Reader – be the practical analysis and discussion of the language in some text, there is no space to discuss this in detail, but see, for example, Barthes (1967, 1970, 1972, 1977); Derrida (1976); Foucault (1970, 1972, 1977); Lacan (1977); Althusser (1969, 1977).

However, I maintain that, as with observation and theory, and description and theory, any writer that supposes that he or she is politically neutral in their writing is merely naively supporting and demonstrating the (largely unseen and unnoticed) political bias of the status quo. What follows from here depends very largely on how you feel about the status quo. Let me state my own political biases as clearly as possible in a simple, bland way. It is clear that we live in a classist, racist and sexist society, and that is, at the very least, a highly unsatisfactory state of affairs. I believe that, of these three major and massive injustices, sexism is the most deep-rooted (psychologically), the most pervasive, the most difficult to perceive, the most resistant to change – yet available as a locus for important and essential radical impetus to the reorganization of all the unequal and oppressive power-structures in our society. (See Millett 1969; Rich 1977; Jaquette 1974; Daly 1978; Berger and Kachuk 1977; Ardener 1975; Delamont and Duffin 1978.) I also believe now that all academic work should be committed in some way (and there are many; see Burton 1981) to influencing long-term improvements in issues of human rights. Each to his or her own, of course – in terms of skills, and powers of perception, analysis, and influence. What we cannot, I think, support any longer is the self-indulgence of the mythological 'knowledge for its own sake'. *All* knowledge is contained and produced within an ideological framework. It is essential to distinguish between work which supports an oppressive dominant ideology and work which challenges it, and to state clearly which it is that you are doing. As all methodological components of theories are intricately related to the goals of those theories, responsible academics must continually state and refer to both the lower-order and higher-order constraints of the particular work they are doing, in order to make sense of that work.

Linguists and literary critics (and therefore also the hybrid stylisticians) have an especially obvious responsibility here. All linguistic work owes ultimate allegiance to the higher-order disciplines of cognitive sociology, political sociology, or the philosophy of mind. Whichever intellectual direction linguists choose, the recurrent questions and problems ultimately to be faced are to do with the specifically *cultural* human issues: thought; consciousness; action; interpretation; meaning; interaction; cultural and historical processes and influences; and so on. To be politically irresponsible in such areas is to be seriously culpable. Similarly, literary criticism (of whatever traditionalist persuasion) is again concerned with products and processes of human society in such a way that *not* to examine and act upon the political implications of literature, Literature and literary criticism *per se* is to be seriously at fault. (See Coward and Ellis 1977; Belsey 1980.)

In that a great deal of highly valued post-Romantic literature is specifically that which co-operates in constructing and maintaining the dominant ideology, and in that a substantial body of literary criticism in general (stylistics in particular) colludes in that construction and maintenance by 'appreciating' and 'describing' texts which hide the problems, conflicts and oppressions in that ideology, this polemical introduction is a plea for a radical rethinking of the contribution that stylisticians could be making to society. In European Marxist-structuralist writing there is a repeatedly stated appreciation of the powers of the non-authoritarian, open literary text in the first instance, a belief in the value of critically deconstructing any text in the second instance. If deconstruction[3] is the means whereby readers may begin to burst the bubble of the dominant ideology, then close analysis of the linguistic construction of texts and their 'realities' is essential, and a linguistic method, by virtue of its generalized tools and procedures, is an excellent strategy with which to begin such work.

13.2 Some general background remarks

The piece of prose fiction I am going to consider in some detail, is a short passage from Sylvia Plath's autobiographical novel *The Bell Jar*. It is a passage which details her experience of electric-shock treatment as a 'remedy' for severe depression. Readers may care to look ahead at this point, to section 13.3 below, where the text is given, in order to contextualize general points made here. Essentially, in section 13.4, I will be analysing aspects of clause construction and, in a preliminary reading of the passage, readers may find it useful to pay specific attention to the simple question 'who does what to whom?'.

Here, then, I want to consider two issues as preliminaries to that analysis. First, I want to map out a model of some relevant features of clause construction in general, against which *any* text can be charted, and our Plath text will be charted. Secondly, I want to discuss why this type of analysis is particularly relevant to the issues raised in the introduction, and similarly why this specific text was chosen for analysis.

The model of processes and participants in the structure of clauses that I shall draw here is adapted from ideas in the work of Michael Halliday (1970, 1973, 1978). Among other things, he offers a model of the underlying semantic options available in English as *types* or processes which are expressed in the clause – the essential unit of construction in any text. My simplified map of those options – with demonstration examples – is reproduced in Figure 13.1. Readers wanting an expanded description should consult Berry (1975, pp. 149ff.) for a clear and precise exposition; a gentle guide. As she says:

> In English grammar we make choices between different types of process, between different types of participant, between different types of circumstance, between different roles for participants and circumstances, between different numbers of participants and circumstances, between different ways of combining processes, participants and circumstances. These choices are known collectively as the *transitivity* choices.
>
> (Berry 1975, p. 150)

Here we shall be dealing with a limited and simplified version of some of these choices, which brings us to several central points which can be made in relation to the semantic map in Figure 13.1. First, it should be understood that the question 'who *does what* to whom?' only makes interesting sense when asked against a background knowledge of all possible options or 'ways of doing' that are available for use in the language. This sign-system relationship is, I take it, a commonplace in linguistic semiotics (Firth 1957; Saussure 1974; Halliday 1978), but the force of it might need restatement here. The point being that, although one might, certainly, approach the processes of the text in an insightful, intuitive way, and observe some relevant patterns of choice there, this map of meaningful options allows us clarity and precision and neatness in analysing the processes

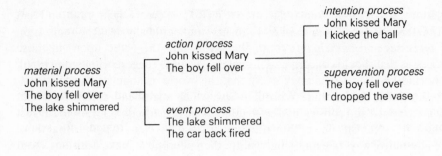

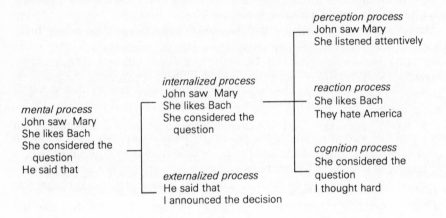

relational process
Truth is Beauty
She is my daughter
They are in the garden

Figure 13.1   Process options.

realized in this text, *compared* with (a) any other text, (b) the absences (Macherey 1978) in this text – the relevant 'other choices' that could have been made – the 'noticeable absences' (Sacks and Schegloff 1973). Thus, it allows us really to see 'what it means' to have chosen particular prominence for, say, one type of process.

Let me quickly also try to explain why processes and participants are a strong place to begin analysis given the arguments in section 13.1 above. If the analyst is interested in 'making strange'[4] the power-relationships that obtain in the socially constructed world – be it the 'real' world of public and private social relationships or the spoken and written texts that we create, hear, read, and that ultimately construct *us* in that 'real' world – then, crucially, it is the realization of *processes* and *participants* (both the actors and the acted upon) in those processes that should concern us. Ultimately, I want to suggest, with Sapir (1956), Whorf (1956) and Vološinov (1973), that the 'world' is linguistically constructed. But rather than a crude Whorfian view, which might lead us to believe that we are trapped and constrained by that linguistic construction, I want to suggest a far more optimistic line of thought. Simply, once it is clear to people that there are alternative ways of expressing 'reality', then people can make decisions about how to express 'reality', both for others and themselves. By this means, we can both deconstruct and *reconstruct* our realities to an enabling degree.

And this brings me to an explanation of why the Plath text seemed peculiarly appropriate to a feminist-linguistic polemic.

Where the topic of 'women and literature' is concerned, there are three immediate areas of thought and study that are being researched:

(a) Images of women in literature written by males – particularly in relation to details of social history. This is, of course, work that draws upon, and contributes to, a 'new' feminist version of that history. (See Rowbotham 1973a, 1973b.)

(b) Images of women in literature written by feminist women. This may well involve *finding* them in the first place. (See Showalter 1977; Rich 1977.)

(c) Images of women in literature by women who were not/are not feminists – either by 'free' choice, or because they were unaware that that choice was available to them.

Sylvia Plath's work and life can clearly be seen in relation to the third point here. Reading her prose, poems and letters, and reading about her, in the context of the raised consciousness and women's support groups of the 1970s and 1980s, is a moving, and disturbing, experience. It is so easy for *us* to locate her contradictions, dilemmas and pressures as they are expressed by her texts. It is so easy to see her writing herself *into* a concept of helpless victim, and eventually, perhaps, into suicide itself.[5] Her texts abound in disenabling metaphors, disenabling lexis, and – I wish to demonstrate here – disenabling syntactic structures.

To return to the mood of section 13.1, I want to assert the importance of perceiving those sorts of forces, pervasive in the language around us, and would maintain that both individuals and social institutions require analytical access to knowledge about the intricacies of the relationship between linguistic structures and reality, such that, with that knowledge, reality might be reconstructed in less damaging ways – and again, I would emphasize, with regard to both individuals and social institutions.

I do not, by any means, wish to suggest that only women 'are' victims, or construct themselves as such. If this were a text written by a man (and there are, of course, similar texts), then it would be open to similar sympathetic analysis and discussion. However, that seems to me to be a job for somebody else to do, given that life is short and we must follow our immediate priorities. My general message is: stylistic analysis is *not* just a question of discussing 'effects' in language and text, but a powerful method for understanding the ways in which all sorts of 'realities' are constructed through language. For feminists who believe that 'the personal is political' there is a burning issue which has to be investigated immediately, and in various triangulated ways. We want to understand the relationships between severe and crippling depression that many women experience and the contradictory and disenabling images of self available for women in models of literature, the media, education, folk-notions of the family, motherhood, daughterhood, work, and so on. It is just these contradictions, it has been argued, that are influential in breakdowns of various sorts. As with so much in this chapter, this is a truncated version of a complex and problematic area of discussion, whose complexities are unfortunately minimized here. Suffice it to say that the contradictions that abound in the language of Sylvia Plath's texts make her an important woman to study from a feminist perspective. Any reader with any other radical political commitment should see what follows as a model to appropriate and to be made relevant to his or her own convictions.

13.3 The text

The wall-eyed nurse came back. She unclasped my watch and dropped it in her pocket. Then she started tweaking the hairpins from my hair.

Doctor Gordon was unlocking the closet. He dragged out a table on wheels with a machine on it and rolled it behind the head of the bed. The nurse started swabbing my temples with a smelly grease.

As she leaned over to reach the side of my head nearest the wall, her fat breast muffled my face like a cloud or a pillow. A vague, medicinal stench emanated from her flesh.

'Don't worry,' the nurse grinned down at me. 'Their first time everybody's scared to death.'

I tried to smile, but my skin had gone stiff, like parchment.

Doctor Gordon was fitting two metal plates on either side of my head. He buckled them into place with a strap that dented my forehead, and gave me a wire to bite.

I shut my eyes.

There was a brief silence, like an indrawn breath.

Then something bent down and took hold of me and shook me like the end of the world. Whee-ee-ee-ee-ee, it shrilled, through an air crackling with blue light, and with each flash a great jolt drubbed me till I thought my bones would break and the sap fly out of me like a split plant.

I wondered what terrible thing it was that I had done.

13.4 Analysis

On reading the passage, readers[6] repeatedly formulate the following sorts of responses:

(a) the persona seems quite helpless;
(b) the persona seems 'at a distance', 'outside herself', 'watching herself', 'detached to being with – and then just a victim';

(c) the medical staff seem more interested in getting the job done than caring.

In order to understand something of what is happening in the language of this passage, that gives rise to such responses, the following instructions enable us to get a firmer grasp of the persona's 'reality' as constructed in the clause-by-clause make-up of the text as a whole:

(a) isolate the processes *per se*, and find which participant (who or what) is 'doing' each process;
(b) find what *sorts* of process they are, and which participant is engaged in which type of process;
(c) find who or what is *affected* by each of these processes.

First, then, here is the text repeated with sentences numbered for ease of reference, and processes isolated and italicized.

(1) The wall-eyed nurse *came back*. (2) She *unclasped* my watch and *dropped* it in her pocket. (3) Then she *started tweaking* the hairpins from my hair.
(4) Doctor Gordon *was unlocking* the closet. (5) He *dragged out* a table on wheels with a machine on it and *rolled* it behind the head of the bed. (6) The nurse *started swabbing* my temples with a smelly grease.
(7) As she *leaned over to reach* the side of my head nearest the wall, her fat breast *muffled* my face like a cloud or a pillow. (8) A vague, medicinal stench *emanated* from her flesh.
(9) 'Don't worry,' the nurse *grinned* down at me. (10) 'Their first time everybody's scared to death.'
(11) I *tried to smile*, but my skin *had gone stiff*, like parchment.
(12) Doctor Gordon *was fitting* two metal plates on either side of my head. (13) He *buckled* them into place with a strap that *dented* my forehead, and *gave me a wire to bite*.
(14) I *shut* my eyes.
(15) There *was* a brief silence, like an indrawn breath.
(16) Then something *bent down* and *took hold* of me and *shook* me like the end of the world. (17) Whee-ee-ee-ee-ee, it *shrilled*, through an air crackling with blue light, and with each flash a great jolt *drubbed* me till I *thought* my bones *would break* and the sap *fly out* of me like a split plant.
(18) I *wondered* what terrible thing it *was* that I *had done*.

Given this simple skeleton analysis, we can abstract out the actors in each process,[7] and spell out the lexical realization of each of the processes associated with them:

Sentence No.	Actor	Process
1	nurse	came back
2a	nurse	unclasped
b	nurse	dropped
3	nurse	started tweaking
4	doctor	was unlocking
5a	doctor	dragged out
b	doctor	rolled

6	nurse	started swabbing
7a	nurse	leaned over to reach
b	nurse's body part	muffled
8	nurse's body contingency	emanated
9a	n.a.	n.a.
b	nurse	grinned
10	n.a.	n.a.
11a	persona	tried to smile
b	persona's body part	had gone stiff
12	doctor	was fitting
13a	doctor	buckled
b	doctor's equipment	dented
c	doctor	gave ... to bite
14	persona	shut
15	–	was
16a	something (electricity)	bent down and took hold
b	something (electricity)	shook
17a	something (electricity)	shrilled
b	electricity part	drubbed
c	persona	thought
d	persona body part	would break
e	persona body part	fly out
18a	persona	wondered
b	–	was
c	persona	had done

The analysis is simple, but the resultant table above gives access to a clear, general picture of who is doing what and when in the persona's description of the 'world' around her. The first half of the text gives the nurse and doctor performing all actions (1–10). We have a brief mention of the persona as actor (11), and then the doctor and his equipment dominate the action (12, 13). We have another brief mention of a negative persona as actor (14), the electricity as actor in a very positive sense (16–17) and finally the persona as actor – in a hypothetical sense at least. We shall be able to say more about the types of process below. A simple counting of actors and their actions shows us very little:

nurse (including body parts) as actor: 8
doctor (including his equipment) as actor: 7
electricity as actor: 4
persona (including body parts) as actor: 7

This is interesting in view of the often expressed pre-analytic response, 'the persona doesn't *do* anything'. Clearly, we can see what readers 'mean' when they say that, but we have to pursue the analysis further, and rephrase the response to capture the 'reality' of the text. What this analysis does lay bare is the *succession* of actors in the scene. The Nurse, for example, drops out after sentence (9), although she has certainly played the major part in the action till then (eight clauses out of eleven), and has been the focus of the persona's (and therefore our) attention. The doctor, his equipment and the persona interact together, then he drops out and is superseded by a succession of clauses where the 'something' takes over very forcefully. Finally the persona is left acting alone.

Charting through the *types* of processes involved allows us much more room for discussion:

1	nurse came back = material-action-intention
2a	nurse unclasped = material-action-intention
b	nurse dropped = material-action-intention
3	nurse started tweaking = material-action-intention
4	doctor was unlocking = material-action-intention
5a	doctor dragged out = material-action-intention
b	doctor rolled = material-action-intention
6	nurse started swabbing = material-action-intention
7a	nurse leaned over to reach = material-action-intention
b	nurse's body part muffled = material-action-supervention
8	nurse's body contingency emanated = material-event
9a	n.a.
b	nurse grinned = material-action-intention
10	n.a.
11a	persona tried to smile = material-action-intention
b	persona's body part had gone stiff = material-event
12	doctor was fitting = material-action-intention
13a	doctor buckled = material-action-intention
b	doctor's equipment dented = material-action-supervention
c	doctor gave ... to bite = material-action-intention
14	persona shut = material-action-intention
15	– was = relational
16a	something took hold = material-action-intention
b	something shook = material-action-intention
17a	something shrilled = material-action-intention
b	something drubbed = material-action-intention
c	persona thought = mental-internalized-cognition
d	persona's body part would break = material-action-supervention
e	persona's body part fly out = material-action-supervention
18a	persona wondered = mental-internalized-cognition
b	– was = relational
c	persona had done = material-action-intention

Here, the overwhelming fact revealed by the analysis is the definite preponderance of the selection of the option material-action-intention; 20 clauses out of 30 make this choice. A closer consideration brings out the following interesting features of the text. First, all the Nurse's actions are material-action-intention processes; though where the Nurse's body is the actor we have supervention or event processes, so that the effect is of her deliberately carrying out determinate actions, in the persona's environment, while her body produces contingent, 'accidental', yet none the less substantial effects on her thought-world also. Similarly all of the doctor's actions are material-action-intention processes, but, like the nurse's body, his equipment produces effects on the environment tangentially, as it were. The electricity is also only represented in terms of material-action-intention processes. Thus, all three of these major actor-participants are seen as overwhelmingly 'in control' of whatever events take place. They are presented and given as being in charge of the construction of the reality that the persona perceives and expresses.

But what of the patient herself? Her attempt at what is (technically) a material-action-intention process (11a) fails. Her related body-part action is similarly only an 'accidental' event, that is, beyond her control (11b). At sentence (14), she succeeds in a material-action-intention process but, whereas all the other actors are doing constructive, concrete tasks by that option, her contribution is to shut her eyes – to remove herself from the scene. At (17c) and (18), she has the only mental-internalized-cognition processes in the passage – a fact which makes it absolutely clear that the piece is very much – and only – from her point of view. At (17d) and (17e) we are given two possible (but hypothetical) supervention processes for her body parts – so, again, material actions that are *not* part of the actual reality, but only subordinated possible outcomes of others' actions. And, finally (18c), her 'successful' material-action-intention process, is located away in the past, in mysterious circumstances.

This further analysis, then, gives us a little more scope in the way of accounting for our understanding of the persona's conception of her world. The next analysis, which isolates who or what is *affected* by each process takes us a little further:

1	nurse affects ϕ by intention process
2a	nurse affects persona's possession by intention process
b	nurse affects persona's possession by intention process
3	nurse affects persona's possession by intention process
4	doctor affects equipment by intention process
5a	doctor affects equipment by intention process
b	doctor affects equipment by intention process
6	nurse affects persona's body part by intention process
7a	nurse affects persona's body part by intention process
b	nurse's body part affects persona's body part by intention process
8	nurse's body contingency affects ϕ by event process
9a	n.a.
b	nurse affects persona by intention process
10	n.a.
11a	persona affects ϕ by intention process
b	persona's body part affects ϕ by event process
12	doctor affects equipment by intention process

13a   doctor affects equipment by intention process
  b   doctor's equipment affects persona's body part by supervention process
  c   doctor affects persona and equipment by intention process
14   persona affects persona's body part by intention process
15   ϕ affects the environment by relational process
16a   something affects persona by intention process
  b   something affects persona by intention process
17a   something affects ϕ by intention process
  b   something affects persona by intention process
  c   persona affects persona's body part by cognition process
  d   persona's body part affects ϕ by supervention process
  e   persona's body part affects ϕ by supervention process
18a   persona affects ϕ by cognition process
  b ϕ affects ϕ by relational process
  c   persona affects ϕ by intention process (hypothetical)

Reading this skeleton gives us a firmer grasp of the abstract reality of the persona's world. Massively, it is the nurse who affects both the persona's possessions and body parts (2a, 2b, 3, 6, 7, 8) and, in one instance, the whole of her (9b). The doctor, on the other hand, uses his intention processes to affect equipment (4, 5a, 5b, 12, 13a, 13c) and, in one localized area, via the persona's body part (13a) and the equipment (13b), the persona herself (13c). At this point he disappears from her world view. The electricity, not surprisingly, continually affects the whole persona (16a, 16b, 17a, 17b).

And the patient herself? At (11a) she affects nothing – despite her intentions. At (11b) her body part affects nothing. At (14) she successfully affects her own body – but remember that this is her escapism clause. At (17c) she again 'successfully' carries out a cognition process on her own body – but remember that the resultant effect is only hypothetical. At (17d), (17e), (18a) and (18c), the remaining clauses which have the persona as actor, the persona and her body parts still affect nothing at all.

This third analysis, then, gives us a much neater and more delicate way of addressing ourselves to readers' responses. Obviously we could discuss much more in this text, and I do not mean to suggest that this is a 'full analysis'.[8] Nevertheless, by pursuing these important sets of related features in this way, we have begun to refine our understanding of the 'reality' presented by this text. Section 13.5 suggests how constructive use might be made of this understanding.

13.5 Follow-up activities

I want, here, to suggest a few follow-up activities that are closely related to the types of analysis in section 13.4, and which have worked well with students recently. I should perhaps stress that I do not see them as optional extras, but as a constructive part of a move towards students' knowledge and power over the relationships that obtain between linguistic structures and socially constructed meanings. I shall include a few pieces of work by them,[9] though, sadly, limitation of space prevents extensive reproductions, and one of the most interesting aspects of this sort of enterprise is the comparison and further analysis of substantial numbers of students' materials.

The first activity is to rewrite the paragraph from the point of view of either the nurse or the doctor, while – and this is crucial – *staying as close to the words of the original text as possible*. 'Do you just mean paraphrasing it?' asked one student, puzzled by that restriction, until, in doing the work, he realized that by considering each word so closely, and in trying to decide whose point of view it represented, he was coming to (a) know the text very thoroughly and (b) see how the semiotic of the text depends heavily on the interplay between networks of syntactic choice and networks of lexical choice. This sort of exercise is the quickest (and most reliable) way I know of demonstrating that the apparent simplicity of the type of analysis given in section 13.4 is – while substantial as an orientation and clarification heuristic – by no means the whole story.

Here, then, are two rewritten versions; (a) the paragraph from the nurse's point of view and (b) the paragraph from the doctor's point of view.

(a)   I returned to the patient's bed. I unclasped her watch and put it safely in my pocket. Then I gently took the hairpins from her hair.

Dr Gordon unlocked the closet. He pulled out the trolly with the EST machine on it, and rolled it behind the head of the bed. I started to swab her temples with protective ointment.

'Don't worry,' I said to her reassuringly. 'The first time everybody's a little nervous.'

She returned a brief smile.

Dr Gordon fitted two metal plates to either side of her head, and buckled them firmly into place with the safety strap. He gave her a wire to bite on.

She closed her eyes.

There was a short silence.

Then, as she lay there, her eyes closed patiently biting the wire, her body suddenly arched upwards into the most perfect 'D' shape, held for a few seconds, then relaxed.

We had commenced treatment!

(b)   Nurse Smith re-entered the room. She began to remove all metal objects from the patient. I unlocked the storage cabinet and, rolling out the equipment, began to prepare it for the treatment.

The patient seemed a little afraid, so Nurse Smith said a few words of encouragement, accompanied by her usual reassuring smile, as she applied the lubricating grease to the girl's forehead. As I fastened the two metal plates in position on her temples, I could see the patient was nervous, but I wasn't unduly worried as this kind of treatment was completely foreign to her. I put the wire between her teeth for her to bite. The girl shut her eyes, and I switched on the equipment to begin the therapy.

A second activity is one that I have only used with students who have not already discussed and analysed the Plath text in class. They were given the final analysis table of section 13.4 – the table which gives actions, affected entities and shorthand labels for processes. I merely said, 'Make something of that,' and refused to answer any questions. What I hoped to get back were texts with different surface structures (obviously), but which would state the 'same' 'state of affairs'. Here is one student's interpretation of the job:[10]

I am no longer me
I must be no longer me
It is not expedient
I am no longer me
In their world I am part of their world
They manipulate me
They use me
I am silent
I am no longer me
They are aliens
Coming at me with instruments
To do what?
To do what?
They wield power, absolute power
There is no escape
I am humiliated, used,
subjugated, enslaved, manipulated
I belong to them.
I become their equipment: experimental equipment,
A flesh machine, only a flesh machine
To be probed
Investigated
Inspected under arc lights
Nurse is a programmed flesh machine
Doctor is a programmed flesh machine.
I too: we understand our roles.
Their programme operates here
Mine operates outside in another world.
We are not men and women in this world: but we have parts to play
I am no longer me.
I am no longer me.
But I will be.

Throughout, I hope it is clear, the emphasis has been away from studying style *qua* style, towards understanding some of the relationships between language, represented thought and the sociolinguistic construction of reality.

13.6 Concluding remarks

It is important to realize that, if I have given the impression that there is any simple set of relationships between language, thought and socially constructed reality, it was an unintentional and artificial contingency of the inevitable gap between the complexities of the world and the simplification process involved in any attempt at a coherent academic statement about the world. Clearly, work in semantics, pragmatics and semiotics has a long way to go before we can hope to chart the networks of meaning and significance which mediate between structure and representations of reality. However, I hope, at least, to have opened up one possible approach to the analysis and understanding of the construction of images of power-relationships in general, and to have urged the motivation for so doing.

To sum up let me offer the following programme of eight points, which I see the teacher of stylistics as pursuing. It assumes students with an interest in literature in general, but little or no linguistic knowledge. Parts (a)–(d) are, I take it, uncontentious; parts (e)–(h) are offered as a programme for radical stylistics.

(a) Stylistics can be part of a programme to enable students to handle competently a coherent and comprehensive descriptive grammar, which can then be used in either literature-oriented studies, or linguistics-oriented studies.
(b) It is always at least a 'way in' to a text.
(c) It can shift discussion to awareness of effects that are intuitively felt to be in a text in the process of reading it, and a contingent 'making strange' of those effects and feelings simultaneously. It is oriented towards 'knowing how' as well as 'knowing that' (Ryle 1949).
(d) It can spell out a shared vocabulary for describing the language of any text – whether those effects are straightforward or ambiguous.
(e) Crucially, stylistics can point the way to understanding the ways in which the language of a given text constructs its own (fictional) reality.
(f) It should then point the way towards understanding the ways in which language constructs the 'reality' of everyday life – and an awareness that it always *must* do so. So that, in a sense, everyday 'reality' can usefully be seen as a series of 'fictional' constructs –. as texts open to analysis and interpretation in just the same way as texts marked out for literary study are.
(g) This would lead to an awareness of the importance of perceiving the constituent parts of the fictions we live *in* and *by*, if only to map them against alternative constructions of reality.
(h) Finally, this would lead to an understanding that the fictions (both large and small) that we live in and by can be rewritten. Both individually and collectively. As reform or revolution, whichever is more appropriate.

As for my title? See it as notes for a poem, on Sylvia Plath, Women, Feminism, Radical Stylistics, academic work in general. Optimistic notes.

Notes

1 I am here following Halliday. See, in particular, Halliday (1978).
2 Throughout I am using single quote marks as 'scare' quotes. They are meant to imply a certain scepticism about the terms encapsulated in them.
3 Readers unfamiliar with the term should see Belsey (1980) for an excellent discussion of this aspect of critical practice. Basically, it is a series of methods for perceiving the *cultural* and *ideological* presuppositions inherent in any text.

4 See Brecht (1964), Garfinkel (1967), Chomsky (1968).
5 Perhaps I should make it clear that I am here acknowledging the pervasive power of the culturation processes, and foregrounding the concept of 'self as an ideological construct' (Lacan 1977).
6 I have taught several undergraduate classes using this text. The responses I quote here are typical, but just happen to be the most recent ones.
7 I am ignoring clauses which represent quoted speech from participants other than the persona, since I am attempting to deconstruct that part of the 'reality' which is specifically 'reality' plus her interpretation. However, compare Anita Thorpe's rewritten version, Section 13.5(a).
8 Compare the argument in Sinclair (1982).
9 My thanks here to Anita Thorpe, Valerie Tiplady, Simon Davies and Pam Burt for permission to quote their work.
10 There is no simple relationship between the surface structure of this piece of writing and the table, since even the sequence of processes has been altered. None the less, the texts are remarkably similar in underlying semantic and cultural propositions.

References

ALTHUSSER, L. 1969: *For Marx*, trans. B. Brewster. Harmondsworth: Penguin.
—1977: *Lenin and philosophy and other essays*, trans. B. Brewster. London: New Left Book.
ARDENER, S. (ed.) 1975: *Perceiving women*. London: Malaby.
BARTHES, R. 1967: *Writing degree zero*, trans. A. Lavers and C. Smith. London: Cape.
—1970: *S/Z*, trans. R. Miller. London: Cape.
—1972: *Mythologies*, trans. A. Lavers. London: Cape.
—1977: *Image, music, text*, trans. S. Heath. London: Fontana.
BELSEY, C. 1980: *Critical practice*. New Accents series. London: Methuen.
BERGER, G. and KACHUK, B. 1977: Sexism, language and social change. *Michigan Papers in Women's Studies* 2.
BERRY, M. 1975: *Introduction to systemic linguistics*, Vol. 1. London: Batsford.
BRECHT, B. 1964(1950): The street scene. In *Brecht on Theatre*, trans. and ed. J. Willett. London: Methuen, 121–9.
BURTON, D. 1981: Pass the Alka-Seltzer: She's swallowed the dictionary. mimeo, English Language Research, University of Birmingham.
CHOMSKY, N. 1968: *Language and mind*. New York: Harcourt Brace and World.
COWARD, R. and ELLIS, J. 1977: *Language and materialism*. London: Routledge and Kegan Paul.
DALY, M. 1978: *Gyn/ecology: The metaethics of radical feminism*. Boston: Beacon Press.
DAVIDSON, D. 1967: Truth and meaning. *Synthese* 17, 304–23.
DELAMONT, S. and DUFFIN, L. (eds) 1978: *The nineteenth century woman: Her cultural and physical world*. London: Croom Helm.
DERRIDA, J. 1976: *Of grammatology*, trans. G. C. Spivak. Baltimore: Johns Hopkins University Press.
FEYERABEND, P. 1975: *Against method*. London: New Left Books.
—1978: *Science in a free society*. London: New Left Books.
FIRTH, J. R. 1957: *Papers in linguistics 1934–1951*. London: Oxford University Press.
FOUCAULT, M. 1970: *The order of things*. London: Tavistock.
—1972: *The archaeology of knowledge*, trans. A. N. Sheridan Smith. London: Tavistock.
—1977: *Language, counter-memory, practice: Selected essays and interviews*, ed. D. F. Bouchard and trans. D. F. Bouchard and S. Simon. Oxford: Blackwell.

GARFINKEL, H. 1967: *Studies in ethnomethodology*. Englewood Cliffs, NJ: Prentice-Hall.

HALLIDAY, M. A. K. 1970: Language structure and language function. In Lyons, J. (ed.), *New horizons in linguistics*. Harmondsworth: Penguin, 140–65.

—1973: *Explorations in the functions of language*. London: Edward Arnold.

—1978: *Language as social semiotic*. London: Edward Arnold.

JAQUETTE, J. (ed.) 1974: *Women in politics*. New York: Wiley.

KUHN, T. 1962: *The structure of scientific revolutions*. Chicago: Chicago University Press.

—1967: *The Copernican revolution*. Cambridge: Cambridge University Press.

LACAN, J. 1977: *Ecrits*, trans. A. Sheridan. London: Tavistock.

LAKATOS, I. 1970: Falsification and the methodology of scientific research programmes. In Lakatos, I. and Musgrave, A. (eds), *Criticism and the growth of knowledge*. Cambridge: Cambridge University Press, 91–6.

—1976: *Proofs and refutations: The logic of mathematical discovery*. Cambridge: Cambridge University Press.

LAKOFF, G. and JOHNSON, P. 1980: *Metaphors we live by*. Chicago: Chicago University Press.

MACHEREY, P. 1978: *A theory of literary production*, trans. G. Wall. London: Routledge and Kegan Paul.

MILLETT, K. 1969: *Sexual politics*. London: Virago.

POPPER, K. 1977: *The logic of scientific discovery*. London: Hutchinson.

—1979: *Objective knowledge*. London: Oxford University Press.

RICH, A. 1972: When we dead awaken: Writing as re-revision. *College English* 34, 18–30.

—1977: *Of woman born: Motherhood as experience and institution*. London: Virago.

ROWBOTHAM, S. 1973a: *Woman's consciousness: Man's world*. Harmondsworth: Penguin.

—1973b: *Hidden from history*. London: Pluto Press.

RYLE, G. 1949: *The concept of mind*. London: Hutchinson.

SACKS, H. and SCHEGLOFF, E. A. 1973: Opening up closings. *Semiotica* 8, 289–327.

SAPIR, E. 1956: *Culture, language and personality*. Berkeley: University of California Press.

SAUSSURE, F. de 1974(1916): *Course in general linguistics*, trans. W. Boskin. London: Fontana.

SHOWALTER, E. 1977: *A literature of their own: British women novelists from Brontë to Lessing*. Princeton: Princeton University Press.

SINCLAIR, J. 1982: Lines about 'Lines'. In Carter R. (ed.), *Language and literature*. London: Allen and Unwin, 163–76.

TARSKI, A. 1956: *Logic, semantics, metamathematics*. Oxford: Clarendon Press.

VOLOŠINOV, V. M. 1973(1930): *Marxism and the philosophy of language*, trans. L. Matejka and I. R. Titunik. New York: Seminar Press.

WHORF, B. L. 1956: *Language, thought and reality*, ed. J. B. Carroll. Cambridge, Mass.: MIT Press.

14

Knowing your place: A Marxist feminist stylistic analysis

Sara Mills

14.1 Introduction

In this essay I would like to attempt to define a Marxist feminist contextualized stylistics. For this purpose I shall be drawing on the distinctly unfashionable work of Louis Althusser, a Marxist literary theorist, together with feminist stylistic and literary theory (Althusser 1984; see also Burton 1982 and Threadgold 1988a, 1988b). It may be argued that the combination of Marxism, feminism, and stylistics is indeed a heady brew, but it is a necessary combination in order to overcome some of the problems encountered both in traditional stylistic analysis and in Marxist analysis. These theoretical positions can be combined to produce an analysis which is theoretically rigorous and which at the same time enables the reader to engage with a text.

14.2 The reader and address in contextualized stylistics

Contextualized stylistics is a radically new departure for stylistics – a move away from text immanent criticism to a more theoretical concern with the factors outside the text that may determine or interact with the elements which appear in the text. This may sound like a rediscovery of traditional literary criticism's concern with sociohistorical context, but a concern with context can be handled in a more interesting theoretical way than has been the case with literary critics. An emphasis on lexical items and the way they interact with their context can help the reader to avoid some of the over-generalized cause-effect relations posited by traditional literary critics.

I wish to present a particular reading of the terms 'context' and 'contextualized' which may not accord with traditional literary models, nor for that matter with the other essays within this book. Most definitions of context centre on the historical and social background in which the text is produced. For example, stylistic analysis has so far shown itself to be largely uninterested in the world outside the text except for the role of the author who plays a determining role in the production and explanation of the linguistic devices which are discovered in the text. As Montgomery (1988) states:

> Stylistics has traditionally been concerned preeminently with the differences between
> or within texts, and those differences have commonly been explored in terms of the
> formal parameters of lexico-grammar.

It is only now with the advent of discourse stylistics that there seems to be a move in the direction of the analysis of context (see Carter and Simpson 1989; and Coupland 1988). However, I would argue that even discourse stylistics is saddled with a very traditional model of context (see Figure 14.1).

Within this model of text, the author is in control of the material s/he produces, that is, there are patterns and effects within the text which the author decides upon and which it is the job of the stylistician to detect. However, there are obvious problems with such a model: first, the writer is clearly not in complete control of her/his material. As many literary theorists such as Culler (1975), Bloom (1975) and Barthes (1977) have shown, there is a range of literary conventions which structure the possibilities of expression at a given time. Authorial choice is made within a limited set of parameters. A second problem with the model is that it is based on the notion of hindsight; it would be impossible to prove that the writer had intended the patterns and effects which the reader succeeded in tracing. Fish (1980) has argued that, in fact, these patternings are largely a result of a literary process which the reader puts into effect when reading texts which have been labelled 'literary'. A third problem with the model is that context does not include the role of the reader, which obviously has a greater role to play in the process of interpretation than this model will allow. However, rather than adopting a Fish approach, which would give the reader the position of the creator of the text, usurping that of the author and thus remaining within the same model, I propose the following model of the text which would avoid some of these problems and broaden our definition of context (see Figure 14.2).

One advantage of this model is that textual production and reception are considered to be part of context and not simply the context of production, which as I have mentioned is the way in which the term is conventionally used. A second advantage is that the reader's role is given more prominence: it is clear that the reader is addressed by the text, and that s/he is affected by and can make an effect on the interpretation of the text. S/he is an active participant, negotiating with the meanings which are being foisted onto her/him, and resisting or questioning some of those meanings. This is in direct contrast to the passive recipient of the text of Figure 14.1.

Context

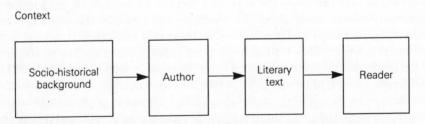

Figure 14.1 The model of context in traditional discourse stylistics.

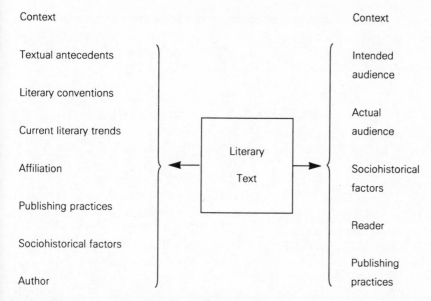

Figure 14.2 A revised model of context in discourse.

I should make it clear at this point that I am not proposing a model of text which is 'open' in Umberto Eco's usage (1979); that is, the text can mean anything and it is up to readers to impose their meanings upon the text. I propose that the reader is positioned by the text in a range of ways which can be accepted or resisted. If there were no dominant reading/s, then there would be no consensus whatsoever as to what texts meant. Although it must be stated that there is a wide range of readings which a text can have, nevertheless the possibilities for dominant readings are certainly not endless. Later in this essay, I will define in more detail the constituents of a dominant reading.

This model takes into account the interactional nature of the relation between texts and their context. Thus, texts are determined by a wide range of pressures on their processes of production and reception, and also have an effect on their audience and on the processes of production of further texts. It will be clear that with a more complex model such as this, it is more difficult to make the straightforward statements beloved of stylisticians, such as, a particular formal pattern leads us to interpret the poem in a particular way. Instead, more modest statements can be made about, for example, the way that the text might be addressing the reader and the limits of resisting that address. It is the way that the reader is addressed by the text which is the focus of this essay. The positioning of the reader has been considered by feminist theorists such as Fetterley (1981), Williamson (1978), Marshment *et al.* (1988), Betterton (1987), and – in feminist film theory – by Kuhn (1982) and Mulvey (1981). However, positioning is simply asserted by these theorists; there is little attempt to trace formal features in the text which might serve as markers, to the reader, of this positioning.

14.3 The positioning of the reader

It is surprising that in literary studies there has been so little work which considers the positioning of the reader at any length. There have been theories of reader-response and reception theories (e.g. Suleiman and Crosman 1981), but they have been primarily concerned with examining a consensus of interpretation through the notion of the implied or ideal reader. Even those critics who do consider reader positioning pay little attention to the formal features in the text which signal the dominant reading to the reader. In order to formulate a mode of analysis which considers formal features and the way they relate to context and reader address, I would like to consider the work of Louis Althusser on interpellation and obviousness and then go on to discuss the work of critics who have been concerned with the notion of positioning of the reader.

Louis Althusser's work on ideological state apparatuses (1984, pp. 1–60) is an interesting combination of Marxist theory and psychoanalysis, and has received a great deal of attention. The basis of his argument is that ideological state apparatuses are those elements whose indirect effect is to reproduce the conditions of production within a society. In order for a capitalist society to continue to function, workers must be made to recognize their position within that society and accept those roles. This happens through two main mechanisms: the repressive state apparatuses, consisting of the police, the army, and the state, which achieve this aim through force or violence; and the ideological state apparatuses, consisting of the educational system, the media, and so on, which achieve this aim through a constant barrage of images and information which map out the role of the subject. The effects of repressive state apparatuses have been well documented and it is on the ideological state apparatuses that Althusser concentrates. He describes the way in which individuals are called into a position of subjecthood – when you recognize your role/s in society, you become a subject in both senses of the word: you are a subject in that you are an individual psyche, and you are also subject to the state and authority. In this way, you are forced to mis/recognize the imaginary (i.e. ideological) conditions of your relation to the means of production. Althusser states that interpellation or hailing is one of the mechanisms whereby this is achieved; he gives the much-cited and maligned example of a police officer in the street calling 'Hey you'. In the process of turning round, the individual has recognized not only her/himself as an individual who may be guilty of something, but also as a subject in relation to a position of authority. Thus, interpellation constructs the subject into a role or position in the very act of hailing it.

Althusser's model has been rightly criticized for being too simplistic an account of the way that interpellation works, because the construction of subjecthood is obviously a much more complicated process than the simple responding to a name or call. With his model of hailing there is a one-to-one fit between the calling and the recognition. However, as Durant (1989) has pointed out, when interpellated by a text, the reader can adopt either the position of the supposed speaker or the role of the supposed addressee, or can be positioned as an overhearer of the interaction. Furthermore, there are clearly other elements in the text which position the reader, but which are more indirect than this model suggests. There is an unending series of hailings, both direct and indirect, to which the reader responds or does not respond. Thus, although certain texts attempt to address themselves to the reader, s/he may be critical of them and may decide not to take them at face value. However, even the hailings which are not intended for the reader, or which are intended for her/him and not received, nevertheless do have an effect on the reader and it is this effect of indirect interpellation which I will attempt to describe in this essay. Despite these problems with the theory of interpellation, rather than rejecting the theory wholesale, it seems more useful to try to work on the theory itself, modifying it slightly so that it will more adequately describe the way that subjects are constituted by texts.

A second point of interest from Althusser's ideological state apparatuses article is the notion of common sense or 'obviousness' which, along with interpellation, is a strong element in the positioning of the reader. In each text, there are elements which are posed as self-evidently true and Althusser asserts that these are the most truly ideological:

> It is indeed a peculiarity of ideology that it imposes (without appearing to do so, since these are 'obviousnesses') obviousnesses as obviousnesses, which we cannot *fail to recognize* and before which we have the inevitable and natural reaction of crying out (aloud or in the 'still, small voice of conscience'): 'That's obvious! That's right! That's true!'
>
> (Althusser 1984, p. 46)

Each text contains an ideological message which we accept (or reject) as given or obvious, and it is in this way that the reader is positioned by what I would like to class as the dominant reading. This is a seemingly coherent message which the text carries, and which the reader is supposed to find as 'obviously' what the text is about. Althusser's notion of obviousness has remarkable similarity to Roland Barthes' (1975) 'cultural code' which I discuss later in the description of dominant readings.

I would now like to consider the ways in which critics, such as Williams, Montgomery, and Durant have treated the idea of address to the reader, or reader positioning. Although these critics are concerned with issues of language, few of them are concerned with issues of gender or politics. It is possible to trace an undercurrent of Althusserian interpellation, but in general this work has not taken on board the political elements of Althusser. Instead, interpellation has been simply used as a term to mean 'hailing', without considering the effects this might have on the subject hailed, as Althusser does. Nor are they concerned with the ways in which the reader is positioned apart from the obvious forms of direct address, that is, when the reader is actually called upon by the narrator, for example, by the use of the pronoun 'you'. Despite these problems, the work of these critics does suggest ways in which the analysis of formal elements may help in the description of reader positioning.

Raymond Williams attempts in his article on monologue and soliloquy (1983) to analyse the ways in which the reader is addressed, either in a direct, semi-direct, or indirect way. Unlike literary theory and stylistics, drama analysis and film theory have considered the way the text addresses the audience to be crucial. Williams tries to map out the linguistic elements in Shakespearean texts which can distinguish between these three kinds of address. However, his work does not seem, in this instance, to be anything other than descriptive, and he does not discuss the effect of these types of address on the audience.

Martin Montgomery's work on DJ talk (1986, 1988) is useful in that it is one of the few examples of an attempt to deal with reader-address using linguistics. Montgomery concentrates on the analysis of direct address to the reader in the form principally of deixis (this/that/I/you, etc.), vocatives (you/Bob Sproat), and selectors (all of you in Edinburgh). He shows the way in which an audience is addressed by a text as 'you' or as a subsection of that 'you', and he notes:

> The audience is not uniformly implicated all in the same way the whole of the time ... while the use of selectors has the effect of singling out sometimes quite specific addressees, the talk is always available for others than those directly named as addressees.
>
> (Montgomery 1988, p. 13)

He draws attention to the fact that there are various sections of the audience who will be overhearing elements of the talk by DJs at various times. He compares this to the case of lyric poetry where he shows that, unlike this direct address, 'the addressee of dramatic lyric poetry is almost always someone other than the actual reader of the text' (1988, p. 14). He also notes that in DJ talk, 'as listeners we are made constantly aware of other (invisible) elements in the audience of which we form a part' (1988, p. 14). This is particularly interesting for the purposes of this essay, as I hope to show that gender is a crucial element for determining whether readers consider that they are being directly addressed or whether in fact they are in the position of overhearing.

Montgomery goes on to state that the same forms of direct address may be used in lyric and romantic poetry and yet, because of the changes in publishing conventions, these forms of address are interpreted in different ways. This is interesting in this context because I shall be arguing that the same forms in the same poem can in fact be interpreted in different ways according to the gender of the reader and the affiliations of that reader. Montgomery's work is interesting because of his attention to the linguistic elements which constitute direct address. However, I would like to argue that the reader is addressed in a much more complex and indirect way. A further element which needs to be integrated into the analysis is that of gender.

Alan Durant (1989) draws on Montgomery's work on address, but uses it for the analysis of pop music lyrics. He distinguishes between the various positions which a listener can adopt when listening to a pop song: for him, there is the position of the singer or the singer's persona, the role of the addressee, or the role of someone who is overhearing this interaction. For Durant, the reader chooses which position to adopt. While this is clearly an advance in that it maps out several alternative positions for the reader if applied to literary texts, the notion of a willed positioning by the reader eliminates any of the ideological positioning described by Althusser. In Althusser's work, the reader is, in the main, unaware of the processes at work in the interpellation; in fact it is the very obviousness of the messages received which prevents the positioned reader becoming aware of his/her ideological nature. Thus, although Durant's work on the varying positions available to the reader seems interesting, within the context of this essay it is not necessary to agree with the notion of reader choice. There are clearly texts which suggest to you what your position is: for example it is unlikely (but not impossible) that a female listener will sing along out loud with the Rolling Stones song 'I can't get no satisfaction' and thus position herself in the role of the singer. It is necessary therefore to draw elements from Durant's work on variable positions of the reader, but to add to this both an analysis of the way roles are foisted onto listeners/readers and also an analysis of the gendering of that reading/listening process.

As I have noted, none of these critics considers gender as a factor in the positioning of the reader, and all of them have tended to use Althusser's terminology without reference to the political framework of the original work. I will attempt to reinscribe that political edge and argue for a gendered reading process.

14.4 Indirect address and dominant reading

One of the major problems with Althusser's concept of interpellation, as I have noted above, is the notion of the *direct* addressing of the subject, and this problem is reinforced by the work of Montgomery and Durant. It is clear that the reader is also addressed in an *indirect* way. Unless readers analyse texts for the way that they are being positioned, this type of address goes largely unnoticed, because it is more difficult to locate. There are, however, several markers of indirect address which I will now describe; I will then go on to discuss the way that indirect address helps to constitute a dominant reading. I will concentrate on two markers of indirect address: mediation, and the cultural code, or obviousness. Colin Mac-Cabe's work on realism (1981) is useful for a discussion of mediation, because he notes that in realist texts there is a hierarchy of discourses or voices within the text. The discourse which occupies the position of truth in this hierarchy is also the one with which the reader aligns herself. He states that in realist texts this dominant voice mediates all of the other voices within the text, that is, the dominant voice gives instructions to the reader about the position she should take on other information or characters within the text. The reader is led to align herself with the voice which is not mediated, that is, the voice or discourse which is not judged by another discourse. In novels, it is clear that there are sub-plots which we are encouraged to view through the dominant discourse, for example, the reader is led to the position where she questions the truth-value of one character's statements, because she has been given a negative description of this character by the narrator, or by another character. This mediation of characters can be traced in texts by analysis of the different voices within the text and can lead the reader to the dominant reading.

A second factor which constitutes indirect address is Barthes' notion of the 'cultural code' referred to above. The cultural code consists of a range of statements at which the reader will nod her head sagely or which she will simply accept as self-evidently 'true' within that culture. Barthes suggests that we can detect these elements of the cultural code since these statements can be prefaced by 'we all know that' or 'it is evident that'. Thus, texts contain a substantial amount of information to which we agree indirectly, and which, in that process, constitutes a role for us as readers. These two factors of indirect address lead to the reader being able to discern the dominant reading which the text offers.

The notion of a dominant reading has been much debated in literary theory. Much post-structuralist work has argued that dominant readings do not exist, or are more unstable than has been suggested. However, even the strongest reading of the 'playful' text, i.e. a deconstructive one, does implicitly rely on the notion of a dominant reading, which is then proved to be unstable by deconstructive analysis. Yet it would seem that most readers can recognize the 'obvious' role/s, positions, and interpretations which the text maps out for them. This dominant reading is not the writer's intention (which is unrecoverable), but a position (or positions) which the text offers or proffers to the reader within a particular historical moment, because of the range of ideological positions available which make that text understandable. This reading will be one which is reinforced by various ideologies circulating within the culture of the time; thus, for example, a text which constructs femininity in a particular way will be made understandable because it is reinforced by a range of other texts and discourses on femininity. Without these other discourses, the text would be difficult to understand or may be incomprehensible. The link between indirect address and dominant readings is therefore that unmediated, seemingly obvious information – ideological information reinforced by other discourses – is one of the factors in the constitution of a dominant reading.

Judith Williamson (1978) has discussed these ideas of dominant readings to some extent in her work on advertisements. She has analysed the ways in which advertisements address the reader, and the way in which the reader is in fact a key element in the making sense of seeming incoherent texts. She gives the example of juxtapositions in advertisements, such as Catherine Deneuve's picture which is fronted by a picture of a bottle of Chanel perfume. The reader makes a cognitive leap to make sense of these juxtaposed images by adopting the message of the advertisement: i.e. that if you want to be as beautiful, rich, and famous as Deneuve, you should use Chanel perfume. It is an interesting form of advertisement, because it does not seem to address the reader directly (there is no text which 'hails' the reader as 'you'), and yet indirectly it is positioning the reader into a discourse of upward aspiration through consumerism. In making that cognitive leap to make sense of the advertisement, Williamson asserts, the reader has in fact made herself into a subject, i.e. a consuming subject. The notion that texts are necessarily incomplete and incoherent and require the reader to resolve that incoherence is suggestive, and it is one which I will be drawing on later in the essay.

To sum up, I would argue that address is, in the main, partial and indirect rather than the successful and complete hailing which Althusser described, and for this reason it is possible to track it down when it is unsuccessful and to construct positions for reading, other than the dominant one. Because texts are always overdetermined, there are always other elements intermingled with the dominant reading. It is these elements which lead to a different oppositional reading, which I would now like to consider.

14.5 Gender and reader position

I have argued that gender is one of the factors that many critics have omitted in their discussion of address and positioning. Judith Fetterley considers the importance of gender in reading: she has described the way that most texts in American literature appear to address a general audience, while in fact they are addressing the reader as a male:

> One of the main things that keeps the design of our literature unavailable to the consciousness of the woman reader, and hence impalpable, is the very posture of the apolitical, the pretense that literature speaks universal truths through forms from which all the merely personal, the purely subjective, has been burned away or at least transformed through the medium of art into the representative.
>
> (Fetterley 1981, p. xi)

Her work is primarily a content-analysis, that is she examines various depictions of female characters which it is difficult for females to read easily unless they adopt the position of a male reader. She states: 'To read the canon of what is currently considered classic American literature is perforce to identify as male' (1981, p. xii). She suggests, and Elaine Showalter's work in this area (1971) would seem to reinforce her point, that it is standard reading practice for women students at university studying literature to position themselves as males in order to make sense of the text. Both Showalter and Fetterley have rather a simplistic model of the relation between literary texts and reality, for they each consider that literary texts reflect reality and this runs the risk of flawing their argument about address. Another problem with both Showalter's and Fetterley's work is that they simply assert that texts address the reader as male on the basis of content analysis and do not provide any language analysis to prove their assertions. It is clear from an analysis of texts which are written by males that there are a large number of elements which can be focused upon which signal to the reader that this is a man-to-man dialogue and it is on these elements that I hope to focus in my analysis below.

However, despite these problems of theoretical position, there are interesting elements in Fetterley's work, for example, when she says:

> While women obviously cannot rewrite literary works so that they become ours by
> virtue of reflecting our reality, we can accurately name the reality that they do reflect
> and so change literary criticism from a closed conversation to an active dialogue.
>
> (Fetterley 1981, p. xxiii)

By describing the position that these texts are addressing and constructing, we
can then go on to challenge literary criticism's avoidance of gender issues in the
analysis of address, and we can also map out a position for ourselves as female
readers in the process of doing so. It is this notion of a 'resisting reader', which
is a space from which female readers can read against the grain, that I find most
suggestive for this essay. Thus, although texts may address us as males, we as
female readers can construct a space of reading which resists the dominant
reading.

It is possible, drawing on the work of other theorists, to use Fetterley's basic
position and to try and discover elements which can justify her assertions. For
example, Deborah Cameron (1985) has shown that by the use of generic pronouns
such as 'he' to refer to both male and female, texts signal to the reader what
gender the dominant reading position is. She goes on to show that generic nouns
are also used to similar effect. She gives the example of a newspaper article which
uses the generic noun 'neighbour' to mean male neighbour, which has to be modified to 'neighbour's wife' if a female neighbour is referred to. She notes that when
texts use generics in this gender-specific way, there is a clear signal to readers that
the position which the text is offering them is male. Female readers are less likely
to feel that the text is addressed to them if generics are used in this way.

A further example of textual markers of indirect address is the work of Robert
Scholes on an Ernest Hemingway short story ('Decoding papa', in Scholes 1982).
He shows that although the focalization in the text appears at first glance to be
equally distributed between the two characters, a man and a woman, on analysis
it is clear that this seemingly neutral narration is focalized on the male. He
demonstrates this by rewriting the text from the male and from the female point
of view, using the pronoun 'I'. In several parts of the text it is impossible to do
this with the female voice and it is therefore clear that the focalization in this
text, as in many others, is gendered; this has an effect on the way that the reader
processes the text and the position which the reader can take up.

However, it must be stated that, despite all of these elements within the text
which lead readers to be positioned as male, it is clear that all women do not
read in the same way; women are not a coherent group and are subject to other
affiliations such as class and race. One major distinction within women readers
which should be made are those who are male-affiliated and those who are
female-affiliated. These categories are ones which may be in play at various
stages within a text, and in different texts; they do not necessarily constitute a
permanent reading position (see also the critique of polarization in Morris 1989).
The term 'female affiliation' was coined by Sandra Gilbert and Susan Gubar
(1988) to describe the problem which women writers face when they decide to
write: whether to align themselves with a male or a female tradition. The same
question poses itself for the female reader, although not necessarily in a

conscious way: whether to take up the position allotted to the male reader of the text, or whether to attempt to resist that position and formulate another position from which to read, as Judith Fetterley has described. Female affiliation is a frame of reference and usually occurs with feminist consciousness-raising; it is a framework of reading adopted in order to resist reading as a male. Therefore, it should be clear that it is a position which is taken up, and not something which is inherent in all females. There are of course texts which position you as female, and there has been a certain amount of feminist work on this area, for example, see Marshment and Gamman (1988). These theorists are concerned to analyse those texts which overtly signal that they are addressed to a female audience. Although this is beyond the scope of my essay it might be interesting to examine the way in which certain texts which position the reader as female are read by males and male-affiliated women. The one problem with these texts is that unless they position the reader within a dominant ideological position, they are difficult to make sense of; thus feminist texts such as *The Color Purple* are frequently misunderstood by male readers as a male-hating diatribe. In some cases, this is the only frame of reference which ideology offers for males reading feminist or female-addressed texts.

To summarize the position which I have attempted to formulate: address to the reader or interpellation is more complex than conventionally described, and I have therefore found it necessary to integrate into this framework the notion of indirect address and its relation to the production of a dominant reading. Furthermore, I have also argued that gender is an important element in the construction of the reader's position. I would like to move now to an analysis of a poem to see how this Marxist feminist stylistics can describe the positioning of the reader.

14.6 Analysis

I have chosen a poem by John Fuller entitled 'Valentine' because, when taught on a summer school by a male colleague, the poem aroused a great deal of discussion. The students seemed to be almost completely polarized: the female students felt anger, but most of the male students found the poem amusing. Subsequent readers have, by and large, repeated this response. This seemed to me to be due at least in part to the way that the reader's position is mapped out as male, with little room for a female reader to manoeuvre.

The editor regrets that he is unable to reproduce the poem here, as the poet, John Fuller, has refused permission to reprint it. **Indeed, we are not even allowed to quote any lines from it, so that Sara Mills' analysis has had to be curtailed in places. It is a sad fact that copyright laws allow authors to exert a form of censorship over any critical assessment of their work that they consider negative.**

Interested readers can find the poem and the full analysis in Michael Toolan (ed.) *Language, Text and Context* (London: Routledge, 1992, pp. 195–205).

The poem consists largely of direct address marked by deixis (I, you); this discourse occupies a dominant position because it is unmediated by any other voice. There are four positions which can be adopted according to gender and affiliation. The male reader is offered a position which I would argue is the dominant reading of this poem; the reader's position is elided with that of the speaking 'I'. That is not to say that the reader and the 'I' become the same, but the reader can adopt that 'I' position without thinking. It would be less likely for a male reader to read the text from the addressed position of the female because of indirect address as I show later. The female reader has three positions: (a) to read the text as if it is addressed to her, the dominant reading for the text, which constitutes her within the dominant male view of femininity; (b) to affiliate as a male, that is to read it as if the text positions her as the speaker. This is a curious position because she can make sense of the poem as a male-affiliated female, and yet there are several points at which she has to read as an overhearing reader. In both cases the female reader laughs at the jokes and is interpellated into a position where certain ideological knowledges about the nature of men and women have to be accepted as true. (c) A third position for the female reader is one of resistance, and is what I will term female affiliated. This is a position outside the dominant readings which are offered by the text.

First, let us consider the dominant reading position: the one that we as readers are encouraged to adopt and to view as natural. This reading, I would argue, is directed to a male reader. It is evident that the poem is directed from a male 'I' to a female 'you'. There are many textual antecedents for this type of love poem, and there are several clues in the text to show that the love-object is female (although there are not as many as you would think). The element which signals the reader as male is the humour which often accompanies poems which make reifying statements about females; there is a long tradition of disguising sexism with humour, so that when challenged, the humour of the text can be cited as a means of deflecting the charges (see, e.g., the dismissals of sexism in Jonson's 'That Women are but Men's Shadows', on the grounds of the poem's prevailing wit and elegance, in Gibbons 1979).

As I noted earlier, Judith Williamson suggests that it is in trying to 'make sense' of the text that the reader's position is constructed. In this poem humour is a central factor in interpellation. The text is humorous in that readers can only make sense of most of the statements if they see that these are exaggerated, and therefore not to be taken at face value. (...) There is also humour in the clash of collocation which can only be resolved if the reader interprets the text as humorous. (...) Furthermore, there are other elements in the text which can be made sense of only if interpreted as humorous, because in a love-poem they would normally be seen as trivial and not fitting in with the literary conventions of love poetry. (...) Humour is also the means by which the text manages to co-opt the reader into aligning with the position of the male 'I' or the female 'you'; in the act of laughing you have positioned yourself in the signifying gap, as Williamson puts it, and thus made yourself into a male or female subject, both of whom would agree with certain ideological statements about women, as I show later in more detail.

There are other elements of humour such as the *doubles entendres*, a specifically sexual form of humour, where the joke rests on the ability of the reader to see that the sentence has two meanings, one of which is sexual. (....)

The rhyme scheme and the metre also reinforce this notion of a funny-clever poem; because of the conventions of twentieth-century poetry, it would be extremely unlikely for a serious, contemporary poem to have a rhyme scheme on the model of the first stanza: aa/bb/ba/ba/ab/ba/ab/aa/b. Variations on this heavily patterned rhyme scheme occur in all of the stanzas, and because the reader is aware of the rarity of this type of rhyme in serious poetry and because s/he knows that it occurs in limericks and children's verse, the reader is led to classify the poem as humorous. (...)

Because of the clumsy rhymes, it has the feel of a schoolboy poem, or even a commercial valentine card with its pedestrian rhymes and plodding metre; therefore the poem seems to retain a certain innocence within this dominant reading. For a male reader it is a very modern love poem in that it falls neither in the tradition of excessive emotion, nor is it totally cynical about love, but mixes excessive emotion with everyday, down-to-earth details. A dominant reading would see strong emotion handled in a funny way so that it can be admitted to without losing face. Because it is written as a valentine, the reader in the dominant reading can align himself with the 'I' position and imagine himself sending the poem to someone he loves.

In terms of indirect address, the poem fits in with a long tradition of extolling the virtues of the loved one, by representing each of her most beautiful parts in turn. Frequently the body parts are likened to parts of nature: doves, sunbeams, flowers, clouds, and so on, and thus objectified. The effect is to reify the woman's body but also to make it safe, since in the main, the elements chosen for comparison are soft, passive and non-threatening. In this poem, the parts of the woman's body are lovingly described, both the ones conventionally described in love poetry: eyes, cheeks, nose, lips, profile, but also more unconventional ones (hence the modern feel to the poem): upper arms, elbows, collar-bones, and even glands. This type of description is seen to be 'normal' within love poetry, and in order to make sense of this listing of body parts, the reader has to draw on elements of the cultural code whereby 'we all know' that female bodies should be described in this way. It is possible to find elements of this type of body part listing in many discourses circulating images of femininity or femaleness, for example, in pornography and advertising (see Betterton 1987). The strangeness of this type of description can be clearly seen if the text is rewritten from a female speaker to a male addressee; there are few textual precedents for women speakers extolling the virtues of a male addressee's body and there are no discourses which would reinforce this type of reading. Therefore the text would appear odd or incomprehensible.

The male reader is also encouraged to align himself with the 'I' figure, because it is in a position of power, a seemingly 'obvious' position given the discourses which circulate through society ratifying the 'naturalness' of male dominance. (...) This position of knowledge and strength is one which has traditionally been granted to the male, and is one which other discourses ratify and reinforce that this is a 'naturally' male position. Thus by reading himself as the 'I' the male reader gratifyingly reassures himself of his subject position and his normality.

For the female reader within the dominant reading, the only viable position available is that of the objectified female addressee. This is a position which, because of the ideological discourses of romantic love and femininity, is very comfortable for many females: being the object of excessive male emotion is structured as a goal for women and a sign of 'normality' (see Modleski 1982). Women's magazines strive to encourage women readers to examine each body part and improve it by buying cosmetics: hair, cheeks, lips, etc., and the reward for this labour is for a male to be intoxicated with the body part. Thus, this poem, in its cataloguing of the body parts, speaks directly to the narcissism encouraged by the ideology of femininity. Each part is described as perfect, even the ones which women's magazines do not normally encourage labour on. (...)

Rosemary Betterton's collection of essays *Looking On* (1987) also discusses this quality of representation of femininity and how it is received by female readers, as does Laura Mulvey in her concept of 'to-be-looked-at-ness' (Mulvey 1981). Valentine cards are part of this view of femininity: they are generally sent by men to women to demonstrate their romantic love, and they are sometimes sent by secret anonymous admirers. This secret voyeuristic admiring is something which the ideology of femininity encourages. As John Berger has noted (1976), women are encouraged to behave as if they have a constant viewer, as if they are always under inspection even at their most private moments. (...)

The female reader in this dominant reading partakes of the humour, realizing that in this way the addresser is able to express excessive emotion, and is able to articulate the excessive admiration which is required by femininity. (...) The speaker expresses excessive emotion, but within an ironic, humorous framework. The poem also contains elements of chivalry which females within a dominant reading are supposed to appreciate. (...) The poem seems to construct the 'I' as a version of the New Man, the mythical beast beloved of journalism: someone who is caring (...), strong (...), aware of his faults (...), and above all, humorous. The final lines of the poem show the reader that the addresser is serious in his intentions; this can be interpreted as showing that the addresser is not simply infatuated with the woman's body, but is prepared to marry her; he will be the final name in her appointment book, and will be with her in her 'future tense'. Thus the poem is a mixture of elements which position a female reader in the role of the 'you' the adored female, and since she draws on discourses of femininity to make sense of the poem, successfully interpellate her into a position of feminine subjecthood.

A female or male reader can also read the poem as 'overhearers' rather than directly aligning themselves with addresser or addressee. Nevertheless I would still argue that even in this slightly distanced form of reading, the ideological messages of indirect address have to be agreed to in order to understand the poem. Thus even here the reader will be interpellated by the poem.

As is well documented, feminists do not have a sense of humour. A female-affiliated resisting reading of this poem would refuse the subject positions proffered by the dominant reading. Refusing the discourses of femininity and the seductions of sex-object status, and refusing to make sense of the poem by being lured by the humour, this reader produces a quite different interpretation and stresses different elements within the text. This resisting reader is prepared to read the poem critically as a series of incoherent statements which can only be made sense of through drawing on ideological discourses of femininity. In this reading, some elements of the text will indeed be left as incoherent, as inexplicable: the aim will be to analyse the way the text proffers a dominant reading, as we have done in the previous sections, and then to produce an alternative reading position. The resisting reader decides consciously to mis-read the poem: to read the poem against the grain of the dominant reading.

Instead of a simple valentine card, this poem can be seen to be portraying a set of strategies akin to those of the protagonist in John Fowles's book *The Collector*. In this novel, the collector of butterflies turns his attention to women; he captures one and keeps her prisoner in his cellar. In Fuller's poem, the collector stalks the victim and catalogues the body parts of his prey, the ones that he has been able to see as he has watched her from a distance. He does not know the woman at all and has never talked to her. (...) In this sense, it is a typical valentine: a card from an admiring male to a woman who is unaware of his attentions.

When read from this position we notice the difference between the 'I'd like' clauses and the 'I like' clauses: the 'I like' clauses are mainly concerned with parts of the body which could be seen by an unknown observer (cheeks, eyes, nose, wrists, fingers, etc.), whereas the 'I'd like' clauses seem to be concerned with sexual activities the observer would like to perform with his unknowing victim. (...) The parallels with pornography and other practices of fetishism are evident: the fragmentation of the woman's body parts, and the dwelling on them, particularly her sexual characteristics, in order to stimulate the male. The speaker is not interested in the simple cataloguing of the woman's body parts as in conventional love poetry, but in seeing each of them as sexual. (...) In addition, as I have already noted, each of the 'I'd like' clauses is also concerned with power through force or violence; this sadism is of a sexual nature. (...)

Read from this position, the reader can see the rather contradictory elements contained in the ideology of romantic love: violence, power, chivalry, attraction, murder, pain, madness. These elements can only be read as coherent if they are positioned within a discourse of romantic love, and if the reader indirectly assents to them as 'obvious'. (...) For example, in this poem, within femininity is classified: madness, murder, physical attractiveness, and religious mysticism. It is clear that what the observer wants is a Woman, a combination of all of the elements of sexual attractiveness, and he is prepared to put up with any of the problematic elements of femininity, such as madness, or murderous intent. (...) Any woman would do. In line with the 'collector' reading, it is possible to read the final lines of the poem in a rather chilling way: the only meeting the woman will have with the speaker will in fact be her last.

Thus, the female-affiliated reader cannot take up either of the positions or roles offered by the poem as the dominant reading; that does not mean to say that she is unaffected by them, but that she is more concerned to describe, analyse, and resist the effects of the poem. By drawing on a description of direct and indirect address, and also attempting to make apparent the incoherences which the reader has to try to resolve in reading the poem, the reader can arrive at a description of the dominant reading. Once that has been located, this dominant reading can be criticized and the reader can move on to developing a position of resistance to those meanings. It is this notion of resistance to the dominant meanings of a text which, if it has hitherto rarely been found in stylistic analysis, can be seen as a starting point for the necessary description of the different interpretations of a text.

References

ALTHUSSER, L. 1984: *Essays on ideology*. London: Verso.

BARTHES, R. 1975: *S/Z*. London: Cape.

—1977: *Image, music, text*, trans. S. Heath. London: Fontana.

BERGER, J. 1976: *Ways of seeing*. Harmondsworth: Penguin.

BETTERTON, R. (ed.) 1987: *Looking on*. London: Pandora.

BLOOM, H. 1975: *The anxiety of influence*. Oxford: Oxford University Press.

BURTON, D. 1982: Through glass darkly: Through dark glasses. In Carter, R. (ed.), *Language and literature*. London: Allen and Unwin, 195–214.

CAMERON, D. 1985: *Feminism and linguistic theory*. London: Macmillan.

CARTER, R. and SIMPSON, P. (eds) 1989: *Language, discourse and literature*. London: Unwin Hyman.

COUPLAND, N. (ed.) 1988: *Styles of discourse*. Beckenham: Croom Helm.

CULLER, J. 1975: *Structuralist poetics*. London: Routledge and Kegan Paul.

DURANT, A. 1989: The position of the listener in popular music lyrics. Unpublished seminar paper, John Logie Baird Centre, University of Strathclyde.

ECO, U. 1979: *The role of the reader*. Bloomington: Indiana University Press.

FETTERLEY, J. 1981: *The resisting reader*. Bloomington: Indiana University Press.

FISH, S. 1980: *Is there a text in this class?* Cambridge, Mass.: Harvard University Press.

GIBBONS, T. 1979: *Literature and awareness*. London: Edward Arnold.

GILBERT, S. and GUBAR, S. 1988: *The war of the words*. New Haven, CT: Yale University Press.

KUHN, A. 1982: *Woman's pictures*. London: Routledge and Kegan Paul.

MacCABE, C. 1981: Realism and cinema: Notes on some Brechtian theses. In Bennett, T., Boyd-Bowman, S., Mercer, C. and Woollacott, J. (eds), *Popular TV and film*. London: Open University British Film Institute, 216–35.

MARSHMENT, M. and GAMMAN, G. (eds) 1988: *The female gaze*. London: Women's Press.

MODLESKI, T. 1982: *Loving with a vengeance*. London: Shoestring.

MONTGOMERY, M. 1986: DJ talk. *Media Culture and Society* 8, 421–40.

—1988: Direct address, mediated text and establishing co-presence. Unpublished discussion paper, Programme in Literary Linguistics, University of Strathclyde.

MORRIS, M. 1989: *The pirate's fiancée*. London: Verso.

MULVEY, L. 1981: Visual pleasure and narrative cinema. In Bennett, T., Boyd-Bowman, S., Mercer, C. and Woollacott, J. (eds), *Popular TV and film*. London: Open University British Film Institute, 206–15.

SCHOLES, R. 1982: *Semiotics and interpretation*. New Haven, CT: Yale University Press.

SHOWALTER, E. 1971: Women and the literary curriculum. *College English* 32, 855.

SULEIMAN, S. and CROSMAN, I. (eds) 1981: *The reader in the text: Essays on audience and interpretation*. Princeton: Princeton University Press.

THREADGOLD, T. 1988a: Language and gender. *Australian Journal of Feminist Studies*, May 1988.

—1988b: Stories of race and gender: An unbounded discourse. In Birch, D. and O'Toole, M. (eds), *Functions of style*. London: Pinter, 169–204.

WILLIAMS, R. 1983: Monologue and *Macbeth*. In Kappeler, S. and Bryson, N. (eds), *Teaching the text*. London: Routledge and Kegan Paul.

WILLIAMSON, J. 1978: *Decoding advertisements: Ideology and meaning in advertising*. London: Marion Boyars.

Part VIII

Cognitive stylistics

15

On verbal irony

Deirdre Wilson *and* Dan Sperber

15.1 Introduction

Some years ago, a referendum was held on whether Britain should enter the Common Market. There was a long campaign beforehand: television programmes were devoted to it; news magazines brought out special issues. At the height of the campaign, an issue of the satirical magazine *Private Eye* appeared. On the cover was a photograph of spectators at a village cricket match, sprawled in deckchairs, heads lolling, fast asleep and snoring; underneath was the caption: 'The Common Market – The Great Debate'.

This is a typical example of verbal irony. As such, it is of interest not only to linguists analysing spontaneous discourse, and to critics analysing literary texts, but also students of humour. It is curious, though, how little attention has been paid, by linguists, philosophers and literary theorists, to the nature of verbal irony. Theories of metaphor abound. By contrast, while there are many illuminating discussions of particular literary examples, the nature of verbal irony is generally taken for granted. Where theoretical definitions are attempted, irony is still essentially seen as a figure of speech which communicates the opposite of what was literally said. In an earlier paper, 'Irony and the use-mention distinction' (Sperber and Wilson 1981), we drew attention to some problems with this definition, and sketched an alternative account. We would now like to return to some of the issues raised in that paper, and propose some developments and modifications.

15.2 Traditional accounts of verbal irony

In classical rhetoric, verbal irony is a trope, and as such involves the substitution of a figurative for a literal meaning. Irony is defined as the trope in which the figurative meaning is the opposite of the literal meaning:

> Irony is the figure used to convey the opposite of what is said: in irony, the words are not taken in their basic literal sense.
>
> (Du Marsais: *Des Tropes*, chapter XIV)

Or, as Dr Johnson put it, irony is 'a mode of speech in which the meaning is contrary to the words'.

Modern pragmatic definitions of verbal irony remain firmly in the classical tradition. According to Grice (1975, p. 53), the ironist deliberately flouts the maxim of truthfulness, implicating the opposite of what was literally said. The only significant difference between this and the classical rhetorical account is that what was classically analysed as a figurative meaning is re-analysed as a figurative implication or implicature.

Yet the traditional definition of irony has many weaknesses. In the first place, there are obvious counterexamples to the claim that an ironical utterance invariably communicates the opposite of what is literally said. Here are some illustrations:

15.2.1 Ironical understatements

We come upon a customer complaining in a shop, blind with rage and making a public exhibition of himself. I turn to you and say:

(1) You can tell he's upset.

This is a typical example of ironical understatement. Understatements are traditionally analysed as saying, not the opposite of what is meant, but merely less than what is meant. Though (1) is intuitively ironical, it does not communicate either (2a) or (2b), as the traditional definition of irony would suggest:

(2a) You can't tell he's upset.
(2b) You can tell he's not upset.

Or take Mercutio's ironical comment on his death-wound:

(3) No, 'tis not so deep as a well, nor so wide as a church door; but 'tis enough, 'twill serve. (*Romeo and Juliet* III.i)

Mercutio did not mean to convey that his wound was not deep enough, and would not serve. Ironical understatements thus fail to fit the traditional definition of irony.

15.2.2 Ironical quotations

Imagine (4) as said in a cold, wet, windy English spring, or (5), as said in a rainy rush-hour traffic jam in London:

(4) Oh to be in England
     Now that April's there. (Browning, 'Home thoughts from abroad')
(5) When a man is tired of London, he is tired of life. (Boswell, *Life of Johnson*)

Either remark could be ironically intended. To succeed as irony, it must be recognized as a quotation, and not treated merely as communicating the opposite of what is literally said. What (4) would communicate when ironically intended is not – as the traditional definition suggests – a desire to be out of England now that April has arrived, but the idea that the English spring does not always live up to expectations, that the memory of home is not always accurate, that romantic thoughts do not always survive reality, and so on. The point of (5) would be not so much – as the traditional definition suggests – to deny the claim that when a man is tired of London he is tired of life, as to make fun of the sentiments that gave rise to it, the vision of London it was originally intended to convey. Ironical quotations thus fail to fit the traditional definition of irony.

15.2.3 Ironical interjections

You have invited me to visit you in Tuscany. Tuscany in May, you write, is the most beautiful place on earth. I arrive in a freak cold spell, wind howling, rain lashing down. As you drive me home along flooded roads, I turn to you and exclaim:

(6)   Ah, Tuscany in May!

My exclamation would almost certainly be ironically intended. Ironical exclamations do not fit the traditional definition of irony. They do not express a complete proposition; hence, they cannot be true or false, and cannot usefully be analysed as deliberate violations of a maxim of truthfulness. Moreover, it is hard to see what the opposite of the interjection 'Ah, Tuscany in May!' would be. Yet verbal irony is clearly present here.

15.2.4 Non-ironical falsehoods

So far, we have considered three cases in which irony is present but the traditional definition is not satisfied. In a fourth case, the traditional definition appears to be satisfied, but irony is absent – which suggests that something is missing from the definition.

This example is taken from Grice (1978, p. 124). We are out for a stroll, and pass a car with a broken window. I turn to you and say:

(7)   Look, that car has all its windows intact.

When you ask me what on earth I mean, I explain that I was merely trying to draw your attention, in an ironical way, to the fact that the car has a broken window. My remark meets the traditional definition of irony. I have said something patently false, intending to communicate the opposite, namely (8):

(8)   That car has one of its windows broken.

Why do you not instantly leap to the conclusion that (8) is what I meant to convey? As Grice points out, though it fits the traditional definition, (7) cannot be understood as ironical in the circumstances. Clearly, something is missing from the definition.

The traditional definition of irony thus fails on the purely descriptive level: some ironical utterances do not communicate the opposite of what is literally said. But there is a more general problem. According to the traditional definition, an ironical utterance communicates a single determinate proposition which could, if necessary, have been conveyed by means of another, purely literal utterance. On this account, the ironical (9) should be pragmatically equivalent to the strictly literal (10):

(9)　　What a wonderful party.

(10)　　What an awful party.

Yet (9) and (10) clearly differ in their pragmatic effects. Intuitively, (9) expresses a certain attitude, creates a certain impression in the hearer. Thus even examples that fit the traditional definition are not adequately described by saying merely that they communicate the opposite of what was literally said. Yet one looks in vain, in either classical rhetoric or modern pragmatics, for attempts to deal with the obvious differences in effects achieved by ironical utterances and their strictly literal counterparts.

The traditional definition of irony raises another, more general problem. An adequate account of irony should provide not just descriptions but explanations. We need to know not just what verbal irony is, but why it exists, how it works, and what is its appeal. Now saying the opposite of what one means is, on the face of it, neither natural or rational. Traditional accounts of verbal irony thus suggest a certain sort of explanation: they suggest that irony is a deviation from the norm; that it should not arise spontaneously; that it is governed by arbitrary rhetorical rules or conventions, which may vary from culture to culture. We believe, on the contrary, that verbal irony is both natural and universal; that it can be expected to arise spontaneously, without having to be taught or learned. If this is so, then we need not only a different definition of verbal irony, but one that suggests a different explanation.

15.3 Irony as echoic mention

In 'Irony and the use-mention distinction', we outlined a new account of irony based on a distinction between *use* and *mention*. This distinction was originally developed to deal with the following sorts of contrasts:

(11a)　Natasha is a beautiful child.

(11b)　'Natasha' is a beautiful name.

(12a)　He deliberately provoked controversy.

(12b)　He deliberately mispronounced 'controversy'.

In (11a), the word 'Natasha' is used to refer to a child; in (11b) it is used to refer to a word of English. In (12a) the word 'controversy' is used to refer to a debate; in (12b) it is used to refer to a word. This self-referential use of words or other linguistic expressions is known in the philosophical literature as 'mention'. Thus, in (11a) and (12a) the words 'Natasha' and 'controversy' are *used*; in (11b) and (12b) they are *mentioned*.

In written English, as in the above examples, quotation marks are often used to mark off cases of mention. In the spoken language, such clues are rarely available. Sometimes, there is little room for doubt as to whether use or mention was intended: for instance, it is hard to see how a rational speaker could have intended 'Natasha' in (11a) to refer to anything other than a child, or in (11b) to refer to anything other than a word. Sometimes, though, matters are less straightforward.

For instance, compare (14a) and (14b) as answers to the question in (13):

(13)   *Peter*: What did Susan say?
(14a) *Mary*: I can't speak to you now.
(14b) *Mary*: 'I can't speak to you now.'

In (14b), as in (11b) and (12b) above, quotation marks are used to distinguish mention from use. In (14a), the sentence 'I can't speak to you now' is used to describe a certain state of affairs; in (14b), it is used to refer to a sentence of English – in other words, it is *mentioned*. Here, either (14a) or (14b) would, on the face of it, be an acceptable response to the question in (13), and in the spoken language some criterion for recognizing the intended interpretation is needed. Notice that, despite their linguistic similarities, the two utterances would be understood in very different ways: for example, in (14a) the referent of 'I' is Mary, the referent of 'you' is Peter, and the referent of 'now' is the time of Mary's utterance; in (14b) the referent of 'I' is Susan, the referent of 'you' is the person Susan was speaking to, and the referent of 'now' is the time of Susan's utterance. In order to understand Mary's reply, Peter must be able to recognize whether the sentence 'I can't speak to you now' was being used or mentioned. A general criterion for resolving this and other linguistic indeterminacies is proposed in section 15.5 below.

Utterance (14b) is, of course, a direct quotation. In direct quotations a sentence or other linguistic expression is mentioned. In 'Irony and the use-mention distinction', we argued that indirect quotations could be analysed as cases of mention too. Consider (15) as a possible reply to (13):

(15)   *Mary*: She couldn't speak to me then.

This utterance has two interpretations, closely parallelling those of (14a) and (14b). On one interpretation, Mary is not reporting what Susan said – Susan may not have said anything at all – but merely explaining why Susan did not speak. This interpretation parallels (14a) above: Mary uses the sentence 'She couldn't speak to me then' to represent a certain state of affairs. On the other interpretation, parallelling (14b) above, Mary is reporting what Susan said. She is not directly quoting Susan's words: for example, Susan would have said 'I', not 'she', 'can't', not 'couldn't', and 'now', not 'then'. On this interpretation, (15) is an indirect quotation, an attempt to reproduce not Susan's words but her meaning.

Now because (15), on this interpretation, is not a direct quotation, it cannot be analysed as involving mention of the *sentence* Susan uttered. Hence, the contrast between the two interpretations of (15) cannot be analysed in terms of a distinction between the use and mention of sentences. In 'Irony and the use-mention distinction', we argued that it should be analysed in terms of a distinction between the use and mention of *propositions*. On both interpretations of (15), we claimed, the sentence 'She couldn't speak to me then' is used to express a proposition; the difference between the two interpretations lay in whether that proposition was itself mentioned or used. On the interpretation parallelling (14a), it was used to represent a certain state of affairs; on the interpretation parallelling (14b), it was mentioned – that is, used to represent itself. On this account, (14b), a direct quotation, mentions the sentence Susan spoke, whereas (15), an indirect quotation, mentions the proposition she expressed.

We went on to argue that verbal irony is a variety of indirect quotation, and thus crucially involves the mention of a proposition. The argument ran as follows. Note first that indirect quotations may be used for two rather different purposes – we called them *reporting* and *echoing*. A report of speech or thought merely gives information about the content of the original: in (15), for example, Mary may simply want to tell Peter what Susan said. An echoic utterance simultaneously expresses the speaker's attitude or reaction to what was said or thought: for example, Mary may use (15) to let Peter know not only what Susan said, but how she reacted to Susan's utterance, what she thought or felt about it. Irony, we argued, is a variety of echoic utterance, used to express the speaker's attitude to the opinion echoed.

Echoic utterances are used to express a very wide range of attitudes. Compare (16b) and (17b):

(16a) *Peter*: Ah, the old songs are still the best.
(16b) *Mary (fondly)*: Still the best.
(17a) *Peter*: Ah, the old songs are still the best.
(17b) *Mary (contemptuously)*: Still the best!

In both cases, Mary's utterance is echoic. In (16b), her attitude to the thought she is echoing is one of approval; from which it follows that she, like Peter, believes the old songs are best. In (17b), her attitude is one of disapproval. She dissociates herself from the thought she is echoing, perhaps indicating indirectly that she believes the old songs are *not* the best.

Verbal irony, we argue, invariably involves the expression of an attitude of disapproval, thus falling into the same broad category as (17b). The speaker echoes a thought she attributes to someone else, while dissociating herself from it with anything from mild ridicule to savage scorn. To illustrate, consider the following scenario. Mary has lent some money to Bill on the understanding that she will get it back next day. She wonders aloud to Peter whether Bill will keep his word. Peter replies as in (18), thus reassuring her that Bill is trustworthy:

(18) Bill is an officer and a gentleman.

Next day, Bill rudely denies all knowledge of his debt to Mary. After telling Peter what has happened, Mary comments:

(19) An officer and a gentleman, indeed.

This utterance is clearly ironical. Mary echoes Peter's earlier reassurance in order to indicate how ridiculous and misleading it turned out to be. To understand (19) as ironical, all that is needed is a realization that it is echoic, and a recognition of the type of attitude expressed.

Not all ironical echoes are as easily recognizable. The thought being echoed may not have been expressed in an utterance; it may not be attributable to any specific person, but merely to a type of person, or people in general; it may be merely a cultural aspiration or norm. For example, because the code of an officer and a gentleman is widely held up for admiration, a failure to live up to it is always open to ironical comment; hence (19) could be ironically uttered even in the absence of an explicit reassurance such as (18).

From both descriptive and explanatory points of view, the echoic account of irony compares favourably with the traditional account. On the descriptive level, it deals with the case where the speaker communicates the opposite of what she says, and with the various cases where she does not. What is common to all these cases is that the speaker echoes an implicitly attributed opinion, while simultaneously dissociating herself from it. What differ from case to case are the reasons for the dissociation.

Perhaps the most obvious reason for dissociating oneself from a certain opinion is that one believes it to be false; in that case, the speaker may implicate the opposite of what was literally said, and the utterance will satisfy the traditional definition of irony. However, as is shown by the ironical understatement in (1), a speaker may dissociate herself from an opinion echoed not because it is false but because it is too mild – because only someone dull-witted and imperceptive could put it forward in the circumstances. As is shown by the ironical quotations (4) and (5) and the ironical exclamation (6), she may dissociate herself from an opinion echoed not because it is false but because to hold it or express it in the circumstances would be patently absurd. The echoic account thus deals both with the examples that fit the traditional definition, and with those that do not.

The echoic account also sheds light on the problematic example (7) above, in which all the traditional conditions for irony are met but no irony is present. On the echoic account, what is wrong with this example is that no-one's views are being echoed and made fun of. As soon as the missing condition is supplied, irony appears. Thus, consider the following scenario. As we set off for a stroll, I complain to you that my street is being used as a dumping ground for broken-down cars. You tell me I'm imagining things: the cars all look in perfect condition to you. Just then, we pass a car with a broken window, and I turn to you and say:

(7)   Look, that car has all its windows intact.

In the circumstances, this remark would certainly be ironical. I am echoing back to you the opinion you have just expressed, but in circumstances where it would clearly be ridiculous to maintain it. Thus, all that is needed to make (7) ironical is an echoic element and an associated attitude of mockery or disapproval.

Notice how inadequate it would be with this example to say that I was merely trying to communicate the opposite of what I had said. The main point of uttering (7) is to express my attitude to the opinion you have just expressed, and in doing so to imply that you were wrong to disagree with me, wrong to think the world is not going to the dogs, and so on. If I had merely wanted to communicate (8) I would, of course, have expressed this proposition directly.

The echoic account of irony also differs from the traditional account in its explanation of irony. If irony is merely a variety of echoic utterance, then it should arise as naturally and spontaneously as echoic utterances in general, and require no separate rhetorical conventions or training. Since echoic utterances are not normally treated as departures from a norm, there is no reason to treat ironical utterances any differently. In fact, the existence of echoic utterances, and the ease with which they are understood, strongly suggests that there *is* no norm or maxim of literal truthfulness, as most modern pragmatists believe. *Any* utterance may be understood in two quite different ways: as expressing the speaker's own opinion, or as echoing or reporting an opinion attributed to someone else; it is up to the hearer to decide which interpretation was intended.

The echoic account of irony has considerable intuitive appeal. Indeed, it seems to accord with the intuitions of that expert ironist Jane Austen, who has Darcy say to that other expert ironist Elizabeth Bennet:

(20)   you find great enjoyment in occasionally professing opinions which ... are
        not your own. (Austen: *Pride and Prejudice*)

However, we would like to modify one aspect of our original treatment. In the next section, we will argue that the use-mention distinction is merely a special case of a more general distinction, which is needed to account for the full range of echoic utterances, and of ironical utterances in particular.

15.4 Irony as echoic interpretation

In 'Irony and the use-mention distinction', we noted that the traditional definition of irony fails to explain the very close links that exist between irony and parody. The *Princeton Encyclopaedia of Poetry and Poetics* (Preminger 1974) defines parody as 'the exaggerated imitation of a work of art':

> Like caricature, it is based on distortion, bringing into bolder relief the salient features of a writer's style or habit of mind. It belongs to the genus *satire* and thus performs the double-edged task of reform and ridicule.
>
> (*Princeton Encyclopaedia*, p. 600)

If parody is exaggerated imitation, and irony is saying one thing and meaning the opposite, it is hard to see what the two can have in common. On the echoic account of irony, their similarities and differences can be brought out. Roughly speaking, parody is to direct quotation what irony is to indirect quotation: both involve an echoic allusion and a dissociative attitude, but in parody the echo is primarily of linguistic form; in irony, as we have seen, it is of content.

However, while both irony and parody intuitively involve echoic allusion, it is hard to see how parody can strictly speaking be analysed as a case of mention. Consider the following, from a parody of the later Henry James:

(21)   It was with the sense of a, for him, very memorable something that he
       peered now into the immediate future, and tried, not without compunc-
       tion, to take that period up where he had, prospectively, left it. (Beerbohm:
       A Christmas Garland, p. 3)

There are clear echoes here of James's style, but in what sense is (21) a *mention*?
Mention, we have seen, involves identical reproduction of an original; but (21)
is not a reproduction of anything James wrote: it merely *resembles* what he wrote.
While direct quotation involves mention in the strict sense – the exact words of
the original are reproduced – parody is typically based on looser forms of
resemblance.

According to the *Princeton Encyclopaedia*, parody may be directed not only
at style, but also at content, or 'habits of mind'. The following, from a parody of
Galsworthy's *Forsyte Saga*, illustrates this aspect of parody:

(22)   Adrian Berridge paused on the threshold, as was his wont, with closed eyes
       and dilated nostrils, enjoying the aroma of complex freshness which the
       dining-room had at this hour ... Here were the immediate scents of dry
       toast, of China tea, of napery fresh from the wash, together with that
       vague, super-subtle scent which boiled eggs give out through their un-
       broken shells. And as a permanent base to these there was the scent of
       much-polished Chippendale, and of bees' waxed parquet, and of Persian
       rugs ...
          Just at that moment, heralded by a slight fragrance of old lace and of
       that peculiar, almost unseizable odour that uncut turquoises have, Mrs
       Berridge appeared. (Beerbohm: *A Christmas Garland*, pp. 110–11)

Clearly, there are echoes here of both form and content: of the sort of thing
Galsworthy said and the way he said it; but in what sense is (22) a mention? It
is not an identical reproduction of anything Galsworthy wrote: it merely resembles what he wrote. Strictly speaking, then, neither parody of form nor parody
of content can be analysed in terms of mention.

In parody, as the *Princeton Encyclopaedia* says, an element of exaggeration is
often involved. The same is true in many standard examples of verbal irony. One
such example is treated in Paola Fanutza's excellent dissertation 'Irony in Jane
Austen's *Emma*' (Fanutza 1985), in which a wide variety of ironical utterances
are insightfully discussed. Emma is playing with her sister's child. Mr Knightley
comments:

> If you were as much guided by nature in your estimate of men and women, and as little
> under the power of fancy and whim in your dealings with them, as you are where these
> children are concerned, we might always think alike.

To which Emma replies:

> To be sure – our discordancies must always arise from my being in the wrong.

(quoted in Fanutza 1985, pp. 47–8)

What Emma ironically echoes back to Mr Knightley is a caricature of the opinions he has just expressed. If mention involves identical reproduction of an original, then where irony involves an element of exaggeration or caricature, an analysis in terms of mention is too narrow.

In fact, what is true of ironical echoes is true of all indirect quotations. Reports of speech are not always identical reproductions of the content of the original: they may be paraphrases or summaries; they may be elaborations, spelling out some assumptions or implications that the original speaker took for granted, or that struck the hearer as particularly relevant. In such cases, the content of the indirect speech report resembles the content of the original without, however, being an identical reproduction of it; and the analysis of indirect speech in terms of mention is too restrictive.

In our book *Relevance* (Sperber and Wilson 1986, ch. 4, sections 7 and 9) we therefore replaced the notion of mention by a notion of *interpretive resemblance*, or resemblance of content. In the appropriate circumstances, we argued, any object in the world can be used to represent any other object it resembles. A uniformed doll can be used to represent a soldier, an arrangement of cutlery and glasses can be used to represent a road accident, a set of vertical lines to represent the heights of students in a class. Such representations are used in communication for two main purposes: to inform an audience about the properties of an original, and for the expression of attitude. I may show you a uniformed doll so that you can recognize a soldier when you see one; I may communicate my attitude to soldiers by, say, kicking the doll.

Utterances, like other objects, enter into a variety of resemblance relations. It is not surprising, therefore, to find these resemblances exploited, and for just the same purposes, in verbal communication. Onomatopoeia is based on resemblances in sound, verbal mimicry on resemblances in phonetic and phonological form, direct quotation and parody on resemblances in syntactic and lexical form, translation on resemblances in propositional content. Where resemblance of propositional content is involved, we talk of *interpretive resemblance*; we reanalyse echoic utterances as echoic *interpretations* of an attributed thought or utterance, and verbal irony as a variety of echoic interpretation. In other respects, the account of verbal irony developed in 'Irony and the use-mention distinction' remains unchanged.

What does it mean to say that one thought or utterance interpretively resembles another? Resemblance in general involves a sharing of properties: the more shared properties, the greater the resemblance. Interpretive resemblance, or resemblance in propositional content, we argue, is best analysed as a sharing of logical and contextual implications: the more shared implications, the greater the interpretive resemblance. It is possible for two propositions to share all their implications; when one of these is interpretively used to represent the other, we say that it is a *literal* interpretation of that other proposition. On this account, literalness is just a special case of interpretive resemblance. However, one representation may interpretively resemble another when the two merely have implications in common.

Let us illustrate these ideas with an example. Mary says to Peter:

(23)   (a) I met an agent last night. (b) He can make me rich and famous.

As we have seen, an utterance such as (23b) has two possible interpretations, (24a) and (24b):

(24a)   He can make me rich and famous, I believe.
(24b)   He can make me rich and famous, he says.

On interpretation (24a), Mary's utterance is a straightforward assertion. On interpretation (24b), it is either an echoic utterance or a report of speech, and must therefore bear some degree of interpretive resemblance to what the agent said.

Suppose that what the agent said was actually (25):

(25)   I can make you rich and famous.

Then Mary's utterance would be a literal interpretation of what the agent said: the propositions expressed by the two utterances would be identical, and hence share all their implications in every context. In that case, it is quite reasonable to see Mary as having *mentioned* the proposition the agent originally expressed.

Suppose, however, that what the agent said was actually (26):

(26)   I can do for you what Michael Caine's agent did for him.

Then Mary's utterance would be a less than literal interpretation of what the agent said, and it would not be reasonable to claim that Mary had mentioned the proposition the agent originally expressed. It may be common knowledge, though, that Michael Caine's agent made him very, very rich and famous. In a context containing this assumption, (26) would contextually imply (23b). The report in (23b) thus interpretively resembles the agent's utterance in (26): the propositions expressed by the two utterances have implications in common. Many reports of speech, and many echoic utterances, are based on this looser form of resemblance.

We propose, then, to analyse indirect speech reports, echoic utterances and irony not as literal interpretations (i.e. mentions) of an attributed thought or utterance, but simply as interpretations, literal or non-literal, of an attributed thought or utterance. This change corrects an over-restrictive feature of our earlier account.

15.5 The recognition of irony

Wayne Booth tells of a puzzling encounter with a graduate student, a sophisticated reader who was arguing that the whole of *Pride and Prejudice* is ironic. This student expressed a dislike of Mr Bennet, and when asked to explain said, 'Well, for one thing, he's really quite stupid, in spite of his claims to cleverness, because he says towards the end that Wickham is his favourite son-in-law'. Booth comments:

> He retracted in embarrassment, of course, as soon as we had looked at the passage together: 'I admire all my three sons-in-law highly,' said he. 'Wickham, perhaps, is my favourite; but I think I shall like *your* husband [Darcy] quite as well as Jane's.' How

could he have missed Mr Bennet's ironic joke when he was in fact working hard to find evidence that the author was *always* ironic?

(Booth 1974, p. 1)

Such failures, even in sophisticated readers, are quite common. Walter Scott, for example, is notorious for having missed the irony in Elizabeth Bennet's remark that she began to appreciate Darcy when she first set eyes on his magnificent estate at Pemberley (see Southam 1976, pp. 155, 159 and 165, footnote 8). The subtler the irony, the greater the risks.

There is no such thing as a fail-safe diagnostic of irony. All communication takes place at a risk. The communicator's intentions cannot be decoded or deduced, but must be inferred by a fallible process of hypothesis formation and evaluation; even the best hypothesis may turn out to be wrong. The standard works on irony (e.g. Booth 1974, Muecke 1969) provide good surveys of the sort of clues that put alert readers or hearers on the track of irony; but the clues themselves have to interact with more general interpretation procedures. In our book *Relevance*, we outline a general criterion for the resolution of linguistic indeterminacies which, we suggest, is used in every aspect of utterance inter-pretation, including the recognition of irony. This criterion is justified by some basic assumptions about the nature of relevance and its role in communication and cognition, which we can do no more than sketch briefly here. (For further details, see *Relevance*; for summary and discussion, see Sperber and Wilson 1987.)

Human information processing, we argue, requires some mental effort and achieves some cognitive effect. Some effort of attention, memory and reasoning is required. Some effect is achieved in terms of alterations to the individual's beliefs: the addition of contextual implications, the cancellation of existing assumptions, or the strengthening of existing assumptions. Such effects we call *contextual effects*. We characterize a comparative notion of *relevance* in terms of effect and effort as follows:

Relevance

(a) Other things being equal, the greater the contextual effect achieved by the processing of a given piece of information, the greater its relevance for the individual who processes it.
(b) Other things being equal, the greater the effort involved in the processing of a given piece of information, the smaller its relevance for the individual who processes it.

We claim that humans automatically aim at maximal relevance: that is, maximal contextual effect for minimal processing effort. This is the single general factor which determines the course of human information processing. It determines which information is attended to, which background assumptions are retrieved from memory and used as context, which inferences are drawn.

To communicate is, among other things, to claim someone's attention, and hence to demand some expenditure of effort. People will not pay attention unless they expect to obtain information that is rich enough in contextual effects to be relevant to them. Hence, to communicate is to imply that the stimulus used (for example, the utterance) is worth the audience's attention. Any utterance addressed to someone automatically conveys a presumption of its own relevance. This fact, we call the *principle of relevance*.

The principle of relevance differs from every other principle, maxim, convention or presumption proposed in modern pragmatics in that it is not something that people have to know, let alone learn, in order to communicate effectively; it is not something that they obey or might disobey: it is an exceptionless generalization about human communicative behaviour. What people do have to know, and always do know when they recognize an utterance as addressed to them, is that the speaker intends that particular utterance to seem relevant enough to them to be worth their attention. In other words, what people have to recognize is not the principle of relevance in its general form, but the particular instantiations of it that they encounter.

Speakers may try hard or not at all to be relevant to their audience; they may succeed or fail; they still convey a presumption of relevance: that is, they convey that they have done what was necessary to produce an adequately relevant utterance.

Relevance, we said, is a matter of contextual effect and processing effort. On the effect side, it is in the interest of hearers that speakers offer the most relevant information they have. However, speakers have their own legitimate aims, and as a result may choose to offer some other information which is less than maximally relevant. Even so, to be worth the hearer's attention, this information must yield at least adequate effects, and the speaker manifestly intends the hearer to assume that this is so. On the effort side, there may be different ways of achieving the intended effects, all equally easy for the speaker to produce, but requiring different amounts of processing effort from the hearer. Here, a rational speaker will choose the formulation that is easiest for the hearer to process, and manifestly intends the hearer to assume that this is so. In other words, the presumption of relevance has two parts: a presumption of adequate effect on the one hand, and a presumption of minimally necessary effort on the other.

As we have seen, the linguistic form of an utterance grossly underdetermines its interpretation. Direct quotations, indirect quotations, echoic utterances and irony are not recognizable from their linguistic form alone. Various pragmatic theories appeal to complex sets of rules, maxims or conventions to explain how this linguistic indeterminacy is contextually overcome. We claim that the principle of relevance is enough on its own to explain how linguistic form and background knowledge interact to determine verbal comprehension.

In a nutshell, for an utterance to be understood, it must have one and only one interpretation consistent with the principle of relevance – one and only one interpretation, that is, on which a rational speaker might have thought it would have enough effects to be worth the hearer's attention, and put the hearer to no gratuitous effort in obtaining the intended effects. The speaker's task is to see to it that the intended interpretation is consistent with the principle of relevance; otherwise, she runs the risk of not being properly understood. The hearer's task is to find the interpretation which is consistent with the principle of relevance; otherwise, he runs the risk of misunderstanding it, or not understanding it at all.

To illustrate these ideas, consider how Peter might set about interpreting Mary's remark in (19) above:

(19)   An officer and a gentleman, indeed.

As we have seen, this remark has two possible interpretations, (27a) and (27b), corresponding to what we originally called use and mention of the proposition expressed:

(27a) Bill is an officer and a gentleman, I believe.
(27b) Bill is an officer and a gentleman, you said.

Suppose that interpretation (27a) is the first to occur to Peter, and thus the first to be tested for consistency with the principle of relevance. To be consistent with the principle of relevance, an interpretation must achieve adequate contextual effects, or at least have been rationally expected to do so. To achieve contextual effects, an interpretation must either have contextual implications, strengthen an existing assumption, or contradict and eliminate an existing assumption. Now the hypothesis that, in the circumstances described, Mary might genuinely believe that Bill is an officer and a gentleman contradicts known facts; rather than eliminating existing assumptions, it is likely itself to be rejected. In the circumstances, Mary could not rationally have expected her utterance, on this interpretation, to achieve adequate contextual effects, and interpretation (27a) must be rejected as inconsistent with the principle of relevance.

Now consider (27b). This could be understood as either a report of speech or an echoic interpretation of an attributed thought or utterance. Suppose Peter decides to test the hypothesis that it is a straightforward report of speech. To be consistent with the principle of relevance on this interpretation, Mary's utterance must achieve adequate contextual effects – for example, by adding contextual implications, or by strengthening an existing assumption – or must at least have been rationally expected to do so. But, unless Peter's memory is defective, he will be able to remember his earlier remark, and will need no reminding of it. Hence, the hypothesis that Mary's utterance was intended as a report of speech is inconsistent with the principle of relevance.

The only remaining possibility is that Mary's utterance was intended as echoic: that is, she was echoing Peter's earlier utterance in order to express her attitude to it. What attitude was she intending to express? The hypothesis that her attitude was one of approval can be ruled out for reasons already given: in the circumstances, the idea that Mary could genuinely believe that Bill is an officer and a gentleman contradicts known facts. Hence, the only possible hypothesis is that Mary was echoing Peter's utterance in order to dissociate herself from the opinion it expressed.

Is Mary's utterance, on this interpretation, consistent with the principle of relevance? Would it achieve adequate contextual effects for the minimum necessary effort, in a way that Mary could manifestly have foreseen? It is easy to see how it might achieve adequate contextual effects: for example, it draws Peter's attention to the various ways in which Bill's behaviour has fallen short of the ideal, and to the fact that he has made a mistake, is possibly responsible for Mary's loss of money, is unlikely to be trusted so readily again in his assessment of character, and so on; moreover, these are effects that Mary might easily have foreseen. As long as no other utterance would have achieved these effects more economically, this interpretation would also be satisfactory on the effort side, and would therefore be consistent with the principle of relevance.

In *Relevance*, we show that having found an interpretation consistent with the principle of relevance, the hearer need look no further: there is never more than one. The first interpretation tested and found consistent with the principle of relevance is the *only* interpretation consistent with the principle of relevance, and is the one the hearer should choose.

15.6 The communication of impressions and attitudes

What do ironical utterances communicate? While rejecting the traditional claim that they invariably communicate the opposite of what was literally said, we have, as yet, offered no alternative account. Ironical utterances, we said, communicate a certain attitude, create a certain impression in the hearer; but how are attitudes and impressions to be dealt with in a theory of communication?

At the end of 'Irony and the use-mention distinction', we were rather sceptical about the possibility of dealing with the communication of impressions and attitudes within the framework of what we called 'logical pragmatics', in which utterance interpretation was seen primarily as an inferential process involving the construction and manipulation of propositional (conceptual) representations:

> An ironical utterance carries suggestions of attitude ... which cannot be made entirely explicit in propositional form. In this respect, a logical-pragmatic model does not provide a better description ... than a semantic model. On the other hand, our analysis of irony ... crucially involves the evocation of an attitude – that of the speaker to the proposition mentioned. This attitude may imply a number of propositions, but it is not reducible to a set of propositions. Our analysis thus suggests that a logical-pragmatic theory dealing with the interpretation of utterances as an inferential process must be supplemented by what could be called a 'rhetorical-pragmatic' or 'rhetorical' theory dealing with evocation.
>
> (Sperber and Wilson 1981, p. 317)

The suggestion was that the representational and computational resources of 'logical pragmatics' would not be adequate to deal with expressions of attitude, which would have to be handled by entirely different mechanisms.

We would not now draw such a sharp distinction between logical and rhetorical pragmatics. We believe that the communication of impressions and attitudes can be handled in much the same terms as the communication of more standard implicatures. In this section, we will suggest how this might be done.

In *Relevance* (chapter 1), we argued that communication involves an intention to modify the audience's *cognitive environment*. The cognitive environment of an individual is a set of assumptions that are *manifest* to him; an assumption is manifest to an individual at a given time if and only if he is capable at that time of representing it conceptually and accepting that representation as true or probably true. Manifest assumptions may differ in their degree of manifestness: the more likely they are to be entertained, the more strongly manifest they are. To modify the cognitive environment of an audience is to make a certain set of assumptions manifest, or more manifest, to him. The intention to modify the cognitive environment of an audience we called the *informative intention*.

Consider now how utterance (28) might be handled in this framework:

(28) *Mary, to Peter*: I can't stay to dinner tonight.

Mary's utterance modifies Peter's cognitive environment by making manifest to him a variety of assumptions. Peter's task, in interpreting (28), is to recognize Mary's informative intention: that is, to decide which set of assumptions she *intended* to make manifest, or more manifest, to him. In recognizing Mary's informative intention, he is guided by the criterion of consistency with the principle of relevance: that is, he looks for an interpretation on which (28) might rationally have been expected to achieve adequate contextual effects for the minimum necessary effort.

Among the assumptions made strongly manifest to Peter by Mary's utterance will be (29):

(29) Mary has said to Peter that she can't stay to dinner that night.

It is easy to see how (29) might achieve contextual effects in a context easily accessible to Peter. For example, by assuming that Mary is a trustworthy communicator, Peter can infer that she is unable to stay to dinner; from this, together with other assumptions, he can infer that some of his plans for the evening will have to be abandoned; depending on the relationship between them, the effort he has gone to in preparing the meal, and the reason for her refusal, further implications would follow. In recognizing Mary's informative intention, Peter is entitled to assume that she intended to make manifest, or more manifest, to him enough of these implications to make her utterance worth his attention. These will be the *implicatures* of her utterance.

Manifestness, we said, is a matter of degree. Among the assumptions made manifest to Peter by Mary's utterance, some will be more strongly manifest than others; moreover, Mary's intentions concerning these assumptions will be more strongly manifest in some cases than in others. In the case of (28), for example, it is hard to see how Mary could have expected her utterance to be relevant enough to be worth Peter's attention if it did not make assumption (29) manifest to him. Let us say that when a communicator makes strongly manifest her intention to make a certain assumption strongly manifest, then that assumption is *strongly communicated*. Then in the circumstances described, (29) will be strongly communicated by (28).

However, not all the speaker's intentions are so easily pinned down. It may be clear, for example, that in saying (28), Mary intended to make manifest to Peter that she couldn't stay to dinner, and fairly clear that she intended him to infer from this that he would have to change his plans for the evening – by inviting someone else, say, by preparing less food, or by abandoning the meal and going out. It may not be so clear, however, that she expected him to follow any particular one of these courses of action, or to carry out the chosen course of action in any particular way. Thus, a wide array of assumptions is made marginally more manifest by Mary's utterance; as the chains of inference grow longer, and the set of possible conclusions wider, Mary's informative intentions become correspondingly less manifest, to the point where they are no longer manifest at all. We might describe this quite standard situation by saying that strong communication shades off into something less determinate, where the hearer is encouraged to think along certain lines, without being forced to any definite conclusion.

Let us say that when the communicator's intention is to increase simultaneously the manifestness of a wide range of assumptions, so that her intention concerning each of these assumptions is itself weakly manifest, each of these assumptions is *weakly implicated*. Then, by saying (28), Mary might weakly implicate a range of assumptions having to do with changes in Peter's plans for the evening, changes in her relationship to Peter, and so on. The less strongly manifest her intentions concerning such assumptions, the weaker the communication will be.

Most recent approaches to pragmatics have concentrated on strong communication. One of the advantages of verbal communication is that it allows the strongest possible form of communication to take place: it enables the hearer to pin down the speaker's intentions about the explicit content of her utterance to a single, strongly manifest candidate, with no alternative worth considering at all. On the other hand, what is implicitly conveyed in verbal communication is generally weakly communicated. Because all communication has been seen as strong communication, the vagueness of most implicatures and of non-literal forms of expression has been idealized away, and the communication of feelings, attitudes and impressions has been largely ignored. The approach just sketched, by contrast, provides a way of giving a precise description and explanation of the weaker effects of communication.

Suppose, for example, that in saying (28) Mary speaks sadly, thus making manifest to Peter assumption (30):

(30)   Mary has spoken sadly.

The effects thus created can be analysed as weak implicatures. Assumption (30) makes manifest, or more manifest, to Peter a wide array of further assumptions. Why is Mary sad? Is it because she can't stay to dinner? Does Peter want her to be sad? How sad is she? Would she cheer up if he invited her for another evening? Would she stay if he cooked dinner immediately? If he offered to drive her home afterwards? If he lit a fire? If he served fish instead of meat? By processing (30) in a context obtained by answering these and other questions, Peter can increase the contextual effects of (28). On the assumption that Mary intended to make (30) manifest to him, Peter is entitled to conclude that she also intended to make manifest to him enough of these effects to make (30) worth processing.

What we are suggesting is that the assumptions made manifest to Peter by Mary's utterance include not only the contextual effects of the proposition she has expressed, but also those of various descriptions of her utterance – her tone of voice, facial expression, accompanying gestures, and so on. Some subset of these may form part of the *intended* interpretation of her utterance, this subset being selected, as usual, by the criterion of consistency with the principle of relevance. The resulting communication will, of course, be weak, but it will not be different in kind from the communication of quite standard implicatures. In either case, the interpretation process will involve the inferential processing of newly presented information in the context of assumptions supplied by the hearer. What makes communication weak is merely the fact that a very wide array of assumptions is made manifest, or more manifest, so that, in forming hypotheses about the speaker's informative intentions, the hearer has a very wide range of contexts and contextual effects to choose from.

Let us return, in the light of this suggestion, to our original example: the magazine cover with the caption 'The Common Market – The Great Debate' printed across a photograph of spectators asleep at a village cricket match. How should this cover be understood?

The caption and photograph would, between them, have made a variety of assumptions manifest to contemporary readers. The caption would give them access to encyclopaedic information about the Common Market, including the information that a referendum on Britain's entry to it was shortly to be held, and that the referendum issue had been repeatedly referred to by politicians and journalists as the 'Great Debate'; the photograph would give them access to a range of assumptions about the length and uneventfulness of village cricket matches, the lack of excitement normally felt by spectators, and so on. What set of assumptions was this cover *intended* to make manifest to contemporary readers? That is, on what interpretation might it have been intended to achieve adequate contextual effects for the minimum necessary effort?

Here, some hypotheses can be automatically eliminated as inconsistent with the principle of relevance. These would include the hypothesis that the designers of the cover merely intended to make manifest, or more manifest, the assumption that the debate on the Common Market would be exciting, together with some subset of its contextual effects. A communicator who merely wanted to achieve these effects could have achieved them without putting readers to the unnecessary effort of processing information about village cricket matches: hence, the use of this cover to achieve these effects would be inconsistent with the principle of relevance.

Consider now the hypothesis that the description 'The Great Debate' was echoically used – a hypothesis that would have come easily to contemporary readers. Clearly, for reasons just given, the attitude being expressed to the opinion echoed cannot have been one of approval. By contrast, the hypothesis that it was one of dissociation or disapproval is strongly confirmed by the accompanying photograph. This photograph conveys an impression of stupefying boredom. On the assumption that the Common Market Debate resembles the village cricket match in relevant respects, readers can infer that this debate too is one of stupefying boredom; that to call it a 'Great Debate' is ridiculous; that it is not, in fact, a great debate. On the assumption that the cover designers intended to make these assumptions manifest to the audience, their behaviour would be consistent with the principle of relevance. This is the interpretation, then, that the audience should choose.

On this account, the magazine cover would achieve a combination of strong and weak communication. It would strongly communicate that it was ridiculous to call the Common Market debate a 'Great Debate', that this debate was very boring, and that it was not, in fact, a great debate. It would weakly implicate a wide array of contextual effects derivable from these assumptions, in terms of which readers would be able to create for themselves an impression of just how ridiculous the media descriptions were, and just how boring the debate was likely to be.

15.7 Concluding remark

In this paper, we have analysed irony as a variety of echoic interpretive use, in which the communicator dissociates herself from the opinion echoed with accompanying ridicule or scorn. The recognition of verbal irony, and of what it communicates, depends on an interaction between the linguistic form of the utterance, the shared cognitive environment of communicator and audience, and the criterion of consistency with the principle of relevance. This approach to irony, which appears to offer both better descriptions and better explanations than traditional accounts, has one surprising consequence which is perhaps worth mentioning here.

It is tempting, in interpreting a literary text from an author one respects, to look further and further for hidden implications. Having found an interpretation consistent with the principle of relevance – an interpretation (which may itself be very rich and very vague) which the writer might have thought of as adequate repayment for the reader's effort – why not go on and look for ever richer implications and reverberations? If we are right, and considerations of relevance lie at the heart of verbal communication, such searches go beyond the domain of communication proper. Though the writer might have *wished* to communicate more than the first interpretation tested and found consistent with the principle of relevance, she cannot rationally have *intended* to. Relevance theory thus explains how irony is (fallibly) recognized, and sets an upper limit to what the ironist can rationally expect to achieve.[1]

Note

1 Deirdre Wilson is grateful to the British Council, the Associazione Italiana di Anglistica and the University of Turin for their hospitality at the AIA conference on Le Forme del Comico, October 1985, at which an earlier version of this paper was presented.

References

BEERBOHM, M. 1950: *A Christmas garland*. London: Heinemann.
BOOTH, W. 1974: *A rhetoric of irony*. Chicago: University of Chicago Press.
FANUTZA, P. 1985: Irony in Jane Austen's *Emma*. Tesi di Laurea (Lingue e Letterature Straniere). Universita Degli Studi Di Cagliari.
GRICE, H. P. 1975: Logic and conversation. In Cole, P. and Morgan, J. (eds), *Syntax and semantics*, Vol. 3, *Speech Acts*. New York: Academic Press, 41–58.
—1978: Further notes on logic and conversation. In Cole, P. (ed.), *Syntax and semantics*, Vol. 9, *Pragmatics*. New York: Academic Press, 113–28.
MUECKE, D. 1969: *The compass of irony*. London: Methuen.
PREMINGER, A. (ed.) 1974: *Princeton encyclopaedia of poetry and poetics*. London: Macmillan.
SOUTHAM, B. C. 1976: *Sense and sensibility, Pride and prejudice and Mansfield Park: A casebook*. London: Macmillan.
SPERBER, D. and WILSON, D. 1981: Irony and the use-mention distinction. In Cole, P. (ed.), *Radical pragmatics*. New York: Academic Press, 295–318.
—1986: *Relevance: Communication and cognition*. Oxford: Blackwell.
—1987: A precis of relevance, and Presumptions of relevance. *Behavioral and Brain Sciences* 10, 697–754.

16

'According to my bond': King Lear and re-cognition

Donald C. Freeman

An emerging theory of cognitive metaphor provides a promising basis for analysing figurative language in literary works.[1] In particular, cognitive metaphor provides accounts of language patterns that are isomorphic with larger imaginative literary structures, as well as particular interpretations that are more explicit and falsifiable than existing interpretations founded upon the language of literary works. I want to demonstrate this theory in a reading of *King Lear* that focuses on its opening scene, where metaphorical structures arise from a competition between the framing bodily experiences of balance and linking that define ways of understanding crucial to the larger patterns of the play.

16.1 Metaphor and schematized bodily experience

The salient features of earlier research in the theory of metaphor are epitomized in the work of Samuel R. Levin, who argued in a seminal essay that, for example, to interpret a metaphor like 'a grief ago' we in effect import the semantic feature [+Time] from 'grief's' syntactic frame into the word itself; the phrase is to that extent a 'confrontation' (Levin 1964, p. 314) between ordinary and metaphoric language. Metaphor thus is part of a figurative language that contrasts with a 'literal', non-figurative language. According to this theory, 'literal' language, including 'dead' (but not literary) metaphors, is unmarked and ordinary, but figurative language, including literary (but not dead) metaphors, is deviant, foregrounded, highlighted, made strange. The 'deviance' is with respect to a language-universal set of semantic features and combinatory rules external to individual cognition. Lakoff (1987, pp. 157–84) has characterized this view as the Objectivist position. Classically, metaphor is seen – and not only in linguistically based theories – as a deviant and parasitic structure; we characterize metaphors in terms of their deviance from ordinary non-metaphorical language.[2]

Precisely these two characterizations of metaphor – that it is a structure parasitic upon ordinary language structure and that it can be explained in terms of its deviance from semantic interpretations of ordinary, non-metaphorical language interpretable by a compositional semantics – are explicitly rejected by cognitive metaphor. The cognitive view arises from the Experientialist position (as articulated, for example, in Lakoff 1987, p. xv) on semantic theory. The Experientialist position claims that we create metaphor by projecting onto an abstract *target domain* the entities and structure of a concrete *source domain*, a schematized real or vicarious bodily experience. Metaphor arises from, in Johnson's (1987, p. xv) cogent formulation, 'embodied human understanding'. As human beings we share a range of physical experiences that take on structure and coherence from the non-propositional schemata we extract from them. Our propensity to extract these schemata is a fundamental property of mind. We project elements of the structure and components of our physical experience onto our non-physical, abstract experience. Precisely this sense of projection from schematized bodily experience constitutes the claim for metaphor as embodied human understanding.

Consider, for example, the famous line from *King Lear*, 'I am a man/More sinn'd against than sinning' (III.ii.59–60). The context, justice, makes it clear that this line epitomizes Lear's sense of a higher justice, that in a truly just universe he would be no more sinned against than he had sinned, that if there were justice, Lear's sins would balance his suffering. This notion of balance is fundamental to our idea of justice: we understand the abstraction of justice in terms of bodily balance. The concept of horizontal balance dominates both our non-verbal and verbal language about justice. Our courts decide civil lawsuits according to 'the preponderance', or greater weight, 'of the evidence'. A witness's testimony can be said to be 'biased'. Our icon for justice is a blindfolded woman holding a two-pan scale. All of these metaphors, and many more besides, having to do with such seemingly disparate notions as mathematical equality, patterns in visual art, and certain kinds of musical progression are projected from a non-verbal, non-propositional, non-representational schema of BALANCE (for general discussion of schema theory, see Johnson 1987, pp. 18–40 and the references he cites; for discussion of musical progression and the BALANCE schema, see Freeman 1991, p. 153). The theory of cognitive metaphor claims that we project the elements of this schema – entities (the items that balance) and the relation-ships among those entities (counteraction or equality) – onto elements of our more abstract experience.

Such an explanation of 'justice' as deriving ultimately from our embodied human understanding of balance explains 'I am a man / More sinn'd against than sinning'. But the BALANCE schema also captures lines like Edgar's, 'He childed as I father'd' (III.vi.108), in which Lear's sufferings at the hands of his daughters are balanced by Edgar's sufferings at the hands of his father Gloucester (and the balance between the plot and major subplot of the play is epitomized); it captures Lear's misunderstanding of the father–child relationship, which persists even to the end, when, awakened from his sleep after he has been brought in from the heath, he implores Cordelia:

Lear	If you have poison for me, I will drink it.
	I know you do not love me; for your sisters
	Have, as I do remember, done me wrong:
	You have some cause, they have not.
Cordelia	No cause, no cause.

(IV.vii.72–5)

Lear persists in understanding the parent-child relationship in terms of the BALANCE schema, even as Cordelia reaches beyond it. But children need no cause to wrong parents; conversely and more importantly, a child whom a parent has wronged need not balance that wrong by committing another. By no means all of the metaphors I have cited are metaphors of justice. But they do derive from a common source, the embodied, culturally reinforced experience of balance.

That source, the schema of BALANCE, underlies a richer, more important, and previously unexplained structure of metaphor in the play: that of financial accounting.[3] Terms and phrases like 'divest', 'prize me at her worth', and 'comes too short' (I.i.48, 69, 71) partake of the BALANCE schema, but they are not metaphors of justice. They can be better explained in the more densely structured, balance-based scenario[4] of financial accounting.

A second rich source of metaphor in *King Lear* is the equally simple LINKS schema, which consists of two entities joined by a bonding element. These three aspects of the LINKS schema's structure, like those of the BALANCE schema, are mapped onto a wide array of non-physical human experiences. The source of the LINKS schema arises from our literal, physical link to our biological mothers. We then proceed to, for example, a 'bonding' with our parents, our relatives, and our friends. Marriages are often celebrated with the proverb 'blest be the tie that binds', and sometimes include the Biblical admonition, 'What therefore God hath joined, let no man put asunder' (*Matthew* 19, verse 6). People without a romantic interest are 'unattached', or free of 'entanglements'. When one event consistently follows another, we hypothesize that the two events are linked by causation. Links of divine ordination and divine love join the elements of the Great Chain which, shorn of its theology, is alive and well today (see Lakoff and Turner 1989, pp. 160–213). The lion is still the king of the beasts, and gold is still the premier investment commodity, whereas platinum, rarer and more expensive, is merely an industrial commodity.

These two powerful perceptual structures give a local habitation and a name to previously unjustified and unrelated critical commonplaces. For example, it is a staple of Shakespearean criticism to say that in the opening scene the playwright establishes the atmosphere of a play's world. What are established, in fact, are the play's dominating schemata. In *King Lear*, Gloucester's cynical account to Kent of his sons' parentage establishes the play's competing schemata of BALANCE and LINKS. Gloucester demonstrates that like Lear, he understands parental relationships through the CHILDREN ARE FINANCIAL ASSETS metaphor, one that the audience is shortly to see played out fully in the ritual of Lear's retirement.

His [Edmund's] breeding, Sir, hath been at my charge:
...
But I have a son [Edgar], Sir, by order of law, some year elder than this, who yet is no dearer to my account:

(I.i.8, 18–19)

The 'charge' that Edmund's breeding constitutes for Gloucester is an analogy from estate accounting, which used the so-called 'Charge and Discharge' method, in which, Green (1930, p. 47) writes, 'the executor "charged" himself with the estate and "discharged" himself of disbursements properly chargeable to the estate'. Edmund, a bastard, is not a financial asset but a cost item that it has embarrassed Gloucester to acknowledge; Edgar, though not an embarrassment (a cost to Gloucester's reputation) is no more highly valued in the balance sheet of his father's affections. From the start of the play, familial LINKS are debased; children are bastards or 'by order of law'; the relationship of child to father, an important source of LINK metaphors in the play, begins with what will result in Edmund's perversion of his filial duty. Charges and accounts, sons and daughters, bastards and legal progeny (and what ought to be but are not the same thing, natural and unnatural children) – these seemingly unrelated facts of language and plot spring from the same impulses: the BALANCE and LINKS schemata.

These competing schemata structure a significant portion of the play's metaphors that traditional accounts of the play's language leave unrelated. More significantly, they and the analyses they make possible, constitute previously undiscovered empirical evidence for relating the play's figurative language to such other structural elements as narrative, plot, and particular constellations of characters. For example, many critics have found parallel structure or balance in the fact that while in the sub-plot Edmund gouges out Gloucester's eyes but Edgar redeems him to a new life, in the main plot Goneril and Regan strip Lear of his retainers but Cordelia awakens him to a restoration, however temporary, of his health, fatherhood, and kingship. But I know of nothing written about *King Lear* that uses one theoretical apparatus to *explain* this balance, the patterns of metaphor I describe, and the relationships among these levels. It is this greater explanatory power that is the major contribution to literary theory of cognitive metaphor.

16.2 The King's account-books

Most accounts of *King Lear*'s opening scene treat it as a trial or a love-test. Yet curiously the scene lacks elements crucial in any trial: an offence, a judge, advocates, juries, opposing parties. It is in no sense an adversarial proceeding. Lear has divided his kingdom before the scene begins.[5] We find none of the legal vocabulary that Shakespeare uses so profusely in the mock trial scene (III.vi.35–83) and elsewhere in those of the sonnets and plays containing unambiguous references to trials.

Rather than a trial, what we have in the first scene of *King Lear* is a semantic frame (in the sense of Fillmore 1982) that depends upon the structure of a quasi-legal proceeding, the auditing of financial record-books, and a more general scenario of financial accounting (the substantial evidence that Shakespeare was familiar with this subject matter is summarized in Knight 1973, p. 248). In financial accounting obligations are recorded both to and from the entity keeping the books. Within this scenario, centrally for Lear and less importantly for other characters, the generative metaphor (in the sense of Schön

1979, p. 264) that controls the scene's 'story' is CHILDREN ARE FINANCIAL ASSETS. Lear understands his daughters in the same way that he understands wealth, real property, assets, and debts. Financial assets are expected to provide a return on capital to their owners (here, their fathers). Hence an important metaphor within this framework is FILIAL LOVE IS INTEREST. Financial assets and organizations are periodically audited to see whether they are providing an adequate return, and how the return from one asset compares with that from another, so that, if need be, the investment strategy can be revised. Assets that provide better returns can be the objects of further capital investment. Assets that do not perform well are disposed of, and the money provided by the sale is re-deployed to those assets that do perform well.

Although the fundamental principles of financial accounting are the same today as they were in Shakespeare's time, some details are quite different. First, although balance sheets of a kind were kept, they were balanced out only 'when some special circumstances required the formal closing of the books' (Yamey 1949, p. 106). Second, audits of financial records were oral (indeed, the term 'audit' comes from the Latin *audire*, 'to hear') because when the financial audit in more or less its modern form came into existence in England in the fourteenth century, most of the participants were illiterate. The steward of another's capital recited, or 'spoke' the accounts, in the customary language, and the auditor 'heard' them. Many early account books contain notations such as the following, describing the appointment in 1456 of two auditors for the accounts of the City of Dublin: 'ther schold be from that tym forward two Audytores assignet upon the tresowrerys saud cytte, to hyr har acownt yerly.'[6]

The model for financial accounting and auditing with which Shakespeare and his audience probably would have been most familiar, if only by report, was the semi-annual settling of the Crown's accounts with the sheriff of every county for subventions from the Crown to the county and revenue from the county due the Crown. At this proceeding, according to a standard history:

> the treasurer representing the Exchequer read from his copy of the Great Pipe Roll [a document amounting to a national ledger] the amount due the crown from the sheriff. The Exchequer attendants placed on the checkered cloth [of the table used for the ceremony] dummy counters representing the amounts due the crown. On the near side of the checkered cloth was the sheriff. As the treasurer called the amounts the sheriff placed in the appropriate columns his tally stick, crown vouchers and money or jewels to balance the dummy counters. This settled the yearly account between the crown and sheriff.

So rich in tradition was this ceremony that it continued from the early Norman period well into the nineteenth century. Even in Shakespeare's time, this event would have been seen not merely as a settling of accounts, but a ceremony in its own right.

Just this ceremony, the hearing, or audit, of state accounts, more satisfactorily explains the curiously ritualistic character of this first major scene of the play. Much of the language crucial to Lear's expression of his 'fast intent' can be simultaneously interpreted in the semantic frames of financial accounting and of statecraft. He wishes to 'divest' himself of rule, of 'interest of territory'. He calls upon his daughters to 'tell' (i.e. count out, as well as relate) which of them 'shall we *say* doth love us most' so that he may invest[7] more parental love, which the frame asks us to understand as capital investment, according to the return on each of the three investments represented in his daughters. Each daughter is enjoined to 'speak' or 'say'. Lear will listen, or audit, as each speaks her account, and 'extend ... [his] largest bounty' where nature, natural affection, filial love, challenges, lays claim to that bounty (which again has a financial, though not an accounting, sense) with merit, with the greatest deserving. Future investment will balance past performance – as Lear perceives that performance.

Goneril is in no doubt how to demonstrate that 'merit'. Like her father, she couches the language of her declaration in financial terms. The love she bears her father is 'dearer', a word with a financial as well as an affectionate sense; that love is 'beyond what can be valued' as more conventional financial assets are appraised; it 'makes breath poor'. Regan's accounting is more concrete. She is made, she asserts, of the same 'metal' (in Shakespearean usage, normally gold metal) as her sister, and appraises herself equally ('and prize me at her worth'). But Goneril, Regan claims, 'comes too short', an idiom directly from the contemporary language of financial accounting.[8] Regan's reckoning is even more unrealistically extravagant: she professes to find happiness only in her father's love.

Underlying all of this, again, is the schema of BALANCE. Lear seeks to balance his 'bounty' against the love his daughters say they have for him; his new investment in them must balance the return he has received on his previous investments. Goneril in turn, seeks to demonstrate a highly valued love (in order to receive a highly valued piece of kingdom); Regan values herself at her sister's worth, but insists that Goneril is short in her accounts. Lear abundantly demonstrates a trait of character to which we will return: an obsession with what Johnson (1987, p. 95) calls 'moral mathematics' – here, the notion that the emotional costs of child-rearing can be quantified, and ought to be balanced by equally quantifiable expressions of love in a verifiable balance sheet of accounts.

Lear's version of the BALANCE schema forces Cordelia from the start into an unpalatable choice:

> Then poor Cordelia!
> And yet not so; since I am sure my love's
> More ponderous than my tongue.

(I.i.75–7)

Compared with Regan, who 'prize[s] [herself] at [Goneril's] worth', Cordelia is both pitiably and financially poor – but she immediately rejects the financial metaphor in favour of her own version of the BALANCE schema, in which the spiritual weighs more, is more ponderous (and hence more valuable), than its literal expression. She must mediate between her father's intense desire for her to express her love in ways that allow him to maintain his account-books of filial devotion, while remaining true to her 'spiritual' notion of love. In her very first words in the play, Cordelia shows the relative value she places on feelings and words: 'What shall Cordelia speak? Love, and be silent.' For her, feelings will always outweigh words; the two can never balance; she refuses to *speak*, a word associated with the financial audit scenario, what is in effect her accounting of filial love and paternal love returned.

Hence when Lear asks Cordelia, who is the object of a financial claim[9] by her two suitors, what she can 'say to draw/[10] A third more opulent than [her] sisters? Speak' (I.i.84–5), Cordelia gives the only response possible for one who thus weighs words and feelings. She rejects the notion that a paternal gift should be 'drawn' like a salary, a usage current in Shakespeare's time. All she can *say* – all she can speak – is 'Nothing'. What counts for her is what she feels, but feelings have no place in financial audits. Understood in terms of the accounting framework that dominates this scene, Cordelia's famous silence is quite unremarkable. Cordelia's 'nothing' is understood by her father only as a number, as his bewildered response makes clear: 'Nothing will come of nothing' (I.i.89).

At this point the process of frame competition begins that undermines Lear's ceremony and results in Cordelia's being disinherited. For the BALANCE schema underlying Lear's scenario of financial accounting, Cordelia seeks to substitute a schema of LINKS. She seeks to redefine her father's understanding of family relationships as items in an accounting balance sheet into an understanding characterized in the generative metaphor FAMILY RELATIONSHIPS ARE LINKS. She begins this process with the polysemous word 'bond', which exists in both competing frames, financial and kinship:

> I love your Majesty
> According to my bond; no more nor less.
>
> (I.i.91–2)

From the beginning, Cordelia makes clear that she understands 'bond' in terms of her father's financial accounting scenario. In Shakespeare's time, a bond, the financial instrument, was what Shylock (*The Merchant of Venice*, I.iii.144) called a 'single bond'. It was a financial or other obligation undertaken solely on the basis of the borrower's credit, without collateral. The obligation memorialized in a single bond is not, in legal language, defeasible (performance of the obligation is the only way the debtor can discharge it; see *Black's Law Dictionary* 1981, p. 163). One performs under a single bond or one does not. Performance under a single bond is, in two words that come to dominate *King Lear*, all or nothing. For Cordelia, to love her father 'according to [her] bond' is to love him completely; that love can be no more (more complete than complete) nor less (partial) because of the nature of financial single bonds.

But for Cordelia the same all-or-nothing property holds of filial bonds, when this term is defined within the LINKS schema through the metaphor FILIAL RELATIONSHIPS ARE PHYSICAL LINKS. I have sketched out how the same metaphor governs our understanding of phrases like 'family ties' and 'parental bonding'. Lear cannot share the richness of Cordelia's metaphorical understanding, and replies in solely financial terms:

> Mend your speech a little,
> Lest you may mar your fortunes.
>
> (I.i.93–4)

Cordelia's reply partakes once again of both schemata, BALANCE and LINKS:

> Good my Lord,
> You have begot me, bred me, lov'd me: I
> Return those duties back as are right fit,
> Obey you, love you, and most honour you.
> Why have my sisters husbands, if they say
> They love you all? Happily, when I shall wed,
> That lord whose hand must take my plight shall carry
> Half my love with him, half my care and duty:
> Sure I shall never marry like my sisters,
> To love my father all.
>
> (I.i.94–103)

Cordelia focuses first on the physical closeness of her filial relationship with Lear, and then relates this closeness to the financial accounting frame with a verb, 'return', that can be interpreted in both frames. Links are by nature biconditional – A is linked to B if and only if B is linked to A. Within the accounting frame we speak of an investment that 'returns' such-and-such per cent. What Cordelia will 'return', she characterizes as 'duties', a term that resonates in both the accounting and the links frames. That 'return' is commensurate with both the intensity of filial relationships and the balanced nature of accounts: here the most fundamental of human ties, blood relationships of begetting, breeding, loving, are expressed in the language of the wedding ceremony: obedience, love, and honour (see Rosinger 1974).

Yet the explicitly financial character of the accounting metaphor is still kept in play. For Cordelia, marriage as a bond (a human relationship) involves a 'plight' or pledge, another word interpretable within both frames, that necessarily, by the laws of both financial accounting and human development, diminishes the line of credit underlying the 'bond' of daughter to father. If a wedded daughter still loves only her father, she has falsely plighted her troth, for she has no credit left for the bond with her husband – and for Cordelia, nothing truly can come from nothing. The protestations of Goneril and Regan that they 'love [their] father all' are thus false in the same ways that Cordelia's is true – within both the accounting and the links scenarios. Lear's daughters cannot plight the half of their love that their husbands deserve without defaulting upon the bonds calling for them to 'love [Lear] all'. In both scenarios, Cordelia is 'So young, my Lord, and true' (I.i.106): i.e. both truthful, bearing a higher loyalty to her filial bond with her father, and true in the sense of having opposed to her sisters' false accounts (their 'bonds' are simultaneously pledged to two different creditors) her own true reckoning under the obligations of her financial and filial bond. In both senses, Cordelia is her family's best auditor.[11]

Characteristically, Lear interprets Cordelia's 'true' only within the financial accounting frame: 'Let it be so; thy truth then be thy dower' (I.i.107). Likewise, Burgundy expresses in financial terms the bargain he now seeks to strike for Cordelia's hand:

Burgundy	Most royal Majesty,
	I crave no more than hath your Highness offer'd,
	Nor will you tender[12] less.
Lear	Right noble Burgundy,
	When she was dear to us, we did hold her so,
	But now her price is fallen.

(I.i.192–6)

France, however, shares Cordelia's view that love cannot be understood as a set of accounts. After Lear offers Cordelia to Burgundy one last time, as 'herself a dowry', only to have Cordelia point up the irreconcilable conflict between balance and link: 'Since that respects and fortunes are his [Burgundy's] love, I shall not be his wife' (I.i.247–8), France, terming Cordelia 'unprized', makes clear that he loves her precisely because she does not fit Lear's balance-sheet vision, harking back to Regan's use of 'prize' as 'appraise':

Fairest Cordelia, that art most rich, being poor;
Most choice, forsaken; and most lov'd, despis'd!
Thee and thy virtues here I seize upon:
...
Not all the dukes of wat'rish Burgundy
Can buy this unpriz'd precious maid of me.

(I.i.249–51, 257–8)

Thus in this opening scene, Shakespeare embeds the play's major themes in the framing scenario of a financial audit, one that depends on the schema of BALANCE. Lear himself sees statecraft and fatherhood in exclusively abstract, numerical terms; Goneril and Regan give an account of their filial love in language dominated by accounting metaphors that derive from the BALANCE schema;[13] the same metaphors dominate the case pleaded unsuccessfully by Burgundy. Cordelia refutes the balance schema in its own terms; she would substitute an understanding of family relationships as arising from a schema of LINKS. For her, to say 'nothing' does not deny a daughter's love but exalts its inexpressibility; for Lear, 'nothing' is merely a nought, a book-keeping entry.

This word resonates more ambiguously for Lear as the Fool redefines it for him during his visit to Goneril:

Kent	This is nothing fool.
Fool	Then 'tis like the breath of an unfee'd lawyer; you gave me nothing for't. Can you make no use of nothing, Nuncle?
Lear	Why no, boy; nothing can be made out of nothing.
Fool	(*to Kent*) Prithee tell him, so much the rent of his land comes to: he will not believe a Fool.

(I.iv.126–32)

The linguistically nimble Fool entraps Lear with a specifically financial phrase, and reminds his king of the deeper sense of the 'nothing' he now has. Lear, the great valuer, is now without value, an '0', a zero, 'without a figure' (I.iv.189–90), a king with no kingdom, a father with no daughters, a man with no standing, a cipher without a number to give it value, to whom the Fool applies Lear's own principle of accounting: 'I am better than thou art now: I am a fool, thou art nothing' (I.iv. 190–1). The currency in which Lear will repay his older daughters' professions of love comes at a much higher rate of exchange than he anticipated:

> *Fool*   But for all this, thou shalt have as many dolours for thy daughters as thou canst tell in a year.
>
> (II.iv.52–3)

Lear's world is destroyed in the same terms of balance and numbers in which he sought to build it, as Goneril and Regan strip him of the numbers of his retainers:

> *Regan*   I have hope
> You [Lear] less know how to value her [Goneril's] desert
> Than she to scant her duty ...
> I cannot think my sister in the least
> Would fail her obligation.
>
> (II.iv.135–9)

Goneril and Regan, however, indeed know how to value their father's desert; they know just the issue that will torment him most – the number of his followers. As his daughters reduce his retainers – and with them, his humanity – from the *number* one hundred to the *number* zero, it dawns on Lear that in family relationships, a deal is not necessarily a deal, irrespective of what the account-books say or what reservations are spelled out in contractual visiting arrangements:

> I gave you all –
> ...
> Made you my guardians, my depositaries,
> But kept a reservation[14] to be follow'd
> With such a number.
>
> (II.iv.248, 249–51)

We recall that the Fool has already told Lear that he is 'an 0 without a figure'; now, Lear begins to realize that the 'all' he has given Regan and Goneril is being balanced – if that is the word – by nothing at all (and will come to know that Cordelia's 'nothing' is everything). With his daughters' final and specifically numerical slashes at his selfhood, 'What need you five-and-twenty? ten? or five? ... What need one?' Lear begins to see the human condition as going beyond what 'moral mathematics' or the balance sheet will justify:

> O! reason not the need; Our basest beggars
> Are in the poorest thing superfluous:
> Allow not nature more than nature needs,

Man's life is cheap as beast's. Thou art a lady;
If only to go warm were gorgeous,
Why, nature needs not what thou gorgeous wear'st,
Which scarcely keeps thee warm. But, for true need, –
You Heavens, give me that patience, patience I need! –

(II.iv.262–9)

Like Cordelia's use of 'bond' in Act I scene i, Lear's agonized 'O! reason not the need' epitomizes the competition between the financial accounting and links metaphors crucial to the play's conceptual structure. Historically, 'reason' had as one of its nominal meanings a monetary reckoning.[15] The term 'need' bespeaks a link of desperate desire between Lear and 'th' name and addition of a king', represented for *this* king by the number of his retainers, which defines for Lear the nature of kingship beyond what a debit-credit, accounts-book, cost-benefit analysis would show, and represented for human beings by more than the entitlement of their mere physical requirements. For the first time, Lear begins to weigh the links of humanity more than account balances. 'True need' cannot be reasoned, accounted for, reckoned up.

16.3 The LINKS schema

Early in the play, the links-based metaphors involving Lear have to do more with breaking links than with creating them. From his first entrance, Lear sees only the financial side of Cordelia's rich-languaged assertion of the 'bond' between them, and ignores her attempt to couch the father-daughter link in language that he will understand ('I return those duties back as are right fit'). Instead, Lear both physically and spiritually breaks the filial bond and denies the bonding structures of both ownership and family:

Here I disclaim all my paternal care,
Propinquity and property of blood,
And as a stranger to my heart and me
Hold thee from this for ever.

(I.i.112–15)

Later, when Goneril begins the process of stripping him of his retainers, Lear seeks to destroy not only the father–daughter link, but the link of common membership in the human race – 'degenerate bastard' – and to extend this curse into the next generation, so that Goneril either may have the mother–child link denied her or have the parental link become for her an instrument of exquisite torture. Lear prays that the gods may give his own daughter a 'child of spleen' who will be 'thwart disnatured torment' to her, yet linked to her by the very constitutive linking structures that she has denied her father: nature, honour, pains and benefits, and thanks.

This severing of links is carried even further in Act II: Lear threatens to deny the bond of marriage with Regan's mother and thus his bond of fatherhood to Regan, and turns this destruction of human bonds upon himself. Lear converts his physical links of flesh and blood to Goneril to highly particularized, loathsome diseases of that same flesh and blood. The bonds that link Lear with Goneril now are only those of 'disease', 'plague', and 'corrupted blood' (II.iv.220, 222, 223). Finally, in the midst of the storm, Lear would shatter the links that hold together the world, the bonds of nature and the human race, the very 'germains' or gene-pool of life itself. He stands alone, 'the pattern of all patience', divested of links of any kind, to his daughters, to his household, to his kingdom, to the elements of the created world. Lear does not 'tax [the] elements with unkindness' (III.ii.16) because they are not of Lear's kind, they are not linked to him as his daughters should be, by gratitude, by blood, by the duty of subjects to their king.

As Lear's reintegration with the human condition begins, we likewise understand that reintegration through the schema of LINKS. As the nature of the metaphors based upon that schema begins to change, Lear first identifies himself with the Fool through shared physical needs of warmth and safety, and sees himself as linked to the Fool in suffering and sympathy:

> Come on, my boy. How dost, my boy? Art cold?
> I am cold myself. Where is this straw, my fellow?
> The art of our necessities is strange,
> And can make vile things precious. Come, your hovel.
> Poor Fool and knave, I have one part in my heart
> That's sorry yet for thee.
>
> (III.ii.68–73)

Lear demonstrates this same pattern – from physical sensation to mental feeling, from concrete to abstract, from his own physical suffering to a spiritual empathy with the suffering of another – as he begins to reverse the operative definition of kingship that has so far dominated the play: a status in which the links between a king and his subjects (and a father and his daughters) are constituted by the abstractions of courtly ceremony, of debits and credits. Lear seeks the ground of human community and kingship in the concrete links of shared physical suffering in the storm, between his nakedness and his subjects' 'loop'd and window'd raggedness' (III.iv.31), between man and man, and between a King and his subjects. When he strips off his garments in the play's climactic scene and stands naked against the elements, he is clothed in his solidarity with the physical nakedness of Tom o'Bedlam, linked to him in spiritual nakedness and vulnerability of 'unaccommodated man' before the random cruelties of the gods.

The progression is crucial. When Lear's understanding of the world in terms of the empty abstractions of the balance sheet and kingly ceremony fails him, he progressively denies first the abstract and then the physical links of fatherhood, his own marriage, his ungrateful daughters' legitimacy, their humanity and their progeny, and finally the linking structures of the created world and the human species. He then re-cognizes and rebuilds his place in that world in terms of these links, bonding himself first with physical feeling (cold), then with spiritual feeling (empathy), then with individuals (the Fool), then with the rags and hunger of his kingdom's subjects ('the poor naked wretches' with 'houseless heads and unfed sides' [III.iv.28, 30]), and finally with the irreducibly human, unaccommodated, primal human condition figured in Mad Tom. This condition and bond are epitomized in Lear's 'We came crying hither' and in that 'very foolish fond old man' of Act IV, linked to Cordelia now in human mortality and imperfection.

16.4 On description and explanation

Few of the critical analyses in the foregoing are startling; indeed, Lear's restoration to humanity is an important part of any discussion of the play. Some of the financial language in *King Lear* (although not its critical significance) has been described before, as have the play's larger structural entities and the relationships between them. But to describe the play's financial language is merely that: description. What I would claim for this article as an analysis from the standpoint of cognitive metaphor is that this theory enables us not merely to describe, but to *explain* patterns of this kind, and to explain them and their interconnections at different structural levels of the play using the same theoretical apparatus. The analyses produced by a cognitive-metaphoric approach are, moreover, better grounded than earlier purely critical work.

As to the first of these assertions, cognitive metaphor proceeds on the hypothesis that metaphor is not just a matter of language, but of thought and reason (see e.g. Lakoff and Turner 1989, p. xi). The same concept, or 'activated pattern inhering in thought' (Turner 1991, p. 45), underlies both the dozens of examples in *King Lear* of metaphors of financial accounting that instantiate the BALANCE schema and many larger structures in the play. These would include, by way of example, the Gloucester–Edmund–Edgar subplot balanced against the main plot, and the play's balanced sets of characters: the 'unnatural' children – Edmund on one side, Goneril and Regan on the other; the rejected, despised, and then redeemed fathers – Gloucester and Lear; the 'natural' children – Edgar and Cordelia; and the good and bad servants – the Fool and Oswald. The connection between these entities and the balance-based metaphors in the text is not accidental, fortuitous, or the product of what Fish (1980, p. 251) criticizes as responsive only to 'the pressure of the question "how do they relate?" and a relation will always be found'. The connection results from the same process, metaphoric projection from the BALANCE schema, into many distinct domains of the play: into the abstractions of Lear's idea of paternal love, and the ways in which his daughters' responses play into and resist it; into the abstractions of plot-construction, character relations, and narrative sequence; into psychological and social settings, and into many other structural elements (for discussion of these elements and cognitive-metaphoric analysis, see Wye 1992, chs 3 and 4).

The second part of my claim for cognitive metaphor is perhaps more important. The metaphoric impulse is grounded not in intellectual abstractions but in the body that is in the mind. Because cognitive-metaphoric analysis proceeds from the elements and structure of schematized bodily experience to their projection into such abstractions as (for *King Lear*) family relationships and parental and filial love, these analytical claims can be confirmed or disconfirmed according to the accuracy with which those elements and structure and their projection are articulated. The same falsifiability applies, *mutatis mutandis*, to claims made for metaphoric projection into larger abstract structural units. In short, this analysis can be falsified if its topological analysis proves to be wrong. It can be invalidated if the patterns it posits exist only at the level of text and not in larger structural units, or if a competing candidate source domain and metaphoric projection better explains these patterns at all levels of the literary work.[16]

On this second point, we can, for example, trace a pattern of textual metaphors in *King Lear* that depend on the core metaphor LIFE IS A JOURNEY, which is based on the PATH schema: 'we came crying hither' (IV.vi.176); 'I have no way, and therefore want no eyes; I stumbled when I saw' (IV.i.18–19); 'she's [Cordelia] gone for ever .... Thou'lt come no more' (V.iii.258, 306), and many others. But very little connects this pattern of metaphoric projection in the text with larger structural elements in the play. The PATH schema entails such salient aspects as starting and terminal points and a sequence of locations that connect the beginning and the end (for discussion, see Johnson 1987, pp. 113–17). The lives of all of *King Lear*'s major characters have terminal points: most of them die. But we see little of the source points of these paths, the beginning of these journeys. A contrasting example, *Macbeth*, is not only replete with textual metaphors based on the PATH schema, but the LIFE IS A JOURNEY metaphoric projection dominates the play's plot and characters (the extreme case is Macduff, who begins the journey of his life by an alternate route to the conventional birth canal – for discussion, see D. C. Freeman forthcoming). Thus for *King Lear* we can make a principled argument *for* two candidate source domains, BALANCE and LINKS (they exist independently and the play manifests both a pattern of projections from them at the textual level and an equally rich pattern of the same projections at different levels) and *against* a third, the PATH (the play manifests a pattern of projections from it at the same level, but few if any at different levels), as the defining 'conceptual universe' (M. H. Freeman forthcoming) of the play.

Of course the choice of dominant source domains and hence of the abstract entities into which they are projected is interpretive, even if we grant the currently all-encompassing sense of that term (see Fish 1989, p. 320). These choices can change over time: for me, they have changed in 35 years of watching, reading and teaching *King Lear* from the SCALE schema ('Thy life's a miracle. Speak yet again ... Do but look up' [IV.vi.55, 59], and 'The worst is not / So long as we can say "This is the worst" ' [IV.i.27–8], both instances of the orientational metaphors GOOD IS UP, BAD IS DOWN) to the PATH schema (in particular, the LIFE IS A JOURNEY metaphor), instantiated in the lines cited above. These changes arise from autobiography, from deepening insight, from changing views that arise from many causes. I have 're-cognized' *King Lear* several times, and I probably will do so again. But these progressive acts of 'interpretation', acts of choice, are far from being unconstrained. My choice of source domains is limited to those that are independently motivated. BALANCE, LINKS, PATH, and SCALE all lead richly documented lives as image-schemata underlying similar source domains outside *King Lear*. My choice of target domains into which a candidate source domain is projected must be consistent in form with that source domain (the source domain for 'I love you according to my bond' cannot arise from a CONTAINER schema because we do not conceive of 'bond' as having the shape of a container).

On the theory of cognitive metaphor, both my changed 'interpretations' over time and the very different 'interpretive' choices that might be made within a different interpretive community from mine are situated in the body and in bodily experience. Interpretations that depend on evidence from cognitive-metaphoric analysis are constrained both by that experience and by the requirement that the topology of that schematized experience in a metaphoric source domain be mapped into the topology of the target domain. The relative validity of particular source domains and metaphoric projection can be assessed with reference to their independent motivation and internal consistency. Of course there is no one valid God's-eye interpretation of a literary work, whether the evidence for such a claim arises from cognitive metaphor or anything else. But there is a range of plausible interpretations and a scale of valid ones. Cognitive metaphor constrains the interpretive community to the body of the embodied imagination.

Notes

1 Research for this article was conducted at the Institute of Cognitive Studies, University of California, Berkeley, while I was on sabbatical leave from the University of Southern California. I am grateful to both institutions for their support of this work, part of a longer study of cognitive metaphor in Shakespeare's major plays. Quotations from *King Lear* are taken from the Arden Shakespeare edition of the play (Muir 1985).

2 The body of recent literature on metaphor is enormous. A brief summary of this field as of a decade ago may be found in Levinson (1983, pp. 147–62). An unsurprisingly partisan account of more recent work may be found in Lakoff (1993).

3 The play's financial language was noted as long ago as 1928 by Fr. Gundolf (*Shakespeare, sein Wesen und Werk*), cited in Clemen (1951, p. 135), and most recently and felicitously in Colie (1974, pp. 185–219). But these studies fail to capture two systematic relationships: first, between that language's source domain in financial accounting and the schema of BALANCE; second, between this source domain and the schema of LINKS.

4 Throughout what follows I use the term 'scenario' for what cognitive grammarians usually call a 'frame' or 'cognitive model' or 'idealized cognitive model', a way of understanding a concept or scene that structures our thinking about it.

5 Frost (1958) perceives that predictable outcomes such as the already determin-

ed awards of territory are the nature of rituals like this scene. Cordelia thus not only disrupts the ritual but, more seriously, disrupts the participants' (and the audience's) settled expectation of its outcome.

6 Reported in Brown (1905, p. 78).

7 Lear is to use precisely this word to describe his actions to Cornwall and Albany after he has disinherited Cordelia:

> I do invest you jointly with my power,
> Pre-eminence, and all the large effects
> That troop with majesty.
>
> (I.i.129–31)

8 See *OED*, s.v. short, III.C.8.c., 1579: 'They will all comme to short in their reckoning.'

9 Cordelia is one

> to whose young love
> The vines of France and milk of Burgundy
> Strive to be interess'd;
>
> (I.i.82–4)

'Interess'd' is glossed in the *OED* (1) as 'To have a right or share'. It is cognate with a noun that captures the modern sense of 'interest' as 'legal concern'.

10 A word that in Shakespeare's time also collocated with 'payment' or 'salary', just as it does today; this passage is cited in *OED* (B.I.45) for the 'payment' sense.

11 But she remains her father's daughter. When Cordelia wields executive authority late in the play she displays some of Lear's bad habits. To any of her retainers who will help the mad Lear she offers 'all [her] outward worth' (IV,iv,10), when by the link of service they should help their mistress's father (who remains, in Cordelia's view, their king as well) gratis. She seeks to balance Kent's service to her with good works of her own, a world-view he rejects with dignified irony:

> *Cordelia* O thou good Kent! how shall I live and work
> To match thy goodness? My life will be too short,
> And every measure fail me.
> *Kent* To be acknowledg'd, Madam, is o'er-paid.
>
> (IV.vii.1–4)

12 A specifically financial sense, meaning in Shakespeare's time as well as ours 'to offer (money, etc.) in discharge of a debt or liability, especially in exact fulfilment of the requirements of the law and of the obligation'. *OED*, s.v. tender, v., 1.

13 They pledge to Lear as consideration for their inheritances a bond that Cordelia demonstrates is already half-encumbered. Cordelia's 'audit' of Lear's balance sheet demonstrates that his assets are subject to an old adage of financial audits: the troubles are usually found in the receivables.

14 A term in English property law conferring a residual right in land, such as an easement, that can have a monetary value (*Black's Law Dictionary* 1981, p. 1175).

15 *OED* 2c. The only citations are late fourteenth century. The same sense is not recorded for the verb, but the functional shift, from noun to verb, is one of the most general in English.

16 I am often taxed on this point with being 'totalizing' or 'essentialist'. Guilty as charged. I take these terms to mean 'general, ignoring particulars that do not fit

the theory'. Noam Chomsky's early work in linguistic theory is often held up to me as an example of this 'fault' (e.g. Chomsky 1957; I blush at the comparison), where he focuses on syntax and gives short shrift to semantics and pragmatics. Chomsky took the strongest position consistent with the reliable facts that he had. Subsequent research produced more, and more reliable, facts, better theoretical accounts of areas of linguistic structure that his early work ignored, etc. But the theory of government and binding, a more recent incarnation (see Chomsky 1981), bears a recognizable resemblance to its 1957 ancestor, as does a libraryful of books and articles produced in the intervening three decades. None of these developments would have been possible, in my view, had not Chomsky been an unrepentant 'totalizer' from the start. Any theory of anything worth anything begins as totalizing, essentialist, and universalist, and progressively qualifies its claims as research proceeds. Among the many problems of contemporary literary 'theory' is that in seeking to keep in play exceptions and purported anomalies it explains nothing, and is less 'theory' than 'general talk'.

References

Black's Law Dictionary, 5th edn. 1981. St. Paul, Minnesota: West.

BROWN, R. 1905: *History of accounting and accountants*. London: Cass.

CHOMSKY, N. 1957: *Syntactic structures*. The Hague: Mouton.

—1981: *Lectures on government and binding*. Dordrecht: Foris.

CLEMEN, W. H. 1951: *The development of Shakespeare's imagery*. Cambridge, Mass.: Harvard University Press.

COLIE, R. 1974: Reason and need: *King Lear* and the 'crisis' of the aristocracy. In *Some facets of King Lear: Essays in prismatic criticism*. Toronto: University of Toronto Press, 185–219.

FILLMORE, C. 1982: Frame semantics. In Linguistic Society of Korea (ed.), *Linguistics in the morning calm*. Seoul: Hanshin, 111–38.

FISH, S. 1980: *Is there a text in this class?* Cambridge, Mass.: Harvard University Press.

—1989: *Doing what comes naturally*. Durham, NC: Duke University Press.

FREEMAN, D. C. 1991: Songs of experience: New books on metaphor. *Poetics Today* 12, 145–64.

—forthcoming: 'Catch[ing] the nearest way': *Macbeth* and cognitive metaphor. In *Proceedings of the XVth international congress of linguists*. Quebec, August 1992.

FREEMAN, M. H. forthcoming: Metaphor making meaning: Dickinson's conceptual universe. In *Proceedings of the XVth international congress of linguists*. Quebec, August 1992.

FROST, W. 1958: Shakespeare's rituals. *Hudson Review* 10, 577–85.

GREEN, W. 1930: *History and survey of accountancy*. Brooklyn, NY: Standard Text Press.

JOHNSON, M. 1987: *The body in the mind*. Chicago: University of Chicago Press.

KNIGHT, W. N. 1973: *Shakespeare's hidden life: Shakespeare at the law, 1585–1595*. New York: Mason and Lipscomb.

LAKOFF, G. 1987: *Women, fire, and dangerous things*. Chicago: University of Chicago Press.

—1993: The contemporary theory of metaphor. In Ortony, A. (ed.), *Metaphor and thought*, 2nd edn. Cambridge: Cambridge University Press, 202–51.

—and TURNER, M. 1989: *More than cool reason: A field guide to poetic metaphor.* Chicago: University of Chicago Press.

LEVIN, S. R. 1964: Poetry and grammaticalness. In Lunt, H. G. (ed.), *Proceedings of the ninth international congress of linguists.* The Hague: Mouton, 308–16.

LEVINSON, S. 1983: *Pragmatics.* Cambridge: Cambridge University Press.

MUIR, K. (ed.) 1985: *King Lear,* revised edn., The Arden Shakespeare. London: Routledge.

ROSINGER, L. 1974: *King Lear. Publications of the Modern Language Association of America* 89, 585.

SCHÖN, D. A. 1979: Generative metaphor: A perspective on problem-solving in social policy. In Ortony, A. (ed.), *Metaphor and thought,* 1st edn. Cambridge: Cambridge University Press, 254–83.

TURNER, M. 1991: *Reading minds: The study of English in the age of cognitive science.* Princeton, NJ: Princeton University Press.

WYE, M. E. 1992: Jane Austen's *Emma:* Embodied metaphor as a cognitive construct. Unpublished Ph.D. dissertation, University of Southern California.

YAMEY, B. S. 1949: Scientific bookkeeping and the rise of capitalism. *Economic History Review,* 2nd series 1, 99–113.

Suggestions for further reading: Some recent titles

1 General collections of essays

BERNSTEIN, C. J. (ed.) 1994: *The text and beyond: Essays in literary linguistics*. Tuscaloosa: University of Alabama Press.
An uneven collection ranging from formalist analyses to studies of power and gender in language.

CARTER, R. and SIMPSON, P. (eds) 1989: *Language, discourse and literature: An introductory reader in discourse stylistics*. London: Routledge.
A good introduction to contextualized, discourse-oriented approaches to stylistic analysis.

SELL, R. and VERDONK, P. (eds) 1994: *Literature and the new interdisciplinarity: Poetics, linguistics, history*. Amsterdam: Rodopi.
The proceedings of a conference of the Poetics and Linguistics Association, aiming at an interdisciplinary broadening of horizons in literary and linguistic research.

TOOLAN, M. (ed.) 1992: *Language, text and context: Essays in stylistics*. London: Routledge.
Like Carter and Simpson (1989), an extremely useful introduction to discourse stylistics.

VERDONK, P. (ed.) 1994: *Twentieth-century poetry: From text to context*. London: Routledge.
VERDONK, P. and WEBER, J. J. (eds) 1995: *Twentieth-century fiction: From text to context*. London: Routledge.
Two useful introductory textbooks in the stylistics of poetry and fiction; a volume on drama will follow in the same series.

And an invaluable reference tool:
WALES, K. 1990: *A dictionary of stylistics*. Harlow: Longman.

The main periodicals in the field of stylistics are:
Journal of Literary Semantics (Julius Groos Verlag)
Language and Literature (Longman)
Language and Style (City University of New York)
Lingua e Stile (Societa Editrice il Mulino)
Poetics (North-Holland)
Poetics Today (Duke University Press)
Social Semiotics (Central Queensland University)
Style (Northern Illinois University)
Stylistica (Alfar, Sevilla)
Stylistyka (University of Opole, Poland)

2 Pedagogical stylistics

CARTER, R. and LONG, M. N. 1991: *Teaching literature*. Harlow: Longman.
— and NASH, W. 1990: *Seeing through language: A guide to styles of English writing*. Oxford: Blackwell.
—WALKER, R. and BRUMFIT, C. (eds) 1989: *Literature and the learner: Methodological approaches*. London: Modern English Publications and the British Council.
DURANT, A. and FABB, N. 1990: *Literary studies in action*. London: Routledge.
MONTGOMERY, M., DURANT, A., FABB, N., FURNISS, T. and MILLS, S. 1992: *Ways of reading: Advanced reading skills for students of English literature*. London: Routledge.
SHORT, M. (ed.) 1989: *Reading, analysing and teaching literature*. Harlow: Longman.
—1995: *Exploring the language of poems, novels and plays*. Harlow: Longman.
WIDDOWSON, H. 1992: *Practical stylistics*. Oxford: Oxford University Press.

3 Pragmatic stylistics

AUSTIN, T. R. 1994: *Poetic voices: Discourse linguistics and the poetic text*. Tuscaloosa: University of Alabama Press.
HICKEY, L. (ed.) 1989: *The pragmatics of style*. London: Routledge.
PETREY, S. 1990: *Speech acts and literary theory*. London: Routledge.
SELL, R. (ed.) 1991: *Literary pragmatics*. London: Routledge.
VENTOLA, E. (ed.) 1991: *Approaches to the analysis of literary discourse*. Åbo: Åbo Academy Press.

4 Critical stylistics:

BIRCH, D. 1989: *Language, literature and critical practice*. London: Routledge.
—1991: *The language of drama*. London: Macmillan.
FOWLER, R. 1991: *Language in the news: Discourse and ideology in the press*. London: Routledge.
GREEN, K. and LE BIHAN, J. 1995: *Critical theory and practice*. London: Routledge.
HODGE, R. 1990: *Literature as discourse*. Cambridge: Polity Press.
LEE, D. 1992: *Competing discourses: Perspective and ideology in language*. Harlow: Longman.
SIMPSON, P. 1992: *Language, ideology and point of view*. London: Routledge.
WEBER, J. J. 1992: *Critical analysis of fiction: Essays in discourse stylistics*. Amsterdam: Rodopi.

5 Feminist stylistics:

JEFFRIES, L. 1993: *The language of twentieth-century poetry*. London: Macmillan.
MILLS, S. 1995: *Feminist stylistics*. London: Routledge.
WALES, K. (ed.) 1994: *Feminist linguistics in literary criticism*. London: D. S. Brewer.

6 Cognitive stylistics:

COOK, G. 1994: *Discourse and literature: The interplay of form and mind.* Oxford: Oxford University Press.

LAKOFF, G. and TURNER, M. 1989: *More than cool reason: A field guide to poetic metaphor.* Chicago: Chicago University Press.

TURNER, M. 1991: *Reading minds: The study of English in the age of cognitive science.* Princeton: Princeton University Press.

Index

Please note that concepts like language, linguistics, literature, style, etc. are discussed throughout the book and are therefore not included in the index.

Ideology
  dominant 226
  and reader positioning 245–8, 251–2
  relation to language 5, 90, 200
  of romantic love 254–5
  of sincerity 184–5
  social/political 4–6, 52n, 219
  and speech-act theory 4, 181–91
  'text in itself' ideology 207–8
  see also Femininity; Function,
    ideological; Metaphor and ideology;
    Power; Value, social/ideological
Illocutionary
  act 190
  force 84n, 106–7, 112n, 113n, 120,
    146–7
  intentions 183
Implication
  contextual 4, 6, 261, 266, 269–75,
    278
  logical 179
Implicature 4, 167–71, 177, 261, 275–6
  conventional 168, 170
  conversational 168–71, 178
  weak 6, 276–8
Implied
  author 185
  reader, *see* Reader
Impression 263, 274–8
Inference
  illegitimate 102
  interpretive 4, 95, 165, 169, 182,
    271
  political 225
Inferential processing 5, 274–8
Initiator 76
Integrated study of language and
    literature 3, 140, 149–55
Integrationalism 122–3
Interpellation 244, 247, 251–2, 254
  indirect 245, *see also* Reader, indirect
    address
Interpretative groundings, *see*
    Groundings
Interpretive community, *see* Community
Interpretive resemblance, *see*
    Resemblance
Intertextuality 3, 5, 6, 154
  reader 206–20

Ironical
  interjection 262, 266
  quotation 261–2, 266
  understatement 261, 266
  non-ironical falsehood 262–3
Irony, verbal 6, 260–78
Itkonen, E. 118

Jacobs, R. 99
Jakobson, R.
  and contiguity disorder 96
  and formalist stylistics 111, 123, 127,
    131, 196, 207
  and the poetic function 1–2, 10–52,
    121, 198–9
James, H. 267–8
Jaquette, J. 226
Jesperson, O. 22
Johnson, K. 153
Johnson, M. 6, 225, 281, 285, 293
Johnson, S. 95, 260
Jones, G. 89
Jones, L. G. 45
Jonson, B.
  The Alchemist 162, 165
  'That Women are but Men's Shadows'
    252
Jonz, J. 207
Joos, M. 12, 104
Joyce, J. 48n
Jung, C. G. 94

Kachuk, B. 226
Kafka, F. 70
  'Metamorphosis' 85n
Karcevskij, S. I. 23
Katz, J. J. 181
Keats, J. 12, 16, 139
Keenan, E. L. 163
Keenan, E. O. 187
Kempson, R. M. 163–4
Kinkead-Weekes, M. 71, 73, 77, 103
Kiparsky, P. 51n
Knapp, S. 126
Knight, W. N. 283
Koerner, K. 118, 119
Kress, G. 89, 189, 199
Kuhn, A. 243
Kuhn, T. 225